Patient Safety Handbook

June M. Sullivan, JD, MEd OT/L, MT (ASCP)
Renee H. Martin, JD, RN, MSN

Patient Safety Handbook

June M. Sullivan, JD, MEd OT/L, MT (ASCP)
Renee H. Martin, JD, RN, MSN

BAR ASSOCIATION
ng Liberty
ng Justice

AMERICAN BAR ASSOCIATION

HEALTH LAW SECTION

Printed in the United States of America.

13 Digit ISBN: 978-1-60442-113-2

Library of Congress Cataloging-in-Publication Data

Martin, Renee H.
  Patient safety handbook / Renee H. Martin.
    p. ; cm.
  Includes bibliographical references.
  ISBN 978-1-60442-113-2
  1. Medical errors—Prevention. 2. Medical errors—Prevention—Law and legislation—United States. I. American Bar Association. II. Title.
  [DNLM: 1. Medical Errors—legislation & jurisprudence—United States.
2. Medical Errors—prevention & control—United States. 3. Patient Care—standards—United States. 4. Safety Management—standards—United States.
WB 33 AA1 M382p 2008]

  R729.8.M375 2008
  362.1068—dc22   2008030275

Discounts are available for books ordered in bulk. Special consideration is given to state and local bars, CLE programs, and other bar-related organizations. Inquire at ABA Publishing, American Bar Association, 321 North Clark Street, Chicago, Illinois 60610.

For a complete list of ABA publications, visit www.ababooks.org.

12 11 10 09 08   5 4 3 2 1

Table of Contents

Introduction

Since the Institute of Medicine report, *To Err Is Human*, was first published in 1999, patient safety and quality of care have become the driving forces in the delivery and payment of health care services in the United States. This emergence has direct consequences for counsel who must provide sound legal advice regarding the myriad emerging legal, regulatory, and accreditation requirements—as well as private-enterprise initiatives—that affect their health care clients' ability to provide and receive payment for the patient-care services they render.

Patient safety and quality of care are interrelated but discrete concepts. Quality refers to ensuring that certain processes are established from which measurable, predictable, and achievable outcomes derive. Patient safety refers to the mitigation of untoward, unanticipated, and preventable occurrences that may or may not result in measurable patient harm. The provision of quality care requires fundamentally the provision of safe care.

This guide is intended to be a practical tool for counsel serving clients in a variety of settings, and as an overview of the key elements involved in implementing a patient safety program. The guide summarizes certain key patient safety requirements implemented by federal, state, and accreditation agencies that affect health care clients, including the federal Patient Safety and Quality Improvement Act of 2005. Further, it describes the various reporting mechanisms implemented by states, which include reporting requirements, data analysis, and "education" of providers.

Provider clients, including their patient safety officers, will look to counsel to assist in structuring their patient safety plans. This guide describes how to establish the patient safety plan and offers practical advice on how best to structure patient safety and compliance functions within the institution. Because counsel will also be called upon to help draft policies and procedures in support of the patient safety plan, we have included what we hope are useful tools and templates.

CHAPTER 1

Federal Regulatory Responses to Patient Error

I. INTRODUCTION

In 1999, a report by the Institute of Medicine (IOM), a section of the National Academy of Sciences, found that medical errors accounted for up to 98,000 deaths per year, far more than the number of deaths caused by highway accidents, breast cancer, or AIDS at that time.[1] In its report entitled *To Err Is Human*, the IOM found that many medical errors are preventable. The report sparked a presidential initiative ordering federal agencies to take action to reduce medical errors. The federal government developed a plan to compel health care providers to collect, analyze, and report medical errors carefully, and ultimately to pinpoint their causes. This system was intended to replace the patchwork of rules that varied from state to state, compliance with which was inconsistent. The IOM found that most medical errors are not the result of carelessness or incompetence of medical professionals, but are the end product of inadequately designed health care systems.

Since that time, there have been significant changes in how health care is delivered, including the rule change by the Centers for Medicare and Medicaid Services—effective in October 2008—that Medicare will no longer pay for certain preventable incidents such as objects left in patients during surgery, blood incompatibility, air embolisms, falls, urinary tract infections associated with catheter use, and pressure ulcers.[2] Certain private health insurers also will not pay for hospital errors.[3] The private insurers initially plan to stop reimbursement for only the most serious mistakes, but it is expected that the companies will soon stop paying for more common patient errors, such as hospital-acquired catheter infections or blood infections.[4]

This chapter will discuss the federal response to patient error, including an overview of the Center for Patient Safety, Medicare Conditions of

Participation and the OIG Supplemental Guidance for Hospitals, Federal Prosecution of Quality of Care as a False Claim, the Patient Safety and Quality Improvement Act, and the Veterans Affairs National Center for Patient Safety.

II. THE CENTER FOR PATIENT SAFETY WITHIN THE AGENCY FOR HEALTHCARE RESEARCH AND QUALITY

One of the most intriguing aspects of the IOM report is the idea that medical errors can be prevented by redesigning systems to make health care delivery less prone to human error. The foreshadowing of this innovative concept occurred many years before the report was written. Prior to the IOM report, many health care institutions in the United States were somewhat successful at addressing medical errors by implementing non-punitive reporting and the use of human-factors principles in the redesign of systems.[5] Ten years prior to the IOM report, in December 1989, the federal government created the Agency for Health Care Policy and Research (AHCPR),[6] which assisted the Department of Health and Human Services (HHS) toward achieving its goal of promoting the widespread use of the National Information Infrastructure (NII) in health care.[7] The AHCPR also provided information to assist HHS in responding to a request of then-Vice President Gore to improve the coordination of federal activities in health-care-data standards development.[8] To that end, AHCPR was an agency within the Department of Health and Human Services that strived to improve the quality, safety, efficiency, and effectiveness of health care by incorporating widespread use of information technology.

AHCPR collected data on the specific health services that Americans used, how frequently they used them, the cost of these services and how they are paid, as well as data on the cost, scope, and breadth of private health insurance held by and available to people throughout the nation.[9] The AHCPR, under the Health Cost and Utilization Program (HCUP), maintained information on inpatient hospital stays.[10] AHCPR and the National Library of Medicine (NLM) formed a partnership "to support eight cooperative agreements on applications of the electronic medical record: for example, defining laboratory and imaging standards, and developing and testing common medical terminology for the electronic patient record."[11] Additionally, AHCPR funded a program to study the "use of clinical practice guidelines as content in computerized clinical decision support systems."[12] However, the IOM's seminal report, *To Err Is*

Human, brought to the forefront a viable solution to the problem of medial errors. The report captured the attention of government leaders and officials who had the ways and means to take steps toward the prevention of medical errors.

The IOM report recommended the establishment of a federal Center for Patient Safety to serve as the research center to determine procedures that could be utilized to achieve a "50% reduction in errors over five years."[13] The president and Congress reacted to the IOM report by supporting the medical safety movement. The AHCPR was reauthorized on December 6, 1999, as the Agency for Healthcare Research and Quality (AHRQ).[14] The reauthorizing legislation directed AHRQ to: improve the quality of health care; promote patient safety and reduce medical errors; advance the use of information technology for coordinating patient care and conducting quality and outcomes research; and establish an Office of Priority Populations to ensure the needs of minorities, women, children, and the elderly are met.[15]

The president adopted the IOM's recommendations and formed an interagency Patient Safety Task Force.[16] Congress designated $50 million to fund the Center for Patient Safety and Quality within the AHRQ.[17] The AHRQ is the nation's leading federal agency for research on health care quality, costs, outcomes, and patient safety.[18] Its mission is to "support health services research that will improve the quality of health care and promote evidence-based decisionmaking."[19] The goals of the AHRQ are to: "reduce the risk of harm by promoting delivery of the best possible health care; improve health care outcomes by encouraging the use of evidence to make informed health care decisions; transform research into practice to facilitate wider access to effective health care services and reduce unnecessary costs; and use efficient and responsive business processes to maximize the Agency's resources and effectiveness of its programs."[20]

In 1999, AHRQ awarded its first grants to "generate new knowledge about approaches which are effective and cost-effective in promoting the utilization of rigorously derived evidence to improve patient care."[21] The studies involved topics on smoking cessation, Chlamydia screening of adolescents, diabetes care in medically underserved areas, and treatment of respiratory distress syndrome in preterm infants.[22] In 2000, the AHRQ grants focused on "continued development of partnerships between researchers and health care systems and organizations (e.g., integrated health service delivery systems, academic health systems, purchaser groups, managed care programs including health maintenance organizations (HMOs), practice networks, worksite clinics) to help accelerate and magnify the impact of practice-based, patient outcome research in applied settings."[23]

In 2001, the AHRQ issued grants to researchers whose work involved creating procedures and protocols that work toward the IOM's goal of reducing patient errors.[24] The grant recipients were involved in six different areas, including examination of medical-error reporting, exploration of utilizing computers and information technology to improve patient safety, analysis of the relationship between the work environment and patient error, development of innovative methods to improve patient safety, education of clinicians and others about patient safety, and support of state and local officials to advance improvement of patient safety.[25] The researchers were located at state agencies, major universities, hospitals, outpatient clinics, nursing homes, physicians' offices, professional societies, and other organizations across the nation.[26]

Also in January 2001, the AHRQ commissioned the University of California at San Francisco (UCSF)-Stanford University Evidence-Based Practice Center (EPC) to analyze the scientific literature on the topic of safety improvement, including evidence-based best patient safety practices.[27] The end result was a report entitled, *Making Health Care Safer: A Critical Analysis of Patient Safety Practices*, published on July 20, 2001.[28] The EPC defined a "patient safety practice" as "[a] type of process or structure whose application reduces the probability of adverse events resulting from exposure to the health care system across a range of diseases and procedures."[29] The results of the EPC study assisted researchers in developing a set of patient safety practices that were known to improve patient care and that could be implemented by hospitals.[30] The study involved the analysis of evidence-based outcomes.[31] In other words, the researchers examined whether patient safety practices actually produced evidence of improved medical care. The aim was to scrutinize patient safety practices and provide a critical assessment of the current research on the topic of patient safety.[32]

The EPC researchers collected data and analyzed the outcomes from previous controlled observational studies, clinical trials, peer-reviewed medical literature, relevant nonhealth care literature, and "gray literature."[33] The researchers summarized the evidence that supported each medical practice or procedure, and then ranked the practices according to the strength of the evidence that supported them.[34]

The researchers found that correcting the technical work of *individual* health care providers does not prevent the majority of medical errors.[35] Rather, it is the coordinated efforts of multiple members of the health care *team* that improves patient safety.[36] The researchers found that changes in the health care delivery system are far more productive in reducing medical errors than punishing individual providers.[37]

The AHRQ anticipated that the research projects would "address key unanswered questions about how errors occur and provide science-based information on what patients, clinicians, hospital leaders, policymakers and others can do to make the health care system safer. The results of this research [would] identify improvement strategies that work in hospitals, doctors' offices, nursing homes and other health care settings across the nation."[38] According to the results of AHRQ research, system-level failures led to three-fourths of adverse drug events in hospital systems.[39] AHRQ research also found that "preventable adverse drug events in a 700-bed teaching hospital accounted for half of the total cost of $5.6 million attributable to such events in 1 year," even though they comprised less than one-third of the total number of events.[40] There is room for improvement of patient safety within the health care system as a whole.

The EPC's report, *Making Health Care Safer: A Critical Analysis of Patient Safety Practices*, lists clinical interventions that decrease the risks associated with hospitalization, critical care, or surgery.[41] The report identified seventy-nine practices that demonstrated better patient outcomes.[42] The primary interventions include:

- Appropriate use of prophylaxis to prevent venous thromboembolism in patients at risk;
- Use of perioperative beta-blockers in appropriate patients to prevent perioperative morbidity and mortality;
- Use of maximum sterile barriers while placing central intravenous catheters to prevent infections;
- Appropriate use of antibiotic prophylaxis in surgical patients to prevent postoperative infections;
- Asking that patients recall and restate what they have been told during the informed consent process;
- Continuous aspiration of subglottic secretions (CASS) to prevent ventilator-associated pneumonia;
- Use of pressure-relieving bedding materials to prevent pressure ulcers;
- Use of real-time ultrasound guidance during central line insertion to prevent complications;
- Patient self-management for warfarin (Coumadin) to achieve appropriate outpatient anticoagulation and prevent complications;
- Appropriate provision of nutrition, with a particular emphasis on early enteral nutrition in critically ill and surgical patients; and
- Use of antibiotic-impregnated central venous catheters to prevent catheter-related infections.[43]

Although developing and implementing practice guidelines is expensive, well-constructed guidelines may play a significant role in reducing medical errors and addressing patient safety issues.[44]

The evidence-based research showed that these practices should be implemented more widely because of strong evidence that these practices supported positive patient outcomes.[45] But beyond this data, the researchers found that additional research is warranted to determine how effective it would be to incorporate certain safety practices currently used in non-medical fields (i.e., use of simulators, bar codes, computerized entry systems, crew resource management, etc.) into the health care field.[46] The report reviewed practices outside of the medical arena, such as commercial aviation, nuclear safety, and aerospace, as well as the disciplines of human-factors engineering and organizational theory, to determine whether they contained promising approaches to improving patient safety.[47] Indeed they did, but the report indicates that more research is needed.

The report, *Making Health Care Safer*, is important for two main reasons. First, the report provides information to health care providers and organizations as to which procedures and protocols would be most beneficial to implement in order to improve patient safety. Additionally, the report helps the AHRQ and other research agencies and foundations identify future areas of research they could support that would potentially yield rewarding outcomes.[48] The report was the first to approach patient safety through research of evidence-based medicine.[49] The report also identified the financial, operational, and political costs of implementing the changes.[50] The report acknowledged that there are tradeoffs between whether such changes are funded by the private sector or the public sector.[51]

Important decisions need to be made about saving lives through improved patient safety and through other health care or nonhealth care practices. Whatever the solution may be, it is certain that Americans are concerned about the risks of medical errors and eagerly anticipate ways to decrease them.[52]

III. MEDICARE CONDITIONS OF PARTICIPATION AND THE OIG SUPPLEMENTAL GUIDANCE FOR HOSPITALS

A. Conditions of Participation

The IOM report, published in 2000, recommended a 50 percent reduction in patient errors within five years.[53] An "error" was ultimately defined as "the failure of a planned action to be completed as intended or the use of a wrong plan to achieve an aim. Errors can include problems in practice, products, procedures, and systems."[54] Errors include: medication mistakes (for example, an incorrect or wrong dose of a medication); surgical oversights (for example, the amputation of the wrong appendage); diagnostic mishaps (for example, misinterpretation of a radiological image resulting in the diagnosis and treatment of a brain tumor instead of brain infection); medical equipment failures (for example, a defibrillator with nonworking batteries); infections from health care practitioners and medical procedures (for example, nosocomial infections and postsurgical infections); blood transfusion reactions (for example, consequences from mismatched blood types); and injuries due to seclusion or the use of restraints (for example, skin abrasions that progress to abscesses as a result of tight lap belts).[55] These errors are not only detrimental to the patient's health and recovery, but also increase the cost of medicine. In 1996, it was estimated that the total national cost of patient errors was approximately 4 percent of all national health expenditures.[56] In 1994, it was estimated that the annual national health care cost of drug-related morbidity and mortality in the ambulatory setting was as much as $76.6 billion.[57] It is no wonder that the government sought to reduce health care expenditures by decreasing patient errors.

Two of the largest government health care insurance programs[58] are Medicare[59] and Medicaid.[60] In order for health care organizations to participate in the Medicare and Medicaid programs, they must meet certain minimum health and safety standards.[61] The Centers for Medicare and Medicaid Services (CMS) develops these standards—referred to as Conditions of Participation (CoPs) and Conditions for Coverage (CfCs)—as a core for the improvement of quality and as protection of the health and safety of its beneficiaries.[62] CMS also verifies that the accrediting organizations it recognizes either meet or exceed the standards set forth in the CoPs and CfCs. Providers and suppliers must meet these standards in order to be Medicare- and Medicaid-certified.[63] The following types of health care organizations must meet the CoPs and CfCs: ambulatory surgical centers; comprehensive outpatient rehabilitations facilities; critical access hospitals; end-stage renal disease facilities; federally qualified health centers; home health agencies; hospices; hospitals; hospital swing beds; intermediate care facilities for persons with mental retardation; nursing facilities; organ procurement organizations; portable X-ray suppliers; programs for all-inclusive care for the elderly organizations; providers of outpatient services (physical and occupational therapists in independent practice; outpatient physical therapy, occupational therapy, and speech pathology services); psychiatric hospitals; religious nonmedical health care institutions; rural health clinics; skilled nursing facilities; and transplant hospitals.

In January 2003, CMS issued a final CoPs rule requiring hospitals to develop and maintain Quality Assessment Performance and Improvement programs (QAPI).[64] This rule mandated that a hospital's QAPI program must be "an ongoing program that shows measurable improvement in indicators for which there is evidence that it will improve health outcomes and identify and reduce medical errors."[65] The program also must incorporate data that indicates the quality of health services. The hospital must use this data to "(i) [m]onitor the effectiveness and safety of services and quality of care; and (ii) [i]dentify opportunities for improvement and changes that will lead to improvement."[66] Additionally, the hospital is required to set priorities to "(i) [f]ocus on high-risk, high-volume, or problem prone areas; (ii) [c]onsider the incidence, prevalence, and severity of problems in those areas; and (iii) [a]ffect health outcomes, patient safety, and quality of care."[67] As part of the QAPI program, the hospital must conduct performance improvement projects that are proportional in scope, number, and complexity to the hospital's services and operations.[68] The hospital must also keep a record of what projects are being performed, the reasons for conducting the projects, and the measurable progress accomplished.[69]

A QAPI program systematically examines the hospital's quality of care and implements improvement projects on a continuous basis.[70] It concentrates "on the actual care delivered to patients, the performance of the hospital as an organization, and the impact of treatment furnished by the hospital on the health status of its patients."[71] The QAPI program involves all aspects of measuring quality of care and keeping it at satisfactory levels.[72] Generally, these include: "identifying and verifying quality-related problems and their underlying cause[s]; designing and implementing corrective action to address deficiencies; and following up to determine the degree of success of an intervention and to detect new problems and opportunities for improvement."[73] There is a presumption that there is no permanent threshold for good performance. The goal is to improve overall performance.

B.   OIG Supplemental Guidance for Hospitals

The federal government actively prosecutes fraud and abuse in the health care industry. Fraud and abuse are high priority issues for the federal government because the government recovers billions of dollars from investigations, prosecutions, and settlements with health care providers and entities.[74] In each of the years 2004, 2005, and 2006, the average annual recovery from health care providers was $2.68 billion.[75] With so much at stake, it is little wonder that health care providers seek guidance from the federal government on how to comply with the number and complexities of the laws and regulations that govern health care.

In response to growing concerns in health care about compliance with anti-fraud and abuse laws and regulations, the United States Department of Health and Human Services (HHS) Office of Inspector General (OIG) issued its first compliance guidance in 1997, which addressed fraud and abuse in the clinical laboratory arena.[76] Subsequently, many additional health care providers wanted to adopt voluntary compliance programs for the purpose of protecting their operations from allegations of fraud and abuse. In order to promote that goal, the OIG issued its second compliance program guidance, which was geared to hospitals.[77] This program guidance was developed by the OIG with the assistance of several provider groups and industry representatives.[78] The OIG intended the program to help hospitals and their agents develop internal controls that promote compliance with federal and state law.[79] The program guidance recommendations were designed as a voluntary guidance tool to prevent fraud, abuse, and waste in health care, while promoting quality health care to patients.[80]

The OIG recommended that a comprehensive compliance program for hospitals include these seven core elements:[81]

1) The development and distribution of written standards of conduct, as well as written polices and procedures that promote the hospital's commitment to compliance (e.g., by including adherence to compliance as an element in evaluating managers and employees) and that address specific areas of potential fraud, such as claims development and submission processes, code gaming, and financial relationships with physicians and other health care professionals;

2) The designation of a chief compliance officer and other appropriate bodies (e.g., a corporate compliance committee) charged with the responsibility of operating and monitoring the compliance program, and who report directly to the CEO and the governing body;

3) The development and implementation of regular, effective education and training programs for all affected employees;

4) The maintenance of a process, such as a hotline, to receive complaints, and the adoption of procedures to protect the anonymity of complainants and to protect whistleblowers from retaliation;

5) The development of a system to respond to allegations of improper/illegal activities and the enforcement of appropriate disciplinary action against employees who have violated internal compliance policies, applicable statutes, regulations, or federal health care program requirements;

6) The use of audits and/or other evaluation techniques to monitor compliance and assist in the reduction of identified problem areas; and

7) The investigation and remediation of identified systemic problems and the development of policies addressing the nonemployment or retention of sanctioned individuals.[82]

The OIG Compliance Program Guidance for Hospitals sets forth specific conduct and risk areas of concern related to each of these elements. The OIG acknowledged that the health care industry is constantly evolving and that compliance is a dynamic process. The OIG issues supplemental guidance to keep pace with the changes. The OIG issued a Supplemental Compliance Program Guidance for Hospitals in January 2005[83] in order to keep the compliance guidance current with market trends.

The OIG Supplemental Compliance Program Guidance for Hospitals continued to discuss additional risk areas of concern, specifically highlighting outpatient procedure coding, admission and discharge policies, supplemental payment considerations, and the use of information technology. It pinpointed the submission of accurate claims and information as the largest risk area for hospitals. It also discussed the hospital's compliance with: the physician self-referral law[84] (commonly known as the "Stark" law"), the Anti-Kickback Statute,[85] payments to reduce or limit services (gainsharing arrangements), the Emergency Medical Treatment and Labor Act (EMTALA),[86] and substandard care.

In the Supplemental Compliance Program Guidance for Hospitals, the OIG reminded medical providers that the OIG has the authority to exclude any individual or entity from participation in federal health care programs if the health care provider or entity supplies unnecessary care (i.e., care beyond the patient's needs) or substandard quality of care (i.e., care below the professional standard of care).[87] The reader should note that it is not necessary for the health care provider or entity to have "knowledge" or "intent" of the substandard care. Most importantly, the "exclusion can be based upon unnecessary or substandard items or services provided to *any patient*, even if that patient is _not_ a Medicare or Medicaid beneficiary."[88] The OIG recommended that hospitals should continually measure performance and compare it to comprehensive standards. Hospitals who participate in Medicare should always meet the Medicare hospital conditions of participation (CoPs), especially the CoP governing a quality assessment and performance improvement program[89] and the CoP governing the medical staff.[90]

State survey agencies or accreditation organizations, such as the Joint Commission on Accreditation of Healthcare Organizations (JCAHO), determine whether hospitals comply with the CoPs. In addition to the CoPs, the OIG recommended that hospitals develop their own quality of care programs that evaluate the quality of nursing care, ancillary services, and medical services. The evaluation of the medical services should include overseeing the credentialing and peer review of the medical staff.

In August 2007, the government went one step further in its efforts to improve care and reduce errors. CMS announced that it would no longer pay for certain "hospital acquired conditions."[91] These conditions are "preventable events" that would be less likely to occur if the hospital staff engaged in certain patient safety protocols through the application of evidence-based prevention guidelines. As of October 1, 2008, CMS will no longer pay for the following conditions if they are acquired by the patient during a hospital stay: foreign objects left in patient during surgical procedures; air embolisms; blood transfusion errors; urine catheter-associated urinary tract infections; pressure sores; vascular catheter-associated infections; surgical site infections; and hospital-acquired injuries.[92] In order to receive payment for any of these conditions, the hospital will have to demonstrate that the patient came to the facility with the condition.

Hospital industry analysts are concerned that hospital staff will scrutinize patients more closely on admission and find more reasons to report preexisting conditions or develop some other means to circumvent the new rule.[93] According to the American Hospital Association, the new rule could force the hospital to absorb the cost of treating certain infections that may have been contracted prior to the patient's admission.[94] The intent is to have this new rule provide incentives for hospitals to engage in patient safety procedures that will significantly decrease patient errors.[95] However, the fear is that this new rule will lead to creative ways to sidestep its requirements.[96]

Additionally, some health care lawyers believe that the new CMS rule is one step toward federalizing medical malpractice law by allowing the government to determine the appropriate standard of care.[97] Some lawyers contend that plaintiffs ultimately will benefit from this new rule by being able to persuade the jury that Medicare did not pay for a particular injury because it deemed the injury a "medical mistake," thus proving malpractice.[98] Others say that this new rule will spark a flurry of litigation based on the Americans with Disabilities Act to determine whether patients were turned away from elective procedures because they were deemed at "high risk" for infections or falls because of their disability.[99] Whatever the ultimate impact of this new rule, there is one thing that is certain: The federal government will actively pursue any false claims for payment. In fact, as the next section explains, federal statutes prohibit such activities.

IV.   FEDERAL PROSECUTION OF QUALITY OF CARE AS A FALSE CLAIM

The Civil False Claim Act (FCA) is a Civil War-era statute that prohibits the knowing submission to the federal government of false or fraudulent claims.[100] The FCA authorizes the government to file a civil action against an alleged false claimant.[101] The FCA also allows individuals to bring a civil action, called a *qui tam* case, through a private attorney general in the name of the United States as a relator.[102] The procedure to file a *qui tam* case is as follows: A relator files the complaint *in camera* and serves the United States with a copy of the complaint and written disclosure of substantially all material evidence and information.[103] The complaint must stay under seal for sixty days, during which time the United States may intervene and move forward with the action.[104] The complaint is only served upon the defendant if the court orders it.[105]

If the government proceeds with the *qui tam* action and it is successful, the relator obtains an award between 15 and 25 percent of the proceeds of the action.[106] If the government decides not to proceed, the private individual may proceed with the *qui tam* action. If the individual is successful, he or she will keep an award of 25 to 30 percent of the judgment or settlement.[107] The government gets the rest of the award. Any person found liable under the FCA will suffer a civil penalty of $5,500 to $11,000 per claim, plus three times the amount of damages that the government sustains because of the act of that person.[108] *Qui tam* cases can be brought by various individuals, including competitors, disgruntled employees, patients, and family members. FCA claims can be brought for a variety of reasons in many different industries.[109] However, a significant amount of FCA litigation is based on fraudulent health care claims.[110]

In fact, "health care and procurement fraud cases constituted about seventy-nine percent of all qui tam cases" from 1987 through 2005.[111] Traditionally, health care fraud claims involved misrepresentations of facts for payment of health care services.[112] For example, health care providers have been found liable for submitting claims for services that were never rendered, such as a claim for services where the health care provider never treated the patient.[113] The court has imposed liability for bills for health care services that were not rendered as indicated, such as when cheaper services were provided but the health care provider billed for a more expensive service.[114] However, a more recent FCA movement involves bringing FCA claims based on the *quality* of health care in institutions that participate in federal health care programs.

United States ex rel. Aranda v. Community Psychiatric Centers[115] was one of the first cases to challenge the quality of health care under the FCA. In that case, the government claimed that a psychiatric hospital failed to provide government-insured patients with a reasonably safe environment and that by submitting bills to Medicaid, the hospital implicitly certified that it was abiding by applicable statues, rules, and regulations that required the provision of an appropriate quality of care and a safe and secure environment for the Medicaid patients.[116] The government argued that the hospital failed to take appropriate precautions and that physical injury to—and sexual abuse of—psychiatric patients occurred because of inadequate conditions, such as understaffed shifts, lack of monitoring equipment, and inappropriate housing assignments.[117] The defendant hospital challenged the claim, arguing that the government failed to state a claim under the FCA because the claim was based on the *quality of care*. The court found that the government stated actionable claims based on the quality of care rendered.[118] The court noted that "[s]tatutes and regulations governing the Medicaid program clearly require health care providers to meet quality of care standards, and a provider's failure to meet such standards is a ground for exclusion from the program."[119] The court denied the hospital's motion to dismiss, but did not address whether the plaintiff would ultimately prevail on the merits of the case.[120] However, this case was one of the earliest cases to use the quality of health care and patient safety as the basis for prosecuting false claims.

In another early case, *United States v. Community Psychiatric Centers,*[121] the government sued a nursing home under the FCA, claiming that the facility was "so severely understaffed that it could not possibly have administered all of the care it was obligated to perform."[122] The defendant nursing home filed a motion to dismiss. However the court denied the motion and held that the FCA applied to the submission of claims for services that were not actually performed. In support of its denial, the court found that the *United States ex rel. Aranda v. Community Psychiatric Centers* case was sufficiently analogous to the *United States v. Community Psychiatric Centers* case.[123]

The common reasoning throughout these cases is that claims based on the quality of care are not regulatory violations *per se*. Rather, they are based on the government's receipt of a bill for services that were never rendered.[124] In the wake of these cases, several federal prosecutors brought claims based on violations of the FCA where quality of health care was at issue.[125] These cases fall under two general categories: violations of technical quality standards and violations of institutional quality of care.[126] A violation of technical standards occurs where the health care provider implicitly certifies that relevant regulatory or legal requirements are met when in fact they were not.[127] Although prosecutors have attempted to persuade the court that these are valid causes of action, the courts repeatedly reject these claims because the violations are not sufficiently linked to the government's payment decision.[128]

The courts are more inclined to recognize causes of actions based on violations of institutional quality of care, such as in the *United States ex rel. Aranda v. Community Psychiatric Centers* and *United States v. Community Psychiatric Centers* cases. These types of cases involve instances where patient care did not meet standards provided under law for federal health care program recipients.[129] Actions based on violations of quality of care are more aligned with the traditional false claims actions. Traditionally, an action under the FCA could be classified into several prime categories: mischarges; false negotiations; false certifications of entitlement; substandard products and services; and reverse false claims.[130]

In the first category, mischarges occur where the federal government is billed for items or services that were not delivered.[131] The second category, false negotiations, involves misrepresentations made during the negotiation of a federal contract.[132] The third category, false certifications of entitlement, happen where an applicant fabricates that he or she has met the criteria for the government benefit for which he or she applied, such as when an applicant falsely certifies that his or her company meets the requirements for a small business loan from the Small Business Administration.[133] The fourth category, substandard products and services, is fairly self-explanatory in that it involves circumstances in which the contractor supplies a mediocre alternative instead of the service or product that was negotiated in the contract.[134] The final category, reverse false claims, deals with situations where the person uses a false record or statement to either lower or escape altogether his or her financial obligation to the government.[135] For example, a reverse false claim would occur where an entity promises to pay the government a percentage of profits but misleads the government by reducing its stated amount of income or overinflating expenses in order to pay less money to the government.[136]

Actions brought under the FCA that involve violations of the quality of patient care, rather than violations of technical quality standards, tend to fit into these five traditional categories. Therefore, courts are more apt to allow this type of litigation under the FCA.

In fact, the FCA is a strong tool that prosecutors use to recoup money for medical services that were never provided to patients, or that were provided in a way that was considerably less than the provider billed.[137] The government has utilized the FCA to pursue actions against health care providers for purportedly false or fraudulent charges that did not meet the level of care that was stated on the bill. These types of FCA claims against health care providers resemble the more traditional false claims actions. The government has more recently tried to broaden the types of medical false claims actions that can be brought under the FCA to include claims involving the quality of health care. The further the allegations move away from the traditional false claims categories, the less likely the courts will recognize that the FCA applies. Despite this attempt to attack substandard medical care by stretching the FCA to its limit, one of the government's top concerns is enforcement of the FCA as it pertains to the quality of health care.[138]

A natural expansion of the government's use of the FCA to address quality of health care is for the government to bring claims that can be traced directly to medical errors. Medical error can result in actual harm to identifiable patients. Medical providers generate bills to the government for identifiable patients who utilize Medicare or Medicaid, and the government pays for those medical services. As a result, there can be a direct link between government payment and medical errors. In order to prevail on an FCA claim, the government must prove that the health care provider knowingly submitted a false or fraudulent bill to the government for payment.[139] Thus, if a health care provider submits a bill for reimbursement by Medicare or Medicaid for inadequate services rendered (i.e., medical errors), theoretically the government may be able to prove that the medical bill was fraud because the government was denied the value of that payment.[140]

As conditions for participation in the Medicare and Medicaid programs, hospitals "must be constructed, arranged, and maintained to ensure the safety of the patient..."[141]; must have a quality assessment and performance improvement program and must "monitor the effectiveness and safety of services and quality of care; and identify opportunities for improvement and changes that will lead to improvement..."[142]; and must "develop policies and procedures that minimize drug errors."[143] Moreover, the hospital patient has the right to "receive care in a safe setting" and to be "free from all forms of abuse and harassment"[144] Just as *United States v. NHC Healthcare Corp.*[145] set forth claims under the FCA for nursing homes to meet federal regulatory requirements and *United States ex rel. Aranda v. Community Psychiatric Centers*[146] permitted FCA claims for substandard psychiatric care, the government can argue that hospitals also may be liable under the FCA for submitting bills where there is medical error.

However, there is considerable controversy as to whether the claims based on quality of health care are actually the government's attempt to broaden its theories of FCA violations or whether they are just efforts to compel health care providers into settling lawsuits that have no merit.[147] One can argue that health care institutions are under tremendous pressure to settle FCA claims for three reasons: The amount of the potential damages;[148] the economic impact the claim could have on the business in terms of legal fees and employees' time required to defend such cases; and the potential exclusion from the government health care program.[149] The enticement to settle the claim and move on with business rather than face protracted litigation proceedings and trial may be too tempting for health care institutions to pass up. The problem with settlements of FCA claims is that they remove the relevant factual and legal issues from the scrutiny of the court and the jury.[150] The settlements result in unchallenged theories of FCA liability, allowing the government to bring more claims based on these same theories.[151]

The government must overcome a substantial hurdle to prove its FCA case based on medical errors. It must show that there was a medical error that occurred due to a lack of systems in place to prevent the error.[152] In other words, the government must show that there was in fact an error and that the error was the result of the medical institution's failure to establish policies and procedures to prevent the error, which was a deviation from the standard of care. However, there is much debate in the medical literature as to which practices result in the best outcomes, so the difficulties arise in not knowing what systems to put in place to avoid the medical errors.[153]

Although prosecuting claims based on medical errors is a logical extension of the government's use of the FCA, all it does is penalize the health care providers without supplying an answer or a resolution to the problem. Focusing on a punitive resolution to medical errors through enforcement of the FCA may only discourage the development of practices that increase patient safety. Health care providers will act to decrease the risk of liability rather than develop and promote methods to improve patient safety. The concern over FCA litigation should not be so great that health care providers engage in safer, but ultimately less effective, medical practices.[154] Additionally, as noted earlier, the pressure to settle FCA claims prevents issues related to medical error from being resolved by the courts. In other words, utilizing the FCA may prove to be a futile effort to resolve the patient safety issues brought to light by the IOM report, *To Err Is Human*.

V.   PATIENT SAFETY AND QUALITY IMPROVEMENT ACT

After the IOM released *To Err Is Human*, the president[155] and the federal government pressed forward to address the problems of medical errors.[156] The president signed an executive memorandum directing the Quality Interagency Coordination Task Force (QuIC) to analyze the Institute of Medicine study and make recommendations.[157] He also signed legislation that reauthorized the Agency for Healthcare Research and Quality and provided $25 million in funding for research to improve health care quality and prevent medical errors.[158] The AHRQ was named as the lead federal agency to develop strategies and tools for reducing medical errors.[159] AHRQ also assumed responsibility for developing a major report to the nation on health quality.[160]

The QuIC released its report in February 2000.[161] The report described the actions that the QuIC agencies[162] would take to build on current programs and create new initiatives to reduce errors.[163] The QuIC concurred with the IOM's opinion that "medical errors are generally due to systematic flaws in health care rather than individual incompetence or neglect."[164] Not surprisingly, the report also noted that medical errors compromise patient safety and quality, and can be avoided.[165] The QuIC recognized that the medical community can learn valuable lessons from other industries—such as aviation, motor vehicle, and manufacturing—to develop systematic safeguards to protect against medical errors.[166] The report acknowledged that medical errors occur in all areas of health care (not only hospital settings) and in all areas of health care practice including disease prevention, surgery, pharmacy, diagnostic testing, and others.[167] The QuIC advised that medical professionals should be provided with opportunities to learn from medical errors in order to avoid future errors.[168] It encouraged public reporting of both certain types of errors and the facilities that use error-reduction techniques to provide the public with information upon which to base their health care choices.[169] Overall, the report focused on the federal government's involvement in the development and implementation of system-wide remedies for preventing medical errors.[170]

After the report was published, the president announced a national action plan to reduce medical errors by 50 percent within five years.[171] The plan included: the establishment of a new Center for Quality Improvement in Patient Safety; a guarantee that each of the 6,000 hospitals that participate in the Medicare program build a safety program to prevent medical errors; and a state-based national system of reporting medical errors, including mandatory reporting of preventable medical errors that cause death or serious injury and voluntary reporting of other medical mistakes.[172] In order to promote a new culture of safety rather than the old culture of silence, legislation was proposed to protect health care providers and shield confidentiality of patients' medical information.[173]

The proposed legislation resulted in the Patient Safety and Quality Improvement Act of 2005 (PSQUIA).[174] The PSQUIA was intended to improve patient safety by creating a foundation for the development of a change in attitude among health care providers. Instead of continuing the customary apprehension and cautiousness about disclosure of patient errors, the PSQUIA was designed to cultivate a new culture of transparency and discussion about patient errors. The PSQUIA created Patient Safety Organizations (PSOs) to collect and analyze confidential information about patient errors from health care providers. A PSO is a private or public entity or component thereof that is listed and certified by the Department of Health and Human Services.[175] In order to qualify to become a PSO, the entity must have policies and procedures in place to perform patient safety activities and agree to comply with certain criteria including: conducting activities that improve patient safety and quality of health care delivery; hiring qualified staff; contracting with more than one provider for the purpose of receiving and reviewing patient safety work product; certifying that it is not a health insurance issuer; agreeing to fully disclose financial or other relationships between the entity and the provider; collecting the data in a standardized manner; and using the patient safety work product for the purpose of providing direct feedback and assistance to providers to minimize patient risk.[176]

"Patient safety work product" is defined as—

> any data, reports, records, memoranda, analyses, or written or oral statements (i) which (I) are assembled or developed by a provider for reporting to a patient safety organization and are reported to a patient safety organization or (II) are developed by a patient safety organization for the conduct of patient safety activities and which could result in improved patient safety, health care quality, or health care outcomes; or (ii) which identify or constitute the deliberations or analysis of, or

identify the fact of reporting pursuant to, a patient safety evaluation system.[177]

This does not include information that is "collected, maintained, or developed separately, or exists separately, from a patient safety evaluation system."[178] Also, if the information is kept separately from a patient evaluation system, it does not become patient safety work product merely by reason of reporting it to a patient safety organization.[179]

The PSQUIA provides a federal legal privilege and confidentiality protections for health care providers that reveal information pertaining to patient errors to a PSO, or who assist in obtaining information that is developed by a PSO (in other words, "patient safety work product") to conduct patient safety activities.[180] The PSQUIA provides a federal legal privilege as follows:

> [P]atient safety work product shall be privileged and shall not be (1) subject to a Federal, State, or local civil, criminal, or administrative subpoena or order, including in a Federal, State, or local civil or administrative disciplinary proceeding against a provider; (2) subject to discovery in connection with a Federal, State, or local civil criminal or administrative proceeding including in a Federal, State, or local civil or administrative disciplinary proceeding against a provider; (3) subject to disclosure pursuant to section 552 of title 5, United States Code (commonly known as the Freedom of Information Act) or any other similar Federal, State, or local law; (4) admitted as evidence in any Federal, State, or local governmental civil proceeding, criminal proceeding, administrative rulemaking proceeding, or administrative adjudicatory proceeding, including any such proceeding against a provider; or (5) admitted in a professional disciplinary proceeding of a professional disciplinary body established or specifically authorized under State law.[181]

The PSQUIA contains the following provision for the confidentiality of patient safety work product: "patient safety work product shall be confidential and shall not be disclosed."[182] There are a few exceptions for the legal privilege and confidentiality. The legal privilege and confidentiality of patient safety work product does not apply to the following disclosures:

- Disclosure of relevant patient safety work product for use in a criminal proceeding after a court makes an *in camera* determination that such patient safety work product contains evidence of a criminal act and that such patient safety work product is material to the proceeding and not reasonably available from any other source.

- Disclosure of patient safety work product to the extent required to carry out civil actions against a provider who makes an adverse employment action against an individual where the individual in good faith reported information either to the employer for purposes of passing the information to the PSO or directly to the PSO.
- Disclosure of patient safety work product if authorized by each provider identified in such work product.[183]

Also, the following disclosures are *not* confidential and are allowed:

- Disclosure of patient safety work product to carry out patient safety activities.
- Disclosure of non-identifiable patient safety work product.
- Disclosure of patient safety work product to grantees, contractors, or other entities carrying out research, evaluation, or demonstration projects that are authorized, funded, certified, or otherwise sanctioned for the purpose of conducting research to the extent that disclosure of protected health information would be allowed for such purpose under the HIPAA confidentiality regulations.
- Disclosure by a provider to the Food and Drug Administration (FDA) for a drug or activity that is regulated by the FDA.
- Voluntary disclosure of patient safety work product by a provider to an accrediting body that accredits that provider.
- Disclosures that the Secretary of Health and Human Services determines are needed for business operations and are consistent with the goals of this section.
- Disclosure of patient safety work product to law enforcement authorities relating to the commission of a crime or to an event reasonably believed to be a crime if the person making the disclosure believes, reasonably under the circumstances, that the patient safety work product that is disclosed is necessary for criminal law enforcement purposes.
- Disclosure by someone other than a patient safety organization.
- Disclosure of patient safety work product that does not contain materials that assess the quality of care of an identifiable provider or describe actions or failures to act by an identifiable provider.[184]

Lastly, there is no federal privilege for voluntary disclosure of nonidentifiable patient safety work product.[185]

Any patient safety work product that is disclosed continues to be privileged and confidential even after it is disclosed.[186] The disclosure is not considered a waiver of privilege or confidentiality.[187] The privileged and confidential nature of the work product also applies to the work product in the possession or control of a person to whom such work product was disclosed.[188] The provider cannot take a detrimental employment action[189] against an individual who, in good faith, either reports information to the provider with the intent that the information will be reported to a patient safety organization or reports the information directly to a patient safety organization.[190]

The PSQUIA also limits the use of the information in legal proceedings.[191] Patient safety work product is not subject to subpoena in federal or state civil, criminal, or administrative proceedings, or in civil or administrative disciplinary proceeding against a provider.[192] It is also not subject to discovery or disclosure, and cannot be admitted in evidence in such proceedings.[193]

There are provisions for monetary penalties for violations of confidentiality or privilege protections.[194] A person who discloses identifiable patient safety work product in a knowing or reckless manner is subject to a civil monetary penalty of up to $10,000 for each act.[195] A person who is given an adverse employment action by virtue of the person's disclosure of information to the provider with the intent that the information would be passed along to the patient safety organization—or disclosure of the information directly to a patient safety organization—may bring a civil action to enjoin any act or practice that creates the adverse employment action.[196] The individual may also obtain other appropriate equitable relief, including reinstatement of employment, back pay, and restoration of employee benefits.[197]

Finally, the PSQUIA required the creation of a "network of patient safety databases that provides an interactive evidence-based management resource for providers, patient safety organizations, and other entities."[198] The Network of Patient Safety Databases (NPSD) has the capacity to accept and collect data across the network to analyze nonidentifiable patient safety work product that is voluntarily reported by PSOs, providers, and other entities.[199] Common formats are used for the reporting of data to and within the NPSD, including work product elements, common and consistent definitions, and a standardized computer interface for the processing of such work product.[200] The information reported to the NPSD is used to analyze national and regional statistics, including trends and patterns of health care errors.[201] The information is then made available to the public and included in the annual quality reports.[202]

AHRQ conducted a survey of 400 hospitals in 2007 to assess hospital staff opinions about patient safety issues, medical error, and event reporting.[203] The survey measured to what extent the hospitals had established a culture of safety in their institutions. The survey indicated that, even after the passage of the PSQUIA, only 43 percent of staff felt that adverse event reports and their own errors would not be held against them or kept in their file. The encouraging news was that 78 percent of staff reported that they treated each other with respect and worked together as a team. When asked to grade their own institution's patient safety, 48 percent felt that their hospital rated "very good"; 24 percent rated their hospital "average"; 22 percent rated their hospital "excellent"; 5 percent rated their hospital "poor"; and only 1 percent rated their hospital "failing." Lastly, the survey indicated that 53 percent of hospital staff did not report any patient errors in the previous twelve months; 27 percent reported one to two patient errors; 13 percent reported three to five errors; 4 percent reported six to ten patient errors; 2 percent reported eleven to twenty patient errors; and only 1 percent reported twenty-one or more patient errors. Query as to whether these statistics reflect a continued culture of silence or an actual sign of increased patient safety and quality improvement.

In an effort to improve patient safety, the AHRQ teamed up with the Department of Veterans Affairs (VA) to provide knowledge and skills to teams of hospital staff.[204] This new partnership is the Patient Safety Improvement Corps (PSIC). The goals of PSIC are to: conduct effective investigations of medical errors; prepare reports on the findings; develop and implement sustainable system interventions based on the report findings; measure and evaluate the impact of the safety intervention (i.e., mitigate, reduce, or eliminate the opportunity for error and patient injury); and ensure the sustainability of effective safety interventions by transforming them into standard clinical practice.[205] The PSIC program is presented to eligible participating organizations through a series of three one-week sessions. The program consists of topics, tools, and methods to help participants reduce patient error and improve safety.[206] Prior to the PSIC, the VA developed the National Center for Patient Safety, which cultivated a shift in attitude from punishment for patient errors to prevention of patient errors.[207] This new view on dealing with patient errors transformed the "name and blame" culture into a systems approach of problem solving. In the next section, we will explore the changes in patient safety that were implemented by the Veterans Administration.

VI.   VETERANS AFFAIRS NATIONAL CENTER FOR PATIENT SAFETY

The Veterans Affairs (VA) health care system is the largest integrated health care system in the nation.[208] There is at least one VA hospital in every state, Puerto Rico, and the District of Columbia.[209] The system has more than 1,300 sites for patient care, including 875 ambulatory care and community-based outpatient clinics, 136 nursing homes, 43 residential rehabilitation treatment programs, 206 Veterans Centers, and 88 home-care programs that provide medical, surgical, and rehabilitative care.[210] In 2005, it serviced 5.3 million people, including 587,000 inpatient and 57.5 million outpatient visits.[211] The system also provides training and education for health care professionals. In fact, the VA manages the largest medical education and health professional training program in the nation.[212] Every year, approximately 83,000 health care professionals receive training in VA medical centers, and more than half of the physicians currently practicing received part of their professional education in the VA health care system.[213] The VA health care system now provides more medical services to veterans and their families than at any time in its history.[214] With its widespread medical services, education, and training, it is not surprising that the government looked to the VA health care system to develop patient safety programs and methods that would decrease patient errors.

One segment of the VA health care system is the Veterans Affairs National Center for Patient Safety (NCPS). The NCPS was established in 1999 with a primary goal of reducing and preventing harm to patients within the VA national system of health care.[215] The NCPS focuses on prevention of patient errors, rather than punishment, by instituting human factors engineering methods from industries such as aviation and nuclear power to create a systems approach to prevention of patient errors.

The systems approach to problem solving analyzes patient errors within the system as a whole, to determine ways to prevent reoccurrence. The approach recognizes that unintentional adverse events generally do not occur for a single reason or because of the actions of one person, but they are attributed to a series of events that culminate in a bad outcome. In the past, patient safety initiatives focused on blaming an individual person for patient error. This type of "person" approach focuses on blaming individuals for forgetfulness, inattention, carelessness, or poor production.[216] Unlike the "person" approach, the "systems" approach focuses on the conditions and environment in which the individuals work.[217] It targets the health care team, tasks, workplace, organization, and physical environment.[218] At first glance, it may seem as though the systems approach relieves individuals from taking responsibility for their actions. On the contrary, the systems approach does include individual account-ability.[219] But instead of jumping to the conclusion that a patient error is someone's "fault," the entire system is analyzed to look for problem areas that can be corrected.[220] All of the 158 Veterans Affairs hospitals through-out the nation participate in this safety initiative.[221]

The NCPS uses a root-cause analysis (RCA) method to examine adverse medical events.[222] In RCA, the objective is to determine what hap-pened, why it happened, and what must be done to prevent it from hap-pening again.[223] In order to achieve this goal, NCPS developed training programs, cognitive aids, companion software, and tools for health care facilities to use.[224] This proactive risk assessment and prevention gives staff an increased ability to recognize solutions to problems.[225] After the staff performed RCA on thousands of reports, they found that communi-cation breakdown was a major root-cause contributing factor, occurring in 78 percent of cases.[226] The NCPS determined that one way to increase patient safety is to increase effective communication among members of the health care team. The NCPS then developed "medical team training" (MTT) to improve patient care through more effective communication and teamwork.[227]

MTT is based on the principles of crew resource management (CRM), which were developed in the aviation industry.[228] CRM is designed to improve communication skills among team members.[229] CRM instruc-tors initially teach a team of medical care providers assertiveness skills and rules of conduct that promote respect and shared responsibility.[230] Thereafter, they teach specific tools for clinical situations.[231] The funda-mental tool is a briefing, which is a conversation facilitated by a team leader to establish a shared understanding of the management of patient care in the operating room, emergency room, intensive care unit, or any other clinical unit.[232] There are three basic types of briefings: patient-centered briefings, which are done with all team members, the patient, and the family prior to a procedure or during grand rounds to facilitate a common understanding of the pending procedure and voice concerns about procedure-related or care-related issues; administrative briefings, which are staff meetings to discuss all relevant issues in the management of patient care on the clinical unit; and debriefings, which are done after a procedure, an event, or a work experience to process what happened and to explore needed improvements.[233] The training also involves educa-tional instruction, interaction with attendees, faculty role play, and vid-eos of clinical vignettes produced by NCPS faculty.[234]

There are a variety of NCPS cognitive aids that can be used by health care facilities to increase patient safety. These include aids for triage, fall prevention and management, escape and elopement management, the "healthcare failure mode effect analysis process," and root-cause analysis tools. Triage cards are used by RCA teams to obtain information needed for the root-cause analysis of a particular type of patient error.[235] The fall prevention and management cognitive aid provides tips and suggestions on interventions that the staff can use to prevent patient falls.[236] If the patient is at risk for falls, it recommends interdisciplinary plans that include medical, nursing, and rehabilitation management that provide a systemic assessment for determining patients' risks for falling and suggested interventions.[237] The escape and elopement management aid provides information to help staff develop ways to prevent patients from getting away from the facility or unit.[238] It recommends first using the least restrictive methods to prevent elopement and customizing the elopement intervention to meet the patient's needs, the time of day, and the level of activities.[239] It encourages staff to be creative and flexible, and to involve the patient's family as much as possible.[240]

The "healthcare failure mode effect analysis process" (HFMEA) aid provides information on how to complete a proactive risk assessment using the model that NCPS developed.[241] This model recommends identifying and improving steps to ensure a safe and desirable outcome.[242] It includes recognizing the patient error, developing a flow chart of what was intended to be accomplished, and if the process is complex, developing subcategories to isolate the smaller tasks.[243] Thereafter, it recommends conducting a hazard analysis, identifying actions that will control the hazard, and identifying the person in charge of taking those actions.[244] It advocates that staff obtain top management approval before implementing the plan.[245]

The NCPS tools for health care facilities include root-cause analysis, close call reporting, and event flow diagramming. The root-cause analysis tools aid provides instruction on how to complete a root-cause analysis using the NCPS analysis process, including "event-flow" and "cause-and-effect" diagramming.[246] It serves as a guide on how to help teams develop a chronological event-flow diagram to understand *what* occurred. In addition, it helps teams develop a cause-and-effect diagram to understand *why* the event occurred.[247]

After the root-cause analysis is done, an action plan is developed to address deficiencies in the system.[248] The goal of the action plan is to find ways to prevent repeats of adverse events or close calls.[249] A close call is a situation in which an adverse event could have occurred but was averted prior to the event.[250] Close calls are also known as "near misses."[251] Close-call reporting is done in the NCPS Patient Safety Information System, and receives the same level of scrutiny as adverse events that cause actual harm.[252] Event-flow diagramming is one of the critical tools for many process improvement activities including root-cause analysis investigation.[253] It gives all members of the team the same understanding of what occurred and helps avoid different interpretations of the same event.[254]

One of the biggest improvements in patient safety is attributed to the internal, confidential, nonpunitive reporting system called the Patient Safety Information System, which staff can access electronically to document patient safety issues and information.[255] The information is then studied so that staff can take corrective actions and share the event across the system so that other staff members will have the benefit of hindsight if they encounter the same situation. The NCPS also developed a voluntary Patient Safety Reporting System (PSRS) so that staff can report adverse events and close calls that would not otherwise be reported elsewhere in the system.[256]

According to the NCPS, one way of increasing patient safety is to identify and control hazards in the health care environment.[257] A "hazard" is defined as "anything in the clinical environment that poses a risk for harm to a patient or provider."[258] A hazard generally exists in the health care environment before a patient error occurs. The difficulty is to spot it before it harms patients. If the hazard is identified before the patient error occurs, NCPS suggests that the health care team take a proactive approach to examine the system and develop methods to eliminate the hazard before an error occurs. If the hazard is identified after the error occurs, NCPS suggests that the health care team do a root-cause analysis to determine where the hazard lies and develop ways to control the hazard to prevent future patient errors.[259]

The NCPS developed a "hierarchy of hazard control," which ranks approaches from the most effective to the least effective. First, the most effective way to control a hazard is to remove it completely from the patient's environment. The next effective way to control the hazard is to instruct the health care team to guard against the hazard. The third most effective way to control the hazard is to avoid the hazard. If none of the above approaches are possible, the last resort to control the hazard is to provide the health care team with warnings against the hazard.[260]

In summary, the NCPS recognizes that people do not come to work in the health care setting to hurt someone or make mistakes.[261] Rather, mistakes occur because of a breakdown in the system. The key to preventing future patient errors is to recognize potential hazards and develop a plan to avoid them in the health care setting.[262] Communication is an essential element in developing a plan to prevent future patient errors. The goal of patient safety is to reduce or eliminate harm to patients through an examination of the system as a whole, in an effort to determine hazards that can be eliminated or controlled. Patient safety is a full-time endeavor that should be modified constantly and evolve to meet the needs of the ever-changing health care system.

The VA is often held up as a model for hospital safety initiatives.[263] Some changes are relatively straightforward, but would *not* have been discovered without the investigative techniques at the NCPS. For instance, in one VA medical center, all wheelchairs have been modified with antitipping devices.[264] The devices prevent the wheelchairs from tipping backward.[265] The cost of the modification was $42 per chair, for a total charge of $6,700.[266] Since the modification, there have not been any tipping accidents or close calls at that facility.[267] The small investment in such a simple modification has saved many injuries and thousands of dollars. The estimated average cost of treating a hip fracture in the VA health system is $33,000.[268] Small changes can amount to big savings not only in money, but also in the patients' physical and emotional well-being and ability to return to productive activities of daily living. Additionally, health care resources can be better focused on those who seek medical care for non-preventable conditions. With such a major influence in the patient safety arena, the NCPS likely will remain a leader in patient safety for many years.

VII.   CONCLUSION

This chapter examined the regulatory responses to the IOM report, *To Err Is Human*. From the start of the Agency for Health Care Policy and Research in 1989 to the new rule in 2007 in which CMS announced that it will no longer pay for certain "hospital acquired conditions,"[269] it is evident that patient safety is now at the forefront of national concern. The federal government has taken steps, and will continue to take steps, to improve patient safety by putting incentives in place for the private sector to reduce patient errors. Although these initiatives will decrease harm to patients, there is little doubt that the federal government has its own motivation behind the patient safety initiative. The federal government will save money by not paying for preventable patient errors. At first glance, this seems like a win-win situation for all: Patients will be better served by incurring fewer preventable injuries, thereby decreasing the cost of unnecessary procedures. But who will pay the price for initially developing and implementing these new measures? Over time, we will be in a better position to determine the impact of these safety initiatives on the economy as a whole and on the quality of patients' lives. But for now, health care providers and administrators must concentrate their efforts on developing reasonable, practical safety programs that achieve the ultimate goal of decreased patient harm and patient error.

NOTES

1. COMMITTEE ON QUALITY OF HEALTH CARE IN AMERICA, INSTITUTE OF MEDICINE, TO ERR IS HUMAN: BUILDING A SAFER HEALTH SYSTEM (Linda T. Kohn et al., eds., 2000) [hereinafter *To Err Is Human*].

2. Robert Pear, *Medicare Says It Won't Cover Hospital Errors*, N.Y. TIMES, Aug. 19, 2007.

3. Vanessa Fuhrmans, *Insurers Stop Paying for Care Linked to Errors*, WALL STREET JOURNAL, Jan. 15, 2008, at D1.

4. *Id.* "Aetna, the country's third largest insurer by number of members, is beginning to stipulate in hospital contracts up for renewal that it will no longer pay nor let patients be billed for 28 different 'never events.' Compiled by the National Quality Forum...these mistakes include leaving an instrument in a patient after surgery, the death of a mother in a low-risk pregnancy, allowing a patient to develop bedsores or using contaminated devices." *Id.* "Wellpoint, the largest insurer, is testing the same approach in Virginia with four errors from the forum's never-event list...It plans to extend the policy soon to its plans in New England, New York and Georgia. UnitedHealth Group, Inc. and Cigna Corp. say they're exploring policies similar to Medicare's. The Blue Cross Blue Shield Association says that its 39 member health plans are looking at approaches similar to Aetna's or working with hospitals on reducing errors." *Id.*

5. Lucian L. Leape, MD, *Foreword: Preventing Medical Accidents: Is "Systems Analysis" The Answer?*, 27 AM. J. L. AND MED. 145, 146 (2001).

6. HHS, Agency for Healthcare Research and Quality, www.ahrq.gov/about/profile.htm.

7. Moshman Associates, Inc., *Healthcare Informatics Standards Activities of Selected Federal Agencies (A Compendium)* (Sept. 1996), http://aspe.hhs.gov/datacncl/fedstds1.htm#AHCPR.

8. *Id.*

9. *Id.*

10. *Id.*

11. *Id.*

12. *Id.*

13. *To Err Is Human, supra*, at 70.

14. HHS, Agency for Healthcare Research and Quality, www.ahrq.gov/about/profile.htm.

15. *Id.*

16. John V. Jacobi, JD, *Competition Law's Role in Health Care Quality*, 11 ANN. HEALTH L. 45, 54-65 (2002).

17. Leape, *supra*, at 146.

18. HHS, Agency for Healthcare Research and Quality, www.ahrq.gov/about/whatis.htm.

19. HHS, Agency for Healthcare Research and Quality, www.ahrq.gov/about/ataglance.htm.

20. *Id.*

21. HHS, Agency for Healthcare Research and Quality, www.ahrq.gov/about/profile.htm.

22. *Id.*

23. *Id.*

24. Jacobi, *supra*, at 65.

25. U.S. DEP'T OF HEALTH & HUMAN SERV., PRESS RELEASE; HHS ANNOUNCES $50 MILLION INVESTMENT TO IMPROVE PATIENT SAFETY, www.hhs.gov/news/press/2001pres/20011011.html (Oct. 12, 2001) [hereinafter "HHS Press Release"].

26. *Id.*

27. HHS, Agency for Healthcare Research and Quality, www.ahrq.gov/clinic/ptsafety/summary.htm, p. 2.

28. UNIVERSITY OF CALIFORNIA AT SAN FRANCISCO (UCSF)-STANFORD UNIVERSITY EVIDENCE-BASED PRACTICE CENTER, MAKING HEALTH CARE SAFER: A CRITICAL ANALYSIS OF PATIENT SAFETY PRACTICES, (Kaveh G. Shojania, MD, et al., eds., 2001) [hereinafter *Making Health Care Safer*].

29. *Id.* at 1.

30. HHS, Agency for Healthcare Research and Quality, www.ahrq.gov/clinic/ptsafety/summary.htm, at 2.

31. *Id.*

32. HHS, Agency for Healthcare Research and Quality, www.ahrq.gov/clinic/ptsafety/summary.htm, at 2.

33. *Making Health Care Safer*, *supra*, at v. Gray literature is a blend of medical literature and nonhealthcare literature.

34. *Id.*

35. HHS, Agency for Healthcare Research and Quality, www.ahrq.gov/clinic/ptsafety/summary.htm, at 3.

36. *Id.*

37. *Id.*

38. HHS Press Release, *supra*.

39. HHS, Agency for Healthcare Research and Quality, www.ahrq.gov/about/profile.htm.

40. *Id.*

41. *Making Health Care Safer*, *supra*, at v.

42. *Id.*

43. *Id.*, *supra*, at 6.

44. *Id.* at 578.

45. *Id.* at v.

46. *Id.*

47. *Id.* at 3.

48. *Making Health Care Safer, supra,* at 4.

49. *Id.* at 8.

50. *Id.*

51. *Id.*

52. *Id.*

53. *To Err Is Human, supra,* at 70.

54. Conditions of Participation for Hospitals: Quality Assessment and Performance Improvement, 68 Fed. Reg. 3435 (Jan. 24, 2003) (codified at 42 C.F.R. 482.21).

55. *Id.*

56. *To Err Is Human, supra,* at 41.

57. *Id.*

58. In 1960, prior to the Medicare and Medicaid programs, an estimated 21.4 percent of all personal health care expenditures came from the public sector and 78.7 percent, including direct patient payments, came from the private sector. By 1990, 41.3 percent of all personal health care expenditures were by the public sector and 58.7 percent by the private sector. Charles Helbing, *Medicare Program Expenditures-Medicare and Medicaid Statistical Supplement,* http://findarticles.com/p/articles/mi_m0795/is_nSUPP_v14/ai_14804344 (last visited on Oct. 7, 2007).

59. Medicare is defined as a "Federal Act (Health Insurance for the Aged Act) to provide hospital and medical insurance for aged persons under Social Security Act. 42 U.S.C. A. § 1395 et seq. BLACK'S LAW DICTIONARY 982 (6th ed. 1990).

60. Medicaid is defined as "[a] form of public assistance sponsored jointly by the federal and state governments providing medical aid for people whose income falls below a certain level." BLACK'S LAW DICTIONARY 981 (6th ed. 1990).

61. 42 C.F.R § 482.1.

62. Centers for Medicare and Medicaid Services, http://cms.hhs.gov/pf (last visited on Oct. 7, 2007).

63. *Id.*

64. Conditions of Participation for Hospitals: Quality Assessment and Performance Improvement, 68 Fed. Reg. 3435 (Jan. 24, 2003) (codified at 42 C.F.R. 482.21).

65. *Id.*

66. *Id.*

67. *Id.*

68. *Id.*

69. Conditions of Participation for Hospitals: Quality Assessment and Performance Improvement, 68 Fed. Reg. 3435 (Jan. 24, 2003) (codified at 42 C.F.R. 482.21).

70. *Id.*

71. *Id.* at 3435.

72. *Id.*

73. *Id.* at 3435.

74. LINDA A. BAUMANN ET AL., HEALTH CARE FRAUD AND ABUSE: PRACTICAL PERSPECTIVES 2-3 (Linda A. Baumann, ed., The Bureau of National Affairs, Inc., 2002); Health and Human Services Office of Inspector General, http://oig.hhs. gov/publications/docs/budget/FY2008.pdf (last visited Oct. 11, 2007).

75. Health and Human Services Office of Inspector General, http://oig.hhs. gov/publications/docs/budget/FY2008.pdf (last visited Oct. 11, 2007).

76. 62 Fed. Reg. 9435 (Mar. 3, 1997).

77. Program Guidance for Hospitals, 63 Fed. Reg. 8987 (Feb. 23, 1998).

78. *Id.*

79. *Id.*

80. *Id.*

81. *Id.* at 8989.

82. Program Guidance for Hospitals, 63 Fed. Reg. 8987, at 8989 (Feb. 23, 1998).

83. Supplemental Compliance Program Guidance for Hospitals, 70 Fed. Reg. 4858 (Jan. 31, 2005).

84. Section 1877 of the Social Security Act.

85. Section 1128B(b) of the Social Security Act.

86. Section 1867 of the Social Security Act.

87. Section 1128(b)(6)(B) of the Social Security Act.

88. Supplemental Compliance Program Guidance for Hospitals, 70 Fed. Reg. 4858, at 4870 (Jan. 31, 2005).

89. *See* 42 C.F.R. § 482.21.

90. *See* 42 C.F.R. § 482.22.

91. 72 C.F.R. § 47130 (Aug. 22, 2007), www.cms.hhs.gov/quarterlyprovide-rupdates/downloads/cms1533fc.pdf.

92. *Id.* at 47217.

93. "Dr. Kenneth W. Kizer, an expert on patient safety who was the top health official at the Department of Veterans Affairs from 1994 to 1999, said: 'I applaud the intent of the new Medicare rules, but I worry that hospitals will figure out ways to get around them. The new policy should be part of a larger initiative to require the reporting of health care events that everyone agrees should never happen. Any such effort must include a mechanism to make sure hospitals comply." Robert Pear, *Medicare Says It Won't Cover Hospital Errors*, N.Y. TIMES, Aug. 19, 2007. www. nytimes.com/2007/08/19/washington/19hospital.html; "'Medicare is trying to nudge hospitals toward better quality care,' said Bear Stearns' Jason Gurda. 'It's hoping that if hospitals have to bear more financial pain they'll put steps in place to reduce errors.'... 'Medicare pays hospitals over $100 billion a year, so $20 million is less than 0.02%,' Gurda said. 'I'm not expecting a significant impact although it is a first step toward paying for quality.'" Gloria Lau, *Analysts Skeptical About New Rules for Hospital Errors*, INVESTOR'S BUISINESS DAILY, Aug. 17, 2007. http://biz.yahoo.com.

94. Erin Donaghue, *Pressure Is on Hospitals to Stamp Out Bacterial Bugs*, USA TODAY, Oct. 16, 2007, at 7D.

95. Tresa Baldas, *New Medicare Rule May Fuel Litigation*, CONNECTICUT LAW TRIBUNE, Vol. 33, No. 42, Oct. 15, 2007, Medical Malpractice Supplement, p. 7; "'Our goal is to improve the quality of care in our nation's hospitals,' says Herb Kuhn, acting deputy administrator for the Center for Medicare and Medicaid Services. 'Let's not reward things that can be prevented with higher payment.'" Erin Donaghue, *Pressure Is on Hospitals to Stamp Out Bacterial Bugs*, USA TODAY, Oct. 16, 2007, at 7D.

96. Robert Pear, *Medicare Says It Won't Cover Hospital Errors*, N.Y. TIMES, Aug. 19, 2007, www.nytimes.com/2007/08/19/washington/19hospital.html.

97. Tresa Baldas, *New Medicare Rule May Fuel Litigation*, CONNECTICUT LAW TRIBUNE, Vol. 33, No. 42, Oct. 15, 2007, Medical Malpractice Supplement, p. 7.

98. *Id.*

99. *Id.*

100. 31 U.S.C. § 3729-3733 (1994).

101. 31 U.S.C. § 3730(a).

102. 31 U.S.C. § 3730(b)(1).

103. *Id.*

104. *Id.* at § 3730(b)(2).

105. *Id.*

106. 31 U.S.C. § 3730(d).

107. *Id.*

108. 31 U.S.C § 3729(a)(7); 28 C.F.R. 85.3(a)(9) (2001).

109. Joan H. Krause, JD, *Promises to Keep: Health Care Providers and the Civil False Claims Act*, 23 CARDOZO L. REV. 1363, 1371-84 (2002); discussing traditional categories of FCA liability [hereinafter *Promises to Keep*].

110. Letter from Laurie E. Ekstrand, Director of Homeland Security and Justice to The Honorable F. James Sensenbrenner, Jr., Chairman on the Judiciary, House of Representatives, The Honorable Chris Cannon, Chairman, Subcommittee on Commercial and Administrative Law, Committee on the Judiciary, House of Representatives, and The Honorable Charles E. Grassley, United States Senate (Jan. 31, 2006) (on file with the author and at www.gao.gov).

111. *Id.*

112. Joan H. Krause, *Medical Error As False Claim*, 27 AM. J. L. AND MED. 181, 184 (2001) (discussing the Civil False Claims Act and theories of FCA liability) [hereinafter "Krause: Medical Error"].

113. *See* Peterson v. Weinberger, 508 F.2d 45, 47-48 (5th Cir. 1975) (physician liable for submitting bills to Medicare for physical therapy services that were not actually performed by him).

114. *See* United States v. Halper, 490 U.S. 435, 437 (1989), *abrogated on other grounds by*, Hudson v. United States, 522 U.S. 93 (1997) (manager of New City Medical Laboratories, Inc., liable for mischaracterizing the medical services performed by the laboratory where he submitted bills for reimbursement at the rate

of $12 per claim when the actual services rendered by the lab entitled him to only $3 per claim); United States v. Krizek, 111 F.3d 934, 936 (D.C. Cir. 1997) (psychiatrist liable for submitting bills for forty-five- to fifty-minute treatment sessions when he could not have spent the time providing such services; for instance, the court found that the psychiatrist submitted claims for over twenty-one hours of patient treatment within a twenty-four-hour period).

115. United States ex rel. Aranda v. Community Psychiatric Centers, 945 F. Supp. 1485 (W.D. Okla. 1996).

116. *Id.* at 1487.

117. *Id.* at 1488.

118. *Id.* at 1488-89.

119. *Id.* at 1488, *citing* 42 U.S.C. § 1320a-7(b)(6)(B) ("the Secretary may exclude anyone who furnishes patient services of a quality which fails to meet professionally recognized standards of health care."); § 1320c-5 ("providers must assure that patient services will be of a quality which meets professionally recognized standards of health care"); and 42 C.F.R. § 455.2 ("Each state must have a fraud detection program, and the state plan must provide for exclusion of persons who have committed fraud or abuse. *Abuse* means provider practices that are inconsistent with sound medical practices, and result in an unnecessary cost to the Medicaid program, or in reimbursement for services that fail to meet professionally recognized standards for health care" (emphasis in original).

120. United States ex rel. Aranda v. Community Psychiatric Centers, 945 F. Supp. at 1488.

121. United States v. Community Psychiatric Centers, 115 F. Supp. 2d 1149 (W.D. Mo. 2000).

122. *Id.* at 1153.

123. *Id.* at 1156.

124. See *Id.* at 1153 (reasoning that "if the Defendant billed the United States for specific services that it never rendered then that claim would be fraudulent and properly actionable under the FCA").

125. *Medical Error, supra,* at 188-90 (discussing FCA and quality of health care cases).

126. *Promises to Keep, supra,* at 1399-1406.

127. *Id.* at 1398-1400.

128. See Luckey v. Baxter Healthcare Corp., 2 F. Supp. 2d 1034 (N.D. Ill. 1998) (dismissing allegations that a blood products manufacturer submitted false claims by wrongly stating that it complied with plasma testing standards); United States ex rel. Mikes v. Straus, 84 F. Supp. 2d 427, 435-38 (S.D.N.Y. 1999) (holding that physicians' alleged failure to meet professionally recognized standards of care in performing spirometry tests for which Medicare reimbursement was sought was not actionable under FCA under implied false certification theory); United States ex rel. Joslin v. Community Home Health of Maryland, Inc., 984 F. Supp. 374, 384-85 (D. Md. 1997) (finding that a billing form did not function as an implied certification of compliance with state laws.)

129. *See* United States v. NHC Healthcare Corp., 115 F. Supp. 2d 1149, 1153 (W.D. Mo. 2000) (allowing a claim under the FCA for services that were not provided by a nursing home because the defendant nursing home "was so severely understaffed that it could not possibly have administered all of the care it was obligated to perform").

130. *Promises to Keep, supra*, at 1371.

131. *Id.* at 1372.

132. *Id.* at 1373.

133. *Id.* at 1376.

134. *Id.* at 1379.

135. *Id.* at 1380.

136. *Id.*

137. *See* United States v. Pani, 717 F. Supp. 1013 (S.D.N.Y. 1989) (government sued a neurosurgeon for submitting 157 claims for surgeries that he did not perform); Peterson v. Weinberger, 508 F.2d 45 (5th Cir.) (government sued for services that were billed in a physician's name that were actually rendered by a physical therapy company that did not participate in the Medicare program); United States v. Lorenzo, 768 F. Supp. 1127 (E.D. Pa. 1991) (government sued a dentist who billed for routine check-ups that were not covered under the Medicare program as "consultations" for oral cancer); United States v. Krizek, 111 F.3d 934 (D.C. Cir. 1997) (government sued psychiatrist who billed for forty-five- to fifty-minute sessions where he actually only spent twenty to thirty minutes with the patient); and United States v. Halper, 490 U.S. 435 (1989) *abrogated on other grounds,* Hudson v. United States, 522 U.S. 93 (1997) (government sued a laboratory that charged twelve dollars for services that were worth only three dollars).

138. *See* Office of Inspector General, Publication of the OIG Compliance Program Guidance for Nursing Facilities, 65 Fed. Reg. 14289, 14295 n.49 (2000) (discussing that nursing facilities that knowingly bill for nonexistent or substandard care, items, or services could be liable under the FCA).

139. 31 U.S.C. § 3729(a)(1).

140. *Medical Error, supra*, at 190-91, *citing Philadelphia Prosecutor Calculates Damages in Quality of Care Cases*, 2 HEALTH CARE FRAUD REP. (BNA) 928-29 (1998).

141. 42 C.F.R. § 482.41.

142. 42 C.F.R. § 482.21.

143. 42 C.F.R. § 482.25.

144. 42 C.F.R. § 482.13.

145. United States v. NHC Healthcare Corp., 115 F. Supp. 2d 1149, 1153 (W.D. Mo. 2000).

146. United States ex rel. Aranda v. Community Psychiatric Centers, 945 F. Supp. 1485 (W.D. Okla. 1996).

147. *See Medical Error, supra*, at 193-98 (discussing controversy of settling FCA claims), *citing* Uwe E. Reinhardt, *Medicare Can Turn Anyone Into a Crook*, WALL ST. J., Jan. 21, 2000, at A18; Timothy P. Blanchard, *Medicare Medical Necessity Determinations Revisited: Abuse of Discretion and Abuse of Process in the War Against*

Medicare Fraud and Abuse, 43 St. Louis U. L. J. 91, 114 (1999) ("arguing that the FCA's threat of draconian...sanctions coerces providers into settlement regarding issues on which providers would most likely prevail"); John T. Boese & Beth McClain, *Why Thompson is Wrong: Misuse of the False Claims Act to Enforce the Anti-Kickback Act,* 51 Ala. L. Rev. 1, 18 (1999) ("arguing that the FCA penalty structure places great pressure on defendants to settle even meritless suits"); Robert Salcido, *DOJ Must Re-evaluate Use of False Claims Act in Medicare Disputes*, Health Care Fraud Litig. Rep. (BNA), Apr. 2000, at 15 ("The dirty little secret underlying FCA enforcement is that given the civil penalty provision and the costs and risks associated with litigation, the rational move for any healthcare provider accused of fraud is to settle the action even if the government's likelihood of success is incredibly small").

148.   31 U.S.C. § 3729(a)(7); 28 C.F.R. § 85.3(a)(9) (2001). Civil penalty of $5,500 to $11,000 per claim plus three times the amount of damages the government sustains because of the act of that person.

149.   *See* 42 U.S.C. § 1320a-7b.

150.   *Medical Error, supra*, at 193-94.

151.   *Id.*

152.   *Id.* at n.83.

153.   *Id.* at 194-95, *citing* David A. Hyman, *Medicine in the New Millennium: A Self-Help Guide for the Perplexed,* Am. J. L. & Med. 143, 146 (2000) ("Several decades of health services research has made clear that American health care is dogged by persistent quality problems relating to overutilization of certain services, underutilization of other services, unexplained variations in service utilization and errors in health care practice"); Eleanor D. Kinney, *Behind the Veil, Where The Action Is: Private Policy Making and American Health Care*, 51 Admin. L. Rev. 145, 164-65 (1999) (arguing that health services research revealed geographical practice variations, which in turn stimulated greater attention to the outcomes of medical care and more rigorous development of standards of care); John E. Wennberg et al., *Are Hospital Services Rationed in New Haven or Over-Utilized in Boston?* Lancet 1185, 1188 (1987) (arguing that attention to variation is essential to improving clinical practice and understanding cost-containment); John Wennberg & Alan Gittelsohn, *Small Area Variations in Health Care Delivery: A Population-Based Health Information System Can Guide Planning and Regulatory Decision Making*, 182 Sci. 1102, 1107 (1973) ("arguing that variations in health care utilization indicate uncertainty about the effectiveness of different levels of health services").

154.   *Medical Error, supra*, at 196, discussing the "detrimental effect of controlled substance laws on physicians' willingness to prescribe necessary pain medication" for fear of disciplinary action.

155.   The president referred to is former President William Jefferson Clinton, who was the forty-second president of the United States and served as president from 1993 to 2001, http://en.wikipedia.org/wiki/Bill_Clinton.

156.   *Remarks by the President on Health Care*, The Rose Garden, Dec. 7, 1999, www.whitehouse.gov; www.ahrq.gov/wh120799.htm (last visited Sept. 13, 2007); *Clinton-Gore Administration Announces New Actions to Improve Patient Safety and Assure*

Health Care Quality: Goal to Reduce Preventable Medical Errors by 50 Percent Within Five Years, Feb. 19, 2000, www.whitehouse.gov; www.ahrq.gov/wh121900.htm (last visited Sept. 13, 2007); and *Remarks by the President on Medical Errors*, Dwight D. Eisenhower Executive Office Building, Feb. 22, 2000, www.whitehouse.gov; www. ahrq.gov/wh22200rem.htm (last visited Sept. 13, 2007).

157. *Remarks by the President on Health Care*, The Rose Garden, Dec. 7, 1999, www.whitehouse.gov; www.ahrq.gov/wh120799.htm (last visited Sept. 13, 2007).

158. *Id.*

159. *The Best Offense Is a Good Defense Against Medical Errors: Putting the Full-Court Press on Medical Errors*, John M. Eisenberg, MD, Director, Agency for Healthcare Research and Quality, at the Duke University Clinical Research Institute, Jan. 20, 2000. Agency for Healthcare Research and Quality, Rockville, MD, www.ahrq. gov/news/spch01200htm.

160. *Id.*

161. *Remarks by the President on Medical Errors*, Dwight D. Eisenhower Executive Office Building, Feb. 22, 2000, www.whitehouse.gov; www.ahrq.gov/wh22200rem. htm (last visited Sept. 13, 2007).

162. The QuIC agencies contributing to the report include: Department of Health and Human Services (Agency for Healthcare Research and Quality, Centers for Disease Control and Prevention, Food and Drug Administration, Health Care Financing Administration, Health Resources and Services Administration, National Institute of Health, Office of the Secretary, and Substance Abuse and Mental Health Services Administration), United States Coast Guard, Department of Commerce, Department of Defense, Department of Labor, Office of Personnel Management, and Department of Veterans Affairs.

163. DOING WHAT COUNTS FOR PATIENT SAFETY: FEDERAL ACTIONS TO REDUCE MEDICAL ERRORS AND THEIR IMPACT, REPORT OF THE QUALITY INTERAGENCY COORDINATION TASK FORCE TO THE PRESIDENT, Feb. 2000. www.quic.gov/report/errors6.pdf (last visited on Sept. 23, 2007) [hereinafter "Doing What Counts for Patient Safety"].

164. *Id.* at p. 26.

165. *Id.*

166. *Id.*

167. *Id.*

168. Doing What Counts for Patient Safety, *supra*, at 26.

169. *Id.*

170. *Id.*

171. *Remarks by the President on Medical Errors*, Dwight D. Eisenhower Executive Office Building, Feb. 22, 2000, www.whitehouse.gov; www.ahrq.gov/wh22200rem. htm (last visited Sept. 13, 2007).

172. *Id.*

173. *Id.* After the release of *To Err Is Human*, multiple bills of legislation were introduced to address the concerns the report created and to implement certain recommendations. *See,* Medication Error Prevention Act of 2000 (H.R. 3672), Medicare Comprehensive Quality of Care and Safety Act of 2000 (H.R. 5404),

Medical Error Reduction Act of 2000 (S. 2038), Stop All Frequent Errors in Medicare and Medicaid Act of 2000 (S. 2378), Patient Safety and Errors Reduction Act (S. 2738), and Error Reduction and Improvement in Patient Safety Act (S. 2743). However, no legislation successfully passed during the 106th, 107th, or 108th Congresses. Then, during the 109th Congress, the Senate passed S. 544 and the House of Representatives approved it, which resulted in Public Law 109-41. President George W. Bush signed Pub. L. No. 109-41 at the Eisenhower Executive Office Building on July 29, 2005, creating the Patient Safety and Quality Improvement Act of 2005.

174. The Patient Safety and Quality Improvement Act of 2005, Pub. L. No. 109-41, 119 Stat. 424 (2005) (codified as amended at 42 U.S.C. 299 et seq. (2005) [hereinafter "Patient Safety and Quality Improvement Act"]. *See* Appendix A. On Feb. 12, 2008, the DHHS issued proposed regulations implementing certain provisions of the PSQUIA. 73 Fed. Reg. 8112 (Feb. 12, 2008). *See* Appendix B.

175. 42 U.S.C. § 299b-21(5) and 42 U.S.C. § 299b-24(D).

176. 42 U.S.C. § 299b-24.

177. 42 U.S.C. § 299b-21(7).

178. *Id.*

179. *Id.*

180. The Patient Safety and Quality Improvement Act of 2005: Overview, June 2006. Agency for Healthcare Research and Quality, Rockville, MD, www.ahrq.gov/qual/psoact.htm (last visited on Sept. 12, 2007).

181. 42 U.S.C. § 299b-22.

182. *Id.*

183. 42 U.S.C. § 299b-22.

184. *Id.*

185. *Id.*

186. The work product continues to be privileged and confidential *except* for patient safety work product that is disclosed in a criminal proceeding or that is nonidentifiable patient safety work product. 42 U.S.C. § 299b-22(d).

187. 42 U.S.C. § 299b-22(d).

188. *Id.*

189. "Detrimental employment action" is an "adverse employment action" and includes loss of employment, an adverse evaluation or decision made in relation to accreditation, certification, credentialing, or licensing of the individual.

190. 42 U.S.C. § 299b-22(e).

191. The Patient Safety and Quality Improvement Act of 2005: Overview, June 2006. Agency for Healthcare Research and Quality, Rockville, MD, www.ahrq.gov/qual/psoact.htm (last visited on Sept. 12, 2007).

192. 42 U.S.C. § 299b-22.

193. *Id.*

194. The Patient Safety and Quality Improvement Act of 2005: Overview, June 2006. Agency for Healthcare Research and Quality, Rockville, MD, www.ahrq.gov/qual/psoact.htm (last visited on Sept. 12, 2007).

195. 42 U.S.C. § 229b-22(f).

196. *Id.*

197. *Id.*

198. 42 U.S.C. § 299b-23.

199. *Id.*

200. *Id.*

201. *Id.*

202. *Id.*

203. Hospital Survey on Patient Safety Culture: 2007 Comparative Database Report, Agency for Healthcare Research and Quality, Rockville, MD, www.ahrq.gov/qual/hospsurveydb (last visited on Oct. 2, 2007).

204. Patient Safety Improvement Corps: An AHRQ/VA Partnership. Apr. 2007. Agency for Healthcare Research and Quality, Rockville, MD, www.ahrq.gov/about/psimpcorps.htm (last visited on Oct. 2, 2007).

205. *Id.*

206. *Id.*

207. VA National Center for Patient Safety, www.va.gov/NCPS/vision.html (last visited on Oct. 2, 2007).

208. VA National Center for Patient Safety, www.va.gov/ncps/NEWS/NCPSBg/bg_brochure.pdf (last visited on Oct. 13, 2007).

209. *Id.*

210. *Id.*

211. *Id.*

212. *Id.*

213. *Id.*

214. *Id.*

215. VA National Center for Patient Safety, www.va.gov/ncps/news.html#fact (last visited on Oct. 13, 2007).

216. VA National Center for Patient Safety, www.va.gov (last visited on Oct. 15, 2007).

217. *Id.*

218. *Id.*

219. *Id.*

220. *Id.*

221. VA National Center for Patient Safety, www.va.gov/ncps/news.html#fact (last visited on Oct. 13, 2007).

222. VA National Center for Patient Safety, www.va.gov/ncps/NEWS/NCPSBg/bg_brochure.pdf (last visited on Oct. 13, 2007).

223. *Id.*

224. *Id.*

225. *Id.*

226. *Id.*

227. *Id.*

228. VA National Center for Patient Safety, www.va.gov/ncps/TIPS/Docs/TIPS_NovDec04.pdf (last visited on Oct. 14, 2007).

229. Id.

230. Id.

231. Id.

232. Id.

233. Id.

234. Id.

235. VA National Center for Patient Safety, www.patientsafety.gov/pubs.html (last visited on Oct. 15, 2007).

236. Id.

237. VA National Center for Patient Safety, www.patientsafety.gov/CogAids/FallPrevention/index.html (last visited on Oct. 15, 2007).

238. VA National Center for Patient Safety, www.patientsafety.gov/pubs.html (last visited on Oct. 15, 2007).

239. VA National Center for Patient Safety, www.patientsafety.gov/CogAids/EscapeElope/index.html (last visited on Oct. 15, 2007).

240. Id.

241. VA National Center for Patient Safety, www.patientsafety.gov/pubs.html (last visited on Oct. 15, 2007).

242. VA National Center for Patient Safety, www.patientsafety.gov/CogAids/HFMEA/index.html (last visited on Oct. 15, 2007).

243. Id.

244. Id.

245. Id.

246. VA National Center for Patient Safety, www.patientsafety.gov/pubs.html (last visited on Oct. 15, 2007).

247. VA National Center for Patient Safety, www.patientsafety.gov/CogAids/RCA/index.html (last visited on Oct. 15, 2007).

248. VA National Center for Patient Safety, www.va.gov/NCPS/glossary.html (last visited on Oct. 17, 2007).

249. Id.

250. Id.

251. Id.

252. Id.

253. VA National Center for Patient Safety, www.patientsafety.gov/CogAids/RCA/index.html (last visited on Oct. 15, 2007).

254. Id.

255. VA National Center for Patient Safety, www.va.gov/ncps/NEWS/NCPSBg/bg_brochure.pdf (last visited on Oct. 13, 2007).

256. Id.

257. VA National Center for Patient Safety, www.va.gov (last visited on Oct. 15, 2007).

258. *Id.*

259. *Id.*

260. *Id.*

261. *Id.*

262. *Id.*

263. Maxine M. Harrington, *Revisiting Medical Error: Five Years After the IOM Report, Have Reporting Systems Made a Measurable Difference?*, 15 HEALTH MATRIX 329, 357-360 (2005).

264. Department of Veterans Affairs, Profile VA National Center for Patient Safety 2006, www.patientsafety.gov (last visited on Oct. 15, 2007).

265. *Id.*

266. *Id.*

267. *Id.*

268. *Id.*

269. 72 C.F.R. § 47130 (Aug. 22, 2007), www.cms.hhs.gov/quarterlyproviderup dates/downloads/cms1533fc.pdf.

CHAPTER 2

State Survey of Patient Safety Initiatives

The IOM's report recommended the establishment of a nationwide mandatory reporting system in which state governments would collect information about patient errors that resulted in death or serious harm.[1] As of January 4, 2007, twenty-six states and the District of Columbia required the report of an adverse event or incident.[2] This chapter provides a brief synopsis of the state reporting systems. However, the reader should consult individual state laws and regulations for the most current information and specific details pertaining to the adverse event reporting requirements.

I. CALIFORNIA

California requires the reporting of adverse events that threaten the welfare, safety, or health of patients. The reportable events fall into six categories: surgical, product or device, patient protection, care management, environmental, and criminal. California health facilities that are licensed pursuant to the Health and Safety Code § 1250 (a), (b), or (f) (i.e., general acute care hospitals, acute psychiatric hospitals, and special hospitals) must report an urgent adverse event within twenty-four hours of discovery and a nonurgent adverse event within five days of discovery. Failure to report such events is punishable by a civil penalty up to $100 per day that the event was not reported.

Additionally, information about reported events and the outcome of investigations or inspections of substantiated adverse events must be made readily accessible to consumers by January 2009, and posted on the state department of health services' Web site and available in written form by January 2015. (Cal. Health & Safety Code § 1279.1, et seq.)

There are also significant fines for patient safety violations. The California Department of Health Services can impose a $50,000 fine on a

41

long-term care facility, general acute care hospital, acute psychiatric hospital, or special hospital for violations if the facility receives a notice of deficiency and is required to submit a plan of correction for a violation that constitutes an immediate jeopardy to the health or safety of a patient. (Cal. Health & Safety Code § 1280.3 (a)). Also, the California Department of Health Services may assess a penalty up to $17,500 per violation that does not constitute immediate jeopardy to a patient. (Cal. Health & Safety Code § 1280.3(a)).

Authorizing statutes or regulations

- CAL. HEALTH & SAFETY CODE § 1279.1, et seq.
- CAL. HEALTH & SAFETY CODE § 1280.3(a)

II. COLORADO

All health care facilities licensed by the Colorado Department of Public Health and Environment (i.e., general hospitals, psychiatric hospitals, maternity hospitals, rehabilitation hospitals, community clinics, rehabilitation centers, convalescent centers, community mental health centers, acute treatment units, facilities for persons with developmental disabilities, habilitation centers for brain-damaged children, chiropractic centers and hospitals, nursing care facilities, the pilot project rehabilitative nursing facility, hospice care, assisted living residences, dialysis treatment clinics, ambulatory surgical centers, birthing centers and other similar facilities) are required to report any occurrence that results in the death of a patient or resident of the facility, or any occurrence that results in serious injuries (i.e., brain or spinal cord injuries; life-threatening complications of anesthesia or transfusions; second- or third-degree burns involving 20 percent or more of the body surface area of an adult patient or 15 percent or more of the body surface area of a child; any time that a patient of the facility cannot be located after a search of the facility and its grounds and there are circumstances that place the patient's health, safety, or welfare at risk or if the patient has been missing for eight hours; any physical, sexual, or verbal abuse of a patient; any neglect to a patient; misappropriation of a patient's property; any time drugs are diverted from the patient to another; and any malfunction or intentional or accidental misuse of patient equipment during treatment or diagnosis that adversely affects or potentially could have affected a patient). The report must be made to the Health Facilities and Emergency Medical Services Division.

Authorizing statutes or regulations
- C.R.S. § 25-1-124
- 6 C.C.R. § 1011-1, ch. II, § 3.2

III. CONNECTICUT

In October 2002, Connecticut began to require that hospitals and outpatient surgical facilities report adverse events (as listed on the National Quality Forum's List of Serious Reportable Events or on a list compiled by the Connecticut Commissioner of Public Health) to the Connecticut Department of Public Health. The facility must file a written report within seven days after the adverse event occurs. The facility must also file a corrective plan of action within thirty days after the adverse event. Emergent reports must be filed with the Connecticut Department of Public Health immediately. Failure to implement a corrective plan of action may cause the facility to be subject to license revocation, suspension, censure, reprimand, probation, or restriction. The commissioner of public health also may compel the facility to implement the corrective plan of action. The information collected by the Department of Public Health cannot be disclosed at any time and is not subject to subpoena or discovery requests, and cannot be introduced in evidence in any judicial or administrative proceeding, except as specifically provided by law.

Authorizing statutes or regulations
- CONN. GEN. STAT. § 19a-127n
- CONN. GEN. STAT. §19a-494

IV. DISTRICT OF COLUMBIA

Effective on March 14, 2007, the District of Columbia requires that either an individual or entity that is a licensed health care provider (or a health care provider authorized under district law) to submit biannual reports of adverse events on January 1 and July 1 of each calendar year to the system administrator. The report should include the patient's full primary health record with the patient's identity redacted. The information submitted is confidential and is not discoverable or admissible in evidence in any civil, criminal, or legislative proceeding. The information cannot be disclosed by anyone under any circumstances, except a court may order a system administrator to provide information in a criminal proceeding in which an individual is accused of a felony if the court determines that disclosure is essential to protect the public interest and that the information being sought can be obtained from no other source. Failure to submit a report is punishable by a penalty of not less than $500 or more than $2,500.

Authorizing statutes or regulations
- D.C. CODE § 7-161 (2007)

V. FLORIDA

Florida requires every licensed facility to have an internal risk management program that investigates and analyzes the frequency and causes of adverse incidents to patients and develops measures to minimize the risks of such incidents. There must be a licensed risk manager who oversees the program. The facility must submit to the Agency for Health Care Administration and the Florida Department of Public Health an annual summary report of all incident reports filed during that year. The report is not discoverable or admissible in any civil or administrative action, except in disciplinary proceedings by the agency or the appropriate regulatory board. The report is not available to the public. However, the report is available to the health care professional against whom probable cause is found if the record forms a basis for the determination of probable cause. Certain adverse events (such as death, brain or spinal damage, surgical procedure on the wrong patient, surgical procedure on the wrong site, wrong surgical procedure, unnecessary surgical procedure, unplanned surgical repair of damage from a planned surgery, and surgical removal of foreign objects) must be reported to the Agency for Health Care Administration within fifteen days.

After reporting the incidents, the facility must provide a written plan of correction within the time frame established by the agency. If the facility fails to provide a plan of correction, the agency may impose a fine of up to $5,000 for any violation of the reporting requirements. The fine for repeated nonwillful violations may not exceed $10,000 for any violation. The fine for each intentional and willful violation may not exceed $25,000 per violation per day. The fine for an intentional and willful violation may not exceed $250,000.

Authorizing statutes or regulations
- FLA. STAT. § 395.0197
- FLA. STAT. § 395.1065(2)(b)

VI.   GEORGIA

In Georgia, hospitals are required to report certain incidents to the Georgia Department of Human Resources Office of Regulatory Services. These include the following conditions when they are not related to the patient's illness: death; rape; surgery on the wrong person or wrong body part; loss of limb or function; second- or third-degree burns in 20 percent or more of an adult or 15 percent or more of a child; patient injury from misuse of patient care equipment; discharge of an infant to the wrong family; patient missing for more than eight hours; and assault on a patient that requires treatment. The report must be made within twenty-four hours or by the next regular business day. The report is not released to the public.

Authorizing statutes or regulations

- GA. COMP. R. & REGS. 290-9-7.07

VII. ILLINOIS

The Illinois Adverse Health Care Events Reporting Law of 2005 requires hospitals and ambulatory surgical centers to report certain errors to the Illinois Department of Public Health within thirty days of discovering the event. These reportable errors include: surgical events (i.e., wrong body part, wrong patient, wrong procedure, unintentional foreign objects, or death during surgery or immediately thereafter); product or device events (i.e., death or serious illness from contaminated drugs or devices, associated with devices in patient care, or from air embolism); patient protection events (i.e., infant discharged to the wrong person, patient disappearance for more than four hours, or patient suicide); care management events (i.e., medication error, incompatible blood transfusion, death from labor and delivery, or death or serious illness from hypoglycemia); environmental events (i.e., electric shock, wrong gas or contaminated gas, burns, falls, or death or serious disability from the use of or lack of restraints); and physical security events (i.e., care ordered by someone impersonating a health care provider, abduction of a patient, and physical or sexual assault of a patient).

The facility must report the findings of a root-cause analysis of the patient error within ninety days of the initial report of the event. The event report, findings of the root-cause analysis, and corrective plan of action are not available to the public and shall not be discoverable or admissible in any civil, criminal, or administrative proceeding against a facility or health care provider. Hospitals have thirty days to make corrections and add explanatory comments about publicly available information before it is published. The facility may be subject to license suspension if it violates this law.

Authorizing public act

- ILL. PUB. ACT 094-0242

VIII. INDIANA

In Indiana, each hospital is required to have a medical error and reporting quality system. The hospital must report patient errors to the Department of Public Health. These reportable events are similar to those required to be reported in Illinois (see above). The hospital must report a serious event within fifteen working days or a potential event within six months after the event is discovered. The patients' and health care professionals' information is kept confidential and is not discoverable in any court or administrative proceeding. The information cannot be used for punishing any health care professional. However, the information is made available on the Department of Public Health's Web site so the public can see which hospitals are most effective at preventing patient errors.

Authorizing statutes or regulations

- IND. EXEC. ORDER 05-10
- Indiana Department of Health: 410 IND. ADMIN. CODE 15-2.4-2.2

IX. KANSAS

In Kansas, a reportable incident is an incident that could be: below the applicable standard of care and has a reasonable probability of causing injury to a patient; or grounds for disciplinary action by the board. Kansas requires that all health care providers, medical care facility agents, and employees who are directly involved in the delivery of health care services report a reportable incident to either the state or county professional society or organization (if the incident did not occur at a health care facility) or to the chief of the medical staff, chief administrative officer, or risk manager (if the incident occurred at a health care facility). The state or county professional society must report the incident to the professional practices review committee for an investigation. The chief of the medical staff, chief administrative officer, or risk manager of a facility must report the incident to the executive committee or professional practices peer review committee for an investigation. The committees must report to the appropriate state licensing agency (if it is a health care professional) or to the department of health and environment (if it is a facility). Every three months, each committee must report to the secretary of health and environment the number of reportable incidents, investigations, and any action taken.

Authorizing statutes or regulations

- KAN. STAT. ANN. § 65-4923
- KAN. ADMIN. REGS. § 25-52-1
- KAN. ADMIN. REGS. § 100-25-1

X. MAINE

In Maine, mandatory reporting of sentinel events began in 2001. Licensed health care facilities must report serious events that are unrelated to the natural course of the patient's condition, the proper treatment of the patient, or the elopement of a patient who lacks capacity. These serious events are referred to as sentinel events. The sentinel events are death; loss of function; surgery on the wrong body part or wrong patient; incompatible blood transfusion; suicide; infant abduction or discharge to the wrong family; and rape of a patient. The facility must report the sentinel events to the Division of Licensing and Regulatory Services within the Department of Health and Human Services. The information is privileged and confidential and cannot be released to the public. A person is immune from civil or criminal liability if he or she, in good faith, reports a sentinel event.

The sentinel event must be reported to the division within twenty-four hours and a written report must be filed within forty-five days. The report must include a root-cause analysis and investigation of the sentinel event. The internal investigation must include: identification of the system or process that may have impacted the event; a corrective action plan; and the process for monitoring the effectiveness of the plan. The report must show the involvement of the facility's leadership and how the correction plan will be communicated to members of the performance improvement committee.

Authorizing statutes or regulations

■ ME. REV. STAT. ANN. tit. 22, § 8753

XI. MARYLAND

Maryland's Hospital Patient Safety Program regulation became effective in 2004. A hospital must report a Level I event (an event that results in death or serious disability) to the Maryland Department of Health and Mental Hygiene within five days, and must submit a root-cause analysis and action plan to the department within sixty days. The root-cause analysis and other medical review committee information is confidential. There is a $500 fine for hospitals that violate the regulation and the possibility that the hospital's license will be revoked.

Authorizing statutes or regulations

■ MD. CODE REGS. 10.07.06

XII. MASSACHUSETTS

Massachusetts has two mandatory reporting systems. One is administered by the Massachusetts Department of Public Health (DPH) and
the other is the Board of Registration in Medicine's Patient Care
Assessment Program (BRM). Each requires health care providers to
report certain adverse events that fall into the broad categories of:
deaths; major or permanent impairments; unexpected outcomes; accidents, incidents, or unknown causes; and surgical errors. The information submitted to BRM is not subject to subpoena, discovery, or
disclosure, and cannot be entered into evidence. The DPH reports of
investigations and all information in the reporting system are available
to the public upon request ten days after the hospital has an opportunity to respond to the deficiencies.

Authorizing statutes or regulations

- 105 MASS. CODE REGS. 130.331
- MASS. GEN. LAWS ch. 111, § 203(d)
- MASS. GEN. LAWS ch. 112, § 5
- MASS. GEN. LAWS ch. 111, § 205

XIII. MINNESOTA

The Minnesota Department of Public Health (MDH) administers the
Adverse Health Care Events Reporting System, which requires all
Minnesota hospitals, ambulatory surgical centers, community behavioral
health hospitals, and licensing boards for physicians, physician assis-
tants, nurses, pharmacists, and podiatrists to report "never" events. The
"never" events are twenty-seven serious events that include: surgery on
the wrong body part; surgery on the wrong patient; wrong surgical procedure; foreign object left in patient during surgery; death during or after
surgery; death or serious disability from drugs, medical devices, or
biologics; death or serious disability associated with a medical device;
death or serious disability associated with an air embolism; infant discharged to the wrong person; death or serious disability associated with
patient disappearance for more than four hours; patient suicide or
attempted suicide; death or serious disability associated with medications; death or serious disability associated with incompatible blood
products; maternal death or serious disability associated with labor or
delivery; death or serious disability associated with hypoglycemia; infant
death or serious disability associated with hyperbilirubinemia; stage three
or four ulcers acquired after admission; death or serious disability associated with spinal manipulative therapy; death or serious disability associated with electric shock; death or serious disability associated with

administration of the wrong or contaminated gas; death or serious disability associated with burns; death or serious disability associated with falls; death or serious disability associated with the use of or lack of restraints or bed rails; care ordered or delivered by someone impersonating a licensed health care provider; abduction of a patient; sexual assault of a patient; and death or serious disability of a patient or staff member associated with physical assault.

These "never" events must be reported to MDH as soon as possible, but no later than fifteen working days after the event is discovered. The information is classified as "non-public" except as required to complete the MDH annual report. The facility or entity must submit its root-cause analysis and action plan within sixty days after the "never" event. If the facility or entity fails to report a "never" event, the MDH has the authority to investigate the facility under the Vulnerable Adult Act or the Maltreatment of Minors Act, or other state, federal, or accreditation reporting requirements.

Authorizing statutes or regulations
- MINN. STAT. § 144.7063 (2005)
- MINN. STAT. § 144.7065 (2005)
- MINN. STAT. § 144.7067 (2005)
- MINN. STAT. § 144.7069 (2005)

XIV. NEW JERSEY

In 2004, New Jersey adopted the New Jersey Patient Safety Act, which requires a health care facility to report every serious and preventable adverse event that occurs at that facility to the Department of Health and Senior Services, or in the case of a state psychiatric facility, to report the event to the Department of Human Services. The facility must report the event within five business days of when the facility discovered or should have discovered the event. The information reported by the facility is not subject to discovery or admissible as evidence and cannot be disclosed in a civil, criminal, or administrative action or proceeding.

Authorizing statutes or regulations
- N.J. STAT. ANN. §§ 26:2H-12.23-.25
- N.J. ADMIN. CODE § 8:43G-5.6

XV. NEVADA

In Nevada, a person employed by a medical facility must notify the patient safety officer of the facility of a "sentinel event" within twenty-four hours. The patient safety officer must report the sentinel event within thirteen days to the Health Division of the Department of Health and Human Services. A "sentinel event" is an unexpected occurrence or risk involving a facility-acquired infection, death, or serious physical or psychological injury. It includes any process variation for which a recurrence would carry a significant chance of a serious adverse outcome, including a loss of limb or function. A report, document, or other information compiled under the mandatory reporting statute is confidential, protected from disclosure, and not subject to subpoena, discovery, or inspection by the general public. The information also is not admissible in evidence in any administrative or legal proceeding conducted in the state of Nevada.

Authorizing statutes or regulations
- NEV. REV. STAT. §§ 439.800-890
- NEV. ADMIN. CODE §§ 439.900-920

XVI.   NEW YORK

All hospitals in New York are required to report: patients' deaths or impairments of bodily functions in circumstances other than those related to the natural course of illness, disease, or proper treatment; fires in the hospital that disrupt the provision of patient care services or cause harm to patients or staff; equipment malfunction during treatment or diagnosis of a patient that adversely affected or could have adversely affected a patient or hospital personnel; poisoning occurring within the hospital; strikes by hospital staff; disasters or other emergency situations external to the hospital that affect hospital operations; and termination of any services that are vital to the safe operation of the hospital or to the health and safety of its patients and personnel. The hospital is required to conduct an investigation of the incident within thirty days and to provide a copy of the report within twenty-four hours after its completion.

Authorizing statutes or regulations
- N.Y. PUB. HEALTH LAW § 2805(L)
- N.Y. COMP. CODES R. & REGS. tit. 10, § 405.8

XVII.   OHIO

Ohio requires that every hospital submit performance measures annually to the Director of Health. The information must be submitted by October 1 of each year, and must reflect the hospital's performance in meeting the measures during the twelve-month period from April 1 of the previous year to March 31 of the current year. The following measures must be reported: the Agency for Health Care Research and Quality's patient safety indicators for iatrogenic pneumothorax (neonate, pediatric, and adult) and for postoperative respiratory failure; the Centers for Medicare and Medicaid Services' pneumonia measures for pneumococcal vaccination and for blood cultures before initial antibiotic; the National Quality Forum's measures for aspirin at arrival for acute myocardial infarction and for beta blocker at arrival for acute myocardial infarction; and the Joint Commission on Accreditation of Healthcare Organizations' heart failure measures for left ventricular function assessment and for angiotensin converting enzyme inhibitors or angiotensin receptor blockers for left ventricular systolic dysfunction. The information is available for purchase by any interested person or government entity ninety days after it is submitted. Failure to comply with this reporting requirement may result in an injunction.

There are also reporting requirements for licensed health care facilities to report on nine specific services including: solid organ and bone marrow transplantation; stem cell harvesting and reinfusion; cardiac catheterization; open-heart surgery; obstetric and newborn care; pediatric intensive care; operation of linear accelerators; operation of cobalt radiation therapy units; and operation of gamma knives. The Director of Health monitors the health care providers for compliance with the safety and quality-of-care standards. The Director of Health may inspect the facilities and require the facility to issue reports and undergo independent audits. Any data reported to the department cannot be made public. The director may impose a civil fine between $1,000 and $250,000 for lesser infractions, and may cease the facility's operation for more serious infractions.

Authorizing statutes or regulations

- OHIO ADMIN. CODE ch. 3701-84
- OHIO REV. CODE ANN. § 3702.11, et seq.
- OHIO ADMIN. CODE § 3701:14-02

XVIII.   OREGON

In Oregon, the legislature created the Oregon Patient Safety Commission, which oversees a confidential serious adverse event reporting system. Participation in the program is voluntary. The entities eligible to participate are: hospitals, long-term care facilities; pharmacies; ambulatory surgical centers; outpatient renal dialysis facilities; freestanding birthing centers; and independent professional health care societies or associations. After a serious adverse event occurs, the participant must disclose:

serious adverse events; root-cause analysis of serious adverse events; action plans to prevent similar serious adverse events; and patient safety plans establishing procedures and protocols.

In general, reportable serious events include any unanticipated consequence of patient care that results in patient death or serious physical injury. Each category of participant has a specific list of reportable serious events. For instance, hospitals must report the following: any unanticipated consequence of patient care that results in patient death or serious physical injury; surgery performed on the wrong body part; surgery performed on the wrong patient; wrong surgical procedure performed on a patient; retention of a foreign object in a patient after surgery or other procedure; patient death during or shortly after surgery; patient death or serious injury associated with the use of contaminated drugs, devices, or biologics; patient death or serious injury associated with the use of a device; patient death or serious injury associated with an air embolism; infant discharged to the wrong person; patient death or serious injury related to patient elopement; patient suicide or suicide attempt; patient death or serious injury associated with a medication error; patient death or serious injury associated with incompatible blood transfusion; maternal death or serious injury associated with labor and delivery; patient death or serious injury associated with hypoglycemia; patient death or serious injury associated with hyperbilirubinimia in neonates; stage three or four pressure ulcers acquired after admission; patient death or serious injury associated with spinal manipulative therapy; perinatal death or serious injury in an infant unrelated to a congenital condition; patient death or serious injury associated with electric shock; patient death or serious injury associated with wrong gas or contaminated gas; patient death or serious injury associated with burns incurred in the facility; patient death or serious injury associated with a fall in the facility; and patient death or serious injury associated with the use of restraints or bedrails.

If the commission believes that the participant is not meeting its participation requirements, the commission may deny, suspend, or revoke the participant's status in the program. Also, participants must provide written notification of a serious reportable event in a timely manner to each patient who is affected by the event. The reports and data are confidential and privileged and not admissible in evidence in any civil action, including judicial, administrative, arbitration, or mediation proceedings. The information is not subject to a civil or administrative subpoena, discovery in a civil action, or disclosure under state public records law.

The participant is encouraged to report less serious adverse events or close calls. The participants are not required to provide a written disclosure of less serious adverse events or close calls to patients or their personal representatives.

Authorizing statutes or regulations

- OR. REV. STAT. §686.1 (2003)
- OR. REV. STAT. §686.9 (2003)
- Oregon Patient Safety Commission Rules, Section 325 et seq.

XIX. PENNSYLVANIA

In Pennsylvania, the legislature established the Patient Safety Authority (PSA) under Act 13 of 2002, referred to as the Medical Care Availability and Reduction Error (Mcare) Act. The PSA is an independent state agency that identifies problems and recommends solutions to promote patient safety in hospitals, ambulatory surgical facilities, birthing centers, and certain abortion clinics. The PSA implemented a mandatory statewide Pennsylvania Patient Safety Reporting System (PA-PSRS, pronounced "PAY-sirs") that requires more than 400 health care facilities to submit reports of actual events and near misses. The PSA analyzes and evaluates the reports and makes recommendations for changes in health care practices and procedures to reduce the number and severity of serious events ("actual occurrences") and incidents ("near misses") within the facility. The PSA does not have regulatory authority to issue punitive measures to the facilities. However, certain PA-PSRS reports must be sent to the Pennsylvania Department of Health. In turn, the Department of Health can issue sanctions and penalties, including fines and license forfeitures to health care facilities in response to individual citizens' complaints. Additionally, the Bureau of Professional and Occupational Affairs responds to citizens' complaints against licensed medical professionals. All information submitted through PA-PSRS is confidential. The information about individual facilities or providers is not made public.

Authorizing statutes or regulations

- 40 PA. STAT. ANN. § 1303.308 (2003)
- 40 PA. STAT. ANN. § 1303.313
- Medical Care Availability and Reduction of Error Act, P.L. 154, No. 13

XX. RHODE ISLAND

All hospitals in Rhode Island must report to the Department of Health Division of Facilities Regulation within twenty-four hours of the occurrence any incidents that include: fires or internal disasters; patient poisoning; infection outbreaks; kidnapping and inpatient psychiatric elopements and elopements by minors; strikes by personnel; external disasters that adversely affect facility operations; and unscheduled termination of any services vital to the continued safe operation of the facility or to the health and safety of its patients and personnel.

Other reportable events must be reported to the department within seventy-two hours or when the hospital has reasonable cause to believe that the incident has occurred. Such reportable events involve: brain injury; mental impairment; paraplegia; quadriplegia; paralysis; loss of use of limb or organ; hospital stay extended due to serious or unforeseen complications; birth injury; impairment of sight or hearing; surgery on the wrong patient; subjecting a patient to a procedure other than that ordered or intended by the patient's attending physician; any other incident that is reported to their malpractice insurance carrier or self-insurance program; suicide of a patient during treatment or within five days after discharge; blood transfusion error; and any serious or unforeseen complication resulting in an extended hospital stay or death of the patient.

In addition to the reporting requirement, the hospital must investigate the incident to determine whether the incident was within the normal range of outcomes given the patient's condition. The hospital must release the internal review to the department of health. If the incident was within the normal range of patient outcomes, no further action is needed. However, if it was not within the normal range, the hospital must perform a root-cause analysis to identify causal factors that may have led to the incident and develop a performance improvement plan to prevent similar incidents. The hospital must also provide: an explanation of the circumstances surrounding the incident; an updated assessment of the effect of the incident on the patient; a summary of current patient status including follow-up care provided and post-incident diagnosis; and a summary of all actions taken to correct the problem(s) to prevent recurrence. All reports and peer review records and proceedings related to reported events are confidential and privileged.

Authorizing statutes or regulations
- R.I. GEN. LAWS § 23-17-40
- R.I. GEN. LAWS § 23-17-15
- R.I. GEN. LAWS § 23-17-25
- R23-17-HOSP R.I. Code Regs. §§ 1.41, 1.42, 34.0

XXI.   SOUTH CAROLINA

South Carolina requires each accident or incident occurring within a health care facility—including medication errors and adverse drug reactions—to be reported to the South Carolina Department of Health and Environmental Control. Incidents resulting in death or serious injury must be reported in writing to the Division of Health Licensing within ten days of the occurrence. Also, each health care facility must file a joint annual report with the Department of Health and Environmental Control.

Authorizing statutes or regulations

- S.C. CODE ANN. REGS. 61-16, § 206

XXII.   SOUTH DAKOTA

In South Dakota, nursing facilities must report: any death not the result of natural causes that originates on the facility's property such as accidents, abuse, negligence, or suicide; any missing patient or resident; or any allegation of abuse or neglect of any patient by any person. The facility must report the results of the investigation of the incident within five working days after the incident. Failure to comply may be grounds for suspension or revocation of the facility's license.

Authorizing statutes or regulations

- S.D. ADMIN. R. 44:04:01:07
- S.D. CODIFIED LAWS § 34-12-19

XXIII.   TENNESSEE

All hospitals in Tennessee must report an unusual event to the Department of Health within seven business days of its identification. An unusual event is an unexpected occurrence or accident resulting in death or life-threatening or serious injury to a patient, and which is not related to a natural course of the patient's illness or underlying condition. Unusual events include: medication errors; aspiration in a non-intubated patient related to conscious/moderate sedation; intravascular catheter events; volume overload leading to pulmonary edema; blood transfusion reactions; delivery of blood to the wrong patient; complications related to operations/procedures; second- or third-degree burns; falls resulting in fractures, subdural or epidural hematoma, cerebral contusion, subarachnoid hemorrhage, and/or internal trauma; procedure-related incidents (i.e., hemorrhage, post-operative wound infections, wrong patient/wrong site surgical procedure, unintentionally retained foreign body, poisoning, etc.).

For health services provided in a home setting, only unusual events that are witnessed by or known to the person delivering the services must be reported.

Within forty days after the event, the facility must file a corrective action report for the unusual event. If the Department of Health is satisfied that the corrective action plan appropriately addresses errors that contributed to the unusual event and takes the necessary steps to prevent the recurrence of the errors, the department shall approve the corrective action plan. If the department does not approve the corrective action plan, the department provides the facility with a list of actions that are necessary to address the errors.

The report received by the department is confidential and not subject to discovery, subpoena, or legal compulsion for release to any person or entity. The report is not admissible in any civil or administrative action, but it may be released to an appropriate regulatory agency with jurisdiction for disciplinary or license sanctions against the facility.

Authorizing statutes or regulations
- TENN. COMP. R. & REGS. 1200-8-1.11

XXIV. TEXAS

In Texas, hospitals, ambulatory surgical centers, and private mental hospitals and other mental health facilities must file an annual report to the Texas Department of Health that lists the number of occurrences at the hospital or an outpatient facility owned or operated by the hospital. A reportable occurrence includes: a medication error resulting in a patient's unanticipated death or major permanent loss of bodily function in circumstances unrelated to the patient's natural course of the illness; a baby's death unrelated to a congenital condition in a baby with a birth weight greater than 2,500 grams; the suicide of a patient in a setting in which the patient received care twenty-four hours a day; the abduction of a newborn infant or the discharge of an infant to someone without legal custody of the infant; the sexual assault of a patient; a hemolytic blood transfusion reaction; a surgical procedure on the wrong patient or on the wrong body part; a foreign object accidentally left in a patient during a procedure; and a patient death or serious disability associated with the use or function of a device designed for patient care that is used or functions other than as intended. The Department of Public Health cannot require the annual report to include any information other than the number of occurrences of each type of event.

All information compiled by or submitted to the Department of Public Health is confidential and not subject to a subpoena or disclosure, and may not be admitted as evidence or otherwise disclosed in any civil, criminal, or administrative proceeding. The confidentiality protection includes the root-causes analysis, the annual hospital report, action plan, best practices report, department summary, and all related information and materials.

Authorizing statutes or regulations

- TEX. HEALTH & SAFETY CODE §§ 241.201-.210
- TEX. HEALTH & SAFETY CODE §§ 243.001-.060
- TEX. HEALTH & SAFETY CODE §§ 577.001-.064

XXV. UTAH

Utah requires that every general acute hospital, critical access hospital, ambulatory surgical center, psychiatric hospital, orthopedic hospital, rehabilitation hospital, chemical dependency/substance abuse hospital, or long-term acute care hospital report all patient safety sentinel events within seventy-two hours to the Utah Department of Health.

Sentinel events include: surgical events (i.e., wrong body part, wrong patient, incorrect procedure, unintentional foreign objects in patient after surgery, or patient's death during surgery or postoperatively); product or device events (i.e., patient's death from contaminated drugs, devices, or biologics; death or disability associated with the off-label use of a device; or patient's death or disability associated with an air embolism); patient protection events (i.e., infant discharged to the wrong person, death or disability resulting from patient elopement, or patient suicide); care management events (i.e., patient death or disability resulting from medication error, hemolytic reaction to incompatible blood transfusion, labor or delivery of infant, hypoglycemia, kernicterus, stage three or four pressure ulcer, spinal manipulative therapy, prolonged fluoroscopy, radiotherapy to the wrong body region, radiotherapy greater than 25 percent above the prescribed radiotherapy dose; health care-acquired infection, or death of full-term baby); environmental events (i.e., contaminated gas, patient death or major permanent loss of function arising from electric shock, burns, use of restraints or bedrails, and falls); and criminal events (i.e., care ordered by someone impersonating a health care provider, abduction of a patient, nonconsensual sexual contact on a patient, staff member, or visitor by another patient, staff member, or unknown perpetrator, or patient death or major permanent loss of function resulting from a criminal assault or battery).

The report must include facility information, patient information, event information, type of occurrence, analysis, and corrective action. The facility must also perform a root-cause analysis. The facility must submit a final report with an action plan within sixty calendar days of discovery of the sentinel event. The information that the Utah Department of

Health has is confidential. Information produced or collected by the facility is confidential and privileged. An entity that violates the patient safety regulations may be assessed a civil money penalty up to $5,000 or be punished for violation of a Class B misdemeanor for the first violation and a Class A misdemeanor for any subsequent similar violation within two years.

Authorizing statutes or regulations

- UTAH ADMIN. CODE r.380-200 R.380-200-3
- UTAH ADMIN. CODE r.380-210 (Health Care Facility Patient Safety R.380-210-1 through R.380-210-6 Program Rule)

XXVI. VERMONT

As of January 1, 2008, each hospital that is licensed by the Vermont Board of Health is required to report "adverse events" to the Patient Safety Surveillance and Improvement System. Adverse events are listed on the Vermont Department of Health Web site (http://healthvermont.gov). Adverse events include: surgical events (i.e., surgery on wrong body part, surgery on wrong patient, wrong surgical procedure, foreign object retained after surgery, or death during or after surgery); product or device events (i.e., death or serious disability associated with contaminated drugs, associated with the function of a device or air embolism); patient protection events (i.e., infant discharged to the wrong person, patient suicide or attempted suicide, and death or serious disability associated with patient elopement; care management events (i.e., death or serious disability associated with: medication errors, hemolytic reactions associated with blood transfusions, maternal death or disability associated with labor and delivery, hypoglycemia, kernicterus, pressure ulcers, death or serious disability associated with spinal manipulations, or artificial insemination with wrong donor sperm or egg); environmental events (i.e., death or serious disability associated with electric shock, wrong gas or contaminated gas, burns, falls, or the use of bedrails or restraints); and criminal events (i.e., care ordered or given by someone impersonating a health care provider, abduction of a patient, sexual assault of a patient, or death or serious disability associated with a physical assault of a patient or staff member).

Each hospital must submit an initial report to the Patient Safety Surveillance and Improvement System no later than seven calendar days after the discovery of the adverse event. The hospital must also submit a causal analysis and corrective action plan within sixty days from the submission of the initial report.

The facility must also report "intentional unsafe acts" to the Patient Safety Surveillance and Improvement System within seven days after the discovery of the act. An intentional unsafe act is an adverse event[3] or near miss[4] that results from a criminal act, a purposefully unsafe act, alcohol or substance abuse, or patient abuse. The Patient Safety Surveillance and Improvement System conducts routine periodic reviews to evaluate the hospital's compliance with these reporting requirements. All information provided to the Vermont Department of Health and Patient Safety Surveillance and Improvement System is confidential and privileged, and exempt from the public access to records law. The information is not discoverable, not subject to subpoena or other disclosure, and cannot be introduced as evidence in any civil or administrative action against a health care provider.

If the commissioner finds that a hospital has knowingly violated the patient safety rules, the commissioner may impose a civil administrative penalty of no more than $10,000 or, in the case of a continuing violation, a civil administrative penalty of no more than $100,000 or one-tenth of 1 percent of the gross annual revenues of the health care facility, whichever is greater.

Authorizing statutes or regulations

- VT. STAT. ANN. tit.18, §§ 1912-19

XXVII. WASHINGTON

Every childbirth center, hospital, psychiatric hospital, or correctional medical facility must notify the Washington Department of Health within forty-eight hours of an adverse event. A subsequent report must be filed within forty-five days after the event. As part of the report, the facility must provide a root-cause analysis and corrective action plan, or provide an explanation of any reasons for not taking corrective action. When the notification or report is made by a health care worker, the information in the notification, report, and supporting documents is confidential.

Reportable adverse events include: surgical events (i.e., surgery on wrong body part, surgery on wrong patient, wrong surgical procedure, foreign object retained after surgery, or postoperative death); product or device events (i.e., death or serious disability associated with contaminated drugs, devices or biologics, or in misuse of a device or associated with air embolism); patient protection events (i.e., infant discharged to the wrong person, patient suicide or attempted suicide, and death or serious disability associated with patient elopement); care management events (i.e., death or serious disability associated with: medication

errors, hemolytic reactions associated with blood transfusions, maternal death or disability associated with labor and delivery, hypoglycemia,
kernicterus, stage three or four pressure ulcers, death or serious disability associated with spinal manipulations, or artificial insemination
with wrong donor sperm or egg); environmental events (i.e., death or
serious disability associated with electric shock, wrong gas or toxic substances, burns, falls, or the use of bedrails or restraints); and criminal
events (i.e., care ordered or given by someone impersonating a health
care provider, abduction of a patient, sexual assault of a patient, and
death or serious disability associated with a physical assault of a patient
or staff member).

Authorizing statutes or regulations
- WASH. REV. CODE § 18.130.160 §§ 104-112
- WASH. ADMIN. CODE 246-320-145

XXVIII.   WYOMING

In 2005, the Wyoming legislature enacted the Mandatory Reporting of
Safety Events statute (Wyoming Statute 35-2-912). The statute requires
that licensed health care facilities report any occurrence of a patient safety
event to the Wyoming Department of Health. A "safety event" is an unexpected occurrence involving death or serious physical or psychological
injury, or the risk of such injury. A violation of the statute may result in
punishment by conditions placed upon the facility's license, suspension
of admissions to the facility, or denial, suspension, or revocation of a
facility's license.

   Reportable patient safety events include: surgical events (i.e., surgery on wrong body part, surgery on wrong patient, wrong surgical procedure, foreign object retained after surgery, or death during surgery or
immediately postoperative); product or device events (i.e., death or serious disability associated with contaminated drugs, devices, or biologics, or in misuse of a device or associated with air embolism); patient
protection events (i.e., infant discharged to the wrong person, patient
death or serious disability associated with patient disappearance for
more than four hours, or patient suicide or attempted suicide); care
management events (i.e., death or serious disability associated with:
medication errors, hemolytic reactions associated with blood transfusions, maternal death or disability associated with labor and delivery
within forty-two days after delivery, hypoglycemia, kernicterus, stage
three or four pressure ulcers, or death or serious disability associated
with spinal manipulations); environmental events (i.e., death or serious

disability associated with electric shock, wrong gas or toxic substances, burns, falls, or the use of bedrails or restraints); and criminal events (i.e., care ordered or given by someone impersonating a health care provider, abduction of a patient, sexual assault of a patient, and death or serious disability associated with a physical assault of a patient or staff member).

Any notice, report, or document, and any other information compiled or disseminated under the statute, is confidential and not discoverable or admissible in evidence in any administrative or legal proceeding conducted in Wyoming, and is not a public record. Contractors, employees, or other members of the Wyoming Department of Health who receive any notice, report, document, or any other information compiled or disseminated under the statute are not permitted or required to testify in any civil action as to any evidence or any other matters or as to any findings, recommendations, evaluation, opinions, or other actions of the Department of Health. However, information, documents, or other records that are available from original sources are not immune from discovery or use in any civil action just because they were submitted to the Department of Health. Also, any person who provides information to the Department of Health is not prevented from testifying as to matters within his or her knowledge, but he or she cannot be asked about communications with the Department of Health.

Authorizing statutes or regulations

- Wyo. Stat. Ann. § 35-2-912
- Department of Health, Health Care Facility Event Reporting, ch. 2

XXIX. CONCLUSION

States are beginning to address the patient safety issue by enacting legislation and regulations that provide for certain adverse event reporting requirements. However, legislative changes to the laws and developments of new laws can come about rapidly. Those states that have not yet implemented adverse event reporting requirements may do so within a short time. The reader should become knowledgeable about relevant state laws, bearing in mind that changes in the laws may occur frequently. In this chapter, we attempted to summarize the state laws that are currently in effect. In order to stay abreast of the most current adverse events reporting requirements, it is advisable to conduct independent legal research and contact the local department of health.

NOTES

1.   COMMITTEE ON QUALITY OF HEALTH CARE IN AMERICA, INSTITUTE OF MEDICINE, TO ERR IS HUMAN: BUILDING A SAFER HEALTH SYSTEM, at 9 (Linda T. Kohn et al., eds., 2000).

2.   According to the National Academy for State Health Policy, which tracks state reporting systems, the states are California, Colorado, Connecticut, Florida, Georgia, Illinois, Indiana, Kansas, Maine, Maryland, Massachusetts, Minnesota, New Jersey, Nevada, New York, Ohio, Oregon, Pennsylvania, Rhode Island, South Carolina, South Dakota, Tennessee, Texas, Utah, Vermont, Washington, and Wyoming. Also included is the District of Columbia. *Patient Safety Toolbox for States*, www.pstoolbox.org (last visited on January 6, 2008).

3.   An adverse event is any untoward incident, therapeutic misadventure, iatrogenic injury, or other undesirable occurrence directly associated with care or services provided by a health care provider or health care facility. VT. STAT. ANN. tit.18, § 1912(1).

4.   A near miss is any process variation that did not affect the outcome but for which a recurrence carries a significant chance of a serious adverse outcome. VT. STAT. ANN. tit.18, § 7.

CHAPTER 3

Private and Public Responses

I. INTRODUCTION

In this chapter, we will examine the private and public responses to the Institute of Medicine's report, *To Err Is Human: Building a Safer Health System*. Since the report was released, there has been a wide variety of reactions throughout the health care system, both in the private and public arenas. The following is a brief overview of what different groups did to revise, amend, adjust, or create patient safety measures for health care providers to implement for the purpose of improving the safety of the health care system.

II. THE JOINT COMMISSION ON THE ACCREDITATION OF HEALTHCARE ORGANIZATIONS

The Joint Commission on the Accreditation of Healthcare Organizations has a rich history. In 1910, Ernest Codman, MD, proposed that all hospitals track their patients to determine whether the treatment they received produced an effective outcome.[1] If the treatment was not effective, the hospital would then determine why, so that procedures could be revised to improve future outcomes.[2] In 1913, Franklin Martin, MD, a colleague of Dr. Codman, proposed the creation of the American College of Surgeons (ACS), which had a stated objective of the "end result system" proposed by Dr. Codman. This "end result system of hospitalization" evolved over time until, in 1951, the ACS joined with the American College of Physicians (ACP), the American Hospital Association (AHA), the American Medical Association (AMA), and the Canadian Medical Association (CMA) to create the Joint Commission on Accreditation of Hospitals (JCAH). Eventually, the CMA withdrew and joined with other organizations in Canada to develop their own accreditation body.

Initially, JCAH's primary purpose was to provide voluntary accreditation.[3] Today, the organization is known as the Joint Commission on the

Accreditation of Healthcare Organizations (JCAHO), and it includes accreditation bodies for health care facilities in several areas, including long-term care, psychiatry, dental, pathology, ambulatory care, home care, managed care, durable medical equipment, and laboratories.[4] JCAHO's mission is to "continually improve the safety and quality of care provided to the public through the provision of health care accreditation and related services that support performance improvement in health care organizations."[5] From its modest beginnings until now, the organization has increased its prominence in the health care field. Health care organizations take great pride in becoming accredited and maintaining their accreditation through JCAHO.

JCAHO accreditation approval indicates that a facility meets high standards. Not all facilities are JCAHO-approved because not all facilities are capable of achieving the level of patient care required under the stringent JCAHO criteria. The accreditation process focuses on operational systems that are critical to the safety and quality of patient care.[6] There are four key elements of the accreditation process: periodic performance review (PPR); tracer methodology; priority focus process (PFP); and unannounced survey.

The PPR is an annual review done by the health care facility to determine the level of its own compliance with the accreditation participation requirements, national patient safety goals, applicable standards, and elements of performance.[7] If the facility discovers that there are areas of noncompliance, the staff must develop a plan of action to correct the deficiencies, which must be approved by JCAHO.[8] Any hospital, laboratory, or organization providing ambulatory care, behavioral health care, home care, or long-term care that intends to continue a JCAHO accreditation must complete a PPR annually.[9] An organization that undergoes an initial JCAHO survey must submit a PPR twelve months after its initial full survey.[10] The PPR provides a framework for the facility to determine its continued compliance with JCAHO standards.[11] However, a PPR does not affect the decision to accredit an organization.[12] A PPR allows the facility to prepare for a survey, and provides information to correct any deficiencies before the JCAHO survey is complete.[13] The PPR helps to keep the accreditation process consistent because the scoring methodology for the PPR is the same as the ones used by the surveyors during the on-site survey.[14]

The tracer methodology follows a number of patients, residents, or clients through the health care organization's means of caring for the individual.[15] The tracers are used to determine whether the organization conforms to the selected standards, and to assess the organization's methods of providing care and services to patients, residents, or clients.[16] Essentially, the surveyor does this by using certain patients' records as a roadmap to move through the organization. Surveyors "trace" the specific care that an individual received by observing and talking to staff in areas where the care was given.[17] As the surveyors trace this roadmap of the patient's care, they gauge the organization's compliance with JCAHO standards.[18] The surveyors also determine whether the organization's system is up to par for delivering safe, quality health care.[19]

During the tracer process, the surveyor looks for compliance issues in various areas of performance.[20] The surveyor identifies trends that could indicate potential system-level problems in the organization.[21] This process creates opportunities for surveyors to educate and inform staff and administrators.[22] It also provides occasions to share best practices from similar health care organizations.[23] The number of patients "traced" depends on the length of the survey.[24] The average three-day survey with three surveyors generally allows for completion of eleven tracers.[25]

If the surveyors identify trends that are potentially problematic, the facility will receive a "requirement for improvement" that indicates what the facility should do to meet the JCAHO standard required for that particular category.[26] The facility then has forty-five days from the end of the survey to submit its "evidence of standards compliance" (ESC), which details the actions the facility has taken to comply with the standards or clarify why it believes it was in compliance with the standards at the time of the survey.[27] Within the same time frame, the facility must also identify "measures of success" that the facility will use over time to assess the facility's continued compliance.[28] Four months after JCAHO approves the ESC, the facility must submit information on its measures of success that indicates the facility's compliance.[29] A measure of success is a "quantifiable measure that demonstrates whether an action was effective and sustained. The Measure of Success Goal is the quantifiable level of compliance (expressed as a percentage) that the organization is striving to achieve as the result of implementation of the corrective action identified in the ESC report."[30]

The priority focus process (PFP) is a tool that helps surveyors concentrate their activities on the issues most relevant to patient safety and quality of care at that particular health care organization.[31] It gathers presurvey data from various sources including the Joint Commission, the health care organization, and other public sources.[32] The PFP then applies rules to identify areas to focus the survey activities appropriately, and guides the selection of tracer patients.[33] The PFP helps to make the on-site sampling consistent and helps surveyors evaluate health care organizations' performance consistently.[34]

The unannounced survey is a random day-long survey on an arbitrary selection of organizations in the ambulatory care, behavioral health care, home care, hospital, and long-term care accreditation programs.[35] JCAHO performs the random surveys anywhere from nine to thirty months after the accreditation date.[36] During the unannounced survey, the surveyor assesses both variable and fixed components.[37] The surveyor addresses the variable components first and, if time permits, moves on to the fixed components.[38] Variable components are specific to the organization and they include presurvey areas such as previous recommendations, demographic data related to clinical-service and diagnostic-related groups, and data from the Joint Commission's quality monitoring system.[39] Fixed components are based on the degree of risk posed to the patients by the organization's noncompliance with standards related to critical performance areas.[40] In 2007, fixed components included patient safety, assessment and care/services, quality improvement expertise/activities, and medication management.[41] The fixed components vary depending on the type of organization that is being surveyed. However, the one consistent fixed component throughout all types of organizations is patient/client safety.[42] Over the past few years, JCAHO has moved patient safety to the forefront of concern. In July 2002, JCAHO issued its first set of national patient safety goals (NPSGs) for each category of health care organization that it accredits.[43]

The purpose of JCAHO's NPSGs is to promote specific improvement in patient safety.[44] The JCAHO NPSGs are established by accruing data from the National Sentinel Event Database.[45] This process identifies trends to see where the shifts occur within the sentinel event data.[46] "A sentinel event is an unexpected death or serious physical—including loss of limb or function—or psychological injury or the risk thereof. 'Risk thereof' means that although no harm occurred this time, any recurrence would carry a significant chance of a serious adverse outcome."[47] Each year JCAHO gathers data from the National Sentinel Event Database, as well as feedback from its staff and individuals working in the field, to determine the topics for the NPSGs for that year.[48] In 2007, the number one most common sentinel event was the wrong surgery site.[49] Sentinel events are often related to operative procedures, infections, transfusions, and inpatient suicide.[50] The three most common causes of sentinel events are poor communication, orientation and training issues, and patient assessment issues.[51] JCAHO reviews the topics carefully and prioritizes them. A committee, the Sentinel Event Advisory Group (SEAG), reviews the information and determines the NPSGs and requirements for that year.[52] The SEAG first began in April 2002, and it consists of experienced physicians, nurses, pharmacists, and others with special expertise in patient safety.[53] The SEAG's recommendations for the NPSGs are forwarded to the Joint Commission's board of commissioners for approval.[54]

The organizations that JCAHO accredits are surveyed to determine whether they implement the NPSGs and requirements (or some acceptable alternatives).[55] There are specific NPSGs that are different for each accreditation program. The ambulatory care program, behavioral health program, critical access hospital program, disease-specific care program, home care program, hospital program, laboratory services program, long-term care program, and office-based surgery program each has its own distinct goals.[56] However, the common theme throughout each of these programs' goals is patient safety. For example, in 2008, all of the accreditation programs share as common goals: improvimg the accuracy of patient identification; improving the effectiveness of communication among caregivers; reducing the risk of health care-associated infections; and encouraging patients' active involvement in their own care as a patient safety strategy.[57]

Some programs are required to comply with more NPSGs than others. For example, in order to be accredited in the critical access hospital program the organization must comply with ten goals, while accreditation in the laboratory services program requires the organization to meet four goals.[58] Also, if some of the requirements are applicable to the program but not relevant to the services provided by a particular organization, then JCAHO allows the organization to disregard those goals that are not relevant.[59] If an organization has no control over whether an outside entity that provides services to the accredited organization complies with the national patient safety goals, then the accredited organization must, at the very least, inform the outside entity about the requirements of the goals and encourage the entity to comply.[60]

JCAHO assesses the organization's compliance with the NPSGs during all full accreditation surveys and, when relevant, during other types of surveys.[61] The assessment is integrated into the survey; there is no separate activity for the determination of compliance.[62] Generally, the surveyors evaluate four areas. First, the surveyors assess the organization's compliance with the NPSGs by speaking with the organization leaders to determine what they have done to implement the NPSGs.[63] The surveyors inquire as to what tools the organization uses, who does what, etc.[64] Second, the surveyors interview the staff during the tracer activities.[65]

The surveyors question staff about whether they understand what is expected of them, how they go about doing it, what problems they run into, how often they are not able to meet expectations, etc.[66] Third, the surveyors review medical/clinical records.[67] Lastly, the surveyors directly observe activities to confirm that the documented activities actually happen.[68] For example, the surveyors will observe the medication use process to determine whether staff performs medication reconciliation during treatment and upon discharge.[69] Although JCAHO reviews documentation of compliance, its main focus is on actual performance in order to demonstrate compliance.[70]

Aside from the NPSGs, almost 50 percent of Joint Commission standards are directly related to safety.[71] These standards are in the areas of medication use, infection control, surgery and anesthesia, transfusions, restraint and seclusion, staffing and staff competence, fire safety, medical equipment, emergency management, and security.[72] The standards also include specific requirements for the response to adverse events, prevention of accidental harm through the analysis and redesign of vulnerable patient systems (i.e., ordering, preparing, and dispensing of medication), and the organization's responsibility to tell a patient about outcomes, whether good or bad.[73] Apart from the standards and the NPSGs, JCAHO also has an Office of Quality Monitoring that tracks complaints and reports of concern about health care organizations that relate to the quality of care.[74] JCAHO offers patient safety resources such as seminars, programs, publications, training, education, and consultation.[75] JCAHO is involved in patient safety research, patient safety initiatives, legislative efforts that promote patient safety, and patient safety coalitions that join JCAHO with other organizations to promote patient safety. In the past few years, JCAHO has integrated patient safety as a requirement for accreditation and made it a priority.

III.   THE LEAPFROG GROUP

One of the recommendations in the Institute of Medicine's 1999 landmark report, *To Err Is Human: Building a Safer Health System*, was to have large corporations get involved in reinforcement of patient safety and to reward those health care providers that demonstrate quality and safety improvements.[76] One private response to this recommendation is the Leapfrog Group (LG). The LG is a consortium of large employers that joined efforts to base their decisions to purchase health care on "principles that encourage quality improvement among providers and consumer involvement."[77] The LG's mission is to "trigger giant leaps forward in the safety, quality and affordability of health care by: supporting informed healthcare decisions by those who use and pay for health care; and, promoting high-value health care through incentives and rewards."[78] The LG was started by a group of major employers in November 2000.[79] It is supported by its members, the Business Roundtable,[80] The Robert Wood Johnson Foundation,[81] and others.[82]

The LG recognized that doctors and hospitals are paid with no regard to the quality or affordability of the care that they provide.[83] It theorized that without any financial incentive to enhance the quality of care, doctors and hospitals are not motivated to improve the delivery of care or to provide more efficient care.[84] The LG seeks to encourage the delivery of better health care by providing financial incentives and persuading health care consumers to select health care providers who deliver higher quality of care.[85]

To that end, the LG's members follow four purchasing principles when selecting health care for their enrollees: educating and notifying employees about safety, quality, and affordability of health care, including the significance of evaluating the level of health care that each provider supplies to the patient; acknowledging and compensating health care providers for major advances in the safety, quality, and affordability of their care; making health care plans accountable for putting the Leapfrog purchasing principles into practice; and increasing the support of health care benefits consultants and brokers to utilize and promote the Leapfrog purchasing principles with all of their clients.[86] The LG also encourages its members to provide rewards to hospitals that utilize the LG's quality and safety practices to increase the quality of health care that they provide.[87]

One incentive is the Leapfrog Hospital Rewards Program (LHRP).[88] Through this rewards system, LHRP encourages hospitals to increase patient safety and provides incentives for improvement in the areas of coronary artery bypass graft (CABG) (commonly known as bypass surgery), percutaneous coronary intervention (PCI) (commonly known as angioplasty), acute myocardial infarction (AMI) (commonly known as heart attack), community acquired pneumonia (CAP), and deliveries/ newborn care.[89] These five clinical areas comprise a significant percentage of commercial inpatient spending and are prime areas for improvement in quality and efficiency.[90] The LG uses Leapfrog Hospital Insights (LHI) performance measures to determine hospital quality and efficiency. It then ranks the hospitals in each of these areas, depending on quality and efficiency.[91] Hospitals that are in the top 25 percent *for both quality and efficiency* are identified as "top performance" hospitals.[92] Only 5 to 8 percent of hospitals across the nation attain the distinction of being in the top performance group of hospitals.[93] This group becomes the gold standard by which all other hospitals are evaluated.[94] The remaining hospitals are ranked according to how close they are to the top quartile of hospitals.[95] While it is not statistically possible for every hospital to be in the top 25 percent, the key is to have *all* hospitals at least strive to achieve the performance levels of the top performance hospitals. The rankings are then used by the LG, health plans, data vendors, and others to publicly recognize the hospitals' performance.[96] They are also used by purchasers and payers to reward hospitals.[97] Hospitals nationwide voluntarily participate in LHI by submitting patient safety data through the Leapfrog Quality and Safety Survey and additional quality and efficiency data through JCAHO.[98]

An example of the ranking method is as follows. For AMI, the Leapfrog Hospital Insights directly measures actual mortality rates and compares each hospital's actual mortality rate to its severity-adjusted "expected" mortality rate. It then computes how many lives a hospital "saves" per patient admission. In other words, the actual number of deaths is compared to the expected number of deaths for the severity of the conditions of those AMI patients. Hospitals with the fewest number of actual deaths compared to the number of expected deaths were ranked as the top performers.[99] Then, the Leapfrog Hospital Insights computes the weighted averages of lives saved for the top 25 percent of hospitals and for all hospitals.[100] When all of the hospitals' data for AMIs were considered as a whole, the hospitals slightly outperformed the LG's expectations. There were 1.3 fewer deaths per thousand admissions than predicted.[101] However, the top 25 percent of those hospitals had forty-five fewer deaths per thousand admissions than expected.[102] This gap indicates that the remaining 75 percent of hospitals have a lot of room for improvement. The LG predicts that, given the 775,000 annual admissions for AMI in the United States, there is a potential to save about 34,000 lives per year with increased implementation of patient safety measures.[103] There are similar calculations for the other four areas of clinical conditions, with similar statistics for the possibility to save lives. The LG estimates that the top performing hospitals saved $18.5 billion compared with other hospitals.[104] The decrease in spending does not reflect a decrease in quality because the top performing hospitals are ranked according to *quality* of care as well as *efficiency* of care.[105]

LHI also measures readmission rates and medication errors. The LG found that if all hospitals performed at the top quartile rate, there would be 144,923 fewer readmissions in the five categories at a savings of $18.5 billion.[106] In the same respect, if all hospitals used the physician order entry for prescriptions, it would avoid 187,000 serious medication errors in the commercially insured population annually.[107]

This rating system helps to identify the differences in the quality of care that different hospitals provide.[108] All hospitals nationwide that provide adult inpatient care are welcome to participate in the LHI.[109]

In addition to LHI, the LG also welcomes all hospitals in the United States to participate in LG's voluntary Hospital Quality and Safety Survey. Additionally, the LG extends a formal invitation to hospitals that are geographically located in regional-roll-out (RRO) areas. RROs are geographic areas where LG members encourage hospitals to meet the LG's recommended quality and safety practices.[110] The RROs comprise over 50 percent of consumers and hospital beds in the United States.[111] In the Hospital Quality and Safety Survey, the LG inquires as to whether the hospitals have the following four quality and safety practices: computerized physician order entry system (CPOE); an ICU staffed by health care providers who are trained in critical care; experienced staff that provides the best results for specific high-risk procedures; and high Leapfrog Safe Practices Score (meaning that the hospital instituted twenty-seven procedures to decrease preventable patient errors).[112] Studies that were commissioned by the LG indicate that if the first three practices were implemented in every nonrural hospital in the nation, there would be over 65,000 lives saved and $41.5 billion saved annually.[113]

The CPOE are electronic prescribing systems that intercept errors at the time the physician orders the medication.[114] When using the CPOE, the physician enters the medication order into a computer rather than using a pen and paper. The computer then integrates the order with the patient information, including laboratory and prescription data. The computer analyzes the medication order against the patient's data and automatically checks for potential errors. The CPOE warns against drug interactions, allergies, or overdose; keeps accurate, current prescription information that assists physicians to keep up to date with new drugs on the market; keeps drug-specific information that eliminates confusion between drug names that sound or are spelled alike; improves communication between physicians and pharmacists; and reduces medication errors as well as health care costs.[115] In order for a hospital to fully comply with the CPOE standard, it must: make certain that 75 percent of all medication orders are entered via a computer system that has prescribing-error prevention software; demonstrate that the CPOE system can alert physicians to 50 percent of the common, serious prescribing errors; and require that physicians electronically document a reason for overriding an interception before the physician overrides it.[116]

Despite the overwhelming benefits of the CPOE, many hospitals are reluctant to implement the practice.[117] One reason is that the upfront cost of implementing the system can be prohibitive. At Brigham and Women's Hospital, the cost of implementing CPOE was about $1.9 million, and it costs an additional $500,000 to maintain the system every year.[118] However, the return on the initial investment was between $5 million and $10 million in annual savings.[119] One drawback is that the physicians must become comfortable with the system and overcome the urge to order medications by hand.[120]

The second area that the LG surveys is whether a hospital staffs the ICU with health care providers who are trained in critical care. Studies have shown that the quality of care in the ICU is affected by whether "intensivists" provide care and by the organization model of the ICU staff.[121] Intensivists are either: board-certified physicians who are additionally board-certified in critical care medicine; physicians board-certified in emergency medicine who complete a critical care fellowship in a program accredited by the American College of Emergency Physicians; or physicians board-certified in medicine, anesthesiology, pediatrics, or surgery who completed training prior to the availability of subspecialty certification in critical care and who have provided at least six weeks of full-time ICU care annually since 1987.[122]

The organization of the ICU staff is also important. There are two general types of ICU staff arrangements. Hospitals either have "open" systems, where the patient receives care primarily from physicians who have responsibilities outside the ICU with the assistance of critical care specialists; or "closed" systems, where patients receive care exclusively from critical care specialists or teams that are close at hand to provide emergency care.[123] Studies show that mortality rates are significantly lower in hospitals with "closed" staff ICU models that are exclusively managed by board-certified intensivists.[124] Hospitals that have ICUs staffed with intensivists have a mortality rate that is 30 percent less and a mortality rate in the ICU that is 40 percent less than hospitals that do not use intensivists to staff ICUs.[125] Additionally, those hospitals that staff ICUs with intensivists have a lower ICU and hospital length of stay.[126]

Hospitals that meet the LG's ICU physician staffing safety standard have an adult and/or pediatric ICU that is staffed by intensivists who are present during daytime hours and provide clinical care exclusively in the ICU. Also, when intensivists in such hospitals are not present or available via telemedicine, they will return pages at least 95 percent of the time within five minutes and make arrangements for a certified physician to reach ICU patients within five minutes.[127] In 2006, only 26 percent of hospitals responding to the survey met the ICU physician staffing safety standard.[128] There are several reasons for not meeting this standard, including a shortage of certified intensivists, lack of funding to hire intensivists, and intensivists choosing not to work in the ICU due to reimbursement issues.[129] Some solutions are to consolidate ICU care into larger hospitals or implement telemedicine for ICU physician staffing at those hospitals currently without it.[130]

Two areas of the Hospital Quality and Safety Survey are the safe practices score (SPS) and evidence-based hospital referral (EBHR). The SPS reflects the revisions suggested by the National Quality Forum (NQF) that were placed on their list of safe practices in health care.[131] The NQF is a not-for-profit organization created to develop and implement a national strategy for health care quality measurement and reporting.[132] The NQF publishes recommendations in its consensus report for improving health care quality.[133] The consensus report contains recommendations for implementation of thirty practices that should be universally used in clinical care to reduce the risk of patient error.[134] The practices include leadership, creating a culture of safety, matching patient care needs to staff capability, communication, medication management, prevention of nosocomial infections, and other specific care processes.[135] A hospital is evaluated for its implementation of each of the practices and given a Leapfrog Safe Practices Score. The hospitals are then ranked into four groups: fully meets progress goal; making good progress; good early-stage effort; and willingness to report.[136] This information is valuable for consumers to make informed hospital choices.

The evidence-based hospital referral (EBHR) involves matching the patient's high-risk condition with an appropriate facility that is associated with better outcomes for that condition.[137] When the referral is made to the proper facility, patients can expect lower mortality rates and higher adherence to clinical practices known to improve outcomes for surgical and high-risk procedures.[138] Studies have shown that choosing hospitals that have higher volumes and surgeons with more experience will result in lower surgical mortality.[139] However, this better outcome does not necessarily reflect more skillful surgeons and fewer technical errors, but it more likely reflects greater proficiency with all aspects of care, including patient selection, anesthesia, and postoperative care.[140] In 2007, the LG added two EBHR procedures—aortic valve and bariatric surgeries—and raised the EBHR standards for clinical areas.[141] These changes increased the acceptable limits for the Hospital Quality and Safety Survey and increased the number of procedures that the LG assesses, making it more difficult for hospitals to meet the LG's standards.[142] Many of those hospitals that scored in the top quartile in 2006 did not do as well in the 2007 survey.[143]

The Hospital Quality and Safety Survey annually measures a range of hospital quality and safety practices. The LG found that the quality and safety practices will significantly reduce preventable medical mistakes.[144] The group also believes that it is possible for the health care industry to implement these practices in the near future.[145] The LG considers health as a long-term investment in businesses and the community. The LG releases the ratings to the public so that consumers have the information to make informed health care decisions.[146] Through the ratings, the health plans, purchasers, or consumers can determine which health care providers have implemented the suggested best quality and safety practices and make their health care choices accordingly.[147] This is one of the first steps in using purchasing power to improve hospital safety and quality.[148]

IV. THE NATIONAL PATIENT SAFETY FOUNDATION

The National Patient Safety Foundation (NPSF) was founded in 1997 by the American Medical Association, CNA HealthPro, and 3M, with significant support from the Schering-Plough Corporation.[149] The NPSF is an independent not-for-profit organization; its mission is to improve the safety of patients.[150] The NPSF does this through research, distribution of new information, multidisciplinary projects, and patient safety tools and programs provided to all sectors of the health care system.[151] The NPSF recognizes that the prevention of health care errors and the elimination or mitigation of patient injuries caused by health care errors are vital to the delivery of quality health care.[152] The key to patient safety is the prevention of patient injury through early and appropriate responses to evident and potential problems.[153] In order to improve patient safety, it is essential to establish a culture of trust, honesty, integrity, and open communications.[154] The NPSF believes that any significant advancement in patient safety requires an integrated body of scientific knowledge and the infrastructure to support its development.[155] Advancement also requires patient involvement in continuous learning and constant communication of information between care givers, organizations, and the general public.[156] The NPSF acknowledges that our health care system is not perfect and that improvement requires fundamental change.[157]

The NPSF initiatives involve individuals and entities that have an interest in improving patient safety.[158] These interested parties include providers, patients, families, academics, researchers, suppliers, educators, payors, insurers, policy-makers, and others who have concerns about the safety of the health care system.[159] One of the NPSF's initiatives is the Stand Up for Patient Safety Program (SUPSP), which was founded in 2002.[160] The seventeen founding members comprise various health care systems throughout the nation.[161] The basic principle behind SUPSP is that partnership is fundamental to the development and continued strength of a patient safety culture.[162] With that in mind, SUPSP facilitates partnerships among all levels of an organization and all groups involved in patient care.[163] Its program materials and resources engage the full spectrum of health care stakeholders.[164] The program encourages a "teamwork" approach by providing materials designed to be coordinated for implementation by administrators, trustees, clinical staff, patients and families, and communities.[165] The SUPSP is also designed to foster partnerships between health care providers, patients, families, and communities by providing materials that are specifically aimed at engaging patients as active participants in the health care process.[166]

The SUPSP encourages collaboration between its member organizations by providing members with a forum to discuss approaches and strategies, pose questions, and exchange information on best practices.[167] The benefits of a yearly membership at the partner level include: a member resource guide that contains articles, slide presentations, brochures, videos with learning guides, etc.; ten audio-Web conferences per year; access to the SUPSP Web site, which includes patient safety resources; a National Patient Safety Awareness Week toolkit that includes resources and information; twice-monthly e-mail notification about current literature on patient safety; a subscription to the journal, *Focus on Safety*, published by NPSF; a subscription to *Journal of Patient Safety*, a peer-reviewed quarterly periodical published by NPSF containing recent research and advancements in patient safety; and attendance at regional seminars focused on patient safety organizations' executive and mid-level management leaders.[168] Yearly memberships at the "charter" level have additional benefits including one complimentary registration to the Annual Patient Safety Congress, which is an annual symposium that brings together health care chief executives, board members, policy makers, practitioners, academics, researchers, and patient advocates to exchange information for the implementation of best practices and the latest research.[169]

Another NPSF initiative is the Lucien Leape Institute (LLI), which was created in May 2007.[170] The institute functions as a think tank that focuses on delineating strategic pathways and identifying areas of concern for patient safety.[171] The goal is to provide vision and context for the various patient safety efforts that are underway in the health care field.[172] The members of the LLI include the president and chief executive officer of the Institute for Healthcare Improvement, the director of the Agency for Healthcare Research and Quality, the senior vice president for the Institute for Healthcare Improvement, the chair of the board of directors of the NPSF, the retired chairman and chief executive officer of Kaiser Foundation Health Plan, Inc., and Kaiser Foundation Hospitals, the chief operating officer of Children's Hospitals and Clinics of Minnesota, and the president of JCAHO.[173] The chair of the LLI is Dr. Lucian Leape, a physician and adjunct professor of heath policy at the Harvard School of Public Health, who provided leadership at the NPSF since its inception.[174]

Another NPSF project is the Partnership for Clear Health Communication (PCHC), at the National Patient Safety Foundation which was created in May 2007.[175] This program is a collaboration between NPSF and the Partnership for Clear Health Communication.[176] Founded in 2002, the Partnership for Clear Health Communication is a nonprofit organization dedicated to improving low health literacy.[177] The partnership of these two organizations seemed natural because the NPSF was intricately involved in the promotion of health literacy. Health literacy is the ability to read, understand, and effectively use basic medical instructions and information.[178] Health literacy is essential for the improvement of patient safety.[179]

Almost half of the U.S. adult population—roughly 90 million people—have low functional health literacy.[180] The average reading level in the U.S. is eighth-grade, and 20 percent of the population reads at or below the fifth-grade level.[181] Most health-related material is written at the tenth-grade reading level or higher.[182] The PCHC found that literacy skills are a better predictor of health status than age, income, employment status, education level, or racial/ethnic group.[183]

A report released by the University of Connecticut in October 2007[184] indicates that low health literacy is a major source of economic inefficiency in the U.S. health care system. In fact, it costs an estimated $106 billion to $238 billion annually to the economy, which is between 7 and 17 percent of all personal health care expenditures.[185] The study showed that if health literacy is improved, the savings would be enough to insure every one of the more than forty-seven million people in the U.S. who lacked health insurance in 2006.[186] The researchers found that while ethnic minority groups were disproportionately affected by low health literacy, the majority of those with low health literacy skills are white and born in America.[187] They also found that health literacy skills significantly impact an individual's ability to manage a chronic illness, such as diabetes or high blood pressure.[188] A person who is able to comprehend and act upon medical instructions makes fewer visits to the emergency room and spends less time in the hospital, thereby lowering the cost of the individual's health care.[189] The study concluded that a national health reform to address the low health literacy problem would result in financial savings as well as better health.[190]

The NPSF integrated its flagship health literacy program, entitled "Ask Me 3," into the PCHC program.[191] "Ask Me 3" promotes the use of three essential questions that patients should ask their providers in every health care visit: What is my main problem?; What do I need to do?; and Why is it important for me to do this? The program is an effective tool designed to improve health communication between patients and their health care providers.[192] Additionally, PCHC works closely with the Centers for Medicare and Medicaid Services (CMS) to increase awareness and improve understanding of the Medicare Part D prescription drug benefit.[193]

The PCHC recommends that health care organizations take steps to improve health literacy so that health care outcomes will improve. This can be done in the following ways. First, the health care provider should educate himself or herself, and other staff, on the scope and impact of low health literacy.[194] Second, the health care provider should educate his or her peers by distributing materials and conducting outreach to promote clear health communication at hospitals and community centers.[195] Third, the health care provider should educate public officials by speaking with state and federal legislators to increase funding to support health literacy research and programs.[196]

The NPSF also provides funding for research grants. The research program fosters the advancement of patient safety by promoting studies by leaders in the field on the prevention of human errors, system errors, patient injuries, and the consequences of adverse events.[197] Since its inception, the program has issued over $2.8 million in funding for more than twenty-eight investigator-driven grants.[198] More than two-thirds of the grants were awarded to interdisciplinary teams to support research on topics such as medication errors, organization design, and disclosure or communication issues.[199] The research committee annually selects several grant recipients that are awarded up to $100,000 each.[200] The funding for the grants is established, in part, through collaboration with other organizations. The James S. Todd Memorial Research Award is funded by the NPSF and the American Medical Association.[201] Other grants are partially funded by the Commonwealth Fund and the Patrick and Catherine Weldon Donaghue Medical Research Foundation.[202] Past research grants have funded projects such as "Understanding Medical Errors in Hospital Psychiatry," "Patient Safety in After-Hours Telephone Medicine," "Automated Maintenance of Problem-Drug Matches in the Electronic Medical Record to Promote Safety," "Post-Surgical Patients Receiving Patient-Controlled Analgesia," "Developing a Knowledge Base for RN Stacking: A Critical Patient Safety Strategy for Nursing Care Delivery," "Improving the Safety and Efficacy of Pediatric Sedation Practice Through the Creation of the Pediatric Sedation Research Consortium," and "Talking to Patients About Medical Errors."

The NPSF announced on October 29, 2007, that effective in January 2008, it would collaborate with the Medical Group Management Association (MGMA) and AIG Healthcare to broaden patient safety and quality improvement services. In this unique collaboration, NPSF will provide its Ambulatory Stand Up for Patient Safety Program tools and resources to MGMA members, who will have automatic access to an exclusive insurance offering from AIG Healthcare that includes risk management/patient safety credit and a retrospectively decreased insurance premium adjustment.[203] Through these types of collaborations, its research grants, and the dissemination of information and materials to promote patient safety, the NPSF plays a vital role in changing the delivery of health care to improve the safety of the entire health care system. These improvements are eagerly anticipated to increase the quality of health care and curb ever-expanding health care costs.

V.   INSTITUTE FOR HEALTHCARE IMPROVEMENT

In 1986, the National Demonstration Project on Quality Improvement in Health Care (NDP) was launched to explore the application of modern quality improvement methods to health care.[204] During the following several years, NDP offered meetings and seminars focused on improving health care quality.[205] Out of those efforts, the Institute for Healthcare Improvement (IHI) was founded in 1991.[206] IHI receives its major funding from its fee-based services and the support of a group of foundations, companies, and individuals.[207] It is a nonprofit organization based in Cambridge, Massachusetts.[208] The IHI promotes change in health care by fostering concepts for improving patient care and transforming those ideas into reality.[209]

IHI seeks to improve the lives of patients, the health of communities, and the satisfaction of the health care workforce through strategies that promote change in health care.[210] These strategies include: motivating people by bringing them together to cooperate, share lessons, and encourage each other; getting results by spreading knowledge and providing methods, tools, and other support that turns knowledge into improved outcomes; inventing new solutions by initiating and supporting innovative efforts; raising enjoyment in the health care workforce by changing the skills, attitudes, and knowledge of the workforce to encourage collaboration and to work toward increasing the well-being of the patient; and remaining viable over the long-term by practicing what it teaches.[211]

The behavior and choices of the IHI staff, faculty, and board of directors are guided by nine core values. First, there are no boundaries at IHI because the people of IHI compose a single organization, with common systems, common knowledge, and unconditional teamwork.[212] Second, staff members change and respond rapidly to modifications in the health care systems, IHI services.[213] Third, staff focus on obtaining improved results for the patients and communities the IHI serves and are open to new approaches to achieve them.[214] Fourth, the staff brings together people who have expertise and knowledge so that they can teach each other, help each other, and improve the work of IHI.[215] Fifth, the IHI strives to serve and satisfy those who shape and deliver health care.[216] Sixth, staff endeavor to earn and preserve the trust of those they help.[217] Seventh, staff make every effort to make those who work with them feel informed and welcomed.[218] Eighth, the IHI works in a streamlined fashion to reduce disorder so that resources are not wasted.[219] Last but not least, staff show appreciation for their colleagues' hard work and take pride in it.[220] Through these goals, the IHI seeks to accelerate the progress of health care systems throughout the world and work toward improved safety, effectiveness, patient-centeredness, timeliness, efficiency, and equity in health care.[221] The IHI aims to achieve health care for all and eliminate needless deaths, needless pain and suffering, helplessness in those it serves, unwanted waiting, and waste.[222] IHI's mission is to hasten the improvement of health care worldwide. The IHI Web site allows quick, easy access to promote this mission.[223]

Much of the information provided by IHI is on its Web site, www.ihi. org. The Web site provides ready-to-use solutions, knowledge about improvement, and information that is focused on health care quality across a broad array of topics.[224] The site is a common place for a community of people who have mutual interests, and it gives them the opportunity to work with experts in the field.[225]

The IHI offers information in the "topics" area of its Web site to the public free of charge.[226] The topics section is the center around which information is organized.[227] There are several topic areas, including information related to improvement methods, spreading changes, chronic conditions, education, end of life, office practices, patient-centered care, patient safety, reducing mortality, and reliability.[228] Under each of the topics, there are subcategories of how to improve, measures for improvement, changes to be tested, improvement stories, tools to use to accelerate improvement, resources, literature, frequently asked questions, and emerging content.[229] There is also an "expert host" for each topic.

To begin implementing improvement methods, the health care facility should use the "model for improvement" on the IHI's site as a guide.[230] The model for improvement was developed by Associates in Process Improvement[231] as a tool for hastening health care improvement.[232] The model was not intended to be a substitute for models of change that an organization may already be using, but it may be used as an adjunct to them.[233] Hundreds of health care organizations in several countries use the model for improvement to improve various health care procedures and results.[234] The model has two parts: three basic questions that can be addressed in any order, and the "plan-do-study-act" (PDSA) cycle, which guides the test of a change to determine if the change is an improvement.[235] Also, it is important to select the correct people for the process improvement team to increase the changes of successful improvement.[236]

The first of the three basic questions is: What are we trying to accomplish? This question addresses the intended goal of the organization. Change can only occur if the staff has a clear vision as to what the team is responsible to improve.[237] The objective is a time-specific, measurable goal aimed at addressing a certain population of patients that will be affected.[238] It is crucial for staff members to agree on the purpose of their efforts so that each team member can work toward that end. The Institute of Medicine (IOM) published a report containing six aims for improvement,[239] which many organizations use to help develop their goals. The IOM report focuses on narrowing the quality gap between what we understand to be good health care and the health care that people actually receive. The report recommends six principles as a guide for policymakers, health care leaders, clinicians, regulators, purchasers, and others to redesign and improve America's health care system.[240] These principles are basic steps to achieve ideal health care.

The six principles are as follows:[241] First, health care must be safe. This principle goes beyond the pledge to "first do no harm." It means that safety must be inherent in the system so that no one is ever harmed by health care. Second, health care must be effective. It should match science with the proper use of the best available techniques. For example, every elderly heart patient who would benefit from beta-blocker drugs should get them. Third, health care should be patient-centered. Staff should take into account and respect the individual patient's culture, social context, and specific needs. Fourth, health care should be timely. Prompt attention should be given to the patient to avoid unintended waiting that does not provide information or time to heal. Fifth, health care should be efficient. Staff should constantly strive to reduce waste of supplies, equipment, space, capital, ideas, time, and opportunities. Lastly, health care should be equitable. Race, ethnicity, gender, and socioeconomic status should not hinder any individual from obtaining high-quality health care. Through the use of these principles, the entire health care system would undergo fundamental changes to improve the quality of health care and reduce patient errors.

Some examples of effective goal statements are: within one year, to achieve more than 95 percent compliance with on-time prophylactic antibiotic administration; within nine months, to reduce waiting time to see a physician to less than fifteen minutes; within ten months, to transfer every patient deemed ready to transfer from the inpatient facility to a long-term care facility within twenty-four hours after the determination is made; within nine months, to reduce intensive care unit mortality by 20 percent; and within one year, to reduce adverse drug events per coronary care unit stay by 75 percent.[242]

The second of the three basic questions is: How will we know that a change is an improvement? It is crucial for the team to measure change so it can determine whether its actions are effective. Measurement of improvement is a critical part of testing and implementing change. However, measurement of improvement is not the same as measurement for research. In research, the goal is to attain new knowledge. In improvement, the goal is to bring new knowledge into daily practice. There are three types of measurement: outcome measures; process measures; and balancing measures. All three should be used to measure improvement. Outcome measures track how well the system performs by determining the results. For instance, if the goal is to reduce the amount of hospital-stay days for patients who receive total knee replacements, measure the average amount of hospital-stay days for that particular surgery. Process measures indicate whether the parts or steps in the process are performing as planned. For instance, if the goal is to reduce the amount of hospital-stay days for patients who receive total knee replacements, measure how soon after surgery the patient begins receiving therapy and the average amount of hours of therapy the total knee replacement patients receive. Balancing measures demonstrate whether the changes that are designed to improve one part of the system cause new problems in other parts of the system. For instance, if the goal is to reduce the amount of hospital-stay days for patients who receive total knee replacements, measure whether readmission rates for patients who receive total knee replacements are increasing. On the IHI Web site, there is a Health System Measures Kit that contains a set of health system performance measures that are linked to the six dimensions of quality outlined in the IOM report.[243]

The last of the three basic questions is: What changes can we make that will result in an improvement? Not all changes lead to improvement, but all improvement requires change.[244] It is vital for the organization to identify the changes that are most likely to result in improvement. There are many types of changes that will lead to improvements, but they are generated from a small number of change concepts.[245] A change concept is an idea that helps in developing specific models for change that lead to improvement.[246] The combination of change concepts with the knowledge about specific subjects can generate plans for ways to test change.[247] After the idea for change is generated, the organization should perform a plan-do-study-act (PDSA) cycle to test the change on a small scale to determine whether the idea for change actually brings about improvement.[248] If the idea for change does bring about improvement, the change should be implemented into larger and larger patient samples until the organization is confident that it should be implemented throughout the system.[249]

The PDSA cycle is the process of testing the change in the real work setting. Essentially, this involves four steps. First, plan the test or observation, including a plan for collecting data.[250] The plan should also include stating the objective of the test, making predictions about what will happen and why, and developing a plan to test the change.[251] Second, perform the test on a small scale. This includes completing the test, documenting problems and unexpected observations, and beginning the evaluation of data.[252] Third, take time to analyze the data and study the results. This includes comparing the data to the predictions and summarizing and processing what was learned.[253] Fourth, modify the change based on what the test demonstrated. This includes establishing the revisions that should be made and preparing a plan for the next test.[254]

Once the organization tests the change on a small scale, analyzes the results of each test, and modifies the change through several PDSA cycles, the organization is ready to implement the change on a much wider scale.[255] Implementation is the process by which the organization institutes a permanent change into the work place.[256] The implementation of a change may affect documentation, written policies, hiring, training, compensation, and aspects of the infrastructure that were not involved in the testing phase.[257] However, implementation also requires the use of the PDSA cycle.[258] The difference between testing a change and implementing a change is demonstrated in the following example: Testing a change involves three nurses on different shifts using a new medication order form; implementing a change involves having all thirty nurses on the pilot nursing unit begin using the new medication order form.[259]

The final phase of the model for improvement is spreading the change. This is the process of taking a successful implementation process from a pilot unit or population and repeating that change in other parts of the organization.[260] The team learns important information for successful spread of change during the implementation stage.[261] This information includes issues regarding key infrastructure matters, optimal sequencing of tasks, and working with people to help the organization adopt and become accustomed to a change.[262] For example, if all thirty nurses on a pilot unit implement a new medication order form successfully, then spreading the change would involve repeating the change in all nursing units in the organization and assisting the units to take on the change.[263]

One critical aspect of having a successful change is to include the proper people on the process team from the start.[264] Each organization should build its team to suit its own needs.[265] However, in order to be effective, the team members should come from three different types of expertise within the organization.[266] First, at least one member of the team should hold a leadership position in the health care system.[267] The team needs a person with enough influence and power in the organization to institute the recommended change and to overcome barriers that might occur.[268] More importantly, the system leader will have the insight to understand how the proposed change will affect the entire system and the consequences that it might cause.[269] The system leader should have enough authority in all of the areas that are affected by the change in order to allocate the time and resources that the team needs to achieve its goal.[270] A member of the team who is a system leader would typically be an administrator or manager in the organization.

Second, the team should have members that have technical or clinical expertise.[271] This type of team member is someone who has working knowledge of the area that is being proposed for change, and who understands the patient care processes in that area. Examples of individuals with technical or clinical expertise are physicians, technologists, therapists, pharmacists, and nurses.

Third, the team should have a person with day-to-day leadership responsibilities.[272] This person will guide the project.[273] The day-to-day leader is responsible for making sure that the tests are implemented. He or she also oversees data collection. This person should know the working details of the system, as well as how the proposed changes will affect the system.[274] A day-to-day leader is likely to be a clinical manager or come from a mid-level management position.

It is essential to have at least one member of the team from each of the three areas mentioned above to have successful and efficient progress toward change for improvement of the system. The other members of the team should include those who work on the front line in the area being studied for change. These include physicians, nurses, aides, technicians, etc.

The IHI provides a significant amount of information, networking, and expertise to organizations that are in the process of improving their systems to decrease patient errors and increase efficiency. This information is given through various programs that IHI offers. These programs include: The 5 Million Lives Campaign, which is a national initiative focused on protecting patients from five million incidents of medical harm in U.S. hospitals between December 2006 and December 2008; conferences and seminars; IMPACT network, which is IHI's "association for change" where members work together and with expert faculty to make improvements in the health care system; Innovation Communities, which are learning laboratories that seek to make improvements at the microsystem level; professional development; audio and Web programs; strategic initiatives, which test the next wave of innovations to be used throughout the health care system; and an archive of past programs previously offered by IHI that can be used as a reference library.

VI.   INSTITUTE FOR SAFE MEDICATION PRACTICES

The Institute for Safe Medication Practices (ISMP) is dedicated to the safe use of medication and the prevention of medication errors.[275] ISMP began as a continuing column on medical safety in the publication *Hospital Pharmacy* in 1975.[276] It was officially incorporated as a nonprofit organization in 1994 and was run by volunteers.[277] Today, it has a paid, full-time staff and is financially supported by charitable contributions, unrestricted grants, subscriptions to its newsletters, fees from consulting and educational services, and volunteer efforts.[278] It does not receive advertising revenue or government support.[279] It is not funded by the pharmaceutical industry. Therefore, it serves as an independent "watchdog" organization to promote medication safety; it is the only organization in the nation to do so.[280]

The ISMP mission is to "advance patient safety worldwide by empowering the healthcare community, including consumers, to prevent medication errors."[281] It achieves this by: collecting and analyzing reports of medication-related hazardous conditions, near-misses, errors, and adverse drug events; distributing information about medication safety, tools for risk reduction, and strategies for preventing errors; informing the public, including the health care community and its consumers, about safe medication practices; joining with other patient safety organizations, educational institutions, governmental agencies, and other health care organizations; promoting the integration of safe medication standards by accrediting bodies, manufacturers, policy makers, regulatory agencies, and organizations that set standards; and conducting research to determine evidence-based safe medication practices.[282] The ISMP strives to establish itself as the leading independent patient safety organization in the movement to prevent medication errors and adverse drug events.[283]

The ISMP collaborates with a variety of organizations to promote medication safety. These organizations include the American Hospital Association, Food and Drug Administration, the Joint Commission, the National Coordinating Council for Medication Error Reporting and Prevention, and U.S. Pharmacopeia (USP).[284] The joint effort between ISMP and USP is a program aimed at collecting data from health care practitioners who voluntarily report medication errors. This program is called USP-ISMP Medication Errors Reporting Program (MERP).[285]

The ISMP learns about medication errors via MERP.[286] It is a confidential national voluntary program for reporting medication errors. USP and ISMP share the medication error report, the identity of the person reporting the information, and the person's location so that the information can be analyzed. However, the identity and location of the person reporting the medication error is not shared with third parties unless the reporter gives his or her permission.[287] USP and ISMP send the report to third parties such as the Food and Drug Administration Drug Watch Program and the pharmaceutical manufacturer or labeler.[288] The report includes: what went wrong; whether it was an actual medication error or a potential error; the patient outcome; the type of setting (i.e., hospital, long-term care facility, etc.); the generic name of the medication; the brand name of the medication; dosage form, concentration, or strength, etc.; how the error was discovered; and the reporter's recommendation for error prevention.[289]

It is important to have the information and analyze it because medication errors or potential medication errors that are left unreported are unrecognized.[290] If they are not reported, there is no possibility to develop epidemiological and preventive measures to prevent future errors.[291] Hundreds of health care professionals report medication errors to MERP every year.[292] ISMP shares the stories of medication errors in its publications and educational efforts, but does not disclose the specific location of an event, the people involved, or the person who reported the error.[293] If a facility requests ISMP's advice about how to respond to a medication error or how to prevent future errors, ISMP does not publicly divulge the recommendations.[294] ISMP has an advisory panel of practicing health care professionals, researchers, and experts in human factors and medication safety to assist it in developing evidence-based error-reduction strategies.[295] Additionally, the ISMP staff spends a considerable amount of time in health care settings to obtain firsthand knowledge about new medication safety practices.[296]

MERP has had a dramatic effect on the use and manufacture of medication. In response to examination of certain types of errors and hazards reported to MERP, the ISMP electronically issues nationwide alerts and press releases to health care professionals in a timely fashion. These alerts serve as an "early warning system" to prevent additional hazardous medication errors. Some recommended early-intervention error-reduction plans have included changing look-alike packaging to stop medication mix-ups, changing confusing labels that can lead to dosage errors, adding labels to unlabeled medications in the sterile field, and sending out warnings about unintentional, potential overdoses.[297]

The ISMP also distributes medication error trends and error-reduction strategies in response to the data collected by MERP.[298] These include information about dangerous drug abbreviations, serious medication errors and drugs most prone to these errors, medication safety, elimination of handwritten prescriptions, and medication safety self assessments for hospitals, community and ambulatory pharmacies, and antithrombotic therapy providers.[299] Additionally, based on the MERP data, ISMP advises USP and the Food and Drug Administration to promote changing labels on pharmaceuticals that have confusing or look-alike packaging and labeling, or look-alike or sound-alike names.[300] Individual organizations establish protocols and monitor compliance based on ISMP's publication of errors submitted to MERP.[301] Also, individual health care practitioners institute changes in their practices based on the ISMP information gleaned from the MERP data.[302]

With the distribution of information pertaining to MERP medication error reports, the ISMP has influenced the adoption of national safety guidelines, standards, and goals by the Joint Commission, USP, and other organizations. These include the elimination of the apothecary system of measurement, greater clarity in prescription writing, medication safety alerts for computerized physician order entry, the use of "tall man" lettering for labeling of products, pediatric pharmacy medication safety guidelines, guidelines for safe electronic communication of medication orders, and elimination of the use of infusion pumps without accidental free-flow protection.[303] The ISMP has also been a leader in advocating for changes in public policy based on the MERP data. These efforts include hosting the first Global Conference on Medication Error Reporting Programs with national and international experts from around the world; partnering with the American Hospital Association in a national initiative to help hospitals scrutinize and increase medication safety; and providing testimony at legislative hearings to promote medication safety.[304]

In October 2006, the ISMP, along with the Health Research and Educational Trust and the Medical Group Management Association, released the "physician practice patient safety assessment" (PPPSA). The PPPSA is a tool on the Web that allows health care practitioners to evaluate their patient safety practices daily.[305] The three entities developed the PPPSA with a grant from the Commonwealth Fund.[306] The PPPSA allows medical practices to assess their effectiveness in six categories.[307] First, information about medications is evaluated, including appropriate medication history, prescribing, storage, labeling, purchasing, dispensing of samples, and administration of vaccines. Second, transition of care between providers is analyzed to determine whether proper procedures are used for care coordination in order to track patients and their clinical information. Third, patient safety issues related to ambulatory surgery, especially sedation and anesthesia, are assessed to be sure proper surgical and invasive procedures are in place. Fourth, there is an assessment of the personal qualifications and competency of caregivers. Fifth, patient education and communication is evaluated to determine whether the practice takes action to help patients understand and carry out their responsibilities. Sixth, there is a determination as to whether the administrative procedures of the practice are geared toward creating a culture of safety.

The use of PPPSA will allow the practices to: pinpoint areas for improvement; determine a baseline of current procedures to track progress over time; measure their own data against practices of similar size, structure, or location nationwide; encourage discussion about patient safety among all staff members; decrease liability exposure; and support activities that lead to improved care and decreased patient error.

According to ISMP, some ways for the consumer to prevent medication errors include the following.[308] The consumer should take an active role in his or her own care by learning about the medications he or she takes. It is in the consumer's best interest to know about the effects of the medication, how and when to take it, and its side-effects. The consumer should always keep an up-to-date medication list with all of the current medications he or she takes. The consumer should not accept a drug that he or she is not familiar with. Nor should the consumer accept a new drug from a health care provider unless the provider can explain why the drug is being prescribed. Consumers also should remind the health care providers about any allergies, including allergies to foods and dyes. Before the consumer is discharged from a hospital, he or she should ask for a complete explanation as to each medication.

It is important for the consumer to read the patient information sheets that accompany many of the medications. If it is difficult to swallow the medication, the consumer should ask for alternate forms of it (for example, a liquid form rather than a pill form). The consumer should throw away expired medication. The consumer should have a "brown bag check-up" for all of the medication he or she is currently taking. A "brown bag check-up" is a meeting with the prescribing physician or pharmacist to evaluate all of the medication the consumer is taking, including over-the-counter medicines. The consumer should have the physician write the reason why the medication is being prescribed on the prescription paper as an additional guide for the pharmacist to dispense the correct medication. The consumer should only use the measuring device provided with liquid prescriptions to measure the dose of the liquid prescription; if none is provided, the consumer should ask the pharmacist to recommend which measuring device should be used. If the consumer uses more than one pharmacy, the consumer should have a primary pharmacy (just like a primary physician) in order to keep an up-to-date personal medication record.

In addition to PPPSA and MERP, the ISMP offers various types of consulting services to assist health care practitioners in navigating the medication systems and providing improved care to their patients.[309] The "proactive risk assessment" consulting team is composed of pharmacists, nurses, and physicians that collect information about the health care practitioner's current medication practices through direct observation and interviews with individuals. The team then analyzes the information to determine the areas of risk exposure and recommends error prevention strategies.[310] Risk assessment can be done comprehensively as a broad organizational project or as a targeted assessment narrowly focused in one area such as pediatrics, oncology, surgical centers, or resolution of issues related to the Joint Commission's Medications Management Standards and National Patient Safety Goals. The assessments can be either preventative or an objective follow-up after serious or near miss events.[311] Also, the Actionable Improvements in the Measurement of medication safety program (AIM) is a one- to two-day on-site support service designed to help organizations improve their collection and use of data related to the safety of medication use.[312] The ISMP consulting team evaluates the organization's current methods of gathering, analyzing, and using facility-specific medication-related data, and then offers advice for improvement.

The ISMP Medication Safety Mentorship Program is a two-day on-site safety assessment. During the program, the ISMP staff offers recommendations about: prioritizing medication safety issues that are unique to the organization; optimizing current knowledge and understanding of principles and strategies for improvement of medication safety; organizing and analyzing existing medication error information; starting internal medication safety initiatives; and maximizing the organization's safety team's efforts to enhance improvements in safety. This program is designed for practitioners who have responsibility for medication safety oversight (e.g., patient safety managers, medication safety managers, quality or risk managers, medical staff leaders, etc.).

Another type of consulting service is ISMP's "rural hospital medication safety connection resource kit."[313] The kit supplies rural and small hospitals with resources to improve medication safety. The kit contains CDs with presentations by ISMP experts and a resource binder that contains information for identifying safety gaps, improving safety in the pediatric population, managing high-alert drugs, and developing a culture of safety.[314]

The ISMP also does technology assessments to determine the best information systems, robotics, and medication-related devices that are most suitable for the organization.[315] Technology assessments can include pharmacy systems, integrated health information systems, computerized prescriber order entry systems, electronic prescribing systems, bar-coded point of care systems, robotics for packaging and filling of pharmaceuticals, infusion pumps, and stand-alone information systems for support care in the emergency department, oncology, and perioperative settings.[316]

The ISMP also provides root-cause analysis consulting for on-site investigation and analysis after a medication event.[317] The team formulates a plan of action to improve the process that led to the medication error. The team consists of two or three practitioners that spend one or two days in the facility. The team generates a report that summarizes and prioritizes the team's recommendations for improvement.[318]

The ISMP offers a collaboration team that can interact with any group that undertakes a medication safety improvement project.[319] The team gives on-site lectures, teleconferences, seminars, or workshops, and participates in regularly scheduled phone calls or face-to-face meetings. The time frame for the group collaborations can vary from a few months to several years, depending on the group and the nature of the project.

Lastly, a subsidiary of ISMP called Med-E.R.R.S. assists manufacturing companies by performing failure mode and effects analysis (FMEA) for device/technology manufacturers seeking to decrease the probability of medication errors and increase the safety and performance of their products.[320] The team evaluates the direct interaction of the practitioner with the device; reviews the safety, efficiency, and function of the device; and analyzes its documentation capabilities.[321] Scrutiny of these areas can lead to improved medication safety.[322] The team provides feedback related to the device's ability to promote safe patient care for an organization in light of the impact the new technology has on other systems within the organization.[323] During the FMEA visit, the team meets with the vendor's research and development team and interviews key people from the company to learn more about the product.[324] The team will also evaluate the product materials and other marketing information, and/or provide practitioner and patient education and assistance.[325] After the product evaluation, the team writes a report and remains available for further consultation.[326]

Through it many services, the ISMP is a valuable resource to provide knowledge about medications, error analysis (preventative as well as post-error), medication safety education, and safety alerts and other communication about medication safety to the health care practitioner and the consumer. The ISMP's accomplishments are many—too many to list in this book. For more information, consult the ISMP's Web site at www.ismp.org.

VII.   THE COMMONWEALTH FUND

Anna Harkness founded the Commonwealth Fund in 1918 with the idea of doing "something for the welfare of mankind."[327] Anna Harkness's husband, Stephen V. Harkness, who died in 1888, was a successful businessman who invested early in the petroleum refining business and provided funding for Standard Oil Company at a critical time in its development.[328] Anna originally began the Commonwealth Fund with her gift of nearly $10 million.[329] With successive gifts to the fund between 1918 and 1959, the Harkness family's total donations to the fund's endowment was more than $53 million.[330] Anna and Stephen's son, Edward Harkness, was the first president of the fund,[331] and he guided the fund through its first twenty-two years.[332] Edward inspired the fund's staff to rethink old ways, try new ideas, and take risks.[333] This innovative way of thinking helped the fund continue to be a catalyst for change by recognizing potential solutions to help the nation toward achieving a high-performance health care system.[334]

The fund seeks to: establish a base of scientific evidence for effective ways to change the health care organization; obtain talented people to develop methods to transform the health care organization; and work together with health care organizations that have the same concerns.[335] The fund primarily focuses its work on developing new ways to overcome the challenges that vulnerable populations face in obtaining high-quality, safe, compassionate, coordinated, and efficiently delivered health care.[336] The fund's publications assist health care policy leaders to work toward creating a health care system that will benefit all members of society. The fund's publications report on areas in which there is already a consensus and explore areas that have a common ground in order to allow policy makers to discuss the areas that need consensus building and discussion in order to create a high-performance health care system.[337]

Historically, the fund supported the construction of hospitals and new medical schools, brought health care to underserved communities, encouraged the patient-centered care movement, and addressed health care issues facing the elderly, youth, and those of lower socioeconomic status.[338] Recently, the fund has focused on addressing the issues of health care coverage and access to health care, as well as improving the quality and efficiency of health care.[339] In 2002, Frances Cooke Macgregor, a long-time contributor, gave $3.1 million to the fund to help support projects aimed at reducing medical errors and improving patient safety.[340] One of the fund's major concerns is health care quality.

The fund's mission is to "promote a high performing health care system that achieves better access, improved quality, and greater efficiency, particularly for society's most vulnerable, including people with low-incomes, the uninsured, minority Americans, young children, people with disabilities, and the elderly."[341] The fund pursues this mission by funding independent research in health care issues and making grants to improve health care practice and policy.[342] The fund has national programs that work to achieve its goals. It also has an international program in health care policy, which is designed to generate groundbreaking policies and practices in other countries as well as in the United States.[343] The fund's current programs are in the following areas: the future of health insurance; Medicare's future; quality improvement and efficiency; patient-centered primary care initiatives; state innovations; quality of care for underserved populations; child development and preventive care; quality of care for frail elders; and international programs in health policy and practice.[344] Grant proposals that seek to clarify the scope of serious and overlooked problems, to develop, test, and evaluate innovative models for addressing such problems, to distribute tools and models of care, or to analyze the impact of policies and trends are given preference.[345]

The fund's Program on Health Quality Improvement strives to improve the quality and efficiency of health care in the United States.[346] The program provides financial support for projects that: promote the improvement and implementation of measures that increase efficiency and quality of health care; analyze and boost health care organizations' capacity to provide improved care more efficiently; and scrutinize payment methods and encourage models that provide incentives that encourage health care providers to improve quality and efficiency.[347] The program leaders recognize that the American health care system is not up to par. "For instance, according to the national health system scorecard released by the Commission on a High Performance Health System, anywhere from 100,000 to 150,000 deaths could be prevented each year if the U.S. was able to raise standards of care to benchmark performance levels achieved within this country and abroad."[348] In order to address this and similar concerns, the Program on Health Quality Improvement has funded several projects including: the Massachusetts Health Quality Partners' (MHQP) study of cost and resource utilization by physician groups, which analyzes factors that affect physicians' performance; Health Management Associates' and CareScience, Inc.'s study of the dynamics of high performance over time and the factors that contribute to continued high performance; Boston University Health Policy Institute's study of hospitals' quality-improvement activities and physicians' and nurses' perceptions of the quality of care at those institutions; and the Harvard School of Public Health's study of quality and efficiency as it relates to pay-for-performance programs.[349] In April 2007, the fund issued fifteen grants addressing various topics that examine ways to increase the performance of America's health system, including issues regarding medical education of health care professionals, policies and regulatory infrastructures that deal with performance, electronic medical records, patient-centered medical home care, the Medicare Part D prescription drug benefit, affordable health care coverage, and universal health care.[350]

The fund established the Commission on a High Performance Health System in 2005 as the board of directors' response to the need for national leadership to revamp, revitalize, and retool the national health care system.[351] The commission is made up of nineteen members who represent every sector of health care, state and federal policy areas, the business sector, professional societies, and academia.[352] The commission's goal is to promote a high-performance health system that provides all Americans with affordable access to high-quality, safe care that maximizes efficiency.[353] The commission focuses on the most vulnerable part of the population: low-income families, the uninsured, racial and ethnic minorities, the young, the aged, and the people with serious medical conditions.[354] To date, the commission's most notable accomplishments have been to highlight specific areas for the public where the health system fails to deliver adequate care and to promote a holistic approach to health care reform.[355]

In September 2006, the commission published the results of its national scorecard on the U.S. health system's performance entitled, *Why Not the Best? Results from a National Scorecard on U.S. Health System Performance* (Scorecard).[356] The Scorecard assessed how well the U.S. health system performed as a whole in comparison to what is achievable.[357] The scores were developed from ratios that compare the national average performance to benchmarks that represent top performance in thirty-seven categories.[358] The U.S. scored an average of sixty-six out of a possible 100.[359] This rating is low, considering the resources that the nation invests in its health care.[360] "Although national health spending is significantly higher than the average rate of other industrialized countries, the U.S. is the only industrialized country that fails to guarantee universal health insurance and coverage is deteriorating, leaving millions without affordable access to preventive and essential health care."[361] Some of the significant findings are:

- Mortality in the U.S. is one-third worse than the best-performing country for deaths that could have been prevented with timely and effective care;
- Less than half of adults receive preventive and screening tests, despite their documented benefits;
- Only half of patients with congestive heart failure receive written discharge instructions regarding care following hospitalization;

- 35 percent of adults under 65 years old (about 61 million) were either underinsured or uninsured during the year 2003;
- 34 percent of all adults under 65 years old have problems paying their medical bills or have medical debt that they are paying off over time;
- Hospital thirty-day readmission rates for Medicare patients ranged from 14 percent to 22 percent across the region; bringing the readmission rates to the level of top-performing regions would save Medicare $1.9 billion annually;
- U.S. insurance administrative costs were more than three times the rate of countries with the most integrated insurance systems;
- Only 17 percent of U.S. doctors use electronic medical records, compared with 80 percent in the top three countries;
- There is a wide gap between low-income or uninsured populations and those with higher incomes and insurance;
- Hispanic risk rates are 20 percent higher than white risk rates on key indicators of quality, access, and efficiency;
- African American rates for mortality, quality, access, and efficiency are 24 percent higher than white rates.[362]

The results of the study illustrate compelling reasons for change in the American medical system. As the researchers point out, the results of the study do not only represent numbers. The results symbolize illnesses that can be avoided, deaths that can be prevented, and money that can be saved.[363] If the gaps were closed in the thirty-seven areas studied, there would be a savings of $50 billion to $100 billion annually in health care spending and 100,000 to 150,000 deaths would be prevented.[364] One key point coming from the study is that more research is needed to develop the methods and means for change in the health care system. To that end, the fund provides grants to support ongoing studies.

The fund can provide either small grants ($50,000 or less) or board-level grants (greater than $50,000). The decisions to issue small grants are made on a monthly basis.[365] They are tied closely to the fund's strategic purposes, which allows the fund to move quickly and provides flexibly to fund the projects.[366] Board-level grants are approved at one of the three board meetings held each year during July, November, and April.[367] In fiscal year 2004-2005, the median award amount for small grants was approximately $18,324; for board-level grants, the median amount was approximately $211,000.[368] Grant time periods can be as small as one month or continue for a few years.[369] The grants are not renewable annually, but rather they are funded for a complete project period.[370]

The fund's policy is to issue 20 percent of its grants for unsolicited proposals and 20 percent to support projects with investigators who are new to the fund so that the program staff remains open to new ideas and new researchers.[371] Generally, the fund issues grants to nonprofit entities. However, when a suitable nonprofit research pool is not available, the fund will issue grants to support projects at for-profit entities.[372] Individuals seeking support must do so through the Foundation Center.[373] The majority of grants are given in support of domestic research projects, but some grants are available for international projects through the fund's International Program in Health Care Policy and Practice.[374] The fund also supports two fellowship programs: the Harkness Fellowships in Health Care Policy; and the Commonwealth Fund/Harvard University Fellowship in Minority Health Policy.[375]

In addition to grants and fellowships, the fund produces more than 100 publications every year, including several different newsletters. The *Commonwealth Fund Digest* is a bimonthly synopsis of fund and fund-supported publications.[376] *Quality Matters* is a Quality Improvement and Efficiency Program publication that provides detailed case studies and commentaries on quality-improvement topics, news briefs, and summaries of the medical and health policy literature.[377] *States in Action: A Bimonthly Look at Innovations in Health Policy* is a bimonthly newsletter that tracks innovative strategies that states use to obtain more value for the health care dollar while improving the quality of care.[378] *Washington Health Policy Week in Review* is a weekly publication that provides selected articles from the daily newsletter *CQ HealthBeat*.[379]

Through research and education, the fund clearly is fulfilling the wishes of its founder to do "something for the welfare of mankind." The research that it funds contributes to improving America's health care system by increasing patient safety. Much more research is needed, but the fund's efforts will have a positive impact to help provide high-quality health care to all members of society.

VIII.   CONCLUSION

This chapter examined the private and public responses to the Institute of Medicine's report, *To Err Is Human: Building a Safer Health System*. These groups perform and fund a wide range of research, education, and methods to implement patient safety policies and protocols. The Joint Commission on the Accreditation of Healthcare Organizations strives to continuously improve the safety and quality of care provided to the public through the provision of health care accreditation and related services that support performance improvement in health care organizations. The Leapfrog Group aims to make giant leaps forward in the safety, quality, and affordability of health care by supporting informed health care decisions by those who use and pay for health care, and by promoting high-value health care through incentives and rewards. The National Patient Safety Foundation seeks to improve the safety of patients through research, education, and multidisciplinary projects and patient safety tools and programs in the health care system. The Institute for Healthcare Improvement advances change in health care by working with patients, health care providers, and organizations to motivate, educate, create solutions, and encourage collaboration to promote ideas for improving patient care and the implementation of those ideas. The Institute for Safe Medication Practices seeks to promote patient safety by focusing the health care community on the prevention of medication errors. The Commonwealth Fund endeavors to bring to light potential solutions that will allow the health care system to better serve the elderly, young children, people with disabilities, minorities, and those with lower socioeconomic status, thus improving health care for all members of society.

Although these groups approach patient safety in different ways, each group makes major contributions to the improvement of the health care system in its own way. The hope is that, through their research, programs, and implementation strategies, patient safety will improve and significant strides will be made toward eliminating preventable patient errors.

NOTES

1. The Joint Commission, www.jointcommission.org/AboutUs (last visited on Oct. 20, 2007).

2. *Id.*

3. *Id.*

4. *Id.*

5. *Id.*

6. The Joint Commission, www.jointcommmission.org/Accreditation Programs/Hospitals/Accredidtaitonprocess (last visited on Oct. 19, 2007).

7. *Id.*

8. *Id.*

9. *Id.*

10. *Id.*

11. *Id.*

12. *Id.*
13. *Id.*
14. *Id.*
15. *Id.*
16. *Id.*
17. *Id.*
18. *Id.*
19. *Id.*
20. *Id.*
21. *Id.*
22. *Id.*
23. *Id.*
24. *Id.*
25. *Id.*
26. *Id.*
27. *Guidelines for Submission of Evidence of Standards Compliance*, The Joint Commission, www.jointcommission.org/AccreditationPrograms/Hospitals/AccreditationProcess (last visited on Oct. 19, 2007).
28. The Joint Commission, www.jointcommission.org/AccreditationPrograms/Hospitals/AccreditationProcess (last visited on Oct. 19, 2007).
29. *Id.*
30. *Guidelines for Submission of Evidence of Standards Compliance*, The Joint Commission, www.jointcommission.org/AccreditationPrograms/Hospitals/AccreditationProcess (last visited on Oct. 19, 2007).
31. The Joint Commission, www.jointcommission.org/Accreditation Programs/Hospitals/AccreditationProcess (last visited on Oct. 22, 2007).
32. *Id.*
33. *Id.*
34. *Id.*
35. *Id.*
36. *Id.*
37. *Id.*
38. *Id.*
39. *Id.*
40. *Id.*
41. *Id.*
42. *Id.*
43. The Joint Commission, www.jointcommission.org/PatientSafety/facts_patient_safety.htm (last visited on Oct. 25, 2007).
44. The Joint Commission, www.jointcommission.org (last visited on Oct. 25, 2007).
45. Telephone conference with Dr. Peter Angood, Vice President and Chief Patient Safety Officer for JCAHO (Sept. 13, 2007), www.jointcommission.org/NR/rdonlyres.

46. *Id.* The Joint Commission, www.jointcommission.org/PatientSafety/facts_patient_safety.htm.

47. The Joint Commission, www.jointcommission.org/PatientSafety/facts_patient_safety.htm.

48. *Id.*

49. Telephone conference with Dr. Peter Angood, Vice President and Chief Patient Safety Officer for JCAHO (Sept. 13, 2007), www.jointcommission.org/NR/rdonlyres.

50. *Id.*

51. *Id.*

52. *Id.*

53. The Joint Commission, www.jointcommission.org/PatientSafety/facts_patient_safety.htm (last visited on Oct. 25, 2007).

54. *Id.*

55. *Id.*

56. The Joint Commission, www.jointcommission.org/PatientSafety/NationalPatientSafetyGoals (last visited on Oct. 25, 2007).

57. *Id.*

58. *Id.*

59. *FAQs for The Joint Commission's 2007 National Patient Safety Goals* (updated January 2007), www.jointcommission.org (last visited on Oct. 25, 2007).

60. *Id.*

61. *Id.*

62. *Id.*

63. *Id.*

64. *Id.*

65. *Id.*

66. *Id.*

67. *Id.*

68. *Id.*

69. *Id.*

70. *Id.*

71. The Joint Commission, www.jointcommission.org/PatientSafety/facts_patient_safety.htm (last visited on Oct. 25, 2007).

72. *Id.*

73. *Id.*

74. *Id.*

75. *Id.*

76. COMMITTEE ON QUALITY OF HEALTH CARE IN AMERICA, INSTITUTE OF MEDICINE, TO ERR IS HUMAN: BUILDING A SAFER HEALTH SYSTEM, pp. 139-140 (Linda T. Kohn et al., eds., 2000) [hereinafter *To Err Is Human*]. "Clearly, there is much opportunity for large employers to place greater emphasis on quality, and specifically patient safety, issues when making decisions to contract with a specific health

plan and in the design of payment and financial incentive systems to reward demonstrated quality and safety improvements." *Id.* at 140.

77. The Leapfrog Group, www.leapfroggroup.org (last visited on Oct. 26, 2007).

78. *Id.*

79. *Id.*

80. "The Business Roundtable (www.businessroundtable.org) is an association of chief executive officers of leading U.S. companies with $4.5 trillion in annual revenues and more than 10 million employees. Member companies comprise nearly a third of the total value of the U.S. stock markets and represent over 40 [forty] percent of all corporate income taxes paid. Collectively, they returned $112 billion in dividends to shareholders and the economy in 2005.... In general, the Roundtable focuses on issues it believes will have an effect on the economic well-being of the nation..." The Business Roundtable, www.businessroundtable.org (last visited on Oct. 27, 2007).

81. The Robert Wood Johnson Foundation is a philanthropic organization that "seeks to improve the health and health care of all Americans." The Robert Wood Johnson Foundation, www. rwjf.org (last visited on Oct. 27, 2007).

82. The Leapfrog Group, www.leapfroggroup.org (last visited on Oct. 26, 2007).

83. *Id.*

84. *Id.*

85. *Id.*

86. *Id.*

87. *Id.*

88. *Id.*

89. *Id.*

90. *Id.*

91. *Id.*

92. *Id.* .

93. *Id.*

94. *Id.*

95. *Id.*

96. *Id.*

97. *Id.*

98. *Id.*

99. *Id.*

100. *Id.*

101. *Id.*

102. *Id.*

103. *Id.*

104. *Id.*

105. *Id.*

106. *Id.*, and John D. Birkmeyer, MD, & Justin B. Dimick, MD, *The Leapfrog Group's Patient Safety Practices, 2003: The Potential Benefits of Universal Adoption* (February 2004).

107. The Leapfrog Group, www.leapfroggroup.org (last visited on Oct. 26, 2007).

108. *Id.*

109. *Id.* Since the focus of the LHI is on adult patient care, children's hospitals are not eligible to participate in LHI.

110. *Id.*

111. *Id.*

112. *Id.*

113. *Id.*

114. *Id.*

115. *Id.*

116. *Id.*

117. The Leapfrog Group, www.leapfroggroup.org (last visited on Oct. 26, 2007). "[F]ewer than 2% of U.S. hospitals have CPOE completely or partially available..." *The Leapfrog Group Factsheet on Computer Physician Order Entry*, www.leapfroggroup.org.

118. *Id.*

119. *Id.*

120. *Id.*

121. The Leapfrog Group, www.leapfroggroup.org (last visited on Oct. 26, 2007). *The Leapfrog Group Factsheet on ICU Physician Staffing*, www.leapfroggroup.org.

122. *Id.*

123. *Id.*

124. *Id.*

125. *Id.*

126. *Id.*

127. *Id.*

128. *Id.*

129. *Id.*

130. *Id.*

131. The Leapfrog Group, www.leapfroggroup.org (last visited on Oct. 26, 2007).

132. *The Leapfrog Group Factsheet on The Leapfrog Safe Practices Score Leap*, www.leapfroggroup.org (last visited on Oct. 26, 2007).

133. The NQF consensus report is entitled *Safe Practices for Better Healthcare: A Consensus Report*, published in May 2003 and updated in October 2006.

134. *The Leapfrog Group Factsheet on The Leapfrog Safe Practices Score Leap*, www.leapfroggroup.org (last visited on Oct. 26, 2007).

135. *Id.*

136. *Id.*

137. The Leapfrog Group Factsheet on Evidence Based Hospital Referral (EBHR) available on the Leapfrog Group, www.leapfroggroup.org (last visited on Oct. 26, 2007).

138. *Id.*

139. *Id.*

140. *Id.*

141. The Leapfrog Group, www.leapfroggroup.org (last visited on Oct. 26, 2007).

142. *Id.*

143. *Id.*

144. *Id.*

145. *Id.*

146. *Id.* The results of the hospital surveys are available for public viewing at www.leapfroggroup.org.

147. *Id.*

148. The Leapfrog Group, www.leapfroggroup.org (last visited on Oct. 26, 2007).

149. The National Patient Safety Foundation, www.npsf.org (last visited on Nov. 2, 2007).

150. *Id.*

151. *Id.*

152. *Id.*

153. *Id.*

154. *Id.*

155. *Id.*

156. *Id.*

157. *Id.*

158. *Id.*

159. *Id.*

160. *Id.*

161. *Id.*

162. *Id.*

163. *Id.*

164. *Id.*

165. *Id.*

166. *Id.*

167. *Id.*

168. *Id.*

169. *Id.*

170. *Id.*

171. *Id.*

172. *Id.*

173. *Id.*

174. *Id.*

175. *Id.*

176. *Id.*

177. *Id.*

178. *Id.*

179. *Id.* A report by the National Center for Education Statistics, entitled *The Health Literacy of America's Adults,* found that only 22 percent of adults have the ability to obtain, process, and understand basic health information and services needed to make appropriate health decisions. It also found that low health literacy is associated with poor health outcomes (increased hospitalization rates, fewer preventive screenings, and higher rates of disease and mortality).

180. The Partnership for Clear Health Communication at the National Patient Safety Foundation, www.askmethree.com (last visited on Nov. 2, 2007).

181. *Id.* Forty percent of seniors and 50 percent of African Americans and Hispanics read at or below the fifth-grade level.

182. *Id.*

183. *Id.*

184. John A. Vernon et al., *Low Health Literacy: Implications for National Health Policy,* Oct. 10, 2007, www.askmethree.org.

185. *Id.*

186. *Id.*

187. *Id.*

188. *Id.*

189. *Id.*

190. *Id.*

191. The National Patient Safety Foundation, www.npsf.org (last visited on Nov. 2, 2007).

192. *Id.*

193. *Id.*

194. *Id.*

195. *Id.*

196. *Id.*

197. *Id.*

198. *Id.*

199. *Id.*

200. *Id.*

201. *Id.* The James S. Todd Memorial Research Award was established in honor of the past executive vice president of the American Medical Association, who was instrumental in founding the NPSF.

202. *Id.*

203. *Id.*

204. The Institute for Healthcare Improvement, www.ihi.org (last visited on Nov. 5, 2007).

205. *Id.*

206. *Id.*

207. *Id.*
208. *Id.*
209. *Id.*
210. *Id.*
211. *Id.*
212. *Id.*
213. *Id.*
214. *Id.*
215. *Id.*
216. *Id.*
217. *Id.*
218. *Id.*
219. *Id.*
220. *Id.*
221. *Id.*
222. *Id.*
223. *Id.*
224. *Id.*
225. *Id.*
226. *Id.*
227. *Id.*
228. *Id.*
229. *Id.*
230. *Id*

231. Associates in Process Improvement helps organizations improve their products and services and increase their capability for continued improvement by: providing guidance for senior leaders on planning and managing improvement; developing methods to accelerate the rate of improvement; teaching philosophy and methods associated with improving products and services; and providing guidance to teams and individuals on specific improvements. The Associates in Process Improvement, www.apiweb.org (last visited on Nov. 8, 2007).

232. The Institute for Healthcare Improvement, www.ihi.org (last visited on Nov. 5, 2007).

233. *Id.*
234. *Id.*
235. *Id.*
236. *Id.*
237. *Id.*
238. *Id.*

239. COMMITTEE ON QUALITY OF HEALTH CARE IN AMERICA, INSTITUTE OF MEDICINE, CROSSING THE QUALITY CHASM: A NEW HEALTH SYSTEM FOR THE 21ST CENTURY (National Academies Press 2001).

240. The Institute for Healthcare Improvement, www.ihi.org (last visited on Nov. 5, 2007).

241. *Id.* The six principles are available at www.ihi.org/IHI/Topics/ImprovementMethods.

242. The Institute for Healthcare Improvement, www.ihi.org (last visited on Nov. 5, 2007).

243. *Id.*

244. *Id.*

245. *Id.* For a list of hundreds of change concepts, as well as examples of how they were applied in process improvement, both in health care and outside of health care, *see* G.J. Langley, K.M. Nolan, T.W. Nolan, C.L. Norman, & L.P. Provost, The Improvement Guide (Jossey-Bass Publishers, Inc., 1996).

246. The Institute for Healthcare Improvement, www.ihi.org (last visited on Nov. 5, 2007).

247. *Id.*

248. *Id.*

249. *Id.*

250. *Id.*

251. *Id.*

252. *Id.*

253. *Id.*

254. *Id.*

255. *Id.*

256. *Id.*

257. *Id.*

258. *Id.*

259. *Id.*

260. *Id.*

261. *Id.*

262. *Id.*

263. *Id.*

264. *Id.*

265. *Id.*

266. *Id.*

267. *Id.*

268. *Id.*

269. *Id.*

270. *Id.*

271. *Id.*

272. *Id.*

273. *Id.*

274. *Id.*

275. The Institute for Safe Medication Practices, www.ismp.org (last visited on Nov. 11, 2007).

276. *Id.*

277. *Id.*

278. *Id.*

279. *Id.*
280. *Id.*
281. *Id.*
282. *Id.*
283. *Id.*
284. *Id.* U.S. Pharmacopeia (USP) is the official public standards-setting authority for all prescription and over-the-counter medicines, dietary supplements, and other health care products manufactured and sold in the United States. It is an independent, science-based public health organization that is funded through the sale of its products and services that are used in promoting good pharmaceutical care. U.S. Pharmacopeia, www.usp.org (last visited on Nov. 11, 2007).
285. The Institute for Safe Medication Practices, www.ismp.org (last visited on Nov. 11, 2007).
286. *Id.*
287. *Id.*
288. *Id.*
289. *Id.*
290. *Id.*
291. *Id.*
292. *Id.*
293. *Id.*
294. *Id.*
295. *Id.*
296. *Id.*
297. *Id.*
298. *Id.*
299. *Id.*
300. *Id.*
301. *Id.*
302. *Id.*
303. *Id.*
304. *Id.*
305. *Id.*
306. *Id.* The Health Research and Educational Trust is a private, not-for-profit organization that addresses health management and policy issues. For more information, go to www.hret.org. The Medical Group Management Association represents 242,000 physicians' practices. Its purpose is to improve the effectiveness of medical group practices. For more information, go to www.mgma.com. The Commonwealth Fund is a private foundation that supports independent research on health and social issues. For more information, read the next section of this book or go to www.cmwf.org.
307. The Institute for Safe Medication Practices, www.ismp.org (last visited on Nov. 11, 2007).
308. *Id.*

309. *Id.*
310. *Id.*
311. *Id.*
312. *Id.*
313. *Id.*
314. *Id.*
315. *Id.*
316. *Id.*
317. *Id.*
318. *Id.*
319. *Id.*
320. *Id.*
321. *Id.*
322. *Id.*
323. *Id.*
324. *Id.*
325. *Id.*
326. *Id.*
327. The Commonwealth Fund, www.commonwealthfund.org (last visited on Nov. 16, 2007).
328. *Id.*
329. *Id.*
330. *Id.*
331. *Id.*
332. *Id.*
333. *Id.*
334. *Id.*
335. *Id.*
336. *Id.*
337. *Id.*
338. *Id.*
339. *Id.*
340. *Id.*
341. *Id.*
342. *Id.*
343. *Id.*
344. *Id.*
345. *Id.*
346. *Id.*
347. *Id.*
348. *Id.*
349. *Id.*
350. *Id.*
351. *Id.*

352. *Id.*

353. *Id.*

354. *Id.*

355. *Id.*

356. The Commonwealth Fund Commission on a High Performance Health System, *Why Not the Best? Results from a National Scorecard on U.S. Health System Performance*, The Commonwealth Fund (Sept. 2006), www.commonwealthfund. org.

357. *Id.*

358. *Id.*

359. *Id.*

360. *Id.*

361. *Id.*

362. *Id.*

363. *Id.*

364. *Id.*

365. The Commonwealth Fund, www.commonwealthfund.org (last visited on Nov. 16, 2007).

366. *Id.*

367. *Id.*

368. *Id.*

369. *Id.*

370. *Id.*

371. *Id.*

372. *Id.*

373. *Id.* The Foundation Center is an organization that matches individuals and nonprofit entities with grantmakers. More information may be obtained by going to the Foundation Center's Web site at http://foundationcenter.org.

374. *Id.*

375. *Id.*

376. *Id.*

377. The Commonwealth Fund, www.commonwealthfund.org (last visited on Nov. 16, 2007).

378. *Id.*

379. *Id.*

CHAPTER 4

Developing a Patient Safety Program

I. SOURCES OF PATIENT SAFETY PROGRAM STANDARDS[1]

Precise mechanisms for achieving patient safety are not mandated. Instead, the federal Medicare regulations, together with private accreditation organizations and advisory groups, have established broad guidelines designed to ensure that organizations develop, implement, and maintain ongoing quality assessment and performance improvement activities that include certain components.

Almost all patient safety program components can be traced to the Institute of Medicine recommendations, which provide that:

> All health care settings should establish comprehensive patient safety programs operated by trained personnel within a culture of safety. These programs should encompass (1) case finding—identifying system failures, (2) analysis—understanding the factors that contribute to system failures, and (3) system redesign—making improvements in care processes to prevent errors in the future. Patient safety programs should invite the participation of patients and their families and be responsive to their inquiries.[2]

A. Medicare Conditions of Participation for Hospitals and QAPI

The Medicare Conditions of Participation for Hospitals (CoPs) contain standards intended to establish minimum requirements to protect the health and safety of beneficiaries.[3] Commencing in 2003, CMS implemented a new CoP that requires hospitals to "develop, implement and maintain an effective, ongoing, hospital-wide, data-driven quality assessment and performance improvement program or QAPI.[4] CMS, in its commentary to the final CoP rule, explicitly acknowledged the impor-tance of the IOM report, *To Err Is Human,* in focusing attention on sys-temic and procedural failures in preventing medical error. CMS specifically adopted a definition of error that "can include problems in practice, products, procedures, and systems."

The CoPs require hospitals to undertake a proactive approach to improving their performance and adhere to the minimum require-ments of both systematically examining their quality and undertaking ongoing improvement projects.[5] A hospital's QAPI program must therefore:

- include an ongoing program that shows measurable improve-ment in relation to indicators for which there is evidence that the program will improve health outcomes and reduce medical errors. Hospitals are required to measure, track and analyze qual-ity indicators, including adverse patient events;
- incorporate quality indicator data. Data the hospital collects should be used for monitoring the effectiveness, safety, and qual-ity of services and identifying improvement strategies;
- *set priorities for improvement activities, which involves focusing on high-risk, high volume areas that affect health outcomes and patient safety. These activities must involve tracking adverse patient events and medical errors, studying their causes, and implementing preventative actions and feedback and learning mechanisms throughout the hospital* (emphasis added);
- include distinct performance improvement projects. The number and scope of the projects conducted by the hospital must be pro-portional to the scope and complexity of the hospital's operation and be similar in effort to projects conducted by CMS contracted quality improvement organizations (QIOs).[6]

The CoPs therefore clearly establish that hospitals must, as an essen-tial component of any quality improvement program, include patient safety activities that at a minimum involve tracking adverse patient events and medical errors, analyzing their causes, and implementing preventative actions and feedback and learning mechanisms throughout the hospital.

The CoP makes the hospital's governing body accountable for ensur-ing the ongoing program for patient safety and quality improvement is well defined, implemented, maintained, and adequately funded.[7] Considerable discretion is given to hospitals to design their programs in an effort to increase flexibility and reduce regulatory burden, while main-taining an appropriate level of accountability.[8]

B.   The Joint Commission

The Joint Commission (JCAHO) has promulgated patient safety standards for all JCAHO-accredited health care organizations.[9] JCAHO's safety standards now form the basis for JCAHO accreditation of health care organizations and drive the accreditation process. The standards are complex and permeate all aspects of an organization's operations. In addition to the patient safety standards, since 2002, JCAHO annually establishes national patient safety goals with which organizations are expected to fully comply. Current goals center on improving the accuracy of patient identification, the effectiveness of communication among caregivers, safe use of high-alert medications, effective clinical alarm systems, reducing health care-associated infections, reconciliation of medications, and patient falls.[10]

JCAHO maintains a preeminent and influential national and international role in accrediting health care organizations as evidenced by JCAHO and the Joint Commission International's formation of a collaborative relationship with the World Health Organization. The WHO, JCAHO, and JCAHO International have founded the WHO Collaborating Centre dedicated solely to patient safety.

C.   The Department of Veterans Affairs

The Department of Veterans Affairs (VHA) is the largest integrated health care system in the U.S. In 1999, the VHA established the National Center for Patient Safety (NCPS) and launched its VHA Patient Safety Program.[11] Since that time, the VHA has become an acknowledged leader in the patient safety movement.[12] The NCPS was established to develop a culture of safety throughout the Veterans Health Administration. Its stated goal is the nationwide reduction and prevention of inadvertent harm to VHA patients as a result of their care. Patient safety managers at 153 VHA hospitals and patient safety officers at twenty-one VA regional headquarters participate in the program.

The VHA's patient safety program focuses particularly on the use of multidisciplinary teams investigating the root cause of medical close calls and adverse events together with confidential staff reporting systems.[13] Particularly useful in assisting health care providers is the VHA Patient Safety Program handbook, which describes patient safety adverse event and root-cause analyses.[14]

The VHA has also partnered with the federal Agency for Healthcare Research and Quality (AHRQ) to form the Patient Safety Improvement Corps (PSIC). The PSIC program provides knowledge and skills to teams of hospital and other staff, including patient safety officers and those responsible for patient safety reporting and analysis.[15]

II. PATIENT SAFETY PROGRAM COMPONENTS

Each patient safety program has as its foundation a well-articulated safety plan. A patient safety plan is designed to support and promote the mission, vision, and values of an organization, with a special focus on the continuous enhancement of safety for all patients. The plan defines an organization's safety priorities and delineates the mechanisms for effectively responding to patient safety concerns in both a proactive and reactive fashion, with the goal of reducing risk, errors, and other adverse events.[16] A safety plan constructs the foundation for a systematic and coordinated approach to integrating patient safety priorities into the design and redesign of all relevant organizational processes, functions, and services. Bringing the plan to fruition requires an organizational safety infrastructure that operationalizes mechanisms and mobilizes resources for effectively addressing patient safety concerns.

The basic components of a patient safety program, as outlined by JCAHO are:[17]

1. **Program Goals and Structure**

   - Determined by the Board and implemented by leadership
   - Consistent with the organization's mission
   - Establish activities & functions relating to patient safety
   - Include all participating sites, settings, and services

2. **Scope of the Program**

   - Management of the Program
   - Components (safety-related offices, committees, functions)
   - Interdisciplinary participation
   - Oversight

3. **Mechanisms for Coordination**

   - Among components of the Program
   - Among the professional disciplines
   - Across the organization

4. **Communicating with Patients about Safety**

   - Patient education
   - Disclosure

5. **Staff Education**

- Safety-related orientation and training
- Expectations for reporting
- Non-punitive environment

6. **Safety Improvement Activities**

- Prioritization of improvement activities
- Routine safety-related data collection and analysis
  o Incident reporting
  o Medication error reporting
  o Infection surveillance
  o Facility safety surveillance
  o Staff perceptions of, and suggestions for, improving patient safety
  o Staff willingness to report errors
  o Patient/family perceptions of, and suggestions for, improvement
- Identification, reporting, and management of sentinel events
- Proactive risk reduction
  o Identification of high-risk processes
  o Failure mode effects and criticality analysis
- Reporting of results
  o To the Patient Safety Committee
  o To organization staff
  o To executive leadership and the governing body.

The remainder of this chapter will describe the implementation of key elements of a patient safety program.

III.   DEFINING PROGRAM GOALS AND MECHANISMS OF COORDINATION

A.   Defining Program Goals

1.   *Role of the Governing Board and Clinical Governance*[18]

Since the seminal IOM Report, *To Err Is Human*, governing boards are increasingly responsible for ensuring the quality of health care provided in their organizations and play a vital role in monitoring and improving care to make certain that it is safe, beneficial, patient-centered, timely, efficient, and equitable.[19] Ensuring that an organization provides safe care requires the board to expand its knowledge base and expertise to clinical, regulatory, and operational issues associated with patient safety and quality of care. Improvement in safety, a key component of quality, does not occur unless the organization's governing body and senior management articulate a commitment to safety through overt, clearly defined efforts that sustain the organization's interest and focus on patient safety.

Health care board oversight obligations of patient safety and quality represent an expansion and evolution of a board's core fiduciary responsibilities rooted in the traditional common law and state statutory fiduciary duty of care. Since quality and safety are emerging regulatory enforcement priorities, the board's duty of care necessarily involves protecting the organization from enforcement exposure.

The duty of care requires the board to act in good faith with the care exercised by an ordinarily prudent person in a manner the board reasonably believes to be in the best interest of the health care organization. Recently, this duty of care has been interpreted to include a director's active and reasonable inquiry into aspects of the corporate operations. This reasonable inquiry means that the board creates sound reporting mechanisms whereby the board properly and timely receives quality and safety operational performance information such that the organization complies with applicable law.[20] Through this duty of care and oversight function, corporate compliance and patient safety board obligations meld.

In addition to the duty of care, nonprofit health care entities have additional obligations under the duty of obedience to follow the organization's specific mission and purpose as expressed in its governing documents. The duty of obedience is implicated by the nonprofit's charitable mission and goal to promote health, which necessarily involves keeping patients safe and attending to quality.

Governing board members should therefore be informed of: emerging quality of care and patient safety issues that affect the organization; specific federal and state quality-of-care measurement and reporting requirements, including how the organization will comply with newly imposed requirements; and reports from senior management on organizational quality-of-care improvement activities and their effectiveness.

Boards can utilize several approaches in achieving effective and meaningful oversight. Minimally, the board can specifically include in member orientation and education the relevance of quality and safety to members' fiduciary responsibilities. Board meetings can allot time to quality oversight of such areas as medical staff credentialing, patient safety improvements, occurrence of sentinel events, and the monitoring of clinical indicators and customer service indicators. Boards that devote at least 25 percent of meeting time to discussing quality issues are more likely to have higher quality indicator scores.[21] Board members should receive key quality performance measures in a dashboard or scorecard format that enables easy understanding and clear comparison of the facility's performance compared to national standards.

Alternatively, the board may formally delegate quality improvement and oversight to a "quality improvement committee" it establishes. The board would charge this committee with helping it fulfill its quality and patient safety responsibilities.[22]

Prior to implementation of the patient safety program, the board should formally adopt and approve the program. The program presented to the board should articulate well-defined executive responsibility and provide for strong, clear, visible organizational commitment and attention to safety. The safety program should include: commitment from senior-level leadership; defined program objectives and plans; dedicated personnel resources; a budget; a provision for the collection and analysis of data; and a provision for the monitoring of progress. Once implemented, relevant information must be regularly communicated to the board and/or a key board committee so that the board is able to monitor the effectiveness of the patient safety program and become aware of any particular adverse events that could negatively impact the organization.

2. Executive Leadership

In addition to board oversight and direction, there must be well-defined executive responsibility for an organization's safety program to be successful. Senior leaders must make patient safety a strategic priority for the organization and take an active role in creating a culture of safety that communicates to everyone that patient safety is part of his or her job description. Further, leaders must ensure that the culture is just (i.e., that the culture is not punitive and supports the self-disclosure of adverse events as well as the discussion of errors so that lessons can be learned from them).

The Joint Commission's leadership standards require accredited organizations to have leaders create and maintain a culture of safety throughout the organization and to regularly evaluate the culture of safety and quality through the use of valid and reliable tools.[23] Prior to implementing a patient safety program and on a routine and regular basis thereafter, executive leadership should assess and evaluate an organization's "culture of safety." The safety culture of an organization is the sum total of the "individual and group values, attitude, perceptions, competencies, and patterns of behavior that determine the commitment to, and the style and proficiency of an organization's health and safety management."[24] When an organization achieves a positive safety culture, management, staff, and executive leadership collectively share perceptions of the importance of patient safety, effectively communicate based on trust, and have confidence in the organization's ability to establish and implement effective safety measures.

The various quality and safety components, departments, or committees should report regularly to executive leadership. At a minimum, this necessitates active review at the executive level of safety performance data and action plans to address proactive and reactive responses by the organization when safety performance levels differ from national benchmarks or fall below expectations. In addition to reviewing data, executives in both clinical and nonclinical areas should be involved in actively monitoring the organization's safety systems, including activities such as walk-throughs and safety rounds. This level of monitoring provides a firsthand opportunity to observe clinical settings, evaluate hazardous conditions, and interact openly with frontline staff about their safety concerns.

3.   Staff Members

Staff members at all levels of the organization, including volunteers, must be aware of their role in creating a culture of safety. Each staff member, whether engaged in providing clinical or nonclinical services, should be encouraged to participate in patient safety activities and made aware of the contribution his or her role plays in carrying out the organization's safety plan. Safety-related job expectations should be incorporated into job descriptions and become an element tied to any merit-pay or performance-evaluation system.

4.   Role of the Medical Staff

For obvious reasons, physicians on the medical staff are integral to the organization's culture of safety. It is therefore crucial to gain buy-in from the medical staff collectively and from individual physician members individually. Enlisting physicians who will "champion" patient safety efforts via a prominent physician leader or small physician group serves to engender acceptance of the program by the larger medical staff. The champion should be selected based on the respect he or she receives from peers, effective communication and social skills, and an ability to take a principled stand when needed. Many organizations also demonstrate the value placed on the physician's role in achieving patient safety by appointing the chief medical officer, the vice president of medical affairs, or a similarly situated physician to chair or to otherwise serve on patient safety committees.[25]

IV. MECHANISM OF COORDINATION

A. Patient Safety Committee and Patient Safety Officer

Traditionally, health care organizations have addressed patient safety with a rather disconnected approach in which separate departments or entities were responsible for individual aspects of safety and quality management. For example, risk management often addressed issues related to legal liability, risk reduction, and loss prevention; quality improvement focused its efforts on improving health care processes and outcomes; and safety management oversaw the physical safety of an organization's environment of care (i.e., fire, security, disaster preparedness, and maintenance of facilities and equipment). Full integration of these individual organizational components into a comprehensive quality and safety program is necessary to provide effective oversight and communication to executive leadership and the governing board such that the organization can effectively achieve its goals and objectives set forth in the organization's safety plan.

JCAHO requires that patient safety activities be integrated into the design and redesign of relevant organizational processes, functions, and services across the organization. JCAHO does not prescribe any specific organizational structure for the patient safety program, nor does JCAHO require the creation of new structures or safety offices within an organization. Instead, JCAHO expects that patient safety and quality activities, both existing and newly created, have an identified focus of accountability within the organization's leadership. The overriding mandate for ensuring the successful implementation and monitoring of compliance with quality and safety standards rests with board leadership. Consequently, there must be a reporting mechanism through which the board receives relevant safety and quality-program performance information.[26]

JCAHO does not define the mechanism through which a safety program must be managed, but does require that the day-to-day oversight and management of an organization's safety program rest with either one or more qualified individuals.[27] Since the emphasis and goal is to ensure that certain patient safety functions are performed, rather than the creation of any one particular structure, patient safety programs can be tailored to the size and complexity of the health care organization. A patient safety committee is one option to provide the necessary structure. Additional options include: expanding the scope of an existing committee, such as quality improvement, to include patient safety; integrating the patient safety-related efforts of several different committees into a coordinating council; or assigning one individual to coordinate patient-safety initiatives in a variety of areas.[28]

The purpose of having one or more dedicated positions for this role is to enable more focused coordination and implementation of the safety program's requisite components. In support of this designated individual, an interdisciplinary collaborative committee with members from a spectrum of clinical and nonclinical services should be formed and charged with safety oversight and management. The safety committee plays an integral role in: developing all aspects of a patient safety program, including educational programs for staff members, patients, and families; assessing the effectiveness of safety initiatives; and developing policies and procedures in support of the safety program.

The interdisciplinary safety committee often includes the safety officer, medical staff, nursing staff, pharmacist, and a layperson or patient representative. The major purpose of the safety committee is to assemble a knowledgeable, empowered core group with members who have authority to speak for their respective areas and make decisions within the context of the committee.

B. Scope of the Program

The "scope" of a patient safety program refers to the types of events that will be addressed by the organization. Events can range from near misses that cause no harm to sentinel events that cause serious harm. The organization's response to safety concerns will, to a large degree, be determined by the scope of the safety plan, which in turn will be dictated by state law or accreditation requirements. The plan's scope will influence the selection and prioritization of organizational safety activities, including the mechanisms necessary to appropriately report and respond to events.

JCAHO requires that the scope of the program, and therefore the scope of the patient safety committee's work, be divided into two areas. The first area is reactive, which means responding to errors that involve actual harm to a patient or a "near miss." The other is proactive, which means developing error-reduction strategies based on the selection of at least one high-risk process as published in the literature (e.g., journal articles, FDA alerts, or JCAHO Sentinel Event Alerts) or on actual data compiled by the provider.[29]

C.   Safety Improvement Activities

1.   *Proactive Risk Assessment and Prioritization of Improvement Activities*

JCAHO requires that accredited organizations use risk assessment techniques proactively to identify weaknesses in a process, predict what might happen as a result of those weaknesses, and initiate process redesigns that minimize the risk of unintended patient harm. The process mandated by JCAHO to conduct this prospective assessment is one used by many other high-risk industries—such as automotive, aerospace, airline, computer software design, and the military—and is called failure mode and effect analysis (FMEA). This technique examines the individual components of a process to determine the manner in which any individual step or component of that process could fail, prioritize where to focus efforts, and then measure the outcomes of process or system change.

JCAHO does not dictate what key processes must undergo FMEA, but JCAHO does expect that a provider annually will conduct at least one FMEA for an identified high-risk process. Providers are to monitor the issuance of Sentinel Event Alerts[30] as an initial step in identifying applicable subject matter for FMEA analysis, or they may set FMEA priorities based on their own risk management experience.

The FMEA process requires the following steps: choose the process to be studied; assemble a multidisciplinary team; organize information about the process being studied; conduct a hazard analysis; and develop and implement actions and outcome measures to be used to analyze and test the redesigned process. A hazard analysis is an assessment conducted for the purpose of identifying potential safety risks in a process and determining what, if any, patient harm might occur if the process failure actually occurs. Hazard analysis allows the team members to make informed decisions about what failure modes should be prioritized and addressed. This is the most detailed step of the FMEA process and the most time-consuming. A hazard analysis involves five activities: identify the failure mode (i.e., anything that could go wrong during the completion of a step in a process); determine the potential effect of the failure mode; rank the severity of failure mode effects; rank the probability of each failure mode; and identify areas of greatest concern or critical failure modes.

Many institutions have adopted a hazard analysis developed by the Veterans Affairs National Center for Patient Safety (VHA NCPS), which is a priority scoring methodology known as the "safety assessment code" (SAC).[31] The SAC uses numerical measures for the severity and probability of events that then drives the level of analysis required. Assessing severity includes criteria such as the extent of injury, increased length of stay, and level of care required to remedy the error. For near misses, the score represents the worst outcome that could have potentially occurred had the event actually transpired. Each hazard or incident is assigned a score based on the severity and probability of occurrence. Scores over a certain number are considered the highest risk, and they automatically require root-cause analysis of the incident.

2. *Reactive Responses and Root-Cause Analysis*

Root-cause analysis (RCA) is a methodology for identifying the contributing factors that underlie variations in performance associated with sentinel or adverse events and near misses. A "root cause" is the most fundamental reason an event or near miss has occurred. It is a structured approach to an investigation that retrospectively examines and dissects the genesis and evolution of an event or near miss to discover why it occurred and uncover its causes. The goal of the process is to identify the most obvious opportunities for improvement that will prevent recurrence.[32] The end product of a root-cause analysis is an action plan that identifies strategies the organization intends to implement to reduce the risks of similar events occurring in the future.

Each health care organization must determine, depending on its available resources, how best to operationalize its RCA processes and methodology. RCA requires the assembly of a multidisciplinary team in order to bring differing perspectives and expertise to the analysis. Typically, the team will include a facilitator with expertise in RCA, as well as a team leader with senior management accountability, each of whom shares responsibility for conducting, coordinating, and reporting each RCA process. Senior management does not need to be involved with all steps or to conduct all aspects of the RCA, but its participation is crucial to demonstrate the organization's commitment, for resource allocation, and for assistance in implementation of the action plan that follows the RCA.

Additionally, the RCA team must include content experts who can speak to the specific details of the situation under investigation and frontline staff members who are familiar with how things "really are," including any hazards and hidden barriers that might not be evident to others. Representation from risk management and quality improvement, as appropriate, is also critical to provide expertise in the RCA process and managing group dynamics.

It is important for an organization to apply its RCA processes consistently and fairly to all staff members, including medical staff, in the manner articulated in its policies and procedures. Failure to adhere to agreed-upon processes, even in an isolated incident, creates the possibility of staff mistrust and adversely affects staff members' willingness to internally report adverse events.[33]

Consistent with the principles of a just culture, certain types of incidents are not recommended for RCA by the RCA team. These events include:

- Those thought to be a result of criminal acts;
- Purposefully unsafe acts where the harm is intended;
- Acts related to substance abuse; and
- Suspected patient abuse of any kind.[34]

These events potentially involve staff discipline, dismissal, or criminal charges, as well as possible licensure sanction and are more appropriately referred to and remedied by an internal or external administrative process or regulatory body.[35] In the event that the organization believes an RCA of such an event would lead to system improvement, a parallel RCA process can be undertaken as long as no information is shared between the participants in the two processes and strict confidentiality is maintained.[36]

While variations exist in how an RCA is conducted, JCAHO has established some basic RCA parameters.[37] In order for JCAHO to find it acceptable, an analysis must focus on systems and processes, rather than on individual performance. JCAHO requires that the RCA be thorough and credible. To be "thorough," the RCA must include:

- A determination of the human and other factors most directly associated with the incident and the processes and systems related to its occurrence;
- Analysis of the underlying systems and processes through a series of "why?" questions to determine where redesign might reduce risk;
- Inquiry into all areas appropriate to the specific type of incident;
- Identification of risk points and their potential contributions to this type of event; and
- A determination of potential improvement in processes or systems that would tend to decrease the likelihood of such events in

the future, or a determination, after analysis, that no such improvement opportunities exist.

To be "credible," a root-cause analysis must:

- Include participation by the leadership of the organization and by the individuals most closely involved in the processes and systems under review;
- Be internally consistent (i.e., not contradict itself or leave obvious questions unanswered);
- Provide an explanation for all findings that a relevant process, system, or function is "not applicable" or offers no opportunity for risk reductions; and
- Include consideration of any relevant literature.[38]

Once the RCA is completed, the next step is to develop an action plan that: identifies the changes that are to be implemented to reduce risk and the planned improvement actions; identifies who is responsible for implementation; determines when the action will be implemented; and states how the effectiveness of the actions will be evaluated.

It is critical to internally disseminate the lessons learned and the plan for correcting necessary systems and processes. A particular group for which this follow-through is important is the staff involved in the original incident. Presenting the action plan and getting the group's reaction to the proposed risk-reduction strategies provides important feedback to the RCA team and serves a secondary purpose of bringing closure to a very difficult situation in a constructive, purposeful fashion.

Some organizations are providing the opportunity for the patient and the patient's family to be informed regarding any interventions put in place to prevent an incident from reoccurring in the future. This may help bring closure for the patient and family, and some sense that their loss or experience was a catalyst for positive change within the organization.

V. COMMUNICATING WITH PATIENTS ABOUT SAFETY

Communicating with patients about safety involves empowering the patient to be actively involved in his or her care and disclosing unanticipated events or incidents to the patient and his or her family.

A.   Empowering the Patient

Empowering the patient to actively participate in his or her care to the degree and extent to which the patient is capable and desires to do so is fundamental to safety. A patient's active involvement has been shown to reduce the incidence of errors and improve outcomes. Many errors result from incomplete or incorrect communication between the provider and patient. Providers frequently do not give enough information to help patients make informed decisions. Uninvolved and uninformed patients are less likely to accept the provider's choice of treatment, and are less likely to comply with the treatment plan.[39]

JCAHO places significant emphasis on patient participation and empowerment. In 2007, JCAHO adopted as a national patient safety goal the idea that all accredited providers encourage active patient involvement in their care.[40] Pursuant to this goal, accredited providers are required to define and communicate the means by which patients and their families are to report concerns about safety, and encourage patients and their families to use those means. Suggested measures for accredited providers include: creating and supporting a culture of safety that encourages and allows patients to inquire and express concerns about their care; posting information in prominent places throughout the organization and on Web sites about reporting concerns; and providing patients with anonymous reporting mechanisms.[41] Going one step further, JCAHO also suggests that patients and families be involved in quality, safety, and/or risk management committees. Patients can be involved either through direct committee participation or in an advisory capacity.

While little research exists to date to support the effectiveness of patient involvement in safety activities, it is consistent with the notion of transparency, and many providers report at least anecdotal positive outcomes. Prior to being included in such committees, patients or family members should be properly oriented to the organization's structure, the role and function of the assigned committee, and confidentiality and HIPAA issues. All participating patients and family members should sign a confidentiality statement. Further, patients and family members should not participate in committee sessions where matters such as potential claims and staff-performance issues may be discussed.[42]

An additional national program devised by JCAHO, together with CMS, is the "Speak Up" campaign, which urges patients to take a role in preventing health care errors by becoming active, involved, and informed participants on the health care team.[43] The program features brochures, posters, and other materials on a variety of patient safety topics, including how to prevent medication errors and avoid contagious diseases such as the common cold and influenza. JCAHO encourages and permits providers to adopt and incorporate these materials for their own use.

B. Disclosure of Errors and Unanticipated Outcomes

Perhaps no element of patient safety has engendered more discussion and deliberation than the disclosure of patient error and unanticipated outcomes.[44] Significant and often cited barriers include:

- Fear of retribution and repercussions due to disclosure;
- Lack of legal protection of the information released;
- Poor publicity;
- Lack of communication skills or education on how to disclose information; and
- Belief that disclosure is unnecessary, and that the outcome would be the same without the error or intervention.[45]

While barriers exist, regulators and accreditation agencies have caused providers to grapple with the new reality of patient disclosure. As counsel to health care providers, the often-ingrained and reflexive posture is to advise clients to withhold information and avoid disclosure. This posture is increasingly being replaced (and in this author's opinion, correctly so) with the provision of guidance to clients such that effective disclosure policies and procedures can be developed and implemented. Increasingly, providers who commit to well-developed disclosure policies have found that such policies have financial benefits, fulfill their ethical duties to patients, and improve public perceptions.

JCAHO requires that accredited organizations disclose to patients information related to "unanticipated outcomes" of care.[46] The intent of this standard is for the "responsible licensed practitioner or his/her designee to clearly explain the outcome of treatment or procedures to the patient, and where appropriate the family, whenever those outcomes differ significantly from the anticipated outcome."[47]

Notably, under this standard, a provider is required to disclose only those outcomes that are unanticipated. Medical errors that occur, but do not result in an unanticipated outcome, do not fit within this disclosure obligation. Also, the standard does not require an explanation of why an outcome transpired or its causal nexus. However, as described below, many providers choose to be fully transparent in their disclosure process, to the extent of their ability.

The National Patient Safety Foundation's statement of principle on patient disclosure bases its disclosure threshold on the "occurrence" of injury and provides:

> When health care injury occurs, the patient and family or representatives are entitled to a prompt explanation of how the injury occurred and its short or long term effects. When an error contributed to injury, the patient and or family representative should receive a truthful and compassionate explanation about the error and the remedies available to the patient. They should be informed that the factors involved in the injury will be investigated so that steps can be taken to reduce the likelihood of similar injury to other patients. Health care professionals and institutions that accept this responsibility are acknowledging their ethical obligation to be forthcoming about health care injuries and error.[48]

Professional medical societies also maintain that disclosure is the physician's ethical obligation, but differ on the type of event that requires disclosure. The American Medical Association advocates for the disclosure of "significant" medical complications that may have resulted from a physician's mistake or judgment.[49] The American College of Physicians-American Society of Internal Medicine ethical code provides that "physicians should disclose to patients information about procedural or judgment errors made in the course of care if such information is material to the patient's well being."[50]

The VHA, in 2005, issued a directive mandating disclosures of adverse events to patients who have been harmed in the course of their care, including where the harm may not be obvious or severe, or where the harm may only become evident in the future.[51] The disclosure is defined as a "discussion of clinically significant facts."[52] Disclosures of close calls are discretionary, but recommended.[53]

As of 2007, Nevada,[54] Pennsylvania,[55] New Jersey,[56] Tennessee,[57] Washington,[58] South Carolina,[59] Maryland,[60] Vermont,[61] and Florida[62] have enacted some form of mandatory serious or adverse-event patient-disclosure requirement.

Many organizations recognize that a clear difference exists between an adverse event that results in an untoward outcome involving patient harm and a near miss or close call that does not. In the absence of mandated disclosure requirements, the threshold question for most providers, then, is what should be disclosed. Developing and implementing criteria that clearly delineate whether or not specific incident types should be disclosed is therefore often the first challenge.

In deciding whether to communicate near misses to patients, organizations often decide to disclose events in which the patient is aware of the circumstances. Common sense dictates that when a patient is aware of a near miss, an explanation is essential to alleviate concerns and maintain trust. Utilizing an objective "reasonable person" standard (i.e., what a reasonable person would want to know under the circumstances) is a useful guiding principle. Near misses that did not result in patient harm but could potentially cause harm in the future (considering the severity of consequences and remoteness of risk) should be considered for disclosure, but disclosure in this circumstance is often treated as discretionary. The probability that harm might occur, the consequences if it should occur, and the extent to which steps can be taken now (such as testing or treatment) to prevent or mitigate the future harm should all be considered. The greater the probability, the more severe the consequences may be, and the greater the opportunity to prevent the future harm, the stronger the impetus is to disclose.[63]

Any determination of implementation criteria necessarily involves achieving consensus among organization leadership, risk management, the medical staff, the organization's ethics committee, and, of course, the board. It is also imperative that the organization's malpractice carrier and defense counsel are included in the process and buy into the disclosure criteria and disclosure program.

Generally, in support of its disclosure activities, an organization should develop policies and procedures that include: an institutional position statement on disclosures; the definitions from the safety plan of adverse events or near misses; the criteria for events warranting disclosure; the disclosure process steps for the disclosure conversation, including designated personnel roles; documentation requirements regarding disclosure; conflict resolution steps; a determination of when and by whom the disclosure will be made; development of a process for continued communication with the patient or legal representative after the initial disclosure is made; provision of staff and provider training; and provision of support to the staff member involved in the event.[64] [65]

Although each situation involving an adverse event is unique, the principles for disclosure are generally the same throughout the disclosure process.[66] Key is the recognition that disclosure is an ongoing process, beginning at the occurrence of the adverse event and continuing through to subsequent disclosure discussions.

In certain treatment settings such as long-term care, mental health, or pediatrics, the policies and procedures should: address when the patient is to be included in the disclosure discussion; determine how to disclose to patients without current or permanent capacity; address notification of legal guardians; and determine to whom disclosure is made if the patient has no family or next of kin.[67]

VI. STAFF EDUCATION, EXPECTATIONS FOR REPORTING, AND CREATION OF A NONPUNITIVE ENVIRONMENT

A. Staff Education

Establishing a safety curriculum is an important means of conveying an organization's commitment to creating a safety culture. Members at all levels of an organization, including leadership, medical staff, and volunteers, must be familiarized with critical aspects of safety through a formal orientation process, ongoing in-services, and other education and training programs as appropriate.[68] Safety curricula should be implemented along a continuum that begins with initial orientation and continues with ongoing in-service, competencies, continuing education programs, and job-related safety training. The safety curricula should ideally encompass the following: the teaching of broad safety and quality principles; proper responses to error; methods of collaboration and cooperation across disciplines and departments; leadership qualities that enhance safety; and how each staff member plays a role in carrying out the organization's safety plan through specific job-related aspects of safety.

JCAHO requires that all accredited providers train staff in the basic approaches to and methods of quality-performance improvement and improvement of patient safety.[69] Acquiring patient safety-related knowledge, per JCAHO, involves "an orientation process, ongoing in-service and other education and training programs that emphasize specific job-related aspects of patient safety. As appropriate, this training incorporates methods of team training to foster an interdisciplinary, collaborative approach to the delivery of patient care, and reinforces the need and way(s) to report medical/health care errors."[70]

B. Nonpunitive Environment and a Just Culture

A critical and fundamental component of any safety plan is the expectation that errors will be reported so that the organization can compile information, analyze data, communicate trends, and develop tools for resolving events and ultimately implement procedural and systematic change. It is therefore imperative to the success of any safety program that the organization's management style in dealing with error ensures that there are no reprisals and no impediments to information flowing freely to management and leadership. Reporting will not occur if staff believes they will be punished for doing so. In fact, punishing employees for making a mistake emanates from the misconception that the individual is to "blame" for his or her mistake and that punishment will lead both to improved performance in that individual and serve as a deterrent to error in others. Abundant evidence in human factors and cognitive psychology literature recognizes that most human errors are symptoms of underlying system failures, not personal failures.

Patient safety necessitates that organizations attain a "just culture," which is an atmosphere of trust where people are encouraged and even rewarded for providing safety-related information, but which is also clear about where the line must be drawn between acceptable and unacceptable behavior. [71]

Organizations must strive to achieve the following characteristics of a blame-free environment, wherein the organization:

- embraces the concept that those under its employ or who practice in its facility do not purposely seek to create errors, that most errors occur as a result of ineffective, improperly designed, or flawed systems;
- seeks to develop human resource polices and procedures that support the realization that most errors are not the result of individual failure, but system failure;
- develops ways to reward, rather than discourage, reporting of errors or patient-safety concerns;
- celebrates success at improvement in the reporting of patient-safety concerns and errors, as well as how such disclosure has been used to make improvements in systems to prevent the future possibility of error;
- purposely works to alter its mindset about errors and its behavior with respect to errors, possibly by changing the language it uses to talk about patient safety and errors;
- seeks to engender an environment where reporting about errors and patient safety is the norm, by actively creating an environment where practitioners and employees do not fear retribution for raising concerns or reporting errors; and
- implements methods of feedback to learn from error.

Further, error reporting must take place through an established reporting system supported by policies and procedures that are endorsed by the governing board and communicated to staff. The reporting system adopted should be clearly articulated to staff and include a description of which events are reportable, the time frame within which they are to be reported, and a readily available, easy-to-use format/form that is universal throughout the organization. The reporting system also should allow for feedback to clinicians and staff on the risk-reduction efforts made by the organization in response to reported events.

JCAHO expressly recognizes that the leaders of an organization are responsible for setting the tone such that internal reporting occurs within a system where there is "minimalization of individual blame or retribution for involvement in a medical/health care error."[72] While JCAHO does not require an amnesty policy for accredited providers, many patient-safety experts recommend a policy that allows staff to come forward and report errors as required by the organization and face no direct impact on their employment for doing so.

This is not to say that an organization that adopts a just culture eliminates individual or organizational accountability. Organizations can and should adopt a disciplinary model that centers on accountability and integrates the notions of individual and organizational culpability (e.g., human error, negligence, recklessness, and intentional acts) with the type of error (e.g., rule-based, skill-based, or knowledge-based).[73] To determine whether a particular behavior is culpable enough to involve disciplinary action, the disciplinary policy should require that each patient-safety event be assessed individually. The disciplinary decision-making model many providers select is based on staff risk-based behavior that incorporates the concepts of the civil tort liability system (i.e., negligence, gross negligence, or recklessness). The threshold for discipline is generally determined to be negligence where the staff member had no conscious disregard of a known risk; instead, the staff member should have known, but was unaware, of the risk he or she was taking. Gross negligence or recklessness should result in disciplinary action to deter intentionally unsafe acts.

Implementing a just culture necessitates the full involvement of all levels of the organization, as well as education and training of all levels of management and leadership. Counsel must work closely with human resources to ensure that applicable personnel policies address corrective and remedial actions that address individual and organizational process weaknesses.

NOTES

1. This chapter highlights three significant sources of patient safety standards: Medicare's CoPs, JCAHO, and the VHA system. These sources are not intended to be exhaustive but are highlighted here because these entities and the patient safety standards developed by them have significantly affected the delivery of health care services. Thus, even if a provider is not subject to these standards, they represent an important benchmark for patient safety plans and serve as useful guidance. The reader is directed to chapter 3 for further discussion of advisory groups whose oversight or activities may influence the choice of patient safety standards.

2. Patient Safety: Achieving a New Standard of Care (National Academies Press 2004), www.nap.edu/catalog.php?record_id=10863.

3. http://cms.hhs.gov/CFCsandCoPs/01Overview.

4. 42 C.F.R. § 482.21.

5 68 Fed. Reg. 3,435-36 (Jan. 24, 2003).

6. 42 C.F.R. § 482.21(e) (2003).

7. Id.

8. 68 Fed. Reg. 3,437 (Jan. 24, 2003).

9. See generally, www.jointcommission.org/.

10. www.jointcommission.org/PatientSafety/NationalPatientSafetyGoals/.

11. www.va.gov/ncps/.

12. Michael D. Cantor, MD, JD, et al., Disclosing Adverse Events to Patients. 31 Journal on Quality and Patient Safety 1 (January 2005).

13. VA Patient Safety Program: A Cultural Perspective at Four Medical Facilities, GAO-0583 (December 2004).

14. www.va.gov/ncps/pubs.html#handbook. See Appendix C for a copy of the VHA's National Patient Safety Improvement Handbook.

15. www.ahrq.gov/about/psimpcorps.htm.

16. See Appendix C for a copy of the VHA's National Patient Safety Improvement Handbook. See also Appendix D.

17. www.jointcommission.org/PatientSafety/pt_safety_plan.htm.

18. In its Supplemental Compliance Guidance for Hospitals, the OIG provides insight into the OIG's approach to fraud and abuse issues and specific risk areas that hospitals should consider. Although this Supplemental Guidance is directly applicable only to hospitals, the broadening of the OIG's compliance focus into quality and safety is instructive for other federally funded providers. In this Guidance, the OIG specifically reminded hospitals of the OIG's ability to exclude them from participation in federal health care programs if a facility provides unnecessary or substandard care. The OIG also asserts that hospitals should adopt quality of care protocols and implement procedures for assessing compliance with them. By including quality and safety as a compliance plan oversight requirement, the OIG clearly signaled the role of the board in ensuring an organization's commitment to safety. The OIG, together with the American Health Lawyer's Association, have cosponsored a series of documents that serve as

valuable educational resources on corporate compliance and responsibility, including the board's responsibility relative to health care quality. *See generally* http://oig.hhs.gov/fraud/complianceguidance.html#2.

19. *See Crossing the Quality Chasm,* Institute of Medicine, 2001.

20. *In re* Caremark International, Inc., Derivative Litigation, 698 A.2d 959 (Del. Ch. 1996).

21. BARRY S. BADER, EDWARD A. KAZEMEK, PAMELA R. KNECHT, & ROGER W. WITALIS, DIFFERENTIATING BOARD AND COMMITTEE WORK ON QUALITY (FACHE October 2007); www.greatboards.org/pubs/advisors-corner-differentiating-board-committee-quality-work.pdf.

22. *See* Appendix E for a sample charter of a Quality Improvement Committee.

23. *See* JCAHO Standards L.D. 3.10 and L.D. 3.60; *see also* Appendix F.

24. J. S. SORRA & V. F. NIEVA, HOSPITAL SURVEY ON PATIENT SAFETY CULTURE (Agency for Healthcare Research and Quality September 2004) (prepared by Westat, under contract no. 290-96-004; AHRQ Publication NO. 04-0041). *See also* Appendix G.

25. For additional information on engaging physicians, *see* J. L. REINERSTEIN, A. G. GOSFIELD, W. RUPP, J. W. WHITTINGTON, ENGAGING PHYSICIANS IN A SHARED QUALITY AGENDA (Institute for Healthcare Improvement 2007) (IHI Innovation Series white paper), www.ihi.org.

26. *See* Appendix H for suggested organizational structures.

27. JCAHO Leadership Standard LD 5. *See* Appendix I for a Patient Safety Officer Job Description.

28. *See Commit to Patient Safety: Create a Structure to Succeed,* Publications Sidebar, Joint Commission Resources, www.jcrinc.com/756/.

29. JCAHO Standard LD 5.5.

30. Sentinel Event Alerts are issued as brief periodic reports by JCAHO that: focus on specific types of reported sentinel events; describe lessons learned from their root-cause analyses; and suggest measures that providers can undertake to avoid occurrence of such events in their own settings.

31. *See* www.patientsafety.gov. *See also* Appendix C for VHA Patient Safety Improvement Handbook.

32. *See Canadian Root Cause Analysis Framework,* Canadian Patient Safety Institute, (March 2006), www.patientsafetyinstitute.ca/uploadedFiles/Resources/March%202006%20RCA%20Workbook.pdf.

33. *Id.*

34. *Id.*

35. *Id.*

36. *Id.*

37. *See* Appendix J, JCAHO Root-Cause Analysis Matrix.

38. *See* Joint Commission Sentinel Event Policy and Procedure, www.joint-commission.org/NR/rdonlyres/F84F9DC6-A5DA-490F-A91F A9FCE26347C4/0/SE_chapter_july07.pdf.

39. *See 20 Tips to Help Prevent Medical Errors,* Patient Fact Sheet (Agency for Healthcare Research and Quality February 2000) (AHRQ Publication No. 00-PO38).

40. The Joint Commission, www.jcipatientsafety.org/24111/.

41. *Id.*

42. One organization that has fully adopted this approach is the Dana-Farber Cancer Institute. *See* www.dana-farber.org/pat/patient-safety/patient-safety-resources/patient-rounding-toolkit.html.

43. www.jointcommission.org/PatientSafety/SpeakUp/about_speakup. htm.

44. A full discussion of the effects of disclosure and liability exposure arising therefrom is beyond the scope of this guideline. There is growing provider acceptance of parallel programs and the use of collaborative law in conjunction with patient safety programs. Parallel programs and collaborative law align the processes of disclosure, safety improvement analysis, and compensation for injuries associated with medical treatment. *See* Charlotte Huff, *The Not So Simple Truth,* TRUSTEE (Jan. 28, 2008), www.trusteemag.com/trusteemag_app/jsp/articledisplay.jsp?dcrpath=TRUSTEEMAG/PubsNewsArticleGen/data/2005/0510TRU_FEA_Errors.

As used herein, disclosure is defined as the process of providing information to a patient and/or other about an outcome or error. Disclosure represents a communication process between individuals of information that is frequently privileged. This is in contrast to the concept of "reporting" patient error, where information is provided to an internal or external authority for purposes of tracking, identifying, or analyzing trends. For an analysis of emerging reporting requirements, *see* chapter 3.

45. AMERICAN SOCIETY FOR HEALTHCARE RISK MANAGEMENT FOR THE AMERICAN HOSPITAL ASSOCIATION, DISCLOSURE OF UNANTICIPATED EVENTS: THE NEXT STEP IN BETTER COMMUNICATION WITH PATIENTS (part1) (2003).

46. JCAHO Standard RI.1.2.2.

47. *Id.*

48. *See* National Patient Safety Foundation, *Talking to Patients about Health Care Injury: Statement of Principle* (2000).

49. American Medical Association, AMA Code of Ethics, A-02 Edition, E-8.00, Opinions on Practice Matters, www.ama-assn.org/apps/pf_new/pf_online?category=CEJA&assn=AMA&f_n=mSearch&s_t=&st_p=&nth=1&.

50. THE AMERICAN COLLEGE OF PHYSICIANS-AMERICAN SOCIETY OF INTERNAL MEDICINE, ETHICS MANUAL, (5th Edition), www.acponline.org/ethics/ethicman5th. htm.

51. DEPARTMENT OF VETERANS AFFAIRS, DISCLOSURE OF ADVERSE EVENTS TO PATIENTS, VHA DIRECTIVE 2005-049, (Oct. 27, 2005), www1.va.gov/vhapublications/ViewPublication.asp?pub_ID=1339. *See also* Appendix K.

52. *Id.*

53. *Id.*

54. NEV. REV. STAT. § 439.835.

55. 40 PA. CONS. STAT. ANN. § 1303.308.

56. N.J. STAT. ANN. § 26:2H-12.25.

57. TENN. CODE ANN. § 68-11-211.

58. WASH. REV. CODE § 70.41.380.

59. S.C. CODE ANN. §61-91-601.

60. MD. CODE REGS. § 10.07.06.11.

61. VT. STAT. ANN. tit. 18, § 43A:1915.

62. FLA. STAT. ANN. § 395.1051

63. *Id.*

64. MONOGRAPH, DISCLOSURE OF UNANTICIPATED EVENTS; CREATING AN EFFECTIVE PATIENT COMMUNICATION POLICY (PT. 2), AMERICAN SOCIETY FOR HEALTHCARE RISK MANAGEMENT (November 2003); MONOGRAPH, WHEN THINGS GO WRONG: RESPONDING TO ADVERSE EVENTS, A CONSENSUS STATEMENT OF THE HARVARD HOSPITALS. HARVARD HOSPITALS, MASSACHUSETTS COALITION FOR THE PREVENTION OF MEDICAL ERRORS (2006).

65. *See* Appendix L for a suggested disclosure process algorithm.

66. *See* Appendix M for suggested elements of a disclosure procedure and a checklist for the disclosure process, as well as Appendix N for a sample disclosure policy.

67. *Id.*

68. JOINT COMMISSION ON ACCREDITATION OF HEALTHCARE ORGANIZATIONS, REVISIONS TO JOINT COMMISSION STANDARDS IN SUPPORT OF PATIENT SAFETY AND MEDICAL/HEALTH CARE ERROR REDUCTION (JCAHO 2002).

69. JCAHO Standard LD 4.4.4.

70. JCAHO Standards HR 4 and HR 4.2.

71. J. REASON, MANAGING THE RISKS OF ORGANIZATIONAL ACCIDENTS (Ashgate Publishing Ltd. 1997).

72. REVISIONS TO JOINT COMMISSION STANDARDS IN SUPPORT OF PATIENT SAFETY AND MEDICAL/HEALTH CARE ERROR REDUCTION (JCAHO 2002).

73. *See generally* D. MARX, PATIENT SAFETY AND THE "JUST CULTURE": A PRIMER FOR HEALTH CARE EXECUTIVES (Columbia University 2001); J. REASON, MANAGING THE RISKS OF ORGANIZATIONAL ACCIDENTS (Ashgate Publishing Ltd. 1997). *See also* Appendix O for a sample disclosure of unanticipated events and outcomes policy, as well as Appendix P for a culpability matrix flowchart. Knowledge-based errors are diagnostic errors where flaws exist in problem solving or decision making. Rule-based errors occur when the individual does not fully understand or apply a correct procedure, or applies the correct procedure in the wrong circumstance. Skill-based errors involve improper execution of a task due to an inadvertent slip, inattention, or some other unintentional omission.

APPENDIX A

Patient Safety and Quality Improvement Act of 2005

119 STAT. 424 PUBLIC LAW 109–41–JULY 29, 2005
Public Law 109–41
109th Congress

An Act

July 29, 2005
[S. 544]

To amend title IX of the Public Health Service Act to provide for the improvement of patient safety and to reduce the incidence of events that adversely effect patient safety.

Patient Safety And Quality

Improvement Act of 2005.

Be it enacted by the Senate and House of Representatives of the United States of America in Congress assembled,

SECTION 1. SHORT TITLE; TABLE OF CONTENTS.

(a) SHORT TITLE.—This Act may be cited as the "Patient Safety and Quality Improvement Act of 2005".

(b) TABLE OF CONTENTS.—The table of contents for this Act is as follows:

SEC. 2. AMENDMENTS TO PUBLIC HEALTH SERVICE ACT.

(a) IN GENERAL.—Title IX of the Public Health Service Act (42 U.S.C. 299 et seq.) is amended—

42 USC 299b-1.

(1) in section 912(c), by inserting, "in accordance with part C," after "The Director shall";

(2) by redesignating part C as part D;

42 USC
299c—299c-7.

(3) by redesignating sections 921 through 928, as sections 931 through 938, respectively;

42 USC 299C-7.

(4) in section 938(1) (as so redesignated), by striking "921"and inserting "931"; and

(5) by inserting after part B the following:

PART C—PATIENT SAFETY IMPROVEMENT "SEC.

42 USC 299B-21 **921. DEFINITIONS.**

In this part:

(1) HIPAA CONFIDENTIALITY REGULATIONS.—The term "HIPAA confidentiality regulations" means regulations promulgated under section 264(c) of the Health Insurance Portability and Accountability Act of 1996 (Public Law 104–191; 110 Stat. 2033).

(2) IDENTIFIABLE PATIENT SAFETY WORK PRODUCT.—The term 'identifiable patient safety work product' means patient safety work product that—

(A) is presented in a form and manner that allows the identification of any provider that is a subject of the work product, or any providers that participate in activities that are a subject of the work product;

(B) constitutes individually identifiable health information as that term is defined in the HIPAA confidentiality regulations; or

(C) is presented in a form and manner that allows the identification of an individual who reported information in the manner specified in section 922(e).

(3) NONIDENTIFIABLE PATIENT SAFETY WORK PRODUCT.—The term 'nonidentifiable patient safety work product' means patient safety work product that is not identifiable patient safety work product (as defined in paragraph (2)).

(4) PATIENT SAFETY ORGANIZATION.—The term 'patient safety organization' means a private or public entity or component thereof that is listed by the Secretary pursuant to section 924(d).

(5) PATIENT SAFETY ACTIVITIES.—The term 'patient safety activities' means the following activities:

(A) Efforts to improve patient safety and the quality of health care delivery.

(B) The collection and analysis of patient safety work product.

(C) The development and dissemination of information with respect to improving patient safety, such as recommendations, protocols, or information regarding best practices.

(D) The utilization of patient safety work product for the purposes of encouraging a culture of safety and of providing feedback and assistance to effectively minimize patient risk.

(E) The maintenance of procedures to preserve confidentiality with respect to patient safety work product.

(F) The provision of appropriate security measures with respect to patient safety work product.

(G) The utilization of qualified staff.

(H) Activities related to the operation of a patient safety evaluation system and to the provision of feedback to participants in a patient safety evaluation system.

(6) PATIENT SAFETY EVALUATION SYSTEM.—The term 'patient safety evaluation system' means the collection, management, or analysis of information for reporting to or by a patient safety organization.

(7) PATIENT SAFETY WORK PRODUCT.—

(A) IN GENERAL.—Except as provided in subparagraph (B), the term 'patient safety work product' means any data, reports, records, memoranda, analyses (such as root cause analyses), or written or oral statements—

(i) which—

(I) are assembled or developed by a provider for reporting to a patient safety organization and are reported to a patient safety organization; or

(II) are developed by a patient safety organization for the conduct of patient safety activities; and which could result in improved patient safety, health care quality, or health care outcomes; or

(ii) which identify or constitute the deliberations or analysis of, or identify the fact of reporting pursuant to, a patient safety evaluation system.

(B) CLARIFICATION.—

(i) Information described in subparagraph (A) does not include a patient's medical record, billing and discharge information, or any other original patient or provider record.

(ii) Information described in subparagraph (A) does not include information that is collected, maintained, or developed separately, or exists separately, from a patient safety evaluation system. Such separate information or a copy thereof reported to a patient safety organization shall not by reason of its reporting be considered patient safety work product.

(iii) Nothing in this part shall be construed to limit—

(I) the discovery of or admissibility of information described in this subparagraph in a criminal, civil, or administrative proceeding;

(II) the reporting of information described in this subparagraph to a Federal, State, or local governmental agency for public health surveillance, investigation, or other public health purposes or health oversight purposes; or

(III) a provider's recordkeeping obligation with respect to information described in this subparagraph under Federal, State, or local law.

(8) PROVIDER.—The term 'provider' means—

(A) an individual or entity licensed or otherwise authorized under State law to provide health care services, including—

(i) a hospital, nursing facility, comprehensive outpatient rehabilitation facility, home health agency, hospice program, renal dialysis facility, ambulatory surgical center, pharmacy, physician or health care practitioner's office, long term care facility, behavior health residential treatment facility, clinical laboratory, or health center; or

(ii) a physician, physician assistant, nurse practitioner, clinical nurse specialist, certified registered nurse anesthetist, certified nurse midwife, psychologist, certified social worker, registered dietitian or nutrition professional, physical or occupational therapist, pharmacist, or other individual health care practitioner; or

(B) any other individual or entity specified in regulations promulgated by the Secretary.

SEC. 922. PRIVILEGE AND CONFIDENTIALITY PRORECTIONS

(a) PRIVILEGE.—Notwithstanding any other provision of Federal, State, or local law, and subject to subsection (c), patient safety work product shall be privileged and shall not be—

(1) subject to a Federal, State, or local civil, criminal, or administrative subpoena or order, including in a Federal, State, or local civil or administrative disciplinary proceeding against a provider;

(2) subject to discovery in connection with a Federal, State, or local civil, criminal, or administrative proceeding, including in a Federal, State, or local civil or administrative disciplinary proceeding against a provider;

(3) subject to disclosure pursuant to section 552 of title 5, United States Code (commonly known as the Freedom of Information Act) or any other similar Federal, State, or local law;

(4) admitted as evidence in any Federal, State, or local governmental civil proceeding, criminal proceeding, administrative rulemaking proceeding, or administrative adjudicatory proceeding, including any such proceeding against a provider; or

(5) admitted in a professional disciplinary proceeding of a professional disciplinary body established or specifically authorized under State law.

(b) CONFIDENTIALITY OF PATIENT SAFETY WORK PRODUCT.—

Notwithstanding any other provision of Federal, State, or local law, and subject to subsection (c), patient safety work product shall be confidential and shall not be disclosed.

(c) EXCEPTIONS.—Except as provided in subsection (g)(3)—

(1) EXCEPTIONS FROM PRIVILEGE AND CONFIDENTIALITY.— Subsections (a) and (b) shall not apply to (and shall not be construed to prohibit) one or more of the following disclosures:

(A) Disclosure of relevant patient safety work product for use in a criminal proceeding, but only after a court makes an in camera determination that such patient safety work product contains evidence of a criminal act and that such patient safety work product is material to the proceeding and not reasonably available from any other source.

(B) Disclosure of patient safety work product to the extent required to carry out subsection (f)(4)(A).

(C) Disclosure of identifiable patient safety work product if authorized by each provider identified in such work product.

(2) EXCEPTIONS FROM CONFIDENTIALITY.—Subsection (b) shall not apply to (and shall not be construed to prohibit) one or more of the following disclosures:

(A) Disclosure of patient safety work product to carry out patient safety activities.

(B) Disclosure of nonidentifiable patient safety work product.

(C) Disclosure of patient safety work product to grantees, contractors, or other entities carrying out research, evaluation, or demonstration projects authorized, funded, certified, or otherwise sanctioned by rule or other means by the Secretary, for the purpose of conducting research to the extent that disclosure of protected health information would be allowed for such purpose under the HIPAA confidentiality regulations.

(D) Disclosure by a provider to the Food and Drug Administration with respect to a product or activity regulated by the Food and Drug Administration.

(E) Voluntary disclosure of patient safety work product by a provider to an accrediting body that accredits that provider.

(F) Disclosures that the Secretary may determine, by rule or other means, are necessary for business operations and are consistent with the goals of this part.

(G) Disclosure of patient safety work product to law enforcement authorities relating to the commission of a crime (or to an event reasonably believed to be a crime) if the person making the disclosure believes, reasonably under the circumstances, that the patient safety work product that is disclosed is necessary for criminal law enforcement purposes.

(H) With respect to a person other than a patient safety organization, the disclosure of patient safety work product that does not include materials that—

    (i) assess the quality of care of an identifiable provider; or

    (ii) describe or pertain to one or more actions or failures to act by an identifiable provider.

(3) EXCEPTION FROM PRIVILEGE.—Subsection (a) shall not apply to (and shall not be construed to prohibit) voluntary disclosure of nonidentifiable patient safety work product.

(d) CONTINUED PROTECTION OF INFORMATION AFTER DISCLOSURE.—

(1) In general.—Patient safety work product that is disclosed under subsection (c) shall continue to be privileged and confidential as provided for in subsections (a) and (b), and such disclosure shall not be treated as a waiver of privilege or confidentiality, and the privileged and confidential nature of such work product shall also apply to such work product in the possession or control of a person to whom such work product was disclosed.

(2) EXCEPTION.—Notwithstanding paragraph (1), and subject to paragraph (3)—

(A) if patient safety work product is disclosed in a criminal proceeding, the confidentiality protections provided for in subsection (b) shall no longer apply to the work product so disclosed; and

(B) if patient safety work product is disclosed as provided for in subsection (c)(2)(B) (relating to disclosure of nonidentifiable patient safety work product), the privilege and confidentiality protections provided for in subsections (a) and (b) shall no longer apply to such work product.

(3) Construction.—Paragraph (2) shall not be construed as terminating or limiting the privilege or confidentiality protections provided for in subsection (a) or (b) with respect to patient safety work product other than the specific patient safety work product disclosed as provided for in subsection (c).

(4) LIMITATIONS ON ACTIONS.—

(A) Patient safety organizations.—

(i) IN GENERAL.—A patient safety organization shall not be compelled to disclose information collected or developed under this part whether or not such information is patient safety work product unless such information is identified, is not patient safety work product, and is not reasonably available from another source.

(ii) NONAPPLICATION.—The limitation contained in clause (i) shall not apply in an action against a patient safety organization or with respect to disclosures pursuant to subsection (c)(1).

(B) Providers.—An accrediting body shall not take an accrediting action against a provider based on the good faith participation of the provider in the collection, development, reporting, or maintenance of patient safety work product in accordance with this part. An accrediting body may not require a provider to reveal its communications with any patient safety organization established in accordance with this part.

(e) REPORTER PROTECTION.—

(1) IN GENERAL.—A provider may not take an adverse employment action, as described in paragraph (2), against an individual based upon the fact that the individual in good faith reported information—

(A) to the provider with the intention of having the information reported to a patient safety organization; or

(B) directly to a patient safety organization.

(2) Adverse Employment Action.—For purposes of this subsection, an 'adverse employment action' includes—

(A) loss of employment, the failure to promote an individual, or the failure to provide any other employment-related benefit for which the individual would otherwise be eligible; or

(B) an adverse evaluation or decision made in relation to accreditation, certification, credentialing, or licensing of the individual.

(f) ENFORCEMENT.—

(1) Civil Monetary Penalty.—Subject to paragraphs (2) and (3), a person who discloses identifiable patient safety work product in knowing or reckless violation of subsection (b) shall be subject to a civil monetary penalty of not more than $10,000 for each act constituting such violation.

(2) Procedure.—The provisions of section 1128A of the Social Security Act, other than subsections (a) and (b) and the first sentence of subsection (c)(1), shall apply to civil money penalties under this subsection in the same manner as such provisions apply to a penalty or proceeding under section 1128A of the Social Security Act.

(3) Relation to hipaa.—Penalties shall not be imposed both under this subsection and under the regulations issued pursuant to section 264(c)(1) of the Health Insurance Portability and Accountability Act of 1996 (42 U.S.C. 1320d-2 note) for a single act or omission.

(4) Equitable Relief.—

(A) In General.—Without limiting remedies available to other parties, a civil action may be brought by any aggrieved individual to enjoin any act or practice that violates subsection (e) and to obtain other appropriate equitable relief (including reinstatement, back pay, and restoration of benefits) to redress such violation.

(B) Against State Employees.—An entity that is a State or an agency of a State government may not assert the privilege described in subsection (a) unless before the time of the assertion, the entity or, in the case of and with respect to an agency, the State has consented to be subject to an action described in subparagraph (A), and that consent has remained in effect.

(g) Rule Of Construction.—Nothing in this section shall be construed—

(1) to limit the application of other Federal, State, or local laws that provide greater privilege or confidentiality protections than the privilege and confidentiality protections provided for in this section;

(2) to limit, alter, or affect the requirements of Federal, State, or local law pertaining to information that is not privileged or confidential under this section;

(3) except as provided in subsection (i), to alter or affect the implementation of any provision of the HIPAA confidentiality regulations or section 1176 of the Social Security Act (or regulations promulgated under such section);

(4) to limit the authority of any provider, patient safety organization, or other entity to enter into a contract requiring greater confidentiality or delegating authority to make a disclosure or use in accordance with this section;

(5) as preempting or otherwise affecting any State law requiring a provider to report information that is not patient safety work product; or

(6) to limit, alter, or affect any requirement for reporting to the Food and Drug Administration information regarding the safety of a product or activity regulated by the Food and Drug Administration.

(h) Clarification.—Nothing in this part prohibits any person from conducting additional analysis for any purpose regardless of whether such additional analysis involves issues identical to or similar to those for which information was reported to or assessed by a patient safety organization or a patient safety evaluation system.

(i) Clarification Of Application Of Hipaa Confidentiality Regulations To Patient Safety Organizations.— For purposes of applying the HIPAA confidentiality regulations—

(1) patient safety organizations shall be treated as business associates; and

(2) patient safety activities of such organizations in relation to a provider are deemed to be health care

operations (as defined in such regulations) of the provider.

(j) REPORTS ON STRATEGIES TO IMPROVE PATIENT SAFETY.—

(1) Draft Report.—Not later than the date that is 18 months after any network of patient safety databases is operational, the Secretary, in consultation with the Director, shall prepare a draft report on effective strategies for reducing medical errors and increasing patient safety. The draft report shall include any measure determined appropriate by the Secretary to encourage the appropriate use of such strategies, including make the draft report available for public comment and submit the draft report to the Institute of Medicine for review.

Public Information.

(2) Final Report.—Not later than 1 year after the date described in paragraph (1), the Secretary shall submit a final report to the Congress.

SEC. 923. NETWORK OF PATIENT SAFETY DATABASES.

2 USC 299b-23.

(a) IN GENERAL.—The Secretary shall facilitate the creation of, and maintain, a network of patient safety databases that provides an interactive evidence-based management resource for providers, patient safety organizations, and other entities. The network of databases shall have the capacity to accept, aggregate across the network, and analyze nonidentifiable patient safety work product voluntarily reported by patient safety organizations, providers, or other entities. The Secretary shall assess the feasibility of providing for a single point of access to the network for qualified researchers for information aggregated across the network and, if feasible, provide for implementation.

(b) DATA STANDARDS.—The Secretary may determine common formats for the reporting to and among the network of patient safety databases maintained under subsection (a) of nonidentifiable patient safety work product, including necessary work product elements, common and consistent definitions, and a standardized computer interface for the processing of such work product. To the extent practicable, such standards shall be consistent with the administrative   simplification provisions of part C of title XI of the Social Security Act.

(c) USE OF INFORMATION.—Information reported to and among the network of patient safety databases under subsection (a) shall be used to analyze national and regional statistics, including trends and patterns of health care errors. The information resulting from Public such analyses shall be made available to the public and included information. in the annual quality reports prepared under section 913(b)(2).

Public
Information.

42 USC 299b–24.

"SEC. 924. PATIENT SAFETY ORGANIZATION CERTIFICATION AND LISTING.

(a) CERTIFICATION.—

(1) Nitial Certification.—An entity that seeks to be a patient safety organization shall submit an initial certification to the Secretary that the entity—

(A) has policies and procedures in place to perform each of the patient safety activities described in section 921(5); and

(B) upon being listed under subsection (d), will comply with the criteria described in subsection (b).

Deadlines.

(2) Subsequent Certifications.—An entity that is a patient safety organization shall submit every 3 years after the date of its initial listing under subsection (d) a subsequent certification to the Secretary that the entity—

(A) is performing each of the patient safety activities described in section 921(5); and

(B) is complying with the criteria described in subsection (b).

(b) CRITERIA.—

'(1) In General.—The following are criteria for the initial and subsequent certification of an entity as a patient safety organization:

(A) The mission and primary activity of the entity are to conduct activities that are to improve patient safety and the quality of health care delivery.

(B) The entity has appropriately qualified staff (whether directly or through contract), including licensed or certified medical professionals.

(C) The entity, within each 24-month period that begins after the date of the initial listing under subsection

(d), has bona fide contracts, each of a reasonable period of time, with more than 1 provider for the purpose of receiving and reviewing patient safety work product.

(D) The entity is not, and is not a component of, a health insurance issuer (as defined in section 2791(b)(2)).

(E) The entity shall fully disclose—

(i) any financial, reporting, or contractual relationship between the entity and any provider that contracts with the entity; and

(ii) if applicable, the fact that the entity is not managed, controlled, and operated independently from any provider that contracts with the entity.

(F) To the extent practical and appropriate, the entity collects patient safety work product from providers in a standardized manner that permits valid comparisons of similar cases among similar providers.

(G) The utilization of patient safety work product for the purpose of providing direct feedback and assistance to providers to effectively minimize patient risk.

(2) Additional Criteria For Component Organizations.— If an entity that seeks to be a patient safety organization is a component of another organization, the following are additional criteria for the initial and subsequent certification of the entity as a patient safety organization:

(A) The entity maintains patient safety work product separately from the rest of the organization, and establishes appropriate security measures to maintain the confidentiality of the patient safety work product.

(B) The entity does not make an unauthorized disclosure under this part of patient safety work product to the rest of the organization in breach of confidentiality.

(C) The mission of the entity does not create a conflict of interest with the rest of the organization.

(c) REVIEW OF CERTIFICATION.—

(1) In General.—

(A) Initial Certification.—Upon the submission by an entity of an initial certification under subsection (a)(1), the Secretary shall determine if the certification meets the requirements of subparagraphs (A) and (B) of such subsection.

(B) Subsequent Certification.—Upon the submission by an entity of a subsequent certification under subsection (a)(2), the Secretary shall review the certification with respect to requirements of subparagraphs (A) and (B) of such subsection.

(2) Notice of Acceptance or Non-acceptance.—If the Secretary determines that—

(A) an entity's initial certification meets requirements referred to in paragraph (1)(A), the Secretary shall notify the entity of the acceptance of such certification; or

(B) an entity's initial certification does not meet such requirements, the Secretary shall notify the entity that such certification is not accepted and the reasons therefor.

(3) Disclosures Regarding Relationship to Providers.—The Secretary shall consider any disclosures under subsection (b)(1)(E) by an entity and shall make public findings on whether the entity can fairly and accurately perform the patient safety activities of a patient safety organization. The Secretary shall take those findings into consideration in determining whether to accept the entity's initial certification and any subsequent certification submitted under subsection (a) and, based on those findings, may deny, condition, or revoke acceptance of the entity's certification.

(d) LISTING.—The Secretary shall compile and maintain a listing of entities with respect to which there is an acceptance of a certification pursuant to subsection (c)(2)(A) that has not been revoked under subsection (e) or voluntarily relinquished.

(e) REVOCATION OF ACCEPTANCE OF CERTIFICATION.—

(1) In General.—If, after notice of deficiency, an opportunity for a hearing, and a reasonable opportunity for correction, the Secretary determines that a patient safety organization does not meet the certification requirements under subsection (a)(2), including subparagraphs (A) and (B) of such subsection, the Secretary shall revoke the Secretary's acceptance of the certification of such organization.

(2) Supplying Confirmation Of Notification To Providers.—Within 15 days of a revocation under paragraph (1), a patient safety organization shall submit to the Secretary a confirmation that the organization has taken all reasonable actions to notify each provider whose patient safety work product is collected or analyzed by the organization of such revocation. *Deadlines.*

(3) Publication of Decision.—If the Secretary revokes the certification of an organization under paragraph (1), the Secretary shall—

(A) remove the organization from the listing maintained under subsection (d); and

(B) publish notice of the revocation in the Federal Register. *Federal Register, publication.*

(f) STATUS OF DATA AFTER REMOVAL FROM LISTING.—

(1) New data.—With respect to the privilege and confidentiality protections described in section 922, data submitted to an entity within 30 days after the entity is removed from the listing under subsection (e)(3)(A) shall have the same status as data submitted while the entity was still listed.

(2) Protection to continue to Apply.—If the privilege and confidentiality protections described in section 922 applied to patient safety work product while an entity was listed, or to data described in paragraph (1), such protections shall continue to apply to such work product or data after the entity is removed from the listing under subsection (e)(3)(A).

(g) DISPOSITION OF WORK PRODUCT AND DATA.—If the Secretary removes a patient safety organization from the listing as provided for in subsection (e)(3)(A), with respect to the patient safety work product or data described in subsection (f)(1) that the patient safety organization received from another entity, such former patient safety organization shall—

(1) with the approval of the other entity and a patient safety organization, transfer such work product or data to such patient safety organization;

(2) return such work product or data to the entity that submitted the work product or data; or

(3) if returning such work product or data to such entity is not practicable, destroy such work product or data.

42 USC 299b–25.

SEC. 925. TECHNICAL ASSISTANCE.

"The Secretary, acting through the Director, may provide technical assistance to patient safety organizations, including convening annual meetings for patient safety organizations to discuss methodology, communication, data collection, or privacy concerns.

42 USC 299b–26.

SEC. 926. SEVERABILITY.

"If any provision of this part is held to be unconstitutional, the remainder of this part shall not be affected."

(b) AUTHORIZATION OF APPROPRIATIONS.—Section 937 of the 42 USC 299c–6. Public Health Service Act (as redesignated by subsection (a)) is amended by adding at the end the following:

(e) PATIENT SAFETY AND QUALITY IMPROVEMENT.—For the purpose of carrying out part C, there are authorized to be appropriated such sums as may be necessary for each of the fiscal years 2006 through 2010."

(c) GAO STUDY ON IMPLEMENTATION.—

(1) Study.—The Comptroller General of the United States shall conduct a study on the effectiveness of part C of title IX of the Public Health Service Act (as added by subsection (a)) in accomplishing the purposes of such part.

(2) Report.—Not later than February 1, 2010, the Comptroller General shall submit a report on the

study conducted under paragraph (1). Such report shall include such recommendations for changes in such part as the Comptroller General deems appropriate.

Approved July 29, 2005.

LEGISLATIVE HISTORY—S. 544 (H.R. 3205):
HOUSE REPORTS: No. 109–197 accompanying H.R. 3205 (Comm. on Energy and Commerce).
CONGRESSIONAL RECORD, Vol. 151 (2005):
    July 21, considered and passed Senate.
    July 27, considered and passed House.
WEEKLY COMPILATION OF PRESIDENTIAL DOCUMENTS, Vol. 41 (2005):
    July 29, Presidential remarks.

Tuesday,
February 12, 2008

PART II

Department of Health and Human Services

42 CFR Part 3
Patient Safety and Quality
Improvement;
Proposed Rule

DEPARTMENT OF HEALTH AND HUMAN SERVICES 42 CFR Part 3
RIN 0919–AA01
Patient Safety and Quality Improvement
AGENCY: Agency for Healthcare Research and Quality, Office for Civil Rights, HHS.
ACTION: Notice of proposed rulemaking.
SUMMARY: This document proposes regulations to implement certain aspects of the Patient Safety and Quality Improvement Act of 2005 (Patient Safety Act). The proposed regulations establish a framework by which hospitals, doctors, and other health care providers may voluntarily report information to Patient Safety Organizations (PSOs), on a privileged and confidential basis, for analysis of patient safety events. The proposed regulations also outline the requirements that entities must meet to become PSOs and the processes for the Secretary to review and accept certifications and to list PSOs. In addition, the proposed regulation establishes the confidentiality protections for the information that is assembled and developed by providers and PSOs, termed "patient safety work product" by the Patient Safety Act, and the procedures for the imposition of civil money penalties for the knowing or reckless impermissible disclosure of patient safety work product.
DATES: Comments on the proposed rule will be considered if we receive them

at the appropriate address, as provided below, no later than April 14, 2008.
ADDRESSES: Interested persons are invited to submit written comments by any of the following methods:
   Federal eRulemaking Portal: http://www.regulations.gov. Comments should include agency name and "RIN 0919–AA01".
   Mail: Center for Quality Improvement and Patient Safety, Attention: Patient Safety Act NPRM Comments, AHRQ, 540 Gaither Road, Rockville, MD 20850.
   Hand Delivery/Courier: Center for Quality Improvement and Patient Safety, Attention: Patient Safety Act NPRM Comments, Agency for Healthcare Research and Quality, 540 Gaither Road, Rockville, MD 20850.
   Instructions: Because of staff and resource limitations, we cannot accept comments by facsimile (FAX) transmission or electronic mail. For detailed instructions on submitting comments and additional information on the rulemaking process, see the "Public Participation" heading of the **SUPPLEMENTARY INFORMATION** section of this document. Comments will be available for public inspection at the AHRQ Information Resources Center at the above-cited address between 8:30 a.m. and 5 p.m. Eastern Time on federal business days (Monday through Friday).
FOR FURTHER INFORMATION CONTACT:
Susan Grinder, Agency for Healthcare Research and

Quality, 540 Gaither Road, Rockville, MD 20850, (301) 427–1111 or (866) 403-3697.
SUPPLEMENTARY INFORMATION:
Public Participation
We welcome comments from the public on all issues set forth in this proposed rule to assist us in fully considering issues and developing policies. You can assist us by referencing the RIN number (RIN: 0919-0AA01) and by preceding your discussion of any particular provision with a citation to the section of the proposed rule being discussed.

A. Inspection of Public Comments

All comments (electronic, mail, and hand delivery/courier) received in a timely manner will be available for public inspection as they are received, generally beginning approximately 6 weeks after publication of this document, at the mail address provided above, Monday through Friday of each week from 8:30 a.m. to 5 p.m. To schedule an appointment to view public comments, call Susan Grinder, (301) 427–1111 or (866) 403-3697. Comments submitted electronically will be available for viewing at the Federal eRulemaking Portal.

B. Electronic Comments

We will consider all electronic comments that include the full name, postal address, and affiliation (if applicable) of the sender and are submitted through the Federal eRulemaking Portal identified in the **ADDRESSES** section of this preamble. Copies of electronically submitted comments will be available for public inspection as soon as practicable at the address provided, and subject to the process described, in the preceding paragraph.

C. Mailed Comments and Hand Delivered/Couriered Comments

Mailed comments may be subject to delivery delays due to security procedures. Please allow sufficient time for mailed comments to be timely received in the event of delivery delays. Comments mailed to the address indicated for hand or courier delivery may be delayed and could be considered late.

D. Copies

To order copies of the **Federal Register** containing this document, send your request to: New Orders, Superintendent of Documents, P.O. Box 371954, Pittsburgh, PA 15250-7954. Specify the date of the issue requested and enclose a check or money order payable to the Superintendent of Documents, or enclose your Visa or Master Card number and expiration date. Credit card orders can also be placed by calling the order desk at (202) 512-1800 (or toll-free at 1-866-512- 1800) or by faxing to (202) 512-2250. The cost for each copy is $10. As an alternative, you may view and photocopy the **Federal Register**

document at most libraries designated as Federal Depository Libraries and at many other public and academic libraries through-out the country that receive the **Federal Register**.

E. Electronic Access

This **Federal Register** document is available from the **Federal Register** online database through GPO Access, a service of the U.S. Government Printing Office. The Web site address is: *http://www.gpoaccess.gov/nara/index.html*. This document is available electronically at the following Web site of the Department of Health and Human Services (HHS): *http://www.ahrq.gov/*.

F. Response to Comments

Because of the large number of public comments we normally receive on **Federal Register** documents, we are not able to acknowledge or respond to them individually. We will consider all comments we receive in accordance with the methods described above and by the date specified in the **DATES** section of this preamble. When we proceed with a final rule, we will respond to comments in the preamble to that rule.

I. Background

A. Purpose and Basis

This proposed rule establishes the authorities, processes, and rules necessary to implement the Patient Safety and Quality

Improvement Act of 2005 (Patient Safety Act), (Pub. L. 109- 41), that amended the Public Health Service Act (42 U.S.C. 299 *et seq.*) by inserting new sections 921 through 926, 42 U.S.C. 299b-21 through 299b-26. Much of the impetus for this legislation can be traced to the publication of the landmark report, "To Err Is Human"[1], by the Institute of Medicine in 1999 (Report). The Report cited studies that found that at least 44,000 people and potentially as many as 98,000 people die in U.S. hospitals each year as a result of preventable medical errors.[2]Based on these studies and others, the Report estimated that the total national costs of preventable adverse events, including lost income, lost household productivity, permanent and temporary disability, and health care costs to be between $17 billion and $29 billion, of which health care costs represent one-half.[3] One of the main conclusions was that the majority of medical errors do not result from individual recklessness or the actions of a particular group; rather, most errors are caused by faulty systems, processes, and conditions that lead people to make mistakes or fail to prevent adverse events.[4] Thus, the Report recommended mistakes can best be

---

1 Institute of Medicine, *"To Err is Human: Building a Safer Health System"*, 1999.
2 *Id.* at 31.
3 *Id.* at 42.
4 *Id.* at 49-66.

prevented by designing the health care system at all levels to improve safety—making it harder to do something wrong and easier to do something right.[5]

As compared to other high-risk industries, the health care system is behind in its attention to ensuring basic safety.[6] The reasons for this lag are complex and varied. Providers are often reluctant to participate in quality review activities for fear of liability, professional sanctions, or injury to their reputations. Traditional state-based legal protections for such health care quality improvement activities, collectively known as peer review protections, are limited in scope: They do not exist in all States; typically they only apply to peer review in hospitals and do not cover other health care settings, and seldom enable health care systems to pool data or share experience between facilities. If peer review protected information is transmitted outside an individual hospital, the peer review privilege for that information is generally considered to be waived. This limits the potential for aggregation of a sufficient number of patient safety events to permit the identification of patterns that could suggest the underlying causes of risks and hazards that then can be used to improve patient safety. The Report outlined a comprehensive strategy to

improve patient safety by which public officials, health care providers, industry, and consumers could reduce preventable medical errors. The Report recommended that, in order to reduce medical errors appreciably in the U.S., a balance be struck between regulatory and market-based initiatives and between the roles of professionals and organizations. It recognized a need to enhance knowledge and tools to improve patient safety and break down legal and cultural barriers that impede such improvement. Drawing upon the broad framework advanced by the Institute of Medicine, the Patient Safety Act specifically addresses a number of these long recognized impediments to improving the quality, safety, and outcomes of health care services. For that reason, implementation of this proposed rule can be expected to accelerate the development of new, voluntary, provider-driven opportunities for improvement, increase the willingness of health care providers to participate in such efforts, and, most notably, set the stage for breakthroughs in our understanding of how best to improve patient safety.

These outcomes will be advanced, in large measure, through implementation of this proposed rule of strong Federal confidentiality and privilege protections for information that is patient safety work product under the Patient Safety Act. For the first time, there will now

be a uniform set of Federal protections that will be available in all states and U.S. territories and that extend to all health care practitioners and institutional providers. These protections will enable all health care providers, including multi-facility health care systems, to share data within a protected legal environment, both within and across states, without the threat of information being used against the subject providers. Pursuant to the Patient Safety Act, this proposed rule will also encourage the formation of new organizations with expertise in patient safety, known as patient safety organizations (PSOs), which can provide confidential, expert advice to health care providers in the analysis of patient safety events.[7] The to

_____

7 As we use the term, patient safety event means an incident that occurred during the delivery of a health care service and that harmed, or could have resulted in harm to, a patient. A patient safety event may include an error of omission or commission, mistake, or malfunction in a patient care process; it may also involve an input to such process (such as a drug or device) or the environment in which such process occurs. Our use of the term patient safety event in place of the more limited concept of medical error to describe the work that providers and PSOs may undertake reflects the evolution in the field of patient safety. It is increasingly recognized that important insights can be derived from the study of patient care processes and their organizational context and environment in order

_____

5 Id.
6 Id. at 75.

confidentiality and privilege protections of this statute attach to "patient safety work product." This term as defined in the Patient Safety Act and this proposed rule means that patient safety information that is collected or developed by a provider and reported to a PSO, or that is developed by a PSO when conducting defined "patient safety activities," or that reveals the deliberations of a provider or PSO within a patient safety evaluation system is protected. Thus, the proposed rule will enable health care providers to protect their internal deliberations and analysis of patient safety information because this type of information is patient safety work product.

The statute and the proposed rule seek to ensure that the confidentiality provisions (as defined in these proposed regulations) will be taken seriously by making breaches of the protections potentially subject to a civil money penalty of up to $10,000. The

combination of strong Federal protections for patient safety work product and the potential penalties for violation of these protections should give providers the assurances they need to participate in patient safety improvement initiatives and should spur the growth of such initiatives.

Patient safety experts have long recognized that the underlying causes of risks and hazards in patient care can best be recognized through the aggregation of significant numbers of individual events; in some cases, it may require the aggregation of thousands of individual patient safety events before underlying patterns are apparent. It is hoped that this proposed rule will foster routine reporting to PSOs of data on patient safety events in sufficient numbers for valid and reliable analyses. Analysis of such large volumes of patient safety events is expected to significantly advance our understanding of the patterns and commonalities in the underlying causes of risks and hazards in the delivery of patient care. These insights should enable providers to more effectively and efficiently target their efforts to improve patient safety.

We recognize that risks and hazards can occur in a variety of environments, such as inpatient, outpatient, long-term care, rehabilitation, research, or other health care settings. In many of these settings, patient safety

analysis is a nascent enterprise that will benefit significantly from the routine, voluntary reporting and analysis of patient safety events. Accordingly, we strive in the proposed rule to avoid imposing limitations that might preclude innovative approaches to the identifica-tion of, and elimination of, risks and hazards in specific settings for the delivery of care, specific health care specialties, or in research settings. We defer to those creating PSOs and the health care providers that enter ongoing relationships with them to determine the scope of patient safety events that will be addressed.

Finally, we note that the statute is quite specific that these protections do not relieve a provider from its obligation to comply with other legal, regulatory, accreditation, licensure, or other accountability requirements that it would otherwise need to meet. The fact that information is collected, developed, or analyzed under the protections of the Patient Safety Act does not shield a provider from needing to undertake similar activities, if applicable, outside the ambit of the statute, so that the provider can meet its obligations with non-patient safety work product. The Patient Safety Act, while precluding other organiza-tions and entities from requiring providers to provide them with patient safety work product, recognizes that the data underlying patient safety

---

prevent harm to patients. We note that patient safety in the context of this term also encompasses the safety of a person who is a subject in a research study conducted by a health care provider. In addition, the flexible concept of a patient safety event is applicable in any setting in which health care is delivered: A health care facility that is mobile (e.g., ambulance), fixed and free-standing (e.g., hospital), attached to another entity (e.g., school clinic), as well as the patient's home or workplace, whether or not a health care provider is physically present.

work product remains available in most instances for the providers to meet these other information requirements.

In summary, this proposed rule implements the Patient Safety Act and facilitates its goals by allowing the health care industry voluntarily to avail itself of this framework in the best manner it determines feasible. At the same time, it seeks to ensure that those who do avail themselves of this framework will be afforded the legal protections that Congress intended and that anyone who breaches those protections will be penalized commensurately with the violation.

B. Listening Sessions

We held three listening sessions for the general public (March 8, 13, and 16, 2006) which helped us better understand the thinking and plans of interested parties, including providers considering the use of PSO services and entities that anticipate establishing PSOs. As stated in the **Federal Register** notice 71 FR 37 (February 24, 2006) that announced the listening sessions, we do not regard the presentations or comments made at these sessions as formal comments and, therefore, they are not discussed in this document.

C. Comment Period

The comment period is sixty (60) days following the publication of the proposed rule.

II. Overview of Proposed Rule

We are proposing a new Part 3 to Title 42 of the Code of Federal Regulations to implement the Patient Safety Act. As described above, the Patient Safety Act is an attempt to address the barriers to patient safety and health care quality improvement activities in the U.S. In implementing the Patient Safety Act, this proposed rule encourages the development of provider-driven, voluntary opportunities for improving patient safety; this initiative is neither funded, nor controlled by the Federal Government.

Under the proposal, a variety of types of organizations— public, private, for-profit, and not-for-profit—can become PSOs, and offer their consultative expertise to providers regarding patient safety events and quality improvement initiatives. There will be a process for certification and listing of PSOs, which will be implemented by the Agency for Healthcare Research and Quality (AHRQ), and providers can work voluntarily with PSOs to obtain confidential, expert advice in analyzing the patient safety event and other information they collect or develop at their offices, facilities, or institutions.

PSOs may also provide feedback and recommendations regarding effective strategies to improve patient safety as well as proven approaches for implementation of such strategies. In addition, to encourage providers to undertake patient safety activities, the regulation is very specific that patient safety work product is subject to confidentiality and privilege protections, and persons that breach the confidentiality provisions may be subject to a $10,000 civil money penalty, to be enforced by the Office for Civil Rights (OCR).

The provisions of this proposed rule greatly expand the potential for participation in patient safety activities.

The proposal, among other things, enables providers across the health care industry to report information to a PSO and obtain the benefit of these new confidentiality and privilege protections.

This proposal minimizes the barriers to entry for listing as a PSO by creating a review process that is both simple and efficient. As a result, we expect a broad range of organizations to seek listing by the Secretary as PSOs. Listing will not entitle these entities to Federal funding or subsidies, but it will enable these PSOs to offer individual and institutional providers the benefits of review and analysis of patient safety work product that is protected by strong Federal confidentiality and privilege protections.

Our proposed regulation will enable and assist data aggregation by PSOs to leverage the possibility of learning from numerous patient safety events across the health care system and to facilitate the identification and correction of systemic and other errors. For example, PSOs are required to seek contracts with multiple providers, and proposed Subpart C permits them, with certain limitations, to aggregate patient safety work product from their multiple clients and with other PSOs. In addition, the Secretary will implement other provisions of the Patient Safety Act that, independent of this proposed rule, require the Secretary to facilitate the development of a network of patient safety databases for the aggregation of nonidentifiable patient safety work product and the development of consistent definitions and common formats for collecting and reporting patient safety work product. These measures will facilitate a new level of data aggregation that patient safety experts deem essential to maximize the benefits of the Patient Safety Act.

The Patient Safety Act gives considerable attention to the relationship between it and the Standards for the Privacy of Individually Identifiable Health Information under the Health Insurance Portability and Accountability Act of 1996 (HIPAA Privacy Rule). We caution that the opportunity for a provider to report identifiable patient safety work product to a PSO does not relieve a provider that is a HIPAA covered entity of its obligations under the HIPAA Privacy Rule. In fact, the Patient Safety Act indicates that PSOs are deemed to be business associates of providers that are HIPAA covered entities. Thus, providers who are HIPAA covered entities will need to enter into business associate agreements with PSOs in accordance with their HIPAA Privacy Rule obligations. If such a provider also chooses to enter a PSO contract, we believe that such contracts could be entered into simultaneously as an agreement for the conduct of patient safety activities. However, the Patient Safety Act does not require a provider to enter a contract with a PSO to receive the protections of the Patient Safety Act. Proposed Subpart A, General Provisions, sets forth the purpose of the provisions and the definitions applicable to the subparts that follow. Proposed Subpart B, PSO Requirements and Agency Procedures, sets forth the requirements for PSOs and describes how the Secretary will review, accept, revoke, and deny certifications for listing and continued listing of entities as PSOs and other required submissions. Proposed Subpart C, Confidentiality and Privilege Protections of Patient Safety Work Product, describes the provisions that relate to the confidentiality protections and permissible disclosure exceptions for patient safety work product. Proposed Subpart D, Enforcement Program, includes provisions that relate to activities for determining compliance, such as investigations of and cooperation by providers, PSOs, and others; the imposition of civil money penalties; and hearing procedures.

III. Section by Section Description of the Proposed Rule

A. Subpart A—General Provision

1. Proposed § 3.10—Purpose The purpose of this proposed Part is to implement the Patient Safety and Quality Improvement Act of 2005 (Pub. L. 109–41), which amended the Public Health Service Act (42 U.S.C. 299 *et seq.*) by inserting new sections 921 through 926, 42 U.S.C. 299b–21 through 299b–26.

2. Proposed § 3.20— Definitions Section 921 of the Public Health Service Act, 42 U.S.C. 299b–21, defines several terms, and our proposed rules would, for the most part, restate the law. In some instances, we propose to clarify definitions to fit within the proposed framework. We also propose some new definitions for convenience and to clarify the application and operation of this proposed rule. Moreover, we reference terms defined under the HIPAA Privacy Rule for ease of interpretation and consistency, given the overlap between the Patient Safety Act protections of patient-identifiable patient safety work product (discussed below) and the HIPAA Privacy Rule. Proposed § 3.20 would establish the basic definitions applicable to this proposed

rule, as follows: *AHRQ* stands for the Agency for Healthcare Research and Quality in the U.S. Department of Health and Human Services (HHS). This definition is added for convenience.

ALJ stands for an Administrative Law Judge at HHS. This definition is added for convenience in describing the process for appealing civil money penalty determinations.

Board would mean the members of the HHS Departmental Appeals Board. This definition is added for convenience in providing for appeals of civil money penalty determinations.

Bona fide contract would mean (a) a written contract between a provider and a PSO that is executed in good faith by officials authorized to execute such contract; or (b) a written agreement (such as a memorandum of understanding or equivalent recording of mutual commitments) between a Federal, State, local, or Tribal provider and a Federal, State, local, or Tribal PSO that is executed in good faith by officials authorized to execute such agreement. In addition to the primary interpretation of an enforceable contract under applicable law as proposed under paragraph (a) of this definition, we propose to make the scope of the term broad enough to encompass agreements between health care providers and PSOs that are components of Federal, State, local or Tribal governments or government agencies. Such entities could clearly perform the same data collection and analytic functions as performed by other providers and PSOs that the Patient Safety Act seeks to foster. Thus, paragraph (b) of the definition recognizes that certain government entities may not enter a formal contract with each other, but may only make a commitment with other agencies through the mechanism of some other type of agreement.

We note that proposed § 3.102(a)(2) incorporates the statutory restriction that a health insurance issuer and a component of a health insurance issuer may not become a PSO. That section also proposes to prohibit the listing of public and private entities that conduct regulatory oversight of health care providers, including accreditation and licensure.

Complainant would mean a person who files a complaint with the Secretary pursuant to proposed § 3.306.

Component Organization would mean an entity that is either: (a) A unit or division of a corporate organization or of a multi-organizational enterprise; or (b) a separate organization, whether incorporated or not, that is owned, managed or controlled by one or more other organizations (i.e., its parent organization(s)). We discuss our preliminary interpretation of the terms "owned," "managed," or "controlled" in the definition of parent organization.

Multi-organizational enterprise, as used here, means a common business or professional undertaking in which multiple entities participate as well as governmental agencies or Tribal entities in which there are multiple components.[8] We anticipate that PSOs may be established by a wide array of health-related organizations and quality improvement enterprises, including hospitals, nursing homes and health care provider systems, health care professional societies, academic and commercial research organizations, Federal, State, local, and Tribal governmental units that are not subject to the proposed restriction on listing in proposed § 3.102(a)(2), as well as joint undertakings by combinations of such organizations. One effect of defining component organization as we propose is that, pursuant to section 924 of the Patient Safety Act, 42 U.S.C. 299b–24, all applicant PSOs that fall within the scope of the definition of component organization must certify to

---

[8] The concept of multi-organizational enterprise as used in this regulation, in case law, and in a legal reference works such as *Blumberg on Corporate Groups*, § 6.04 (2d ed. 2007 Supplement) refers to multi-organizational undertakings with separate corporations or organizations that are integrated in a common business activity. The component entities are often, but not necessarily, characterized by interdependence and some form of common control, typically by agreement. Blumberg notes that health care providers increasingly are integrated in various forms of multi-organizational enterprises.

the separation of confidential patient safety work product and staff from the rest of any organization or multi-organizational enterprise of which they (in the conduct of their work) are a part. Component organizations must also certify that their stated mission can be accomplished without conflicting with the rest of their parent organization(s). A subsidiary corporation may, in certain circumstances, be viewed as part of a multi-organizational enterprise with its parent corporation and would be so regarded under the proposed regulation. Thus, an entity, such as a PSO that is set up as a subsidiary by a hospital chain, would be considered a component of the corporate chain and a component PSO for purposes of this proposed rule. Considering a subsidiary of a corporation to be a "component" of its parent organization may seem contrary to the generally understood separateness of a subsidiary in its corporate relationship with its parent.[9]

That is, where two corporate entities are legally separate, one entity would ordinarily not be considered a component of the other entity, even when that other entity has a controlling interest or exercises some management control. However, we have preliminarily determined that viewing a subsidiary entity that seeks to be a PSO as a component of its parent organization(s) would be consistent with the objectives of the section on certifications required of component organizations in the Patient Safety Act and appears to be consistent with trends in the law discussed below. We invite comment on our interpretation. Corporations law or "entity law," which emphasizes the separateness and distinct

rights and obligations of a corporation, has been supplemented by the development of "relational law" when necessary (e.g., to address evolving organizational arrangements such as multi-organizational enterprises). To determine rights and obligations in these circumstances, courts weigh the relationships of separate corporations that are closely related by virtue of participating in the same enterprise, (i. e., a common chain of economic activity fostering and characterized by interdependence).[10] There has been a growing trend in various court decisions to attribute legal responsibilities based on actual behavior in organizational relationships, rather than on corporate formalities.

We stress that neither the statute nor the proposed regulation imposes any legal responsibilities, obligations, or liability on the organization(s) of which a component PSO is a part. The focus of the Patient Safety Act and the regulation is principally on the entity that voluntarily seeks listing by the Secretary as a PSO. We note that two of the three certifications that the Patient Safety Act and the proposed regulation requires component entities to make—relating to the security and confidentiality of patient safety work product—are essentially duplicative of attestations

---

9 Corporations are certain types of organizations that are given legal independence and rights, (e.g. the right to litigate). Subsidiary corporations are corporations in which a majority of the shares are owned by another corporation, known as a parent corporation. Thus, subsidiaries are independent corporate entities in a formal legal sense, yet, at the same time, they are controlled, to some degree, by their parent by virtue of stock ownership and control. Both corporations and subsidiaries are legal constructs

designed to foster investment and commerce by limiting entrepreneurial risks and corporate liabilities. In recognition of the legitimate utility of these objectives, courts have generally respected the separateness of parent corporations and subsidiaries, (e. g., courts do not ordinarily allow the liabilities of a subsidiary to be attributed to its parent corporation, despite the fact that by definition, parent corporations have a measure of control over a subsidiary). However, courts have looked behind the separate legal identities that separate parent and subsidiary to impose liability when individuals in litigation can establish that actual responsibility rests with a parent corporation by virtue of the degree and manner in which it has exercised control over its subsidiary. Under these circumstances, courts permit "the corporate veil to be pierced."

10 See Phillip I. Blumberg Et Al., Blumberg On Corporate Groups §§ 6.01 and 6.02.

that are required of all entities seeking listing or continued listing as a PSO (certifications made under section 924(a)(1)(A) and (a)(2)(A) of the Public Health Service Act, 42 U.S.C. 299b–24(a)(1)(A) and (a)(2)(A) with respect to patient safety activities described in section 921(5)(E) and (F) of the Public Health Service Act, 42 U.S.C. 299b–21(5)(E) and (F)). That is, under the Patient Safety Act, all PSOs have to attest that they have in place policies and procedures to, and actually do, perform patient safety activities, which include the maintenance of procedures to preserve patient safety work product confidentiality and the provision of appropriate security measures for patient safety work product. The overlapping nature of these confidentiality and security requirements on components suggests heightened congressional concern and emphasis regarding the need to maintain a strong "firewall" between a component PSO and its parent organization, which might have the opportunity and potential to access sensitive patient safety work product the component PSO assembles, develops, and maintains. A similar concern arises in the context of a PSO that is a unit of a corporate parent, a subsidiary or an entity affiliated with other organizations in a multi-organizational enterprise. Requiring entities seeking listing to disclose whether they have a parent organization or are part of a multi-

organizational enterprise does not involve "piercing the corporate veil" as discussed in the footnote above. The Department would not be seeking this information to hold a parent liable for actions of the PSO, but to ensure full disclosure to the Department about the organizational relationships of an entity seeking to be listed as a PSO. Accordingly, we propose that an entity seeking listing as a PSO must do so as a component organization if it has one or more parent organizations (as described here and in the proposed definition of that term) or is part of a multi-organizational enterprise, and it must provide the names of its parent entities. If it has a parent or several parent organizations, as defined by the proposed regulation, the entity seeking to be listed must provide the additional certifications mandated by the statute and by the proposed regulation at § 3.102(c) to maintain the separateness of its patient safety work product from its parent(s) and from other components or affiliates[11] of its parent(s). Such certifications are consistent with the above-cited body of case law that permits and makes

_____

11 Corporate affiliates are commonly controlled corporations; sharing a corporate parent, they are sometimes referred to as sister corporations. Separate corporations that are part of a multi-organizational enterprise are also referred to by the common terms "affiliates" or "affiliated organizations".

inquiries about organizational relationships and practices for purposes of carrying out statutes and statutory objectives. It may be helpful to illustrate how a potential applicant for listing should apply these principles in determining whether to seek listing as a component PSO. The fundamental principle is that if there is a parent organization relationship present and the entity is not prohibited from seeking listing by proposed § 3.102(a)(2), the entity must seek listing as a component PSO. In determining whether an entity must seek listing as a component organization, we note that it does not matter whether the entity is a component of a provider or a nonprovider organization and, if it is a component of a provider organization, whether it will undertake patient safety activities for the parent organization's providers or providers that have no relationship with its parent organization(s). The focus here is primarily on establishing the separateness of the entity's operation from any type of parent organization. Examples of entities that would need to seek listing as a component organization include: A division of a provider or nonprovider organization; a subsidiary entity created by a provider or nonprovider organization; or a joint venture created by several organizations (which could include provider organizations, non-provider organizations, or a mix of such organizations) where any or all of the organizations have a measure of control over the joint venture.

Other examples of entities that would need to seek listing as a component PSO include: a division of a nursing home chain; a subsidiary entity created by a large academic health center or health system; or a joint venture created by several organizations to seek listing as a PSO where any or all of the organizations have a measure of control over the joint venture.

Component PSO would mean a PSO listed by the Secretary that is a component organization.

Confidentiality provisions would mean any requirement or prohibition concerning confidentiality established by Sections 921 and 922(b)–(d), (g) and (i) of the Public Health Service Act, 42 U.S.C. 299b-21 and 299b-22(b)–(d), (g) and (i), and the proposed provisions, at §§ 3.206 and 3.208, by which we propose to implement the prohibition on disclosure of identifiable patient safety work product. We proposed to define this new term to provide an easy way to reference the provisions in the Patient Safety Act and in the proposed rule that implements the confidentiality protections of the Patient Safety Act for use in the enforcement and penalty provisions of this proposed rule. We found this a useful approach in the HIPAA Enforcement Rule, where we defined "administrative simplification provision" for that purpose. In determining

how to define "confidentiality provisions" that could be violated, we considered the statutory enforcement provision at section 922(f) of the Public Health Service Act, 42 U.S.C. 299b-22(f), which incorporates by reference section 922(b) and (c).[12] Thus, the enforcement authority clearly implicates sections 922(b) and (c) of the Patient Safety Act, 42 U.S.C. 299b-22(b) and (c), which are implemented in proposed § 3.206. Section 922(d) of the Patient Safety Act, 42 U.S.C. 299b- 22(d), is entitled the "Continued Protection of Information After Disclosure" and sets forth continued confidentiality protections for patient safety work product after it has

_____

12 Section 922(f) of the Public Health Service Act, 42 U.S.C. 299b-22(f), states that "subject to paragraphs (2) and (3), a person who discloses identifiable patient safety work product in knowing or reckless violation of subsection (b) shall be subject to a civil money penalty of not more than $10,000 for each act constituting such violation" (emphasis added). Subsection (b) of section 922 of the Public Health Service Act, 42 U.S.C. 299b-22(b), is entitled, "Confidentiality of Patient Safety Work Product" and states, "Notwithstanding any other provision of Federal, State, or local law, and subject to subsection (c), patient safety work product shall be confidential and shall not be disclosed" (emphasis added). Section 922(c) of the Public Health Service Act, 42 U.S.C. 299b-22(c), in turn, contains the exceptions to confidentiality and privilege protections.

been disclosed under section 922(c) of the Public Health Service Act, 42 U.S.C. 299b-22(c), with certain exceptions.

Thus, section 922(d) of the Public Health Service Act, 42 U.S.C. 299b- 22(d), is a continuation of the confidentiality protections provided for in section 922(b) of the Public Health Service Act, 42 U.S.C. 299b-22(b).

Therefore, we also consider the continued confidentiality provision at proposed § 3.208 herein to be one of the confidentiality provisions. In addition, our understanding of these provisions is based on the rule of construction in section 922(g) of the Public Health Service Act, 42 U.S.C. 299b-22(g), and the clarification with respect to HIPAA in section 922(i) of the Public Health Service Act, 42 U.S.C. 299b-22(i); accordingly, these provisions are included in the definition.

In contrast to the confidentiality provisions, the privilege provisions in the Patient Safety Act will be enforced by the tribunals or agencies that are subject to them; the Patient Safety Act does not authorize the imposition of civil money penalties for breach of such provisions. We note, however, that to the extent a breach of privilege is also a breach of confidentiality, the Secretary would enforce the confidentiality breach under 42 U.S.C. 299b-22(f).

Disclosure would mean the release, transfer, provision of access to, or divulging in any other manner of patient safety work product by a person holding patient safety work product to another person. An impermissible disclosure (i.e., a disclosure of patient safety work product in violation of the confidentiality provisions) is the action upon which potential liability for a civil money penalty rests. Generally, if the person holding patient safety work product is an entity, disclosure occurs when the information is shared with another entity or a natural person outside the entity. We do not propose to hold entities liable for uses of the information within the entity, (i.e., when this information is exchanged or shared among the workforce members of the entity) except as noted below concerning component PSOs. If a natural person holds patient safety work product, except in the capacity as a workforce member, a disclosure occurs whenever exchange occurs to any other person or entity. In light of this definition, we note that a disclosure to a contractor that is under the direct control of an entity (i. e., a workforce member) would be a use of the information within the entity and, therefore, not a disclosure for which a permission is needed. However, a disclosure to an independent contractor would not be a disclosure to a workforce member, and thus, would be a disclosure for purposes of this proposed rule and the proposed enforcement provisions under Subpart D.

For component PSOs, we propose to recognize as a disclosure the sharing or transfer of patient safety work product outside of the legal entity, as described above, and between the component PSO and the rest of the organization (i.e., parent organization) of which the component PSO is a part. The Patient Safety Act demonstrates a strong desire for the separation of patient safety work product between a component PSO and the rest of the organization. See section 924(b)(2) of the Public Health Service Act, 42 U.S.C. 299b–24(b)(2). Because we propose to recognize component organizations as component PSOs which exist within, but distinct from, a single legal entity, and such a compo-nent organization as a component PSO would be required to certify to limit access to patient safety work product under proposed § 3.102(c), the release, transfer, provision of access to, or divulging in any other manner of patient safety work product from a component PSO to the rest of the organization will be recognized as a disclosure for purposes of this proposed rule and the proposed enforcement provisions under Subpart D. We considered whether or not we should hold entities liable for disclosures that occur within that entity (uses) by defining disclosure more discretely, (i.e., as between persons within an entity). If we were to define disclosure in this manner, it may promote better

safeguarding against inappropriate uses of patient safety work product by providers and PSOs. It may also allow better control of uses by third parties to whom patient safety work product is disclosed, and it would create additional enforcement situations which could lead to additional potential civil money penalties. We note that HIPAA authorized the Department to regulate both the uses and disclosures of individually identifiable health information and, thus, the HIPAA Privacy Rule regulates both the uses and disclosures of such information by HIPAA covered entities. See section 264(b) and (c)(1) of HIPAA, Public Law 104–191. The Patient Safety Act, on the other hand, addresses disclosures and authorizes the Secretary to penalize disclosures of patient safety work product. Nonetheless, we do not propose to regulate the use, transfer or sharing by internal disclosure, of patient safety work product within a legal entity. We also decline to propose to regulate uses because we would consider regulating uses within providers and PSOs to be intrusive into their internal affairs. This would be especially the case given that this is a voluntary program. Moreover, we do not believe that regulating uses would further the statutory goal of facilitating the sharing of patient safety work product with PSOs. In other words, regulating uses would not advance the ability of any entity to share patient safety work product for patient safety activities. Finally, we presume that there are sufficient incentives in place for providers and PSOs to prudently manage the uses of sensitive patient safety work product. We are not regulating uses, whether in a provider, PSO, or any other entity that obtains patient safety work product.

Because we are not proposing to regulate uses, there will be no federal sanction based on use of this information. If a provider or other entity wants to limit the uses or further disclosures (beyond the regulatory permissions) by a PSO or any future recipient, a disclosing entity is free to do so by contract. See section 922(g)(4) of the Public Health Service Act, 42 U.S.C. 299b–22(g)(4), and proposed § 3.206(e). We seek comment about whether this strikes the right balance.

The proposed definition mirrors the definition of disclosure used in the HIPAA Privacy Rule concerning disclosures of protected health information. Although we do not propose to regulate the use of patient safety work product, HIPAA covered entities that possess patient safety work product which contains protected health information must comply with the use and disclosure requirements of the HIPAA Privacy Rule with respect to the protected health information. Patient safety work product containing protected health information could only be used in accordance with the HIPAA Privacy Rule use permissions, including the minimum necessary requirement.

Entity would mean any organization, regardless of whether the organization is public, private, for-profit, or not-forprofit. The statute permits any entity to seek listing as a PSO by the Secretary except a health insurance issuer and any component of a health insurance issuer and § 3.102(a)(2) proposes, in addition, to prohibit public or private sector entities that conduct regulatory oversight of providers.

Group health plan would mean an employee welfare benefit plan (as defined in section 3(1) of the Employee Retirement Income Security Act of 1974 (ERISA) to the extent that the plan provides medical care (as defined in paragraph (2) of section 2791(a) of the Public Health Service Act, 42 U.S.C. 300gg–91(a)(1)) and including items and services paid for as medical care) to employees or their dependents (as defined under the terms of the plan) directly or through insurance, reimbursement, or otherwise. Section 2791(b)(2) of the Public Health Service Act, 42 U.S.C. 300gg–91(b)(2) excludes group health plans from the defined class of 'health insurance issuer.' Therefore, a group health plan may establish a PSO unless the plan could be considered a component of a health insurance issuer, in which case such a plan would be precluded from being a PSO by the Patient Safety Act.

Health insurance issuer would mean an insurance company, insurance service, or insurance organization (including a health maintenance organization, as defined in 42 U.S.C. 300gg–91(b)(3)) which is licensed to engage in the business of insurance in a State and which is subject to State law which regulates insurance (within the meaning of 29 U.S.C. 1144(b)(2)). The term, as defined in the Public Health Service Act, does not include a group health plan.

Health maintenance organization would mean (1) a Federally qualified health maintenance organization (as defined in 42 U.S.C. 300e(a)); (2) an organization recognized under State law as a health maintenance organization; or (3) a similar organization regulated under State law for solvency in the same manner and to the same extent as such a health maintenance organization. Because the ERISA definition relied upon by the Patient Safety Act includes health maintenance organizations in the definition of health insurance issuer, an HMO may not be, control, or manage the operation of a PSO.

HHS stands for the United States Department of Health and Human Services. This definition is added for convenience.

HIPAA Privacy Rule would mean the regulations promulgated under section 264(c) of the Health

Insurance Portability and Accountability Act of 1996 (HIPAA), at 45 CFR Part 160 and Subparts A and E of Part 164.

Identifiable Patient Safety Work Product would mean patient safety work product that: (1) Is presented in a form and manner that allows the identification of any provider that is a subject of the work product, or any providers that participate in activities that are a subject of the work product; (2) Constitutes individually identifiable health information as that term is defined in the HIPAA Privacy Rule at 45 CFR 160.103; or (3) Is presented in a form and manner that allows the identification of an individual who in good faith reported information directly to a PSO, or to a provider with the intention of having the information reported to a PSO ("reporter").

Identifiable patient safety work product is not patient safety work product that meets the nonidentification standards proposed for "nonidentifiable patient safety work product".

Nonidentifiable Patient Safety Work Product would mean patient safety work product that is not identifiable in accordance with the nonidentification standards proposed at § 3.212. Because the privilege and confidentiality protections of the Patient Safety Act and this Part do not apply to nonidentifiable patient safety work product once disclosed, the restrictions and data protection rules in

this proposed rule phrased as pertaining to patient safety work product generally only apply to identifiable patient safety work product.

OCR stands for the Office for Civil Rights in HHS. This definition is added for convenience.

Parent organization would mean a public or private sector organization that, alone or with others, either owns a provider entity or a component PSO, or has the authority to control or manage agenda setting, project management, or day-to-day operations of the component, or the authority to review and override decisions of a component PSO. We have not proposed to define the term "owns." We propose to use the term "own a provider entity" to mean a governmental agency or Tribal entity that controls or manages a provider entity as well as an organization having a controlling interest in a provider entity or a component PSO, for example, owning a majority or more of the stock of the owned entity, and expressly ask for comment on whether our further definition of controlling interest as follows below is appropriate. Under the proposed regulation, if an entity that seeks to be a PSO has a parent organization, that entity will be required to seek listing as a component PSO and must provide certifications set forth in proposed § 3.102(c), which indicate that the entity maintains patient safety work product separately from the rest of the organization(s) and

establishes security measures to maintain the confidentiality of patient safety work product, the entity does not make an unauthorized disclosure of patient safety work product to the rest of the organization(s), and the entity does not create a conflict of interest with the rest of the organization(s). Traditionally, a parent *corporation* is defined as a corporation that holds a controlling interest in one or more subsidiaries. By contrast, parent *organization,* as used in this proposed rule, is a more inclusive term and is not limited to definitions used in corporations law. Accordingly, the proposed definition emphasizes a parent organization's control (or influence) over a PSO that may or may not be based on stock ownership.[13] Our approach to interpreting the statutory reference in section 924(b)(2) of the Patient Safety Act, 42 U.S.C. 299b-24(b)(2) to "another organization" in which an entity is a "component" (i.e., a "parent organization") is analogous to the growing attention in both statutory and case law, to the nature and conduct of business organizational relationships, including multi-organizational enterprises. As

---

13 *Cf.* 17 CFR 240.12b-2 (defining "control" broadly as "* * * the power to direct or cause the direction of the management and policies of an * * * [entity] whether through the ownership of voting securities, by contract, or otherwise.")

discussed above in the definition of "component," the emphasis on actual organizational control, rather than the organization's structure, has numerous legal precedents in legislation implementing statutory programs and objectives and courts upholding such programs and objectives.[14] Therefore, the definition of a "parent organization," as used in the proposed regulation would encompass an affiliated *organization* that participates in a common enterprise with an entity seeking listing, and that owns, manages or exercises control over the entity seeking to be listed as a PSO.

As indicated above, affiliated *corporations* have been legally defined to mean those who share a corporate parent or are part of a common corporate enterprise.[15] Parent

organization is defined to include affiliates primarily in recognition of the prospect that otherwise unrelated organizations might affiliate to jointly establish a PSO. We can foresee such an enterprise because improving patient safety through expert analysis of aggregated patient safety data could logically be a common and efficient objective shared by multiple potential cofounders of a PSO. It is fitting, in our view, that a component entity certify, as we propose in § 3.102(c), that there is "no conflict" between its mission as a PSO and all of the rest of the parent or affiliated organizations that undertake a jointly sponsored PSO enterprise.[16] Similarly, it is also

appropriate that the additional certifications required of component entities in proposed § 3.102(c) regarding separation of patient safety work product and the use of separate staff be required of an entity that has several cofounder parent organizations that exercise ownership, management or control, (i.e. to assure that the intended "firewalls" exist between the component entity and the rest of any affiliated organization that might exercise ownership, management or control over a PSO).

To recap this part of the discussion, we would consider an entity seeking listing as a PSO to have a parent organization, and such entity would seek listing as a component organization, under the following circumstances: (a) The entity is a unit in a corporate organization or a controlling interest in the entity is owned by another corporation; or (b) the entity is a distinct organizational part of a multi-organizational enterprise and one or more affiliates in the enterprise own, manage, or control the entity seeking listing as a PSO. An example of an entity described in (b) would be an entity created by a joint venture in which the entity would be managed or controlled by several cofounding parent organizations.

The definition of provider in the proposed rule (which will be discussed below) includes the parent organization of

---

14 14 *Blumberg on Corporate Groups §13* notes that, where applications for licenses are in a regulated industry, information is required by states about the applicant as well as corporate parents, subsidiaries and affiliates. In the proposed regulation, pursuant to the Patient Safety Act, information about parent organizations with potentially conflicting missions would be obtained to ascertain that component entities seeking to be PSOs have measures in place to protect the confidentiality of patient safety work product and the independent conduct of impartial scientific analyses by PSOs.

15 See for example the definition of affiliates in regulations jointly promulgated by the Comptroller of the Currency, the Federal

Reserve board, the FDIC, and the Office of Thrift Supervision to implement privacy provisions of Gramm Leach Bliley legislation using provisions of the Fair Credit Reporting Act (dealing with information sharing among affiliates): "any company that is related or affiliated by common ownership, or affiliated by corporate control or common corporate control with another company." Blumberg, supra note 2, at § 122.09[A] (citing 12 CFR pt.41.3, 12 CFR pt.222.3(1), 12 CFR pt.334.3(b) and 12 CFR pt.571.3(1) (2004)).

16 We note that the certifications from a jointly established PSO could be supported or substantiated with references to protective procedural or policy walls that have been established to preclude a conflict of these organizations' other missions with the scientific analytic mission of the PSO.

any provider entity. Correspondingly, our definition of parent organization includes any organization that "owns a provider entity." This is designed to provide an option for the holding company of a corporate health care system to enter a multi-facility or system-wide contract with a PSO.

Patient Safety Act would mean the Patient Safety and Quality Improvement Act of 2005 (Pub. L. 109–41), which amended Title IX of the Public Health Service Act (42 U.S.C. 299 *et seq.*) by inserting a new Part C, sections 921 through 926, which are codified at 42 U.S.C. 299b–21 through 299b–26.

Patient safety activities would mean the following activities carried out by or on behalf of a PSO or a provider:
(1) Efforts to improve patient safety and the quality of health care delivery;
(2) The collection and analysis of patient safety work product;
(3) The development and dissemination of information with respect to improving patient safety, such as recommendations, protocols, or information regarding best practices;
(4) The utilization of patient safety work product for the purposes of encouraging a culture of safety and of providing feedback and assistance to effectively minimize patient risk;
(5) The maintenance of procedures to preserve confidentiality with respect to patient safety work product;

(6) The provision of appropriate security measures with respect to patient safety work product;
(7) The utilization of qualified staff; and
(8) Activities related to the operation of a patient safety evaluation system and to the provision of feedback to participants in a patient safety evaluation system. This definition is taken from the Patient Safety Act. See section 921(5) of the Public Health Service Act, 42 U.S.C. 299b–21(5). Patient safety activities is used as a key reference term for other provisions in the proposed rule and those provisions provide descriptions related to patient safety activities. See proposed requirements for PSOs at §§ 3.102 and 3.106 and the proposed confidentiality disclosure permission at § 3.206(b)(4).

Patient safety evaluation system would mean the collection, management, or analysis of information for reporting to or by a PSO. The patient safety evaluation system is a core concept of the Patient Safety Act through which information, including data, reports, memoranda, analyses, and/or written or oral statements, is collected, maintained, analyzed, and communicated. When a provider engages in patient safety activities for the purpose of reporting to a PSO or a PSO engages in these activities with respect to information for patient safety purposes, a patient safety evaluation system exists regardless of whether the provider or PSO has

formally identified a "patient safety evaluation system". For example, when a provider collects information for the purpose of reporting to a PSO and reports the information to a PSO to generate patient safety work product, the provider is collecting and reporting through its patient safety evaluation system (see definition of *patient safety work product*). Although we do not propose to require providers or PSOs formally to identify or define their patient safety evaluation system—because such systems exist by virtue of the providers or PSOs undertaking certain patient safety activities—a patient safety evaluation system can be formally designated by a provider or PSO to establish a secure space in which these activities may take place. The formal identification or designation of a patient safety evaluation system could give structure to the various functions served by a patient safety evaluation system. These possible functions are:
1. For reporting information by a provider to a PSO in order to generate patient safety work product and to protect the fact of reporting such information to a PSO (see section 921(6) and (7)(A)(i)(I) of the Public Health Service Act, 42 U.S.C. 299b–21(6) and (7)(A)(i)(I));
2. For communicating feedback concerning patient safety events between PSOs and providers (see section 921(5)(H) of the Public Health Service Act, 42 U.S.C. 299b–21(5)(H));

3. For creating and identifying the space within which deliberations and analyses of information and patient safety work product are conducted (see section 921(7)(A)(ii) of the Public Health Service Act, 42 U.S.C. 299b–21(7)(A)(ii));

4. For separating patient safety work product and information collected, maintained, or developed for reporting to a PSO distinct and apart from information collected, maintained, or developed for other purposes (see section 921(7)(B)(ii) of the Public Health Service Act, 42 U.S.C. 299b–21(7)(B)(ii)); and, 5. For identifying patient safety work product to maintain its privileged status and confidentiality, and to avoid impermissible disclosures (see section 922(b) of the Public Health Service Act, 42 U.S.C. 299b–22(b)).

A provider or PSO need not engage in all of the above-mentioned functions in order to establish or maintain a patient safety evaluation system. A patient safety evaluation system is flexible and scalable to the individual needs of a provider or PSO and may be modified as necessary to support the activities and level of engagement in the activities by a particular provider or PSO. *Documentation.* Because a patient safety evaluation system is critical in identifying and protecting patient safety work product, we encourage providers and PSOs to document what constitutes their patient safety evaluation system.

We recommend that providers and PSOs consider documenting the following: How information enters the patient safety evaluation system; What processes, activities, physical space(s) and equipment comprise or are used by the patient safety evaluation system; Which personnel or categories of personnel need access to patient safety work product to carry out their duties involving operation of, or interaction with the patient safety evaluation system, and for each such person or category of persons, the category of patient safety work product to which access is needed and any conditions appropriate to such access; and, What procedures or mechanisms the patient safety evaluation system uses to report information to a PSO or disseminate information outside of the patient safety evaluation system.

A documented patient safety evaluation system, as opposed to an undocumented or poorly documented patient safety evaluation system, may accrue many benefits to the operating provider or PSO. Providers or PSOs that have a documented patient safety evaluation system will have substantial proof to support claims of privilege and confidentiality when resisting requests for production of, or subpoenas for, information constituting patient safety work product or when making requests for protective orders against requests or subpoenas for

such patient safety work product. Documentation of a patient safety evaluation system will enable a provider or PSO to provide supportive evidence to a court when claiming privilege protections for patient safety work product. This may be particularly critical since the same activities can be done inside and outside of a patient safety evaluation system.

A documented and established patient safety evaluation system also gives notice to employees of the privileged and confidential nature of the information within a patient safety evaluation system in order to generate awareness, greater care in handling such information and more caution to prevent unintended or impermissible disclosures of patient safety work product. For providers with many employees, an established and documented patient safety evaluation system can serve to separate access to privileged and confidential patient safety work product from employees that have no need for patient safety work product. Documentation can serve to limit access by non-essential employees. By limiting who may access patient safety work product, a provider may reduce its exposure to the risks of inappropriate disclosures. Given all of the benefits, documentation of a patient safety evaluation system would be a prudent business practice. Moreover, as part of our enforcement program, we would expect entities to be following sound business practices in maintaining adequate documentation regarding their patient safety evaluation systems to demonstrate their compliance with the confidentiality provisions. Absent this type of documentation, it may be difficult for entities to satisfy the Secretary that they have met and are in compliance with their confidentiality obligations. While we believe it is a sound and prudent business practice, we have not required a patient safety evaluation system to be documented, and we do not believe it is required by the Patient Safety Act. We seek comment as to these issues.

Patient Safety Organization (PSO) would mean a private or public entity or component thereof that is listed as a PSO by the Secretary in accordance with proposed § 3.102.

Patient Safety Work Product is a defined term in the Patient Safety Act that identifies the information to which the privilege and confidentiality protections apply. This proposed rule imports the statutory definition of patient safety work product specifically for the purpose of implementing the confidentiality protections under the Patient Safety Act. The proposed rule provides that, with certain exceptions, patient safety work product would mean any data, reports, records, memoranda, analyses (such as root cause analyses), or written or oral statements (or copies of any of this material) (A) which could result in improved patient safety,

health care quality, or health care outcomes and either (i) is assembled or developed by a provider for reporting to a PSO and is reported to a PSO; or (ii) is developed by a PSO for the conduct of patient safety activities; or (B) which identifies or constitutes the deliberations or analysis of, or identifies the fact of reporting pursuant to, a patient safety evaluation system. The proposed rule excludes from patient safety work product a patient's original medical record, billing and discharge information, or any other original patient or provider information and any information that is collected, maintained, or developed separately, or exists separately, from a patient safety evaluation system. Such separate information or a copy thereof reported to a PSO does not by reason of its reporting become patient safety work product. The separately collected and maintained information remains available, for example, for public health reporting or disclosures pursuant to court order. The information contained in a provider's or PSO's patient safety evaluation system is protected, would be privileged and confidential, and may not be disclosed absent a statutory or regulatory permission.

What can become patient safety work product. The definition of patient safety work product lists the types of information that are likely to be exchanged between a provider and PSO to

generate patient safety work product:

"Any data, reports, records, memoranda, analyses (such as root cause analyses), or written or oral statements" (collectively referred to below as "information" for brevity). Congress intended the fostering of robust patient safety evaluation systems for exchanges between providers and PSOs. We expect this expansive list will maximize provider flexibility in operating its patient safety evaluation system by enabling the broadest possible incorporation and protection of information by providers and PSOs.

In addition, information must be collected or developed for the purpose of reporting to a PSO. Records collected or developed for a purpose other than for reporting to a PSO, such as to support internal risk management activities or to fulfill external reporting obligations, cannot become patient safety work product. However, copies of information collected for another purpose may become patient safety work product if, for example, the copies are made for the purpose of reporting to a PSO. This issue is discussed more fully below regarding information that cannot become patient safety work product.

When information is reported by a provider to a PSO or when a PSO develops information for patient safety activities, the definition assumes that the protections apply to information that "could result in improved patient safety, health care quality, or health care outcomes." This phrase imposes few practical limits on the type of information that can be protected since a broad range of clinical and nonclinical factors could have a beneficial impact on the safety, quality, or outcomes of patient care. Because the Patient Safety Act does not impose a narrow limitation, such as requiring information to relate solely, for example, to particular adverse or "sentinel" incidents or even to the safety of patient care, we conclude Congress intended providers to be able to cast a broad net in their data gathering and analytic efforts to identify causal factors or relationships that might impact patient safety, quality and outcomes. In addition, we note that the phrase "could result in improved" requires only potential utility, not proven utility, thereby allowing more information to become patient safety work product.

How information becomes patient safety work product. Paragraphs (1)(i)(A), (1)(i)(B), and (1)(ii) of the proposed regulatory definition indicate three ways for information to become patient safety work product and therefore subject to the confidentiality and privilege protections of the Patient Safety Act.

Information assembled or developed and reported by providers. By law and as set forth in our proposal, information that is assembled or developed by a provider for the purpose of reporting to a PSO and is reported to a PSO is patient safety work product. Section 921(7)(A)(i)(I) of the Public Health Service Act, 42 U.S.C. 299b- 21(7)(A)(i)(I).

As noted, to become patient safety work product under this section of the definition, information must be reported by a provider to a PSO. For purposes of paragraph (1)(i)(A) of this definition, "reporting" generally means the actual transmission or transfer of information, as described above, to a PSO. We recognize, however, that requiring the transmission of every piece of paper or electronic file to a PSO could impose significant transmission, management, and storage burdens on providers and PSOs. In many cases, providers engaged in their own investigations may desire to avoid continued transmission of additional related information as its work proceeds.

To alleviate the burden of reporting every piece of information assembled by a provider related to a particular patient safety event, we are interested in public comment regarding an alternative for providers that have established relationships with PSOs. We note that the reporting and generation of patient safety work product does not require a contract or any other relationship for a PSO to receive reports from a provider, for a PSO to examine patient safety work product, or for a PSO to provide feedback to a provider based upon the examination of reported information.

Nonetheless, we anticipate that providers who are committed to patient safety improvements will establish a contractual or similar relationship with a PSO to report and receive feedback about patient safety incidents and adverse events. Such a contract or relationship would provide a basis to allow providers and PSOs to establish customized alternative arrangements for reporting.

For providers that have established contracts with PSOs for the review and receipt of patient safety work product, we seek comment on whether a provider should be able to "report" to the PSO by providing its contracted PSO access to any information it intends to report (i.e., "functional reporting"). For example, a provider and a PSO may establish, by contract, that information put into a database shared by the provider and the PSO is sufficient to report information to the PSO in lieu of the actual transmission requirement. We believe that functional reporting would be a valuable mechanism for the efficient reporting of information from a provider to a PSO. We are seeking public comment about what terms and conditions may be necessary to provide access to a PSO to be recognized as functional reporting. We also seek comment about whether this type of functional reporting arrangement should only be available for subsequent related information once an initial report on a specific topic or incident has been transmitted to a PSO.

We do not intend a PSO to have an unfettered right of access to any provider information. Providers and PSOs are free to engage in alternative reporting arrangements under the proposed rule, and we solicit comments on the appropriate lines to be drawn around the arrangements that should be recognized under the proposed rule.

However, our proposals should not be construed to suggest or propose that a PSO has a superior right to access information held by a provider based upon a reporting relationship. If a PSO believes information reported by a provider is insufficient, a PSO is free to request additional information from a provider or to indicate appropriate limitations to the conclusions or analyses based on insufficient or incomplete information.

We seek public comment on two additional aspects regarding the timing of the obligation of a provider to report to a PSO in order for information to become protected patient safety work product and for the confidentiality protections to attach. The first issue relates to the timing between assembly or development of information for reporting and actual reporting under the proposed definition of patient safety work product. As currently proposed,

information assembled or developed by a provider is not protected until the moment it is reported, (i.e., transmitted or transferred to a PSO). We are considering whether there is a need for a short period of protection for information assembled but not yet reported. We note that in such situations, a provider creates and operates a patient safety evaluation system. (See discussion of the definition of patient safety evaluation system at proposed § 3.20.) We further note that even without such short period of protection, information assembled or developed by a provider but not yet reported may be subject to other protections in the proposed rule (e.g., see section 921(7)(A)(ii) of the Public Health Service Act, 42 U.S.C. 299b–21(7)(A)(ii)).Our intent is not to relieve the provider of the statutory requirement for reporting pursuant to section 921(7)(A)(i) of the Public Health Service Act, 42 U.S.C. 299b–21(7)(A)(i), but to extend to providers flexibility to efficiently transmit or transfer information to a PSO for protection. A short period of protection for information assembled but not yet reported could result in greater operational efficiency for a provider by allowing information to be compiled and reported to a PSO in batches. It could also alleviate the uncertainty regarding the status of information that is assembled, but not yet reported for administrative reasons. If we do address this

issue in the final rule, we seek input on the appropriate time period for such protection and whether a provider must demonstrate an intent to report in order to obtain protections. If we do not address this issue in the final rule, such information held by a provider would not be confidential until it is actually transmitted to a PSO under this prong of the definition of patient safety work product.

Second, for information to become patient safety work product under this prong of the definition, it must be assembled or developed for the purpose of reporting to a PSO and actually reported. We solicit comment on the point in time at which it can be established that information is being collected for the purpose of reporting to a PSO such that it is not excluded from the definition of patient safety work product as a consequence of it being collected, maintained or developed separately from a patient safety evaluation system. See section 921(7)(B)(ii) of the Public Health Service Act, 42 U.S.C. 299b–21(7)(B)(ii). To assemble information with the purpose of reporting to a PSO, a PSO must potentially exist, and thus, we believe that collection efforts cannot predate the passage of the Patient Safety Act on July 29, 2005.

Information that is developed by a PSO for the conduct of patient safety activities. By law and as set forth in our proposal, information that is developed by a PSO for patient safety activities is patient safety work product. Section 921(7)(A)(i)(II) of the Public Health Service Act, 42 U.S.C. 299b–21(7)(A)(i)(II). This section of the definition does not address information discussed in the previous section that is assembled or developed by a provider and is reported to a PSO which becomes patient safety work product under that section. Rather, this section addresses other information that a PSO collects for development from third parties, non-providers and other PSOs for patient safety activities. For example, a PSO may be asked to assist a provider in analyzing a complex adverse event that took place. The initial information from the provider is protected because it was reported. If the PSO determines that the information is insufficient and conducts interviews with affected patients or collects additional data, that information is an example of the type of information that would be protected under this section of the definition. Even if the PSO ultimately decided not to analyze such information, the fact that the PSO collected and evaluated the information is a form of "development" transforming the information into patient safety work product. Such patient safety work product would be subject to confidentiality protections, and thus, the PSO would need safe disposal methods for any such information in accordance with its confidentiality obligations.

Information that constitutes the deliberations or analysis of, or identifies the fact of reporting pursuant to, a patient safety evaluation system. By law and as set forth in our proposal, information that constitutes the deliberations or analysis of, or identifies the fact of reporting pursuant to, a patient safety evaluation system is patient safety work product. Section 921(7)(A)(ii) of the Public Health Service Act, 42 U.S.C. 299b–21(7)(A)(ii). This provision extends patient safety work product protections to any information that would identify the fact of reporting pursuant to a patient safety evaluation system or that constitutes the deliberations or analyses that take place within such a system. The fact of reporting through a patient safety evaluation system (e.g., a fax cover sheet, an e-mail transmitting data, and an oral transmission of information to a PSO) is patient safety work product. With regard to providers, deliberations and analyses are protected while they are occurring provided they are done within a patient safety evaluation system. We are proposing that under paragraph (1)(ii) of this definition, any "deliberations or analysis" performed within the patient safety evaluation system becomes patient safety work product. In other words, to determine whether protections apply, the primary question is whether a patient safety evaluation system, which by law and as set forth in this proposed rule, is the

collection, management, or analysis of information for reporting to a PSO, was in existence at the time of the deliberations and analysis. To determine whether a provider had a patient safety evaluation system at the time that the deliberations or analysis took place, we propose to consider whether a provider had certain indicia of a patient safety evaluation system, such as the following: (1) The provider has a contract with a PSO for the receipt and review of patient safety work product that is in effect at the time of the deliberations and analysis; (2) the provider has documentation for a patient safety evaluation system demonstrating the capacity to report to a PSO at the time of the deliberations and analysis; (3) the provider had reported information to the PSO either under paragraph (1)(i)(A) of the proposed definition of patient safety work product or with respect to deliberations and analysis; or (4) the provider has actually reported the underlying information that was the basis of the deliberations or analysis to a PSO. For example, if a provider claimed protection for information as the deliberation of a patient safety evaluation system, and had a contract with the PSO at the time the deliberations took place, it would be reasonable to believe that the deliberations and analysis were related to the provider's PSO reporting activities. This is not an exclusive list. We note therefore that a provider may still be able to show that information was patient safety work product using other indications.

We note that the statutory protections for deliberations and analysis in a patient safety evaluation system apply without regard to the status of the underlying information being considered (i.e., it does not matter whether the underlying information being considered is patient safety work product or not). A provider can fully protect internal deliberations in its patient safety evaluation system over whether to report information to a PSO.

The deliberations and analysis are protected, whether the provider chooses to report the underlying information to a PSO or not. However, the underlying information, separate and apart from the analysis or deliberation, becomes protected only when reported to a PSO. See section 921(7)(A)(i)(1) of the Public Health Service Act, 42 U.S.C. 299b–21(7)(A)(i)(1).

To illustrate, consider a hospital that is reviewing a list of all near-misses reported within the past 30 days. The purpose of the hospital's review is to analyze whether to report any or part of the list to a PSO. The analyses (or any deliberations the provider undertakes) are fully protected whether the provider reports any near-misses or not. The status of the near-misses list does not change because the deliberations took place. The fact that the provider deliberated over reporting the

list does not constitute reporting and does not change the protected status of the list.

Separate and apart from the analysis, this list of near misses is not protected unless it is reported. By contrast, this provision fully protects the provider's deliberations and analyses in its patient safety evaluation system regarding the list. *Delisting.* In the event that a PSO is delisted for cause under proposed § 3.108(b)(1), a provider may continue to report to that PSO for 30 days after the delisting and the reported information will be patient safety work product. Section 924(f)(1) of the Public Health Service Act, 42 U.S.C. 299b–24(f)(1). Information reported to a delisted PSO after the 30-day period will not be patient safety work product. However, after a PSO is delisted, the delisted entity may not continue to generate patient safety work product by developing information for the conduct of patient safety activities or through deliberations and analysis of information. Any patient safety work product held or generated by a PSO prior to its delisting remains protected even after the PSO is delisted. See discussion in the preamble regarding proposed § 3.108(b)(2) for more information. We note that proposed § 3.108(c) outlines the process for delisting based upon an entity's voluntary relinquish-ment of its PSO listing. As we discuss in the accompany-ing preamble, we tentatively

conclude that the statutory provision for a 30-day period of continued protection does not apply after delisting due to voluntary relinquishment. Even though a PSO may not generate new patient safety work product after delisting, it may still have in its possession patient safety work product, which it must keep confidential. The statute establishes require-ments, incorporated in proposed § 3.108(b)(2) and (b)(3), that a PSO delisted for cause must meet regarding notification of providers and disposition of patient safety work product. We propose in § 3.108(c) to implement similar notification and disposition measures for a PSO that voluntarily relinquishes its listing. For further discussion of the obligations of a delisted PSO, see proposed § 3.108(b)(2), (b)(3), and (c). *What is not patient safety work product.* By law, and as set forth in this proposed rule, patient safety work product does not include a patient's original medical record, billing and discharge information, or any other original patient or provider record; nor does it include information that is collected, maintained, or developed separately or exists separately from, a patient safety evaluation system. Such separate information or a copy thereof reported to a PSO shall not by reason of its reporting be considered patient safety work product. The specific examples cited in the Patient Safety Act of what is not patient safety work product—the patient's original medical record, billing and discharge information, or any other original patient record—are illustrative of the types of information that providers routinely assemble, develop, or maintain for purposes and obligations other than those of the Patient Safety Act. The Patient Safety Act also states that information that is collected, maintained, or developed separately, or exists separately from a patient safety evaluation system, is not patient safety work product. Therefore, if records are collected, maintained, or developed for a purpose other than for reporting to a PSO, those records cannot be patient safety work product. However, if, for example, a copy of such record is made for reporting to a PSO, the copy and the fact of reporting become patient safety work product. Thus, a provider could collect incident reports for internal quality assurance purposes, and later, determine that one incident report is relevant to a broader patient safety activity.

If the provider then reports a copy of the incident report to a PSO, the copy of the incident report received by the PSO is protected as is the copy of the incident report as reported to the PSO that is maintained by the provider, while the original incident report collected for internal quality assurance purposes is not protected.

The proposed rule sets forth the statutory rule of construction that prohibits construing anything in this Part from limiting (1) the discovery of or admissibility of information that is not patient safety work product in a criminal, civil, or administrative proceeding; (2) the reporting of information that is not patient safety work product to a Federal, State, or local governmental agency for public health surveillance, investigation, or other public health purposes or health oversight purposes; or (3) a provider's recordkeeping obligation with respect to information that is not patient safety work product under Federal, State or local law. Section 921(7)(B)(iii) of the Public Health Service Act, 42 U.S.C. 299b-21(7)(B)(iii). Even when laws or regulations require the reporting of the information regarding the type of events also reported to PSOs, the Patient Safety Act does not shield providers from their obligation to comply with such requirements.

As the Patient Safety Act states more than once, these external obligations must be met with information that is not patient safety work product, and, in accordance with the confidentiality provisions, patient safety work product cannot be disclosed for these purposes. We note that the Patient Safety Act clarifies that nothing in this Part prohibits any person from conducting additional analyses for any purpose regardless of whether such additional analysis involves issues identical to or similar to those for which information was reported to or assessed by a PSO or a patient safety evaluation system.

Section 922(h) of the Public Health Service Act, 42 U.S.C. 299b-22(h). A copy of information generated for such purposes may be entered into the provider's patient safety evaluation system for patient safety purposes although the originals of the information generated to meet external obligations do not become patient safety work product. Thus, information that is collected to comply with external obligations is not patient safety work product. Such activities may include: State incident reporting requirements; adverse drug event information reporting to the Food and Drug Administration (FDA); certification or licensing records for compliance with health oversight agency requirements; reporting to the National Practitioner Data Bank of physician disciplinary actions; or complying with required disclosures by particular providers or suppliers pursuant to Medicare's conditions of participation or conditions of coverage. In addition, the proposed rule does not change the law with respect to an employee's ability to file a complaint with Federal or State authorities regarding quality of care, or with respect to any prohibition on a provider's threatening or carrying out retaliation against an individual for doing so; the filing of any such complaint would not be deemed to be a violation of the Patient

Safety Act, unless patient safety work product was improperly disclosed in such filing.

Health Care Oversight Reporting and Patient Safety Work Product. The Patient Safety Act establishes a protected space or system of protected information in order to allow frank discussion about causes and remediation of threats to patient safety. As described above, this protected system is separate, distinct, and resides alongside but does not replace other information collection activities mandated by laws, regulations, and accrediting and licensing requirements as well as voluntary reporting activities that occur for the purpose of maintaining accountability in the health care system. Information collection activities performed by the provider for purposes other than for reporting to a PSO by itself do not create patient safety work product. In anticipation of questions about how mandatory and voluntary reporting will continue to be possible, a brief explanation may be helpful regarding how this new patient safety framework would operate in relation to health care oversight activities (e.g., public health reporting, corrective actions, etc.). Situations may occur when the original (whether print or electronic) of information that is not patient safety work product is needed for a disclosure outside of the entity but cannot be located while a copy of the needed information resides in the patient safety evaluation system. If the reason for which the original information is being sought does not align with one of the permissible disclosures, discussed in proposed Subpart C, the protected copy may not be released. Nevertheless, this does not preclude efforts to reconstruct the information outside of the patient safety evaluation system from information that is not patient safety work product. Those who participated in the collection, development, analysis, or review of the missing information or have knowledge of its contents can fully disclose what they know or reconstruct an analysis outside of the patient safety evaluation system.

The issue of how effectively a provider has instituted corrective action following identification of a threat to the quality or safety of patient care might lead to requests for information from external authorities. The Patient Safety Act does not relieve a provider of its responsibility to respond to such requests for information or to undertake or provide to external authorities evaluations of the effectiveness of corrective action, but the provider must respond with information that is not patient safety work product. To illustrate the distinction, consider the following example. We would expect that a provider's patient safety evaluation system or a PSO with which the provider works may make recommen-dations from time to time to the provider for changes it should make in the way it manages and delivers health care. The list of recommendations for changes, whether they originate from the provider's patient safety evaluation system or the PSO with which it is working, are always patient safety work product. We would also note that not all of these recommendations will address corrective actions (i.e., correcting a process, policy, or situation that poses a threat to patients). It is also possible that a provider with an exemplary quality and safety record is seeking advice on how to perform even better. Whatever the case, the feedback from the provider's patient safety evaluation system or PSO may not be disclosed to external authorities unless permitted by the disclosures specified in Subpart C of this proposed rule.

The provider may choose to reject the recommendations it receives or implement some or all of the proposed changes. While the recommendations always remain protected, whether they are adopted or rejected by a provider, the actual changes that the provider implements to improve how it manages or delivers health care services (including changes in its organizational management or its care environments, structures, and processes) are not patient safety work product. In a practical sense, it would be virtually impossible to keep such changes confidential in any event, and we stress that if there is any distinction between the change that was adopted and the recommendation that the provider received, the provider can only describe the change that was implemented. The recommendation remains protected.

Thus, if external authorities request a list of corrective actions that a provider has implemented, the provider has no basis for refusing the request. Even though the actions are based on protected information, the corrective actions themselves are not patient safety work product. On the other hand, if an external authority asks for a list of the recommendations that the provider did not implement or whether and how any implemented change differed from the recommendation the provider received, the provider must refuse the request; the recommendations themselves remain protected.

Person would mean a natural person, trust or estate, partnership, corporation, professional association or corporation, or other entity, public or private. We propose to define "person" because the Patient Safety Act requires that civil money penalties be imposed against "person[s]" that violate the confidentiality provisions. However, the Patient Safety Act does not provide a definition of "person". The Definition Act at 1 U.S.C. 1 provides, "in determining any Act of Congress, *unless the context indicates otherwise* * * *

the words 'person' and 'whoever' include corporations, companies, associations, firms, partnerships, societies, and joint stock companies, as well as individuals" (emphasis added).

The Patient Safety Act indicates that States and other government entities may hold patient safety work product with the protections and liabilities attached, which is an expansion of the Definition Act provision. For this reason, we propose the broader definition of the term "person". We note that this proposed approach is consistent with the HHS Office of Inspector General (OIG) regulations, 42 CFR 1003.101, and the HIPAA Enforcement Rule, 45 CFR 160.103.

Provider would mean any individual or entity licensed or otherwise authorized under State law to provide health care services. The list of specific providers in the proposed rule includes the following: institutional providers, such as a hospital, nursing facility, comprehensive outpatient rehabilitation facility, home health agency, hospice program, renal dialysis facility, ambulatory surgical center, pharmacy, physician or health care practitioner's office (including a group practice), long term care facility, behavior health residential treatment facility, clinical laboratory, or health center; or individual clinicians, such as a physician, physician assistant, registered nurse, nurse practitioner, clinical

nurse specialist, certified registered nurse anesthetist, certified nurse midwife, psychologist, certified social worker, registered dietitian or nutrition professional, physical or occupational therapist, pharmacist, or other individual health care practitioner. This list is merely illustrative; an individual or entity that is not listed here but meets the test of state licensure or authorization to provide health care services is a provider for the purpose of this proposed rule.

The statute also authorizes the Secretary to expand the definition of providers. Under this authority, we propose to add the following to this list of providers: (a) Agencies, organizations, and individuals within Federal, State, local, or Tribal governments that deliver health care, organizations engaged as contractors by the Federal, State, local or Tribal governments to deliver health care, and individual health care practitioners employed or engaged as contractors by the Federal government to deliver health care. It appears that all of these agencies, organizations, and individuals could participate in, and could benefit from, working with a PSO.
(b) A corporate parent organization for one or more entities licensed or otherwise authorized to provide health care services under state law. Without this addition, hospital or other provider systems that are controlled by a parent organization that is not recognized as a

provider under State law might be precluded from entering into system-wide contracts with PSOs. This addition furthers the goals of the statute to encourage aggregation of patient safety data and a coordinated approach for assessing and improving patient safety. We particularly seek comments regarding any concerns or operational issues that might result from this addition, and note that a PSO entering one system-wide contract still needs to meet the two contract minimum requirement based on section 924(b)(1)(C) of the Public Health Service Act, 42 U.S.C. 299b–24(b)(1)(C), and set out and discussed in proposed § 3.102(b). The PSO can do this by entering into two contracts with different providers within the system. (c) A Federal, State, local, or Tribal government unit that manages or controls one or more health care providers described in the definition of provider at (1)(i) and (2). We propose this addition to the definition of "provider" for the same reason that we proposed the addition of parent organization that has a controlling interest in one or more entities licensed or otherwise authorized to provide health care services under state law.

Research would have the same meaning as that term is defined in the HIPAA Privacy Rule at 45 CFR 164.501. In the HIPAA Privacy Rule, research means a systematic investigation, including research development, testing, and evaluation, designed to develop or contribute to generalizable knowledge. This definition is used to describe the scope of the confidentiality exception at proposed § 3.206(b)(6). We propose to use the same definition as in the HIPAA Privacy Rule to improve the level of coordination and to reduce the burden of compliance. At the same time, if there is a modification to the definition in the HIPAA Privacy Rule, the definition herein will automatically change with such regulatory action.

Respondent would mean a provider, PSO, or responsible person who is the subject of a complaint or a compliance review.

Responsible person would mean a person, other than a provider or PSO, who has possession or custody of identifiable patient safety work product and is subject to the confidentiality provisions. We note that because the Patient Safety Act has continued confidentiality protection at 42 U.S.C. 299b–22(d), many entities other than providers and PSOs may be subject to the confidentiality provisions. Thus, for example, researchers or law enforcement officials who obtain patient safety work product under one of the exceptions to confidentiality would be considered a "responsible person".

Workforce would mean employees, volunteers, trainees, contractors, and other persons whose conduct, in the performance of work for a provider, PSO or responsible person, is under the direct control of such provider, PSO or responsible person, whether or not they are paid by the provider, PSO or responsible person. We use the term workforce member in several contexts in the proposed rule. Importantly, in proposed § 3.402 where we discuss principal liability, we propose that an agent for which a principal may be liable can be a workforce member. We have included the term "contractors" in the definition of workforce member to clarify that such permitted sharing may occur with contractors who are under the direct control of the provider, PSO, or responsible person. For example, a patient safety activity disclosure by a provider to a PSO may be made directly to the PSO or to a consultant, as a workforce member, contracted by the PSO to help it carry out patient safety activities.

B. Subpart B—PSO Requirements and Agency Procedures Proposed Subpart (B) sets forth requirements for Patient Safety Organizations (PSOs). This proposed Subpart specifies the certification and notification requirements that PSOs must meet, the actions that the Secretary may and will take relating to PSOs, the requirements that PSOs must meet for the security of patient safety work product, the processes governing correction of PSO deficiencies, revocation, and voluntary relinquishment, and related administrative authorities and implementation responsibilities. The requirements of this proposed Subpart would apply to PSOs, their workforce, a PSO's contractors when they hold patient safety work product, and the Secretary.

This proposed Subpart is intended to provide the foundation for new, voluntary opportunities to improve the safety, quality, and outcomes of patient care. The Patient Safety Act does not require a provider to contract with a PSO, and the proposed rule does not include such a requirement. However, we expect that most providers will enter into contracts with PSOs when seeking the confidentiality and privilege protections of the statute.

Contracts offer providers greater certainty that a provider's claim to these statutory protections will be sustained, if challenged. For example, the statutory definition of patient safety work product describes the nature and purpose of information that can be protected, the circumstances under which deliberations or analyses are protected, and the requirement that certain information be reported to a PSO.

Pursuant to a contractual arrangement, providers can require and receive assistance from PSOs to ensure that these requirements are fully met.

Contracts can provide clear evidence that a provider is taking all reasonable measures to operate under the ambit of the statute in collecting, developing, and maintaining patient safety work product. Contracts enable providers to specify even stronger confidentiality protections in how they report information to a PSO or how the PSO handles and uses the information. Contracts can also give providers greater assurance that they will have access to the expertise of the PSO to provide feedback regarding their patient safety events. While some providers may have patient safety expertise inhouse, a PSO has the potential to offer providers considerable additional insight as a result of its expertise and ability to aggregate and analyze data from multiple providers and multiple PSOs. Experience has demonstrated that such aggregation and analysis of large volumes of data, such as a PSO has the ability to do, will often yield insights into the underlying causes of the hazards and risks associated with patient care that are simply not apparent when these analyses are limited to the information available from only one office, clinic, facility, or system.

Pursuant to a contract with a PSO, a provider may also be able to obtain from a PSO operational guidance or best practices with respect to operation of a patient safety evaluation system. Such a contract also provides a mechanism for a provider to control the nature and extent of a PSO's aggregation of its data with those of other providers or PSOs, and the nature of related analysis and discussion of such data. A provider can also require, pursuant to its contract with a PSO, that the PSO will notify the provider if improper disclosures are made of patient safety work product relating to that provider.

This proposed Subpart enables a broad variety of health care providers to work voluntarily with entities that have certified to the Secretary that they have the ability and expertise to carry out broadly defined patient safety activities of the Patient Safety Act and, therefore, to serve as consultants to eligible providers to improve patient care. In accordance with the Patient Safety Act, we propose an attestation-based process for initial and continued listing of an entity as a PSO. This includes an attestation-based approach for meeting the statutory requirement that each PSO, within 24 months of being listed and in each sequential 24-month period thereafter, must have bona fide contracts with more than one provider for the receipt and review of patient safety work product.

This streamlined approach of the statute and the proposed rule is intended to encourage the rapid development of expertise in health care improvement. This framework allows the marketplace to be the principal arbiter of the capabilities of each PSO. Listing as a PSO by the Secretary does not entitle an entity to Federal funding. The financial viability of most PSOs will derive from their ability to attract and retain contracts with providers or to attract financial support from other organizations, such as charitable foundations dedicated to health system improvement. Even when a provider organization considers establishing a PSO (what this proposed rule terms a component PSO) to serve the needs of its organization, we expect it will weigh the value of, and the business case for, such a PSO.

Proposed Subpart B attempts to minimize regulatory burden while fostering transparency to enhance the ability of providers to assess the strengths and weaknesses of their choice of PSOs. For example, we encourage, but do not require, an entity seeking listing to develop and post on their own Web sites narrative statements describing the expertise of the personnel the entity will have at its disposal, and outlining the way it will approach its mission and comply with the statute's certification requirements. We similarly propose to apply transparency to our implementation of the statute's requirement for disclosure by PSOs of potential conflicts of interest with their provider clients. While the statute only requires public release of the findings of the Secretary after review of such disclosures, we propose to make public, consistent with applicable law, including the Freedom of Information Act, a PSO's disclosure state-

ments as well. In our view, in addition to having the benefit of the Secretary's determination, a provider, as the prospective consumer of PSO services, should be able to make its own determination regarding the appropriateness of the relationships that a PSO has with its other provider clients and the impact those relationships might have on its particular needs. For example, a provider might care if a PSO—despite the Secretary's determination that it had been established with sufficient operational and other independence to qualify for listing as a PSO— was owned, operated, or managed by the provider's major competitor.

The provisions of this proposed Subpart also emphasize the need for vigilance in providing security for patient safety work product. To achieve the widespread provider participation intended by this statute, PSOs must foster and maintain the confidence of providers in the security of patient safety work product in which providers and patients are identified. Therefore, we propose to require a security framework, which each PSO must address with standards it determines appropriate to the size and complexity of its organization, pertaining to the separation of data and systems and to security management control, monitoring, and assessment. The Patient Safety Act recognizes that PSOs will need to enter business associate agreements to

receive protected health information from providers that are covered entities under the HIPAA Privacy Rule. As a business associate of such a provider, a PSO will have to meet certain contractual requirements on the use and disclosure of protected health information for compliance with the HIPAA Privacy Rule that are in addition to the requirements set forth in this proposed rule. Those requirements include the notification of a covered entity when protected health information is inappropriately disclosed in violation of the HIPAA Privacy Rule.

We do not propose to require reporting of impermissible disclosures of other patient safety work product that does not contain protected health information. We solicit comments on whether to parallel the business associate requirements of the HIPAA Privacy Rule. Such a requirement, if implemented, would require a PSO to notify the organizational source of patient safety work product if the information it shared has been impermissibly used or disclosed. Note that such reporting requirements could be voluntarily agreed to by contract between providers and their PSO.

Section 924(b)(2)(A) and (B) of the Public Health Service Act, 42 U.S.C. 299b–24(b)(2)(A) and (B), suggests Congressional concern that a strong firewall must be maintained between a component PSO and the rest of the organization(s) of which it is a part. This proposed subpart proposes specific safeguards that such component PSOs must implement to effectively address those concerns.

As this discussion suggests, in developing this proposed Subpart, we have proposed the most specific requirements in the areas of security and disclosure of potential conflicts of interest. We expect to offer technical assistance and encourage transparency wherever possible to promote implementation, compliance, and correction of deficiencies. At the same time, this proposed Subpart establishes processes that will permit the Secretary promptly to revoke a PSO's certification and remove it from listing, if such action proves necessary.

1. Proposed § 3.102—Process and Requirements for Initial and Continued Listing of PSOs Proposed § 3.102 sets out: The submissions that the Department, in carrying out its responsibilities, proposes to require, consistent with the Patient Safety Act, for initial and continued listing as a PSO; the certifications that all entities must make as part of the listing process; the additional certifications that component organizations must make as part of the listing process; the requirement for biennial submission of a certification that the PSO has entered into the required number of contracts; and the circumstances under which a PSO must submit a disclosure

statement regarding the relationships it has with its contracting providers.

(A) Proposed § 3.102(a)—Eligibility and Process for Initial and Continued Listing In this section, we propose to establish a streamlined certification process that minimizes barriers to entry for a broad variety of entities seeking to be listed as a PSO. With several exceptions, any entity—public or private, for-profit or not-for profit—may seek initial or continued listing by the Secretary as a PSO. The statute precludes a health insurance issuer and a component of a health insurance issuer from becoming a PSO (section 924(b)(1)(D) of the Public Health Service Act, 42 U.S.C. 299b–24(b)(1)(D)).

In addition, we propose to preclude any other entity, public or private, from seeking listing as a PSO if the entity conducts regulatory oversight of health care providers, including accreditation or licensure. We propose this restriction for consistency with the statute, which seeks to foster a "culture of safety" in which health care providers are confident that the patient safety events that they report will be used for learning and improvement, not oversight, penalties, or punishment. Listing organizations with regulatory authority as PSOs would be likely to undermine provider confidence that adequate separation of PSO and regulatory activities would be maintained.

We note that the Patient Safety Act permits a component organization of an entity to seek listing as a PSO if the component organization establishes a strong firewall between its activities as a PSO and the rest of the organization(s) of which it is a part. As drafted, this proposed regulation permits a component organization of an entity with any degree of regulatory authority to seek listing as a component PSO. We have not proposed any restrictions on such component organizations for several reasons. First, we expect that the statutory requirement for a strong firewall between a component PSO and its parent organization(s) with respect to its activities as a PSO and the protected information it holds will provide adequate safeguards. Second, providers will have access to the names of parent organizations of component PSOs. We propose in § 3.102(c) that any component organization must disclose the name of its parent organization(s) (see the proposed definitions of component and parent organizations in § 3.20). We intend to make this information publicly available and expect to post it on the PSO Web site we plan to establish (see the preamble discussion regarding proposed § 3.104(d)). This will provide transparency and enable providers to determine whether the organizational affiliation(s) of a component PSO are of concern. Finally, we believe that allowing the marketplace to determine whether a component PSO has acceptable or unacceptable ties to an entity with regulatory authority is consistent with our overall approach to regulation of PSOs.

At the same time, we recognize that some organizations exercise a considerable level of regulatory oversight over providers and there may be concerns that such organizations could circumvent the firewalls proposed below in § 3.102(c) or might attempt to require providers to work with a component PSO that the regulatory entity creates. Accordingly, we specifically seek comment on the approach we have proposed and whether we should consider a broader restriction on component organizations of entities that are regulatory. For example, should components of state health departments be precluded from seeking listing because of the broad authority of such departments to regulate provider behavior? If a broader restriction is proposed, we would especially welcome suggestions on clear, unambiguous criteria for its implementation.

We will develop certification forms for entities seeking initial and continued listing that contain or restate the respective certifications described in proposed § 3.102(b) and § 3.102(c). An individual with authority to make commitments on behalf of the entity seeking listing would be required to acknowledge each of the certification requirements, attest that the entity meets each of the certification requirements on the form, and provide contact information for the entity. The certification form would also require an attestation that the entity is not subject to the limitation on listing proposed in this subsection and an attestation that, once listed as a PSO, it will notify the Secretary if it is no longer able to meet the requirements of proposed § 3.102(b) and § 3.102(c).

To facilitate the development of a marketplace for the services of PSOs, entities are encouraged, but not required, to develop and post on their own Web sites narratives that specify how the entity will approach its mission, how it will comply with the certification requirements, and describe the qualifications of the entity's personnel. With appropriate disclaimers of any implied endorsement, we expect to post citations or links to the Web sites of all listed entities on the PSO Web site that we plan to establish pursuant to proposed § 3.104(d). We believe that clear narratives of how PSOs will meet their statutory and regulatory responsibilities will help providers, who are seeking the services of a PSO, to assess their options. The Department's PSO Web site address will be identified in the final rule and will be available from AHRQ upon request.

(B) Proposed § 3.102(b)— Fifteen General Certification Requirements In accordance with section 924(a) of the Public Health Service Act, 42 U.S.C. 299b–24(a), the proposed rule would require all entities seeking initial or continued listing as a PSO to meet 15 general certification requirements: eight requirements related to patient safety activities and seven criteria governing their operation. At initial listing, the entity would be required to certify that it has policies and procedures in place to carry out the eight patient safety activities defined in the Patient Safety Act and incorporated in proposed § 3.20, and upon listing, would meet the seven criteria specified in proposed § 3.102 (b)(2). Submissions for continued listing would require certifications that the PSO is performing, and will continue to perform, the eight patient safety activities and is complying with, and would continue to comply with, the seven criteria.

(1) Proposed § 3.102(b)(1)— Required Certification Regarding Eight Patient Safety Activities Proposed § 3.102(b)(1) addresses the eight required patient safety activities that are listed in the definition of patient safety activities at proposed § 3.20 (section 921(5) of the Public Health Service Act, 42 U.S.C. 299b– 21(5)). Because certification relies primarily upon attestations by entities seeking listing, rather than submission and review of documentation, it is critical that entities seeking listing have a common and shared

understanding of what each certification requirement entails. We conclude that five of the eight required patient safety activities need no elaboration. These five patient safety activities include: Efforts to improve patient safety and quality; the collection and analysis of patient safety work product; the development and dissemination of information with respect to improving patient safety; the utilization of patient safety work product for the purposes of encouraging a culture of safety and providing feedback and assistance; and the utilization of qualified staff. We address a sixth patient safety activity, related to the operation of a patient safety evaluation system, in the discussion of the definition of that term in proposed § 3.20. We provide greater clarity here regarding the actions that an entity must take to comply with the remaining two patient safety activities, which involve the preservation of confidentiality of patient safety work product and the provision of appropriate security measures for patient safety work product.

We interpret the certification to preserve confidentiality of patient safety work product to require conformance with the confidentiality provisions of proposed Subpart C as well as the requirements of the Patient Safety Act.

Certification to provide appropriate security measures require PSOs, their workforce members,

and their contractors when they hold patient safety work product to conform to the requirements of proposed § 3.106, as well as the provisions of the Patient Safety Act. (2) Proposed § 3.102(b)(2)—Required Certification Regarding Seven PSO Criteria Proposed § 3.102(b)(2) lists seven criteria that are drawn from the Patient Safety Act (section 924(b) of the Public Health Service Act, 42 U.S.C. 299b–24(b)), which an entity must meet during its period of listing. We conclude that the statutory language for three of the seven required criteria is clear and further elaboration is not required. These three criteria include: The mission and primary activity of the entity is patient safety, the entity has appropriately qualified staff, and the entity utilizes patient safety work product for provision of direct feedback and assistance to providers to effectively minimize patient risk. Two of the criteria are addressed elsewhere in the proposed rule: the exclusion of health insurance issuer or components of health insurance issuers from being PSOs is discussed above in the context of the definition of that term in proposed § 3.20 and the requirements for submitting disclosure statements are addressed in the preamble discussion below regarding proposed § 3.102(d)(2) (the proposed criteria against which the Secretary will review the disclosure statements are set forth in § 3.104(c)).

The remaining two PSO criteria—the minimum contract requirement and the collection of data in a standardized manner—are discussed here.

The Minimum Contracts Requirement. First, we propose to clarify the requirement in section 924(b)(1)(C) of the Public Health Service Act, 42 U.S.C. 299b–24(b)(1)(C) that a PSO must enter into bona fide contracts with more than one provider for the receipt and review of patient safety work product within every 24-month period after the PSO's initial date of listing. We note that the statutory language establishes four conditions that must be met for a PSO to be in compliance with this requirement. We propose to interpret two of them for purposes of clarity in the final rule: (1) The PSO must have contracts with more than one provider, and (2) the contract period must be for "a reasonable period of time." Most contracts will easily meet the third requirement: that contracts must be "bona fide" (our definition is in proposed § 3.20). Finally, the fourth requirement, that contracts must involve the receipt and review of patient safety work product, does not require elaboration.

We propose that a PSO would meet the requirement for "contracts with more than one provider" if it enters a minimum of two contracts within each 24-month period that begins with its initial date of listing. We note that the statutory requirement in section 924(b)(1)(C) of the Public Health Service Act, 42 U.S.C. 299b-24(b)(1)(C), unambiguously requires multiple contracts (i.e., more than one). One contract with two or more providers would not fully meet the statute's requirement. To illustrate, one contract with a 50-hospital system would not meet the requirement; two 25-hospital contracts with that same hospital system would meet the requirement. We believe that the statutory requirement was intended to encourage PSOs to aggregate data from multiple providers, in order to expand the volume of their data, thereby improving the basis on which patterns of errors and the causes for those errors can be identified. This statutory objective is worth noting as a goal for PSOs. A PSO can achieve this goal by aggregating data from multiple providers or by pooling or comparing data with other PSOs, subject to statutory, regulatory, and contractual limitations. The statute requires that these contracts must be "for a reasonable period of time." We propose to clarify in the final rule when a PSO would be in compliance with this statutory requirement. The approach could be time-based (e.g., a specific number of months), task-based (e.g., the contract duration is linked to completion of specific tasks but, under this option, the final rule would not set a specific time period), or provide both options. We seek comments on the operational implica-

tions of these alternative approaches and the specific standard(s) for each option that we should consider. By establishing standard(s) in the final rule, we intend to create certainty for contracting providers and PSOs as to whether the duration requirement has been met. We note that whatever requirement is incorporated in the final rule will apply only to the two required contracts. A PSO can enter other contracts, whether time-based or task-based, without regard to the standard(s) for the two required contracts.

Apart from the requirements outlined above, there are no limits on the types of contracts that a PSO can enter; its contracts can address all or just one of the required patient safety activities, assist providers in addressing all, or just a specialized range, of patient safety topics, or the PSO can specialize in assisting specific types of providers, specialty societies, or provider membership organizations. Because of the limits on the extraterritorial application of U.S. law and the fact that privilege protections are limited to courts in the United States (Federal, State, etc.), the protections in the proposed rule apply only to protected data shared between PSOs and providers within the United States and its territories; there is only this one geographical limitation on a PSO's operations.

If they choose to do so, providers and PSOs may enter into contracts that

specify stronger confidentiality protections than those specified in this proposed rule and the Patient Safety Act (section 922(g)(4) of the Public Health Service Act, 42 U.S.C. 299b-22 (g)(3)). For example, a provider could choose to de-identify or anonymize information it reports to a PSO.

We note that the Secretary proposes to exercise his authority to extend the definition of "provider" for the purposes of this statute to include a provider's "parent organization" (both terms are defined in proposed § 3.20).

This proposed addition is intended to provide an option for health systems (e.g., holding companies or a state system) to enter system-wide contracts with PSOs if they choose to do so. This option would not be available in the absence of this provision because the parent organizations of many health care systems are often corporate management entities or governmental entities that are not considered licensed or authorized health care providers under state law.

Collecting data in a standardized manner. Section 924(b)(1)(F) of the Public Health Service Act, 42 U.S.C. 299b-24(b)(1)(F), requires PSOs, to the extent practical and appropriate, to collect patient safety work product from providers in a standardized manner, to permit valid comparisons of similar cases among similar providers. One of the goals of the legislation is to facilitate a PSO aggregating sufficient data to identify and to address underlying causal factors of patient safety problems.

A PSO is more valuable if it is able to aggregate patient safety work product it receives directly from multiple providers, and if it chooses to do so, aggregate its data with patient safety work product received from other PSOs and/or share nonidentifiable patient safety work product with a network of patient safety databases described in section 923 of the Public Health Service Act, 42 U.S.C. 299b-23. We recognize that if patient safety work product is not collected initially using common data elements and consistent definitions, it may be difficult to aggregate such data subsequently in order to develop valid comparisons across providers and potentially, PSOs. We also recognize, however, that the providers who work with PSOs may have varying levels of sophistication with respect to patient safety issues and that reporting patient safety work product to a PSO in a standardized manner or using standardized reporting formats may not be initially practicable for certain providers or in certain circumstances.

The discussion which follows outlines the timetable and the process to which we are committed.

The Secretary intends to provide ongoing guidance to PSOs on formats and definitions that would facilitate the ability of PSOs to aggregate patient safety

work product. We expect to provide initial guidance beginning with the most common types of patient safety events, before the final rule is issued, to facilitate the ability of PSOs to develop valid comparisons among providers.

The Department will make such formats and definitions available for public comment in a non-regulatory format via publication in the Federal Register. We are considering, and we seek comment on, including a clarification in the final rule, that compliance with this certification requirement would mean that a PSO, to the extent practical and appropriate, will aggregate patient safety work product consistent with the Secretary's guidance regarding reporting formats and definitions when such guidance becomes available. *The process for developing and maintaining common formats.* AHRQ has established a process to develop common formats that: (1) Is evidence-based; (2) harmonizes across governmental health agencies; (3) incorporates feedback from the public, professional associations/ organizations, and users; and (4) permits timely updating of these clinically-sensitive formats.

In anticipation of the need for common formats, AHRQ began the process of developing them in 2005. That process consists of the following steps: (1) Develop an inventory of functioning patient safety reporting systems to inform the

construction of the common formats (an evidence base). Included in this inventory, now numbering 64 systems, are the major Centers for Disease Control and Prevention (CDC) and Food and Drug Administration (FDA) reporting systems as well as many from the private sector.

(2) Convene an interagency Patient Safety Work Group (PSWG) to develop draft formats. Included are major health agencies within the Department—CDC, Centers for Medicare and Medicaid Services, FDA, Health Resources and Services Administration, the Indian Health Service (IHS), the National Institutes of Health—as well as the Department of Defense (DoD) and the Veterans Administration (VA). (3) Pilot test draft formats—to be conducted in February–March of 2008 in DoD, IHS, and VA facilities. (4) Publish version 0.1 **(beta) of the formats in the Federal Register, along with explanatory material, and solicit public comment—planned for July/August 2008. (5) Let a task order contract (completed) with the National Quality Forum (NQF) to solicit input from the private sector regarding the formats. NQF's role will be periodically to solicit input from the private sector to assist the Department in updating its versions of the formats.**

NQF will begin with version 0.1 (beta) of the common formats and solicit public comments (including from providers, professional organizations, the general public, and PSOs), triage them in terms of immediacy of importance, set priorities, and convene expert panel(s) to offer advice on updates to the formats. This process will be a continuing one, guiding periodic updates of the common formats. (6) Accept input from the NQF, revise the formats in consultation with the PSWG, and publish subsequent versions in the **Federal Register**. Comments will be accepted at all times from public and governmental sources, as well as the NQF, and used in updating of the formats.

This process ensures intergovernmental consistency as well as input from the private sector, including, most importantly, those who may use the common formats. This latter group, the users, will be the most sensitive to and aware of needed updates/ improvements to the formats.

The PSWG, acting as the fulcrum for original development and continuing upgrading/maintenance, assures consistency of definitions/formats among government agencies. For instance, the current draft formats follow CDC definitions of healthcare associated infections and FDA definitions of adverse drug events.

AHRQ has been careful to promote consensus among Departmental agencies on all draft common formats developed to date. The NQF

is a respected private sector organization that is suited to solicit and analyze input from the private sector. We welcome comments on our proposed approach to meeting statutory objectives. (C) Proposed § 3.102(c)— Additional Certifications Required of Component Organizations Section 924(b)(2) of the Public Health Service Act, 42 U.S.C. 299b-24(b)(2) and the proposed definition of component organization in proposed § 3.20 requires an entity that is a component of another organization or multi-organizational enterprise that seeks initial or continued listing to certify that it will meet three requirements in addition to certifying that it will meet the 15 general requirements specified in proposed § 3.102(b). We have indicated the types of entities that would be required to seek listing as a component organization in our discussion of the proposed definitions in proposed § 3.20 of the terms "component organization" and "parent organization." To be listed as a component PSO, an entity would also be required to make three additional certifications regarding the entity's independent operation and separateness from the larger organization or enterprise of which it is a part: the entity would certify to (1) the secure maintenance of documents and information separate from the rest of the organization(s) or enterprise of which it is a part; (2) the avoidance of unauthorized

disclosures to the organization(s) or enterprise of which it is a part; and (3) the absence of a conflict between its mission and the rest of the organization(s) or enterprise of which it is a part. We propose in § 3.102(c) specific requirements that will ensure that such component PSOs implement the type of safeguards for patient safety work product that the three additional statutory certification requirements for component organizations are intended to provide. First, the statute requires a component PSO to maintain patient safety work product separate from the rest of the organization(s) or enterprise of which it is a part (section 924(b)(2)(A) of the Public Health Service Act, 42 U.S.C. 299b-24(b)(2)(A)). To ensure compliance with this statutory requirement, we considered, but did not include here, a proposal to prohibit a component PSO from contracting, subcontracting, or entering any agreement with any part of the organization(s) or enterprise of which it is a part for the performance of any work involving the use of patient safety work product. We seek comment on the limited exception proposed in § 3.102(c) here that would permit such contracts or subcontracts only if they can be carried out in a manner that is consistent with the statutory requirements of this section. This means that, while a component PSO could enter such arrangements involving the use of patient safety work product with a unit of the organization(s) or enterprise of which it is a part, the component PSO would maintain the patient safety work product and be responsible for its security (i.e., control the access and use of it by the contracting unit). In addition, under our proposal, while allowing access to the contracting unit of the identifiable patient safety work product necessary to carry out the contractual assignment would be a permissible disclosure, the component PSO would remain responsible for ensuring that the contracting unit does not violate the prohibitions related to unauthorized disclosures required under 924(b)(2)(B) of the PHS Act, 42 U.S.C. 299b-24(b)(2)(B), (i.e., disclosures to other units of the organization or enterprise) and that there is no conflict between the mission of the component PSO and the contracting unit, as required under 924(b)(2)(C) of the PHS Act, 42 U.S.C. 299b-24(b)(2)(C). We invite comment on whether such a limited exception is necessary or appropriate and, if so, the appropriateness of the restrictions we have proposed.

Second, a component PSO would not be permitted to have a shared information system with the rest of the organization(s) since this might provide unauthorized access to patient safety work product. For example, we intend to prohibit a component PSO from storing any patient safety work product in information systems or databases to which the rest of the organization(s) or enterprise of which it is a part would have access or the ability to remove or transmit a copy. We preliminarily conclude that most security measures, such as password protection of the component PSO's information, are too easily circumvented.

Third, the proposed rule provides that the workforce of the component PSO must not engage in work for the rest of the organization(s) if such work could be informed or influenced by the individual's knowledge of identifiable patient safety work product. For example, a component PSO could share accounting or administrative support staff under our proposal because the work of these individuals for the rest of the organization(s) would not be informed or influenced by their knowledge of patient safety work product. By contrast, if the rest of the organization provides health care services, a physician who served on a parent organization's credentialing, hiring, or disciplinary committee(s) could not also work for the PSO. Knowledge of confidential patient safety work product could influence his or her decisions regarding credentialing, hiring, or disciplining of providers who are identifiable in the patient safety work product.

We provide one exception to the last prohibition. It is not our intent to prohibit a clinician, whose work for the rest of the organization is solely the provision of patient care, from undertaking work for the component PSO. We see no conflict if the patient care provided by the clinician is informed by the clinical insights that result from his or her work for the component PSO. If a clinician has duties beyond patient care, this exception only applies if the other duties do not violate the general prohibition (i.e., that the other duties for the rest of the organization(s) cannot be informed by knowledge of patient safety work product). As part of the requirement that the PSO must certify that there is no conflict between its mission and the rest of the organization(s), we propose that the certification form will require the PSO to provide the name(s) of the organization(s) or enterprise of which it is a part (see the discussions of our definitions of parent and component organizations in proposed § 3.20).

We have not proposed specific standards to determine whether conflicts exist between a PSO and other components of the organization or enterprise of which it is a part. We recognize that some industries and particular professions, such as the legal profession through state-based codes of professional responsibility, have specific standards or tests for determining whether a conflict exists.

We request comments on whether the final rule should include any specific standards, and, if so, what criteria should be put in place to determine whether a conflict exists.

(D) Proposed § 3.102(d)—Required Notifications Proposed § 3.102(d) establishes in regulation two required notifications that implement two statutory provisions: a notification to the Secretary certifying whether the PSO has met the biennial requirement for bona fide contracts with more than one provider (section 924(b)(1)(C) of the Public Health Service Act, 42 U.S.C. 299b–24(b)(1)(C)); and the submission of a disclosure statement to the Secretary whenever a PSO has established specific types of relationships (discussed below) with a contracting provider, in particular where a PSO is not managed or controlled independently from, or if it does not operate independently from, a contracting provider (section 924(b)(1)(E) of the Public Health Service Act, 42 U.S.C. 299b–24(b)(1)(E)). (1) Proposed § 3.102(d)(1)—Notification Regarding PSO Compliance With the Minimum Contract Requirement Proposed § 3.102(d)(1) requires a PSO to notify the Secretary whether it has entered at least two bona fide contracts that meet the requirements of proposed § 3.102(b)(2). The notification requirement implements the statutory requirement in section 924(b)(1)(C) of the Public Health Service Act, 42 U.S.C. 299b–24(b)(1)(C), that a PSO must have contracts with more than one provider.

Notification to the Secretary will be by attestation on a certification form developed pursuant to proposed § 3.112.

Prompt notification of the Secretary that a PSO has entered two or more contracts will result in earlier publication of that information by the Secretary and this may be to the PSO's benefit.

We propose that the Secretary receive initial notification from a PSO no later than 45 calendar days before the last day of the period that is 24 months after the date of its initial listing and 45 calendar days prior to the last day of every 24-month period thereafter. While each PSO will have the full statutory period of 24 months to comply with this requirement, we propose an earlier date for notification of the Secretary to harmonize this notification requirement with the requirement, established by section 924(e) of the Public Health Service Act, 42 U.S.C. 299b–24(e), that the Secretary provide each PSO with a period of time to correct a deficiency. If the Secretary were to provide a period for correction that begins after the 24-month period has ended, the result would be that some PSOs would be granted compliance periods that extend beyond the unambiguous statutory deadline for compliance. To avoid this unfair result, we propose that a PSO certify to the Secretary whether it has complied with this requirement 45 calendar

days in advance of the final day of its applicable 24-month period.

If a PSO notifies the Secretary that it cannot certify compliance or fails to submit the required notification, the Secretary, pursuant to proposed § 3.108(a)(2), will then issue a preliminary finding of deficiency and provide a period for correction that extends until midnight of the last day of the applicable 24-month assessment period for the PSO. In this way, the requirement for an opportunity for correction can be met without granting any PSO a period for compliance that exceeds the statutory limit. We invite comments on alternative approaches to harmonize these two potentially conflicting requirements. We note that contracts that are entered into after midnight on the last day of the applicable 24-month period do not count toward meeting the two contract requirement for that 24-month assessment period. If a PSO does not meet the requirement by midnight of the last day of the applicable 24-month assessment period, the Secretary will issue a notice of revocation and delisting pursuant to proposed § 3.108(a)(3). (2) Proposed § 3.102(d)(2)—Notification Regarding PSO's Relationships With ItsContracting Providers Proposed § 3.102(d)(2) establishes the circumstances under which a PSO must submit a disclosure statement to the Secretary regarding its relationship(s) with any contracting provider(s) and the deadline for such required submissions.

The purpose of this disclosure requirement is illuminated by the statutory obligation of the Secretary, set forth in section 924(c)(3) of the Public Health Service Act, 42 U.S.C. 299b- 24(c)(3), to review the disclosure statements and make public findings "whether the entity can fairly and accurately perform the patient safety activities of a patient safety organization." To provide the Secretary with the information necessary to make such a judgment, section 924(b)(1)(E) of the Public Health Service Act, 42 U.S.C. 299b–24(b)(1)(E), requires a PSO to fully disclose information to the Secretary if the PSO has certain types of relationships with a contracting provider and, if applicable, whether the PSO is not independently managed or controlled, or if it does not operate independently from, the contracting provider.

The statutory requirement for a PSO to submit a disclosure statement applies only when a PSO has entered into a contract with a provider; if there is no contractual relationship between the PSO and a provider pursuant to the Patient Safety Act, a disclosure statement is not required. Even when a PSO has entered a contract with a provider, we propose that a PSO would need to file a disclosure statement regarding a contracting provider only when the circumstances, specified in section 924(c)(3) of the Public Health Service Act, 42 U.S.C. 299-24(c)(3), and discussed here, are present. A PSO is first required to assess whether a disclosure statement must be submitted to the Secretary when the PSO enters a contract with a provider, but we note that the disclosure requirement remains in effect during the entire contract period. Even when a disclosure statement is not required at the outset of the contract period, if the circumstances discussed here arise, a disclosure statement must be submitted at that time to the Secretary for review.

With respect to a provider with which it has entered a contract, a PSO is required to submit a disclosure statement to the Secretary only if either or both of the following circumstances are present. First, a disclosure statement must be filed if the PSO has any financial, reporting, or contractual relationships with a contracting provider (other than the contract entered into pursuant to the Patient Safety Act). Second, taking into account all relationships that the PSO has with that contracting provider, a PSO must file a disclosure statement if it is not independently managed or controlled, or if it does not operate independently from, the contracting provider. With respect to financial, reporting or contractual relationships, the proposed rule states that contractual relationships that must be disclosed are not limited to formal contracts but encompass any oral or written arrangement that imposes responsibilities on the PSO. For example, the provider may already have a contract or other arrangement with the PSO for assistance in implementation of proven patient safety interventions and is now seeking additional help from the PSO for the review of patient safety work product. A financial relationship involves almost any direct or indirect ownership or investment relationship between the PSO and the contracting provider, shared or common financial interests, or direct or indirect compensation arrangement, whether in cash or in-kind. A reporting relationship includes a relationship that gives the provider access to information that the PSO holds that is not available to other contracting providers or control, directly or indirectly, over the work of the PSO that is not available to other contracting providers. If any such relationships are present, the PSO must file a disclosure statement and describe fully all of these relationships. The other circumstance that triggers the requirement to disclose information to the Secretary is the provision of the Patient Safety Act that requires the entity to fully disclose "if applicable, the fact that the entity is not managed, controlled, and operated independently from any provider that contracts with the entity." See section 924(b)(1)(E) of the Public

Health Service Act, 42 U.S.C. 299b–24(b)(1)(E). We propose to interpret this provision as noted above because we believe that the adverb "independently" modifies all three verbs—that is, that the entity is required to disclose when it is not managed independently from, is not controlled independently from, or is not operated independently from, any provider that contracts with the entity.

Disclosure would be required, for example, if the contracting provider created the PSO and exercises a degree of management or control over the PSO, such as overseeing the establishment of its budget or fees, hiring decisions, or staff assignments. Another example of such a relationship that would require disclosure would be the existence of any form of inter-locking governance structure. We recognize that contracts, by their very nature, will enable a contracting provider to specify tasks that the PSO undertakes or to direct the PSO to review specific cases and not others. These types of requirements reflect the nature of any contractual relationship and do not trigger a requirement to file such a disclosure statement. The focus of this provision as indicated in section 924(c)(3) of the Public Health Service Act, 42 U.S.C. 299b–24(c)(3), and here is on the exercise of the type of control that could compromise the ability of the PSO to fairly and accurately carry out patient safety activities.

If the contracting provider exercises this type of influence over the PSO, the PSO must file a disclosure statement and fully disclose the nature of the influence exercised by the contracting provider.

To meet the statutory requirement for full disclosure, a PSO's submission should attempt to put the significance of the financial, reporting, or contractual relationship in perspective (e.g., relative to other sources of PSO revenue or other types of contractual or reporting relationships). We would also encourage PSOs to list any agreements, stipulations, or procedural safeguards that might offset the influence of the provider and that might protect the ability of the PSO to operate independently. By doing so, a PSO can ensure that its disclosure statements present a full and, if applicable, balanced picture of the relationships and degree of independence that exist between the PSO and its contracting provider(s). We propose to require that, whenever a PSO determines that it must file a statement based upon these requirements, the Secretary must receive the disclosure statement within 45 calendar days. The PSO must make an initial determination on the date on which a contract is entered. If the PSO determines that it must file a disclosure statement, the Secretary must receive the disclosure statement no later than 45 days after the date on which the contract was entered. During the contract

period, the Secretary must receive a disclosure statement within 45 calendar days of the date on which either or both of the circumstances described above arise. If the Secretary determines, after the applicable 45-day period, that a required disclosure statement was not received from a PSO, the Secretary may issue to the PSO a notice of a preliminary finding of deficiency, the first step in the revocation process established by proposed § 3.108.

2. Proposed § 3.104—Secretarial Actions Proposed § 3.104 describes the actions that the Secretary may and will take regarding certification submissions for listing or continued listing, the required notification certifying that the PSO has entered the required minimum of two contracts, and disclosure statements, including the criteria that the Secretary will use in reviewing such statements and the determinations the Secretary may make. This proposed section also outlines the types of information that the Secretary will make public regarding PSOs, specifies how, and for what period of time, the Secretary will list a PSO whose certification he has accepted and establishes an effective date for Secretarial actions under this proposed subpart. See section 924(c) of the Public Health Service Act, 42 U.S.C. 299b– 24(c). (A) Proposed § 3.104(a)—Actions in Response to Certification Submissions for Initial and

Continued Listing as a PSO Proposed § 3.104(a) describes the actions that the Secretary may and will take in response to certification for initial or continued listing as a PSO (section 924(c)(1)–(2) of the Public Health Service Act, 42 U.S.C. 299b- 24(c)(1)–(2)), submitted to the Secretary pursuant to the requirements of proposed § 3.102. The decision on whether and how to list an entity as a PSO will be based upon a determination of whether the entity meets the applicable requirements of the Patient Safety Act and this proposed part. In most cases, it is anticipated that the Secretary will either accept the submission and list the entity or deny the listing on this basis.

In determining whether to list an entity as a PSO, the proposed rule requires the Secretary to consider the submitted certification and any relevant history, such as prior actions the ecretary has taken regarding the entity or PSO including delisting, any history of or current non-compliance by the entity or PSO with statutory or regulatory requirements or requests by the Secretary, relationships of the entity or PSO with providers and any findings by the Secretary in accordance with proposed § 3.104(c). Initially, the Secretary will rely solely on the submitted certification; entities seeking listing will not have any applicable history of the type specified for the Secretary to consider. Even over time, we anticipate that the Secretary would normally rely upon the

submitted certification in making a listing determination.

There may be occasions in future years when the Secretary may need to take into account the history of an entity or PSO in making a determination for initial or continued listing. Examples of such situations might include: A PSO seeking continued listing that has a history of deficiencies; an entity seeking initial listing may be a renamed former PSO whose certifications had been revoked for cause by the Secretary; or the leadership of an entity seeking listing may have played a leadership role in a former PSO that failed to meet its obligations to providers during voluntary relinquishment (see proposed § 3.108(c)). In such circumstances, it may not be prudent for the Secretary to rely solely upon the certification submitted by the entity or PSO and this proposed subsection would enable the Secretary to seek additional information or assurances before reaching a determination on whether to list an entity. To ensure that the Secretary is aware of any relevant history before making a listing determination, without imposing additional burden on most entities seeking listing, we propose to include an attestation on the certification form that would require acknowledgement if the entity (under its current name or another) or any member of its workforce have been party to a delisting determination by the

Secretary. We welcome comment on this proposal, or alternative approaches, for ensuring that the Secretary can carry out the requirements of this proposed section.

The Secretary also has the authority, under certain circumstances, to condition the listing of a PSO under section 924(c)(3) of the Public Health Service Act, 42 U.S.C. 299b-24(c)(3). The Secretary may establish conditions on the listing of a PSO following a determination, pursuant to proposed § 3.104(c), that such conditions are necessary to ensure that the PSO can fairly and accurately perform patient safety activities. A decision to impose such conditions will typically occur after the listing of a PSO, when the PSO submits a disclosure statement about its relationships with a contracting provider. It also could occur at the time of initial or continued listing based upon a Secretarial review of a disclosure statement submitted contemporaneously with the review of an entity's certification submission.

The Secretary expects to be able to conclude review of an application for initial or continued listing within 30 days of receipt unless additional information or assurances, as described above in the paragraph discussing the history of an entity or PSO, are required, or the application as initially submitted is incomplete. The Secretary will notify each entity that requests listing of the action taken on its certification submission for initial or continued listing. The Secretary will provide reasons when an entity's certification is not accepted and, if the listing is conditioned based upon a determination made pursuant to proposed § 3.104(c), the reasons for imposing conditions.

(B) Proposed § 3.104(b)—Actions Regarding PSO Compliance With the Minimum Contract Requirement Proposed § 3.104(b) sets forth the required Secretarial action regarding PSO compliance with the requirement of the proposed rule for a minimum of two bona fide contracts. If a PSO attests, in the notification required by proposed § 3.102(d)(1), that it has met the requirement, the Secretary will acknowledge in writing receipt of the attestation and include information on the list established pursuant to proposed § 3.104(d) that the PSO has certified that it has met the requirement.

If the PSO notifies the Secretary that it has not yet met the requirement, or if notification is not received from the PSO by the date required under proposed § 3.102(d)(1), the Secretary, pursuant to proposed § 3.108(a)(2), will issue a notice of a preliminary finding of deficiency to the PSO and provide an opportunity for correction that will extend no later than midnight of the last day of its applicable 24-month assessment period. Under this authority, the Secretary will require notification of correction

and compliance from a PSO by midnight of the final day of the applicable 24-month period. If the deficiency has not been corrected by that date, the Secretary will issue promptly a notice of proposed revocation and delisting pursuant to the requirements of proposed § 3.108(a)(3).

(C) Proposed § 3.104(c)—Actions Regarding Required Disclosures by PSOs of Relationships With Contracting Providers. Proposed § 3.104(c) establishes criteria that the Secretary will use to evaluate a disclosure statement submitted pursuant to proposed § 3.102(d)(2), specifies the determinations the Secretary may make based upon evaluation of any disclosure statement, and proposes public release, consistent with the Freedom of Information Act, of disclosure statements submitted by PSOs as well as the Secretary's findings (see section 924(c)(3) of the Public Health Service Act, 42 U.S.C. 299b–24(c)(3)).

In reviewing disclosure statements and making public findings, we propose that the Secretary consider the nature, significance, and duration of the relationship between the PSO and the contracting provider. We seek input on other appropriate factors to consider.

Following review of the disclosure statement, the Secretary will make public findings regarding the ability of the PSO to carry out fairly and accurately defined patient safety activities as

required by the Patient Safety Act. The Secretary may conclude that the disclosures require no action on his part or, depending on whether the entity is listed or seeking listing, may condition his listing of the PSO, exercise his authority under proposed § 3.104(a) to refuse to list, or exercise his authority under proposed § 3.108 to revoke the listing of the entity. The Secretary will notify each entity of his findings and decision regarding each disclosure statement.

This subsection proposes to make this process transparent, recognizing that providers seeking to contract with a PSO may want to make their own judgments regarding the appropriateness of the disclosed relationships. Therefore, with the exception of information, such as information that would be exempt from disclosure under the Freedom of Information Act, we propose to make public each disclosure statement received from a PSO by including it on the list of PSOs maintained pursuant to proposed § 3.104(d) and we may post such statements on the PSO Web site we plan to establish. Public release of PSO disclosure statements would be in addition to the statutory requirement in section 924(c)(3) of the Public Health Service Act, 42 U.S.C. 299b–24(c)(3), that the Secretary's findings regarding disclosure statements must be made public. Greater transparency is intended to promote more informed decision making by providers, who are the primary customers for PSO services.

(D) Proposed § 3.104(d)— Maintaining a List of PSOs Proposed § 3.104(d) implements the statutory requirement in section 924(d) of the Public Health Service Act, 42 U.S.C. 299b–24(d), that the Secretary compile and maintain a list of those entities whose PSO certifications have been accepted in accordance with proposed § 3.104(a) and which certifications have not been revoked or voluntarily relinquished in accordance with proposed § 3.108(b) or (c). The list will include contact information for each PSO, the effective date and time of listing of the PSO, a copy of each certification form and disclosure statement that the Secretary receives from the entity, and information on whether the PSO has certified that it has met the two contract requirement in each 24-month assessment period. The list will also include a copy of the Secretary's findings regarding any disclosure statements filed by each PSO, including whether any conditions have been placed on the listing of the entity as a PSO, and other information that this proposed subpart authorizes the Secretary to make public. To facilitate the development of a marketplace for the services of PSOs, we plan to establish a PSO Web site (or a future technological equivalent) and expect to post the list of PSOs on the PSO Web site, reserving the

right to exclude information contained in disclosure statements that would be exempt from disclosure under the Freedom of Information Act. We seek comment on whether there are specific types of information that the Secretary should consider posting routinely on this Web site for the benefit of PSOs, providers, and other consumers of PSO services.

(E) Proposed § 3.104(e)— Three-Year Period of Listing Proposed § 3.104(e) states that, when the Secretary has accepted certification submitted for initial or continued listing, the entity will be listed as a PSO for a period of three years (section 924(a)(2) of the Public Health Service Act, 42 U.S.C. 299b–24(a)(2)), unless the Secretary revokes the listing or the Secretary determines that the entity has volun-tarily relinquished its status as a PSO (see proposed § 3.108). This subsection also provides that the Secretary will send a written notice of imminent expiration to a PSO no later than 45 calendar days before the date on which the PSO's three-year period of listing expires if the Secretary has not received a certification seeking continued listing. This notice is intended to ensure that a PSO does not let its listing lapse inadver-tently. We expect that the Secretary will include in the notice a date by which the PSO should submit its certifications to ensure that the Secretary has sufficient time to act before the current period of listing expires.

We are considering including in the final rule, and seek comment on, a requirement that the Secretary include information on the public list of PSOs maintained pursuant to § 3.104(d), that identifies the PSOs to which a notice of imminent expiration has been sent. The intent of such a requirement would be to ensure that a provider reporting data to such a PSO has adequate notice and time to ascertain, if it chooses to do so, whether that PSO intends to seek continued listing and, if not, to make alternative arrangements for reporting data to another PSO.

(F) Proposed § 3.104(f)— Effective Date of Secretarial Actions Proposed § 3.104(f) states that, unless otherwise specified, the effective date of each action by the Secretary pursuant to this proposed subpart will be specified in the written notice that is sent to the entity. To ensure that an entity receives prompt notification, the Department anticipates sending such a notice by electronic mail or other electronic means in addition to a hard copy version. We are confident that any entity seeking listing as a PSO will have electronic mail capacity. For listing and delisting, the Secretary will specify both an effective time and date for such actions in the written notice. Our intent is to ensure clarity regarding when the entity can receive information that will be protected as patient safety work product.

3. Proposed § 3.106—Security Requirements Proposed § 3.106 identifies the entities and individuals that are subject to the security requirements of this section and establishes the considerations that entities and individuals specified in subsection (a) should address to secure patient safety work product in their possession. This section provides a common framework for compliance with the requirement in section 921(5)(F) of the Public Health Service Act, 42 U.S.C. 299b-21(5)(F), that a PSO provide appropriate security measures with respect to patient safety work product. In light of the importance of data security to those who supply patient safety work product to any PSO, maintenance of data security will be a high and ongoing priority for PSOs. (A) Proposed § 3.106(a)— Application Proposed § 3.106(a) states that the security requirements in proposed § 3.106(b) apply to each PSO, its workforce members, and its contractors when the contractors hold patient safety work product. This proposed subsection applies the requirements at all times and at any location at which patient safety work product is held. We expect that it will be more efficient for most PSOs to contract for at least a portion of the expertise they need to carry out patient safety activities, including the evaluation of certain types of patient safety events. In such situations, when a PSO discloses patient safety work product to a

contractor to assist the PSO in carrying out patient safety activities and the contractor maintains such patient safety work product at locations other than those controlled by the PSO, our intent is to ensure that these same security requirements apply. We recognize that some contractors that a PSO chooses to employ may not want to, or may not have the resources to, meet these requirements at other locations. In such circumstances, the contractors will need to perform their services at locations at which the PSO can ensure that these security requirements can be met.

We note that this regulation does not impose these requirements on providers, but agreements between PSOs and providers may by contract call for providers to adopt equivalent standards. (B) Proposed § 3.106(b)— Security Framework Proposed § 3.106(b) establishes a framework consisting of four categories for the security of patient safety work product that a PSO must consider, including security management, separation of systems, security control and monitoring, and security assessment.

This framework is consistent with the standards of the National Institute of Standards and Technology (NIST) that federal agencies must follow but this section does not impose on PSOs the specific NIST standards that Federal agencies must meet. We recognize that it is not

likely that PSOs will have the scale of operation or the resources to comply with Federal data security standards. Instead, we propose to require that each PSO must consider the four categories of the NIST framework set forth in this section by developing appropriate and scalable standards that are suitable for the size and complexity of its organization. We seek comment on the extent to which this proposal adequately and appropriately identifies the most significant security issues, with respect to patient safety work product that PSOs receive, develop, or maintain, and which PSOs should be expected to address with due diligence, and the extent to which our approach provides PSOs with sufficient flexibility to develop scalable standards. (1) Proposed § 3.106(b)(1)— Security Management Proposed § 3.106(b)(1) requires the PSO to approach its security requirements by: documenting its security requirements for patient safety work product; taking steps to ensure that its workforce and contractors as specified in proposed § 3.106(a) understand their responsibilities regarding patient safety work product and the confidentiality requirements of the statute, including the potential imposition of civil money penalties for impermissible disclosures; and monitoring and improving the effectiveness of its security policies and procedures.

(2) Proposed § 3.106(b)(2)—Separation of Systems Under the statute, to preserve the confidentiality of patient safety work product, it is important to maintain a clear separation between patient safety work product and information that is not protected, and a clear separation between patient safety activities and other activities. As a result, we have incorporated requirements in proposed § 3.106(b)(2) that PSOs must ensure such separation. The specific requirements for which a PSO must develop appropriate standards include: maintaining functional and physical separation of patient safety work product from other systems of records; protection of patient safety work product while it is held by the PSO; appropriate disposal or sanitization of media that have contained patient safety work product; and preventing physical access to patient safety work product by unauthorized users or recipients. (3) Proposed § 3.106(b)(3)—Security Control and Monitoring Proposed § 3.106(b)(3) requires that policies and procedures adopted by a PSO related to security control and monitoring must enable the PSO to identify and authenticate users of patient safety work product and must create an audit capacity to detect unlawful, unauthorized, or inappropriate activities involving access to patient safety work product. To ensure accountability, controls should be designed to preclude unauthorized removal, transmission or disclosures of patient safety work product. (4) Proposed § 3.106(b)(4)—Security Assessment Proposed § 3.106(b)(4) requires a PSO to develop policies and procedures that permit it to assess periodically the effectiveness and weaknesses of its overall approach to security of patient safety work product. A PSO needs to determine the frequency of security assessments, determine when it needs to undertake a risk assessment exercise so that the leadership and the workforce of the PSO are aware of the risks to PSO assets from security lapses, and specify how it will assess and adjust its procedures to ensure the security of its communications involving patient safety work product to and from providers and other authorized parties. Such communications are potentially vulnerable weak points for any security system and require ongoing special attention by a PSO. 4. Proposed § 3.108—Correction of Deficiencies, Revocation and Voluntary Relinquishment Proposed § 3.108 describes the process by which PSOs will be given an opportunity to correct deficiencies, the process for revocation of acceptance of the certification submitted by an entity for cause and its removal from the list of PSOs, and specifies the circumstances under which an entity will be considered to have voluntarily relinquished its status as a PSO.

This section would establish procedural opportunities for a PSO to respond during the process that might lead to revocation. When the Secretary identifies a possible deficiency, the PSO would be given an opportunity to correct the record if it can demonstrate that the information regarding a deficiency is erroneous, and if the existence of a deficiency is uncontested, an opportunity to correct it. The PSO is encouraged to alert the Department if it faces unanticipated challenges in correcting the deficiency; we propose that the Secretary will consider such information in determining whether the PSO has acted in good faith, whether the deadline for corrective action should be extended, or whether the required corrective action should be modified. If the Secretary determines that the PSO has not timely corrected the deficiency and issues a notice of proposed revocation and delisting, the PSO will be given an automatic right of appeal to present its case in writing. If the Secretary makes a decision to revoke acceptance of the entity's certification and remove it from the list of PSOs, this proposed section specifies the required actions that the Secretary and the entity must take following such a decision. The proposed rule implements the statutory requirements for the establishment of a limited period during which providers can continue to report information to the

former PSO and receive patient safety work product protections for these data, and establishes a framework for appropriate disposition of patient safety work product or data held by the former PSO.
See section 924(e)–(g) of the Public Health Service Act, 42 U.S.C. 299b–24(e)–(g). This section also describes two circumstances under which an entity will be considered to have voluntarily relinquished its status as a PSO: (1) Notification of the Secretary in writing by the PSO of its intent to relinquish its status voluntarily; and (2) if a PSO lets its period of listing expire without submission of a certification for continued listing that the Secretary has accepted. In both circumstances, we propose that such a PSO consult with the source of the patient safety work product in its possession to provide notice of its intention to cease operations and provide for appropriate disposition of such patient safety work product. When the Secretary removes a PSO from listing as a result of revocation for cause or voluntarily relinquishment, the Secretary is required to provide public notice of the action.
We note that section 921 of the Public Health Service Act, 42 U.S.C. 299b–21, and, therefore, the proposed rule, defines a PSO as an entity that is listed by the Secretary pursuant to the requirements of the statute that are incorporated into this proposed rule.

This means that an entity remains a PSO for its three-year period of listing unless the Secretary removes the entity from the list of PSOs because he revokes acceptance of its certification and listing for cause or because the entity voluntarily relinquishes its status as described below.
Accordingly, even when a deficiency is identified publicly or the proposed requirements of this section have been initiated, we stress that an entity remains a PSO until the date and time at which the Secretary's removal of the entity from listing is effective. Until then, data that is reported to a listed entity by providers shall be considered patient safety work product and the protections accorded patient safety work product continue to apply following the delisting of the PSO.
(A) Proposed § 3.108(a)—Process for Correction of a Deficiency and Revocation Proposed § 3.108(a) describes the process by which the Secretary would provide an opportunity for a PSO to correct identified deficiencies and, if not timely corrected or if the deficiencies cannot be "cured," the process that can lead to a determination by the Secretary to revoke acceptance of a PSO's certification. This section proposes a two-stage process. The first stage would provide an opportunity to correct a deficiency. Under the proposal, when the Secretary identifies a deficiency, the Secretary would send the PSO a notice of preliminary

determination of a deficiency. The PSO would then have an opportunity to demonstrate that the information on which the notice was based is incorrect. The notice would include a timetable for correction of the deficiency and may specify the specific corrective action and the documentation that the Secretary would need to determine if the deficiency has been corrected. The PSO would be encouraged to provide information for the administrative record on unexpected challenges in correcting the deficiency, since the Secretary has great flexibility to work with a PSO to facilitate correction of deficiencies. We anticipate that most PSO deficiencies would be resolved at this stage.
Under the proposal, the second stage would occur when the Secretary would conclude that a PSO has not timely corrected a deficiency or has a pattern of non-compliance and issues the PSO a notice of proposed revocation and delisting. Rather than requiring a PSO to seek an opportunity to appeal, the proposed rule would provide an automatic period of 30 days for a PSO to be heard in writing by submitting a rebuttal to the findings in the Secretary's notice of revocation and delisting. The Secretary may then affirm, modify, or reverse the notice of revocation and delisting.
In light of the procedures in the proposed rule to ensure due process, we have not proposed to incorporate any

further internal administrative appeal process beyond the Secretary's determination regarding a notice of proposed revocation and delisting pursuant to proposed § 3.108(a)(5). We invite comments on our proposed approach.

(1) Proposed § 3.108(a)(1)— Circumstances Leading to Revocation Proposed § 3.108(a)(1) lists four circumstances, each of which is statutorily based, that may lead the Secretary to revoke acceptance of a PSO's certification and delist the entity: the PSO is not meeting the obligations to which it certified its compliance as required by proposed § 3.102; the PSO has not certified to the Secretary that it has entered the required minimum of two contracts within the applicable 24-month period pursuant to proposed § 3.102(d)(1); the Secretary, after reviewing a PSO's disclosure statement submitted pursuant to proposed § 3.102(d)(2), determines that the PSO cannot fairly and accurately perform its duties pursuant to proposed § 3.104(c); or the PSO is not in compliance with any other provision of the Patient Safety Act or this proposed part. (See section 924(c) and (e) of the Public Health Service Act, 42 U.S.C. 299b–24(c) and (e).)

(2) Proposed § 3.108(a)(2)— Notice of Preliminary Finding of Deficiency and Establishment of an Opportunity for Correction of a Deficiency Under proposed § 3.108(a)(2), when the Secretary has reason to believe that a PSO is not in compliance with the requirements of the statute and the final rule, the Secretary would send a written notice of a preliminary finding of deficiency to the PSO (see section 924(c) and (e) of the Public Health Service Act, 42 U.S.C. 299b–24(c) and (e)). The notice would specifically state the actions or inactions that describe the deficiency, outline the evidence that a deficiency exists, specify the possible and/or required corrective action(s) that must be taken, establish an opportunity for correction and a date by which the corrective action(s) must be completed, and, in certain circumstances, specify the documentation that the PSO would be required to submit to demonstrate that the deficiency has been corrected.

We propose that, absent other evidence of actual receipt, we would assume that the notice of a preliminary finding of deficiency has been received 5 calendar days after it was sent. Under the proposal, if a PSO submits evidence to the Secretary that demonstrates to the Secretary that the preliminary finding is factually incorrect within 14 calendar days following receipt of this notice, the preliminary finding of deficiency would be withdrawn; otherwise, it would be the basis for a finding of deficiency. We stress that this would not be an opportunity to file an appeal regarding the proposed corrective actions, the period allotted for correcting the deficiency, or the time to provide explanations regarding why a deficiency exists. This 14-day period would only ensure that the PSO has an opportunity, if the information on which the notice is based is not accurate, to correct the record immediately. For example, a notice of a preliminary finding of deficiency may be based on the fact that the Secretary has no record that the PSO has entered the required two contracts.

In this case, if a PSO can attest that it submitted the certification as required or can attest that it has entered the required two contracts consistent with the requirements of proposed § 3.102(d)(1), the Secretary would then withdraw the notice. If a notice of deficiency is based on the failure of the PSO to submit a required disclosure statement within 45 days, the PSO might submit evidence that the required statement had been sent as required. If the evidence is convincing, the Secretary would withdraw the notice of preliminary finding of deficiency. If the Secretary does not consider the evidence convincing, the Secretary would so notify the PSO and the notice would remain in effect. The PSO would then need to demonstrate that it has met the requirements of the notice regarding correction of the deficiency.

We anticipate that in the vast majority of circumstances in

which the Secretary believes there is a deficiency, the deficiency can and will be corrected by the PSO. In those cases, as discussed above, the PSO will be given an opportunity to take the appropriate action to correct the deficiency, and avoid revocation and delisting. However, we can anticipate situations in which a PSO's conduct is so egregious that the Secretary's acceptance of the PSO's certification should be revoked without the opportunity to cure because there is no meaningful cure. An example would be where a PSO has a policy and practice of knowingly and inappropriately selling patient safety work product or where the PSO is repeatedly deficient and this conduct continues despite previous opportunities to cure. We are considering adding a provision whereby an opportunity to "cure" would not be available in this type of situation.

Providing the PSO with an opportunity for correction, as provided in the Patient Safety Act, would entail providing an opportunity to correct the preliminary factual findings of the Department.

Thus, the PSO would have the chance to demonstrate that we have the facts wrong or there are relevant facts we are overlooking. We invite comments regarding this approach and how best to characterize the situations in which the opportunity to "cure" (e.g., to change policies, practices or procedures, sanction employees, send out correction notices) would not be sufficient, meaningful, or appropriate. (3) Proposed § 3.108(a)(3)— Determination of Correction of a Deficiency Proposed section § 3.108(a)(3) addresses the determination of whether a deficiency has been corrected, including the time frame for submission of the required documentation that the deficiency has been corrected, and the actions the Secretary may take after review of the documentation and any site visit(s) the Secretary deems necessary or appropriate (see sections 924(c) and (e) of the Public Health Service Act, 42 U.S.C. 299b–24(c) and (e)).

Under the proposal, during the period of correction, we would encourage the PSO to keep the Department apprised in writing of its progress, especially with respect to any challenges it faces in implementing the required corrective actions. Such communications would become part of the administrative record. Until there is additional experience with the operational challenges that PSOs face in implementing specific types of corrective actions, such information, if submitted, would be especially helpful for ensuring that the time frames and the corrective actions specified by the Secretary are reasonable and appropriate. As noted below, such information would be considered by the Secretary in making a determination regarding a PSO's compliance with the correction of a deficiency. Unless the Secretary specifies a different submission date, or approves such a request from the PSO, we propose that documentation submitted by the PSO to demonstrate correction of the deficiency must be received by the Secretary no later than 5 calendar days after the final day of the correction period.

Under the proposed rule, in making a determination, the Secretary would consider the documentation and other information submitted by the PSO, the findings of any site visit that might have been conducted, recommendations of program staff, and any other information available regarding the PSO that the Secretary deems appropriate. After completing his review, the Secretary may make one of the following determinations: (1) The action(s) taken by the PSO have corrected any deficiency, in which case the Secretary will withdraw the notice of deficiency and so notify the PSO; (2) the PSO has acted in good faith to correct the deficiency but an additional period of time is necessary to achieve full compliance and/or the required corrective action specified in the notice of a preliminary finding of deficiency needs to be modified in light of the actions undertaken by the PSO so far, in which case the Secretary will extend the period for correction and/or modify the specific corrective action required; or (3) the PSO has not completed the corrective action because it has not acted with reasonable diligence or timeliness to ensure that the corrective action was completed within the allotted time, in which case the Secretary will issue to the PSO a notice of proposed revocation and delisting.

When the Secretary issues a notice of proposed revocation and delisting, this notice would include those deficiencies that have not been timely corrected. The notice would be accompanied by information concerning the manner in which the PSO may exercise its opportunity to be heard in writing to respond to the deficiency findings described in the notice.

(4) Proposed § 3.108(a)(4)— Opportunity to be Heard in Writing Following a Notice of Proposed Revocation and Delisting Proposed § 3.108(a)(4) sets forth our approach to meeting the statutory requirement established in section 924(e) of the Public Health Service Act, 42 U.S.C. 299b–24(e), for a PSO to have an opportunity to dispute the findings of deficiency in a notice of proposed revocation and delisting.

Absent other evidence of actual receipt, we would assume that the notice of proposed revocation and delisting has been received by a PSO five calendar days after it was sent.

Under the proposed rule, unless a PSO chooses to waive its right to contest a notice of proposed revocation and delisting and so notifies the Secretary, a PSO would not need to request an opportunity to appeal a notice of proposed

revocation and delisting. A PSO would automatically have 30 calendar days, beginning the day the notice is deemed to be received, to exercise its opportunity to be heard in writing. The Secretary would consider, and include in the administrative record, any written information submitted by the PSO within this 30-day period that responds to the deficiency findings in the notice of proposed revocation and delisting. If a PSO does not take advantage of the opportunity to submit a substantive response in writing within 30 calendar days of receipt of the notice of proposed revocation and delisting, the notice would become final as a matter of law at midnight of the date specified by the Secretary in the notice. The Secretary would provide the PSO with policies and rules of procedures that govern the form or transmission of the written response to the notice of proposed revocation and delisting. We are considering incorporating in the final rule an exception to our proposed policy of automatically providing a PSO with a 30-day period in which to submit a written response to a notice of proposed revocation and delisting. The one exception we are considering relates to failure to meet the requirement for a minimum of two contracts. The statutory requirement is unambiguous that this requirement must be met within every 24-month period after the initial date of listing of the

PSO. We propose elsewhere that a PSO submit its notification 45 calendar days early so that a period for correction can be established that concludes at midnight of the last day of the applicable 24-month period established by the statute for compliance. The Secretary would then need to receive notification from a PSO that this requirement has been met no later than midnight of that last day (see proposed § 3.102(d)(1) and proposed § 3.104(b)).

Other than verifying that the PSO has not entered into and reported the required two bona fide contracts by midnight on the last day of the applicable 24-month period, we see no basis for a written rebuttal of such a deficiency determination. The language we are considering, therefore, would authorize the Secretary, when the basis for a notice of proposed revocation and delisting is the failure of a PSO to meet this very specific requirement, to proceed to revocation and delisting five calendar days after the notice of proposed revocation and delisting would be deemed to have been received.

(5) Proposed § 3.108(a)(5)— The Secretary's Decision Regarding Revocation If a written response to the deficiency findings of a notice of proposed revocation and delisting is submitted by a PSO, proposed § 3.108(a)(5) provides that the Secretary will review the entire administrative record pertaining to the notice of

proposed revocation and delisting and any written materials submitted by the PSO under proposed § 3.108(a)(4). The Secretary may affirm, reverse, or modify the notice of proposed revocation and delisting. The Secretary will notify the PSO in writing of his decision with respect to any revocation of the acceptance of its certification and its continued listing as a PSO. (See section 924(e) of the Public Health Service Act, 42 U.S.C. 299b- 24(e).)

(B) Proposed § 3.108(b)— Revocation of the Secretary's Acceptance of a PSO's Certification

When the Secretary makes a determination to remove the listing of a PSO for cause pursuant to proposed § 3.108(a), proposed § 3.108(b) specifies the actions that the Secretary and the entity must take, and implements the protections that the statute affords to data submitted to such an entity.

(1) Proposed § 3.108(b)(1)— Establishing Revocation for Cause Under our proposal, after following the require-ments of proposed § 3.108(a), if the Secretary determines pursuant to paragraph (a)(5) of this section that revocation of the acceptance of a PSO's certification is warranted for failure to comply with the requirements of the Patient Safety Act, or the regulations implementing the Patient Safety Act, the Secretary would establish, and notify the PSO of, the date and time at which the Secretary will revoke the acceptance of its certification and remove

the entity from the list of PSOs. The Secretary may include information in the notice on the statutory requirements, incorporated in proposed § 3.108(b)(2) and § 3.108 (b)(4) and discussed below, that apply to the entity following the Secretary's actions, and the Secretary would provide public notice as required by proposed § 3.108(d).

(2) Proposed § 3.108(b)(2)— Required Notification of Providers and Status of Data Proposed § 3.108(b)(2) incorporates in the proposed rule the statutory require-ments that are intended to ensure that providers receive a reasonable amount of notice that the PSO with which they are working is being removed from the list of PSOs (section 924(e)(2) of the Public Health Service Act, 42 U.S.C. 299b-24(e)(2)) and to clarify the status of data submitted by providers to a PSO whose listing has been revoked (section 924(f) of the Public Health Service Act, 42 U.S.C. 299b-24(f)).

As required by the statute, within 15 calendar days of the date established in the Secretary's notification of action under paragraph (b)(1) of this section, the entity subject to proposed § 3.108(b)(1) shall confirm to the Secretary that it has taken all reasonable actions to notify each provider whose patient safety work product has been collected or analyzed by the PSO that the entity has been removed from the list of PSOs. We would recommend, but do not propose to require, that

PSOs make a priority of notifying providers who report most frequently to the PSO, especially providers with contracts with the PSO. These providers would need to close out any current contract they have with the PSO, determine if they wish to enter a contract with another PSO, and if so, they would need time to identify another PSO and then negotiate another contract. We also recognize that, even when this statutory notification requirement is met, the notification period is short.

While we do not have the authority to require a PSO to undertake notification of providers more quickly than the statute specifies, we invite comment on whether there are any other steps the Secretary should take to ensure that affected providers receive timely notice.

We are considering requiring notice by electronic or priority mail if no notice has been given at the end of seven days.

Confidentiality and privilege protections that applied to patient safety work product while the former PSO was listed continue to apply after the entity is removed from listing. Furthermore, section 924(f)(1) of the Public Health Service Act, 42 U.S.C. 299b-24(f)(1) provides that data submitted to an entity within 30 calendar days of the date on which acceptance of its certification is revoked and it is removed from the list of PSOs, shall have the same status as data submitted while the entity was still listed. Thus, data that would otherwise be patient safety work product had it been submitted while the PSO was listed, will be protected as patient safety work product if submitted during this 30-day period after delisting. We stress that the statutory language in section 924(f)(1) of the Public Health Service Act, 42 U.S.C. 299b-24(f)(1), pertains only to data submitted to such an entity within 30 calendar days after such revocation and removal. This provision does not enable an entity that has been removed from listing to generate patient safety work product on its own pursuant to section 921(7)(A)(i)(II) of the Public Health Service Act, 42 U.S.C. 299b-21(7)(A)(i)(II); the entity loses that authority on the effective date and time of the Secretary's action to remove it from listing. (3) Proposed § 3.108(b)(3)—Disposition of Patient Safety Work Product and Data Proposed § 3.108(e) incorporates in the proposed rule statutory requirements regarding the disposition of patient safety work product or data following revocation and delisting of a PSO (section 924(g) of the Public Health Service Act, 42 U.S.C. 299b-24(g)). This proposed subsection would require that the former PSO provide for the disposition of patient safety work product or data in its possession in accordance with one or more of three alternatives described in section 924(g) of the Public Health Service Act, 42 U.S.C. 299b-24(g).

The three alternatives include: transfer of the patient safety work product with the approval of the source from which it was received to a PSO which has agreed to accept it; return of the patient safety work product or data to the source from which it was received; or, if return is not practicable, destroy such work product or data.

The text of the proposed rule refers to the "source" of the patient safety work product or data that is held by the former PSO, which is a broader formulation than the statutory phrase "received from another entity." While the statutory requirement encompasses PSOs as well as institutional providers, we tentatively conclude that the underlying intent of this statutory provision is to require the appropriate disposition of patient safety work product from all sources, not merely institutional sources. We note that the statute, and therefore the proposed rule, permits individual providers to report data to PSOs and individual providers are able to enter the same type of ongoing arrangements, or contractual arrangements, as institutional providers.

Moreover, proposed § 3.108(b)(2) would require PSOs to notify all providers (individual as well as institutional providers) from whom they receive data about the Secretary's revocation and delisting decision. We preliminarily conclude, therefore, that it is consistent with the statute that a former PSO consult

with all sources (individuals as well as entities) regarding the appropriate disposition of the patient safety work product or data that they supplied. Moreover, it is a good business practice. If workforce members of a former PSO retain possession of any patient safety work product, they would incur obligations and potential liability if it is impermissibly disclosed. We welcome comments on our interpretation.

The statutory provision indicates that these requirements apply to both patient safety work product or 'data' described in 924(f)(1) of the Public Health Service Act, 42 U.S.C. 299b-24(f)(1). Subsection (f)(1), entitled 'new data' and incorporated in proposed § 3.108(b)(2), describes data submitted to an entity within 30 calendar days after the entity is removed from listing as a PSO and provides that this data "shall have the same status as data submitted while the entity was still listed." The proposed regulation mirrors this formulation.

While the statute and this proposed rule would permit destruction of patient safety work product, we would encourage entities that have their listing as a PSO revoked to work with providers to ensure that patient safety work product remains available for aggregation and further analysis whenever possible, either by returning it to the provider or, with concurrence of the provider, transferring it to a PSO willing to accept it.

The statute does not establish a time frame for a PSO subject to revocation and delisting to complete the disposition of the patient safety work product or data in its possession. We invite comment on whether we should include a date by which this requirement must be completed (for example, a specific number of months after the date of revocation and delisting).

(C) Proposed § 3.108(c)— Voluntary Relinquishment
The statute recognizes the right of an entity to relinquish voluntarily its status as a PSO, in which case the Secretary will remove the entity from the list of PSOs. See section 924(d) of the Public Health Service Act, 42 U.S.C. 299b-24(d).

We stress that, if the Secretary determines that an entity has relinquished voluntarily its status as a PSO and removes the entity from listing, the confidentiality and privilege protections that applied to patient safety work product while the former PSO was listed continue to apply after the entity is removed from listing. (1) Proposed § 3.108(c)(1)—Circumstances Constituting Voluntary Relinquishment Proposed § 3.108(c)(1) provides that an entity would be considered to have relinquished voluntarily its status as a PSO under two circumstances: when a PSO advises the Secretary in writing that it no longer wishes to be a PSO, and when a PSO permits its three-year period of listing to expire without

timely submission of the required certification to the Secretary for continued listing. To ensure that such a lapse is not inadvertent, we provide in proposed § 3.104(e)(2) that the Secretary would send a notice of imminent expiration to any PSO from which the Secretary has not received a certification for continued listing by the date that is 45 calendar days before the expiration of its current period of listing. This notice is intended to ensure that the PSO has sufficient time to submit a certification for continued listing if it chooses to do so and that, if a lapse occurs, it is not inadvertent.

(2) Proposed § 3.108(c)(2)— Notification of Voluntary Relinquishment Proposed § 3.108(c)(2) would require an entity that seeks to relinquish voluntarily its status as a PSO to include attestations in its notice to the Secretary that it has made all reasonable efforts to provide for the orderly termination of the PSO. First, the PSO must attest that it has made—or will have made within 15 calendar days of the date of this notification to the Secretary—all reasonable efforts to notify organizations or individuals who have submitted data to the PSO of its intent to cease operation and to alert providers that they should cease reporting or submitting any further information as quickly as possible. We preliminarily conclude that, when a PSO voluntarily relinquishes its status, data

submitted by providers to the entity after the date on which the Secretary removes it from listing is not patient safety work product. The statutory provision, incorporated in the proposed rule at § 3.108(b)(2), that permits providers to submit data to an entity for an additional 30 days after the date of its removal from listing applies only to PSOs for which the Secretary has revoked acceptance of its certification for cause. It does not apply to a PSO that voluntarily relinquishes its status. We welcome comment on our interpretation.

Second, the PSO would be required to attest that, in consultation with the organizations or individuals who submitted the patient safety work product in its possession, it has established—or will have made all reasonable efforts within 15 calendar days of the date of this notification to establish—a plan for the appropriate disposition of such work product, consistent to the extent possible with the statutory requirements incorporated in proposed § 3.108(b)(3). Finally, the individual submitting the notification of voluntary relinquishment would provide appropriate contact information for further communications that the Secretary deems necessary.

We caution any PSO considering voluntary relinquishment that its status remains in effect until the Secretary removes the entity from listing. The

PSO's responsibilities, including those related to the confidentiality and security of the patient safety work product or data in its possession, are not discharged by the decision of a PSO to cease operations. Accordingly, we urge PSOs that are experiencing financial distress or other circumstances that may lead to voluntary relinquishment, to contact AHRQ program staff as early as possible so that the PSO's obligations can be appropriately discharged.

(3) Proposed § 3.108(c)(3)— Response to Notification of Voluntary Relinquishment In response to the submission of a notification of voluntary relinquishment, proposed § 3.108(c)(3) provides that the Secretary would respond in writing and indicate whether the proposed voluntary relinquishment is accepted. We anticipate that the Secretary would normally approve such requests but the text provides the Secretary with discretion to accept or reject such a request from a PSO that seeks voluntary relinquishment during or immediately after revocation proceedings. Our proposal is intended to recognize that, in certain circumstances, for example, when the deficiencies of the PSO are significant or reflect a pattern of non-compliance with the Patient Safety Act or the proposed rule, the Secretary may decide that giving precedence to the revocation process may be more appropriate.

(4) Proposed § 3.108(c)(4)— Implied Voluntary Relinquishment Proposed § 3.108(c)(4) enables the Secretary to determine that implied voluntary relinquishment has taken place if a PSO permits its period of listing to expire without receipt and acceptance by the Secretary of a certification for continued listing. In our view, the statute does not permit an entity to function as a PSO beyond its 3-year period of listing unless it has submitted, and the Secretary has accepted, a certification for a 3-year period of continued listing. To ensure that such a lapse is not inadvertent, we propose a requirement in § 3.104(e)(2) that the Secretary would send a notice of imminent expiration to any PSO from which the Secretary has not received the required certification for continued listing by the date that is 45 calendar days prior to the last date of the PSOs current period of listing. Accordingly, we propose that the Secretary would determine that a PSO under these circumstances has relinquished voluntarily its status at midnight on the last day of its current period of listing, remove the entity from the list of PSOs at midnight on that day, make reasonable efforts to notify the entity in writing of the action taken, and promptly provide public notice in accordance with proposed § 3.108(d). Under the proposed rule, the notice of delisting would request that the entity make reasonable efforts to comply

with the requirements of proposed § 3.108(c)(2). Compliance with these requirements in this circumstance would mean that the former PSO would be required to notify individuals and organizations that routinely reported data to the entity during its period of listing that it has voluntarily relinquished its status as a PSO and that they should no longer report or submit data, and make reasonable efforts to provide for the disposition of patient safety work product or data in consultation with the sources from which such information was received in compliance with the statutory requirements incorporated in proposed § 3.108(b)(3)(i)–(iii). The former PSO would also be expected to provide appropriate contact information for further communications from the Secretary.

We are aware that, if a PSO does not give appropriate notice to providers from which it receives data, that it does not intend to seek continued listing, this could jeopardize protections for data that these providers continue to report.

To address this issue, we are seeking comment in proposed § 3.104(e) on a proposal that would ensure that providers have advance notice that a PSO is approaching the end of its period of listing but has not yet sought continued listing.

(5) Proposed § 3.108(c)(5)— Non-Applicability of Certain Procedures and Requirements

Proposed § 3.108(c)(5) provides that neither a decision by a PSO to notify the Secretary that it wishes to relinquish voluntarily its status as a PSO, nor a situation in which a PSO lets its period of listing lapse, constitutes a deficiency as referenced in the discussion regarding proposed § 3.108(a). As a result, neither the procedures and requirements that apply to the Secretary or a PSO subject to the revocation process outlined in that proposed subsection, nor the requirements that apply to the Secretary or a PSO following action by the Secretary pursuant to proposed § 3.108(b)(1), would apply in cases of voluntary relinquishment. Adoption of this proposal would mean that a PSO has no basis for appealing decisions of the Secretary in response to a request for voluntary relinquishment or challenging its removal from listing if its period of listing lapses and the Secretary determines that implied voluntary relinquishment has occurred. We specifically welcome comment on this proposal.

(D) Proposed § 3.108(d)—Public Notice of Delisting Regarding Removal From Listing Proposed § 3.108(d) incorporates the proposed rule the statutory requirement that the Secretary must publish a notice in the **Federal Register** regarding the revocation of acceptance of certification of a PSO and its removal from listing pursuant to proposed § 3.108(b)(1) (see section

924(e)(3) Public Health Service Act, 42 U.S.C. 299b-24(e)(3)). This proposal also would require the Secretary to publish such a notice if delisting results from determination of voluntary relinquishment pursuant to proposed § 3.108(c)(3) or (c)(4). The Secretary would specify the effective date and time of the actions in these notices.

5. Proposed § 3.110—Assessment of PSO Compliance Proposed § 3.110 provides that the Secretary may request information conduct spot-checks (reviews or site visits to PSOs that may be unannounced) to assess or verify PSO compliance with the requirements statute and this proposed subpart. anticipate that such spot checks will involve no more than 5–10% of PSOs any year. The legislative history of patient safety legislation in the 108th and 109th Congress suggests that the Senate Health, Education, Labor and Pensions (HELP) Committee assumed that the Secretary had the inherent authority to undertake inspections necessary to ensure that PSOs were meeting their obligations under the statute. In fact, in reporting legislation in 2004, the Senate HELP Committee justified its proposal for an expedited process for listing PSOs—that is substantially the same as the one incorporated in the Patient Safety Act that was enacted in 2005 and is incorporated in this proposed rule—the basis that the Secretary

could and would be able to conduct such inspections. The ability of the Secretary to "examine any organization at any time to see whether it in fact is performing those required activities" the Senate HELP Committee wrote, enables the Committee to "strike the right balance" in adopting an expedited process for listing of PSOs by the Secretary (Senate Report 108-196). Accordingly, we tentatively conclude that this proposed authority for undertaking inspections a spot-check basis is consistent with Congressional intent and the overall approach of the proposed rule of using regulatory authority sparingly.

While patient safety work product would not be a focus of inspections conducted under this proposed authority, we recognize that it may not be possible to assess a PSO's compliance with required patient safety activities without access to all of a PSO's records, including some patient safety work product. This proposed section references the broader authority of the Department to access patient safety work product as part of its proposed implementation and enforcement of the Patient Safety Act.

We also note that the inspection authority of this proposed subpart is limited to PSOs and does not extend to providers.

6. Proposed § 3.112—Submissions and Forms Paragraphs (a) and (b) of proposed § 3.112 explain

how to obtain forms and how to submit applications and other information under the proposed regulations. Also, to help ensure the timely resolution of incomplete submissions, proposed paragraph (c) of this section would provide for requests for additional information if a submission is incomplete or additional information is needed to enable the Secretary to make a determination on the submission.

C. Subpart C—Confidentiality and Privilege Protections of Patient Safety Work Product

Proposed Subpart C would establish the general confidentiality protections for patient safety work product, the permitted disclosures, and the conditions under which the specific protections no longer apply. The proposed Subpart also establishes the conditions under which a provider, PSO, or responsible person must disclose patient safety work product to the Secretary in the course of compliance activities, and what the Secretary may do with such information. Finally, proposed Subpart C establishes the standards for nonidentifiable patient safety work product. The privilege and confidentiality protections set forth in this proposed Subpart apply to the PSO framework established by the Patient Safety Act and this proposed Part, which will involve providers, PSOs, and responsible persons who possess patient safety work product. The Patient Safety Act and this proposed

Subpart seek to balance key objectives. First, it seeks to address provider concerns about the potential for damage from unauthorized release of such information, including the potential for the information to serve as a roadmap for provider liability from negative patient outcomes. Second, it seeks to promote the sharing of information about adverse patient safety events among providers and PSOs for the purpose of learning from those events to improve patient safety and creating a culture of safety. To address these objectives, the Patient Safety Act established that patient safety work product would be confidential and privileged, with certain exceptions.

Thus, the Patient Safety Act allows sharing of patient safety work product for certain purposes, including for patient safety activities, but simultaneously attaches strict confidentiality and privilege protections for that patient safety work product. To further strengthen the confidentiality protections, the Patient Safety Act imposes significant monetary penalties for violation of the confidentiality provisions, as set forth in proposed Subpart D. Moreover, patient safety work product that is disclosed generally continues to be privileged and confidential, that is, it may only be permissibly disclosed by the receiving entity or person for a purpose permitted by the Patient Safety Act and this proposed Subpart. The only way that

patient safety work product is no longer confidential is if the patient safety work product disclosed is nonidentifiable or when an exception to continued confidentiality exists. See section 922(d)(2)(B) of the Public Health Service Act, 42 U.S.C. 299b-22(d)(2)(B). A person disclosing such work product outside of these statutory permissions in violation of the Patient Safety Act and this proposed Subpart may be subject to civil money penalties. Proposed § 3.204, among other provisions, provides that patient safety work product is privileged and generally shall not be admitted as evidence in Federal, State, local, or Tribal civil, criminal or administrative proceedings and shall not be subject to a subpoena or order, unless an exception to the privilege applies; the exceptions are discussed in proposed § 3.204(b). Proposed § 3.206 provides that patient safety work product is confidential and shall not be disclosed except as permitted in accordance with the disclosures described in proposed §§ 3.206(b)-(e), 3.208 and 3.210. Under proposed § 3.208, patient safety work product continues to be privileged and confidential after disclosure with certain exceptions. Under proposed § 3.210, providers, PSOs, and responsible persons must disclose to the Secretary such patient safety work product as required by the Secretary for the purposes of investigating or determining compliance with this proposed Part, enforcing the confidentiality provisions, or making determinations on certifying and listing PSOs. Proposed § 3.210 also provides for disclosure to the Secretary. Proposed § 3.212 describes the standard for determining that patient safety work product is nonidentifiable.

Throughout the proposed rule, the term patient safety work product means both identifiable patient safety work product and nonidentifiable patient safety work product, unless otherwise specified. In addition, if a disclosure is made by or to a workforce member of an entity, it will be considered a disclosure by or to the entity itself.

Finally, throughout our discussion we note the relationship between the Patient Safety Act and the HIPAA Privacy Rule. Several provisions of the Patient Safety Act recognize that the patient safety regulatory scheme will exist alongside other requirements for the use and disclosure of protected health information under the HIPAA Privacy Rule. For example, the Patient Safety Act establishes that PSOs will be business associates of providers, incorporates individually identifiable health information under the HIPAA Privacy Rule as an element of identifiable patient safety work product, and adopts a rule of construction that states the intention not to alter or affect any HIPAA Privacy Rule implementation provision (see section

922(g)(3) of the Public Health Service Act, 42 U.S.C. 299b-22(g)(3)). We anticipate that most providers reporting to PSOs will be HIPAA covered entities under the HIPAA Privacy Rule, and as such, will be required to recognize when requirements of the HIPAA Privacy Rule apply. Because this proposed rule focuses on disclosures of identifiable patient safety work product which may include protected health information, we discuss where appropriate the overlaps between the proposed Patient Safety Act permitted disclosures and the existing HIPAA Privacy Rule use and disclosure permissions.

1. Proposed § 3.204—Privilege of Patient Safety Work Product Proposed § 3.204 describes the privilege protections of patient safety work product and when the privilege protections do not apply. The Patient Safety Act does not give authority to the Secretary to enforce breaches of privilege protections. Rather, we anticipate that the tribunals, agencies or professional disciplinary bodies before whom these proceedings take place will adjudicate the application of privilege as set forth in section 922(a)(1)-(5) of the Public Health Service Act, 42 U.S.C. 299b-22(a)(1)-(5). Even though the privilege protections will be enforced through the court systems, and not by the Secretary, we repeat the statutory privilege provisions and exceptions for convenience. We note,

however, that the same exceptions are repeated in the confidentiality context, which the Secretary does enforce; so these are repeated at proposed § 3.206 and such impermissible disclosure may be penalized under proposed Subpart D.

To determine the permissible scope of disclosures under the Patient Safety Act, it is important to understand the application of the privilege protection and its exceptions described in conjunction with the related proposed confidentiality disclosures. The admission of patient safety work product as evidence in a proceeding or through a subpoena, court order or any other exception to privilege, whether permissibly or not, amounts to a disclosure of that patient safety work product to all parties receiving or with access to the patient safety work product admitted. Thus, we use the term disclosure to describe the transfer of patient safety work product pursuant to an exception to privilege, as well as to an exception to confidentiality. In addition, although the Secretary does not have authority to impose civil money penalties for violations of the privilege protection, a violation of privilege may also be a violation of the confidentiality provisions. For these reasons, we include the privilege language in the proposed implementing regulations.

Finally, as discussed in proposed § 3.204(c), we include a regulatory exception to privilege for

disclosures to the Secretary for the purpose of enforcing the confidentiality provisions and for making or supporting PSO certification or listing decisions.
(A) Proposed § 3.204(a)—Privilege Proposed § 3.204(a) would repeat the statutory language at section 922(a) of the Public Health Service Act, 42 U.S.C. 299b-22(a), establishing the general principle that patient safety work product is privileged and is not subject to Federal, State or local civil, criminal or administrative proceedings or orders; is not subject to disclosure under the Freedom of Information Act or similar Federal, State or local laws; and may not be admitted into evidence in any Federal, State or local civil, criminal or administrative proceeding or the proceedings of a disciplinary body established or specifically authorized under State law. In addition, we have clarified that patient safety work product shall be privileged and not subject to use in Tribal courts or administrative proceedings. Because the Patient Safety Act is a statute of general applicability, it applies to Indian Tribes. In addition, the application of the Federal privilege to Tribal proceedings implements the strong privilege protections intended under section 922 of the Public Health Service Act, 42 U.S.C. 299b-22. (See section 922(g)(1)-(2) of the Public Health Service Act, 42 U.S.C. 299b-22(g)(1)-(2), preserving more stringent Federal, State, and local confidentiality laws).

(B) Proposed § 3.204(b)—Exceptions to Privilege

Proposed § 3.204(b) describes the exceptions to the privilege protection at proposed § 3.204(a) that are established in section 922(c) of the Public Health Service Act, 42 U.S.C. 299b-22(c), as added by the Patient Safety Act. When the conditions set forth in proposed § 3.204(b) are met, then privilege does not apply and would not prevent the patient safety work product from, for example, being entered into evidence in a proceeding or subject to discovery. In all cases, the exceptions from privilege are also exceptions from confidentiality.
For proposed § 3.204(b)(1)-(4) and § 3.204(c), we discuss the scope of the applicable confidentiality protection in proposed § 3.206(b) and § 3.206(d). (1) Proposed § 3.204(b)(1)—Criminal Proceedings

Proposed § 3.204(b)(1) would permit disclosure of identifiable patient safety work product for use in a criminal proceeding, as provided in section 922(c)(1)(A) of the Public Health Service Act, 42 U.S.C. 299b-22(c)(1)(A). Such patient safety work product is not subject to the privilege prohibitions described in proposed § 3.204(a) or the confidentiality protection described in proposed § 3.206(a). See proposed § 3.206(b)(1). Prior to a court determining that an exception to privilege applies pursuant to this provision, a court must make an in

camera determination that the identifiable patient safety work product sought for disclosure contains evidence of a criminal act, is material to the proceeding, and is not reasonably available from other sources. See section 922(c)(1)(A) of the Public Health Service Act, 42 U.S.C. 299b-22(c)(1)(A). We discuss in full the requirements of this disclosure under the confidentiality disclosure discussion below.
(2) Proposed § 3.204(b)(2)—Equitable Relief for Reporters Proposed § 3.204(b)(2) permits the disclosure of identifiable patient safety work product to the extent required to carry out the securing and provision of specified equitable relief as provided for under section 922(f)(4)(A) of the Public Health Service Act, 42 U.S.C. 299b-22(f)(4)(A). This exception is based on section 922(c)(1)(B) of the Public Health Service Act, 42 U.S.C. 299b-22(c)(1)(B).
The Patient Safety Act permits this disclosure as an exception to privilege and confidentiality to effectuate the provision that authorizes equitable relief for an employee who has been subjected to an adverse employment action for good faith reporting of information to a PSO directly or to a provider for the intended report to a PSO. We discuss in full the requirements of this disclosure under the confidentiality disclosure discussion below.
(3) Proposed § 3.204(b)(3)—Authorized by Identified Providers

Proposed § 3.204(b)(3) describes when identifiable patient safety work product may be excepted from privilege when each of the providers identified in the patient safety work product authorizes the disclosure. This provision is based on section 922(c)(1)(C) of the Public Health Service Act, 42 U.S.C. 299b–22(c)(1)(C). Such patient safety work product is also not subject to the confidentiality protections described in proposed § 3.206(a). We discuss in full the requirements of this disclosure under the confidentiality disclosure discussion below.

(4) Proposed § 3.2049(b)(4)— Nonidentifiable Patient Safety WorkProduct Proposed § 3.204(b)(4) permits patient safety work product to be excepted from privilege when disclosed in nonidentifiable form. This provision is based on section 922(c)(3) of the Public Health Service Act, 42 U.S.C. 299b–22(c)(3). As with other privilege protections, we expect the tribunals for which the information is sought to adjudicate the application of this exception. We discuss in full the requirements of this disclosure in the confidentiality disclosure discussion below.

(C) Proposed § 3.204(c)— Implementation and Enforcement of thePatient Safety Act Proposed § 3.204(c) excepts from privilege disclosures of relevant patient safety work product to or by the Secretary as needed for investigation or determining

compliance with this Part or for enforcement of the confidentiality provisions, or for making or supporting PSO certification or listing decisions, under the Patient Safety Act. We propose that the Secretary may use and disclose patient safety work product when pursuing civil money penalties for impermissible disclosures. This is a privilege exception in the same manner as exceptions listed in proposed § 3.204(b), but we state it separately to provide specific emphasis for the inclusion of this exception to privilege by the Secretary for enforcement activities. This information is also a permissible disclosure under proposed § 3.206(d), discussed below.

The Patient Safety Act provides for broad privilege and confidentiality protections, as well as the authority for the Secretary to impose civil money penalties on persons who knowingly or recklessly disclose identifiable patient safety work product in violation of those protections. However, in order to perform investigations and compliance reviews to determine whether a violation has occurred, the Secretary may need to have access to privileged and confidential patient safety work product. We believe that Congress could not have intended that the privilege and confidentiality protections afforded to patient safety work product operate to frustrate the sole enforcement mechanism Congress provided for the punishment of impermis-

sible disclosures and to preclude the imposition of civil money penalties. As a matter of public policy, the creation of a confidentiality protection is meaningless without the capacity to enforce a breach of those protections.

For these reasons, we propose a privilege exception narrowly drawn to permit the Secretary to perform the enforcement and operational duties required by the Patient Safety Act, which include the submission of patient safety work product to administrative law judges (ALJs), the Departmental Appeals Board (Board), and the courts.

This proposed provision would permit the disclosure of patient safety work product to the Secretary or disclosure by the Secretary so long as such disclosure is for the purpose of implementation and enforcement of these proposed regulations. Such disclosure would include the introduction of patient safety work product into proceedings before ALJs or the Board under proposed Subpart D by the Secretary, as well as the disclosure during investigations by OCR or activities in reviewing PSO certifications by AHRQ. Moreover, disclosures of patient safety work product made to the Board or other parts of the Department that are received by workforce members, such as contractors operating electronic web portals or mail sorting and paper scanning services, would be permitted as a disclosure to the Secretary under this proposed provision. This provision would also permit the Board to disclose any patient safety work product in order to properly review determinations or to provide records for court review. Patient safety work product disclosed under this exception remains protected by both privilege and confidentiality protections as proposed in § 3.208. This exception does not limit the ability of the Secretary to disclose patient safety work product in accordance with the exceptions under proposed § 3.206(b) or this Part. Rather, this proposed section provides a specific permission by which patient safety work product may be disclosed to the Secretary and the Secretary may further disclose such patient safety work product for compliance and enforcement purposes.

We believe strongly in the protection of patient safety work product as provided in the Patient Safety Act and the proposed regulation, and seek to minimize the risk of improper disclosure of patient safety work product by using and disclosing patient safety work product only in limited and necessary circumstances. We intend that any disclosure made pursuant to this proposed provision be limited in the amount of patient safety work product disclosed to accomplish the purpose of implementation, compliance, and enforcement. Proposed § 3.312 discusses the limitations on what the Secretary may do with any patient safety work product

obtained pursuant to an investigation or compliance review under proposed Subpart D. As discussed in the preamble to proposed § 3.312, section 922(g)(3) of the Public Health Service Act, 42 U.S.C. 299b-22(g)(3), provides that the Patient Safety Act does not affect the implementation of the HIPAA confidentiality regulations. Accordingly, the privilege provisions in the Patient Safety Act would not bar the Secretary from introducing patient safety work product in a HIPAA enforcement proceeding.

2. Proposed § 3.206—Confidentiality of Patient Safety Work Product Proposed § 3.206 describes the confidentiality protection of patient safety work product as well as exceptions from confidentiality protection. The following discussion generally refers to an act that falls within an exception from confidentiality as a permissible disclosure. (A) Proposed § 3.206(a)—Confidentiality Proposed § 3.206(a) would establish the overarching general principle that patient safety work product is confidential and shall not be disclosed. The principle applies to patient safety work product held by anyone. This provision is based on section 922(b) of the Public Health Service Act, 42 U.S.C. 299b-22(b). (B) Proposed § 3.206(b)—Exceptions to Confidentiality Proposed § 3.206(b) describes the exceptions to confidentiality, or the permitted disclosures.

Certain overarching principles apply to the proposed confidentiality standards.

First, we consider these exceptions to be "permissions" to disclose patient safety work product and the holder of the patient safety work product retains full discretion whether or not to disclose.

Thus, similar to the disclosures permitted under the HIPAA Privacy Rule, we are defining a uniform federal baseline of protection that is enforceable by federally imposed civil money penalties. We are not encouraging or requiring disclosures, except to the Secretary as provided in this proposed rule. Therefore, a provider, PSO, or responsible person, may create confidentiality policies and procedures with respect to patient safety work product that are more stringent than these proposed rules and are free to otherwise condition the release of patient safety work product that comes within these exceptions by contract, employment relationship, or other means. See, for example, section 922(g)(4) of the Public Health Service Act, 42 U.S.C. 299b-22(g)(4). However, the Secretary will not enforce such policies or private agreements.

Second, when exercising the discretion to disclose patient safety work product, we encourage providers, PSOs, and responsible persons to consider the purposes for which the disclosures are made. Disclosures should be narrow and consistent with the overarching goals of the privilege and confidentiality protections, even though these protections generally continue to apply to patient safety work product after disclosure. We encourage any entity or person making a disclosure to consider both the amount of patient safety work product that is being disclosed, as well as the amount of identifiable information disclosed. Even though not required, entities or persons should attempt to disclose the amount of information commensurate with the purposes for which a disclosure is made. We encourage the disclosure of the least amount of identifiable patient safety work product that is appropriate for the purpose of the disclosure, which might mean the disclosure of less information than all of the information that would be permitted to be disclosed under the confidentiality provisions. We also encourage the removal of identifiable information when feasible regardless of whether protection under this rule continues. While a provider, PSO, or responsible person need not designate a workforce member to determine when a disclosure of patient safety work product is permitted, such a designation may be a best practice to ensure that a disclosure complies with the confidentiality provisions, and contains the least amount of patient safety work product necessary. Third, we have addressed the scope of redisclosure by persons receiving patient safety work product. Persons

receiving patient safety work product would only be allowed to redisclose that information to the extent permitted by the proposed regulation. For example, we propose that accrediting bodies receiving patient safety work product pursuant to the accrediting body disclosure at proposed § 3.206(b)(8) may not further disclose that patient safety work product. We seek public comment on the subject of whether there are any negative implications associated with limiting re-disclosures in this way. Additionally, agencies subject to both the Patient Safety Act and the Privacy Act, 5 U.S.C. 552a, must comply with both statutes when disclosing patient safety work product. Under the Patient Safety Act, see section 922(b) of the Public Health Service Act, 42 U.S.C. 299b–22(b), if another law, such as the Privacy Act, permits or requires the disclosure of patient safety work product, disclosure of this information would be in violation of the Patient Safety Act unless the Patient Safety Act also permits this disclosure. However, if the Privacy Act prohibits the disclosure of information that is patient safety work product, the permissible disclosure of this informa-tion under the Patient Safety Act would be in violation of the Privacy Act. Therefore, for agencies subject to both statutes, patient safety work product must be disclosed in a manner that is permissible under both statutes. The Privacy Act does permit agencies to make disclosures

pursuant to established routine uses. See 5 U.S.C. 552a(a)(7); 552a(b)(3); and 552a(e)(4)(D). We recom-mend that Federal agencies that maintain a Privacy Act system of records containing information that is patient safety work product include routine uses that will permit disclosures allowed by the Patient Safety Act. Finally, for HIPAA covered entities, when individually identifiable health informa-tion is encompassed within the patient safety work product, the disclosure must also comply with the HIPAA Privacy Rule. Thus, for patient safety work product disclosures that contain individually identifiable health information, as defined in 45 CFR 160.103, we note some of the comparable HIPAA Privacy Rule permissions for consideration.

(1) Proposed § 3.206(b)(1)— Criminal Proceeding Proposed § 3.206(b)(1) would establish the permitted criminal proceeding disclosure which parallels the privilege exception disclosure for use in a criminal proceeding, proposed § 3.204(b)(1). Proposed § 3.206(b)(1) would permit disclosure of identifiable patient safety work product for use in a criminal proceeding. Prior to a court determining that an exception to privilege applies pursuant to this provision, a court must make an in camera determination that the identifiable patient safety work product sought for disclosure contains evidence of a criminal act, is material

to the proceeding, and is not reasonably available from other sources. See section 922(c)(1)(A) of the Public Health Service Act, 42 U.S.C. 299b–22(c)(1)(A).

After such determinations by a court, the patient safety work product may be permissibly disclosed within the criminal proceeding. This provision and these limitations are based on section 922(c)(1)(A) of the Public Health Service Act, 42 U.S.C. 299b–22(c)(1)(A). When considering claims that confidentiality protection has been breached, we intend to defer to, and not review, the court's in camera determinations made in context of determining the privilege exception. The Secretary has not been authorized to enforce the underlying privilege protection or make determinations regarding its applicability. The Secretary's authority is limited to investigating and enforcing violations of the confidentiality protections parallel to this privilege exception at proposed § 3.206(b)(1). The Patient Safety Act establishes that patient safety work product, once disclosed, will generally continue to be privileged and confidential as discussed in proposed § 3.208. See section 922(d)(1) of the Public Health Service Act, 42 U.S.C. 299b–22(d)(1). However, the Patient Safety Act limits the continued protection of the specific patient safety work product disclosed for use in a criminal proceeding. Patient safety work product

disclosed for use in a criminal proceeding continues to be privileged and cannot be reused as evidence or in any context prohibited by the privilege protection, but is no longer confidential. See section 922(d)(2)(A) of the Public Health Service Act, 42 U.S.C. 299b–22(d)(2)(A). For example, law enforcement personnel who obtain patient safety work product used in a criminal proceeding may further disclose that patient safety work product because the confidentiality protection does not apply. However, if law enforcement sought to enter the information into another criminal proceeding, it would need a new in camera determination for the new criminal proceeding. For a further discussion of continued confidentiality, see discussion of proposed § 3.208 below.

For entities that are subject to the HIPAA Privacy Rule and this Part, disclosures must conform to 45 CFR 164.512(e) of the HIPAA Privacy Rule.

We expect that court rulings following an in camera determination would be issued as a court order, which would satisfy the requirements of 45 CFR 164.512(e). So long as such legal process is in compliance with 45 CFR 164.512(e), the disclosure would be permissible under the HIPAA Privacy Rule.

(2) Proposed § 3.206(b)(2)— Equitable Relief for Reporters Proposed § 3.206(b)(2) would permit the

disclosure of identifiable patient safety work product to the extent required to carry out equitable relief as provided for under section 922(f)(4)(A) of the Public Health Service Act, 42 U.S.C. 299b–22(f)(4)(A). See section 922(c)(1)(B) of the Public Health Service Act, 42 U.S.C. 299b–22(c)(1)(B). This proposed provision parallels the privilege exception to carry out equitable relief at proposed § 3.204(b)(2). The Patient Safety Act permits this disclosure to effectuate the provision that authorizes an employee to seek redress for adverse employment actions for good faith reporting of information to a PSO directly or to a provider with the intended disclosure to a PSO.

The Patient Safety Act prohibits a provider from taking an adverse employment action against an individual who, in good faith, reports information to the provider for subsequent reporting to a PSO, or to a PSO directly. See section 922(e)(1) of the Public Health Service Act, 42 U.S.C. 299b–22(e)(1). Adverse employment actions are described at section 922(e)(2) of the Public Health Service Act, 42 U.S.C. 299b–22(e)(2), and include loss of employment, failure to promote, or adverse evaluations or decisions regarding credentialing or licensing. The Patient Safety Act provides adversely affected reporters a civil right of action to enjoin such adverse employment actions and obtain other equitable relief, including back pay or reinstatement, to redress the prohibited actions. As part of that right to seek equitable relief, the Patient Safety Act provides that patient safety work product is not subject to the privilege protections described in section 922(a) of the Public Health Service Act, 42 U.S.C. 299b–22(a), and as similarly described in proposed § 3.204(a), or to the confidentiality protection in section 922(b) of the Public Health Service Act, 42 U.S.C. 299b–22(b), and as similarly described in proposed § 3.206(a), to the extent such patient safety work product is necessary to carry out the equitable relief.

Although such disclosure is excepted from both confidentiality and privilege as to efforts to seek equitable relief, the identifiable patient safety work product remains subject to confidentiality and privilege protection in the hands of all subsequent holders and the protections apply to all subsequent potential disclosures. See section 922(d)(1) of the Public Health Service Act, 42 U.S.C. 299b–22(d)(1). Thus, even though the reporter is afforded discretion to disclose the relevant patient safety work product to seek and obtain equitable relief, all subsequent holders receiving the patient safety work product from the reporter are bound by the continued privilege and confidentiality protections. Thus, this provision would allow the reporter seeking equitable relief from an adverse employment action to include patient safety work product in briefs and in open court. To protect the patient safety work product as much as possible in these circumstances, we could condition the disclosure of identifiable patient safety work product in these circumstances on a party's, most likely the reporter's, obtaining of a protective order in these types of proceedings.

Such a protective order could take many forms that preserve the confidentiality of patient safety work product. For example, it could limit the use of the information to case preparation, but not make it evidentiary. Such an order might prohibit the disclosure of the patient safety work product in publicly accessible proceedings and in court records to prevent liability from moving to a myriad of unsuspecting parties (for example, parties in a courtroom may not know that they may be liable for civil money penalties if they share the patient safety work product they hear).

We solicit comments on whether a protective order should be a condition for this disclosure, imposed by regulation, or whether instead we should require a good faith effort to obtain a protective order as a condition for this disclosure and use our enforcement discretion to consider whether to assess a penalty for anyone who cannot obtain such an order and thus breaches the statutory continued confidentiality protection of this informa-tion. See discussion below at proposed § 3.402(a).

We also address the intersection of the HIPAA Privacy Rule herein because identifiable patient safety work product may contain individually identifiable health information and be sought for disclosure under this exception from a HIPAA covered entity or that HIPAA covered entity's business associate.

Under the HIPAA Privacy Rule at 45 CFR 164.512(e), when protected health information is sought to be disclosed in a judicial proceeding via subpoenas and discovery requests without a court order, the disclosing HIPAA covered entity must seek satisfactory assurances that the party requesting the information has made reasonable efforts to provide written notice to the individual who is the subject of the protected health information or to secure a qualified protective order. A protective order that meets the qualified protective order under 45 CFR 164.512(e) would be permissible under the HIPAA Privacy Rule and render a disclosure under this exception in compliance with the HIPAA Privacy Rule.

(3) Proposed § 3.206(b)(3)—Authorized by Identified Providers Proposed § 3.206(b)(3) would establish a permitted disclosure parallel to the privilege exception at proposed § 3.204(b)(3), when each of the providers identified in the patient safety work product authorizes the disclosure in

question. This provision is based on section 922(c)(1)(C) of the Public Health Service Act, 42 U.S.C. 299b-22(c)(1)(C).

In these circumstances, patient safety work product may be disclosed, not withstanding the privilege protections described in proposed § 3.204(a) or the confidentiality protections described in proposed § 3.206(a). However, patient safety work product disclosed under this exception continues to be confidential pursuant to the continued confidentiality provisions at section 922(d)(1) of the Public Health Service Act, 42 U.S.C. 299b-22(d)(1), and persons are subject to liability for further disclosures in violation of that confidentiality.

This exception applies to patient safety work product that contains identifiable provider information. Under the proposed language, each provider identified in the patient safety work product sought to be disclosed must separately authorize the disclosure. For example, if patient safety work product sought to be disclosed by an entity or person pursuant to this exception describes an incident involving three physicians, each physician would need to authorize disclosure of the patient safety work product, in order for the entity or person to disclose it. Making information regarding one provider nonidentifiable in lieu of obtaining an authorization is not sufficient.

We considered whether the rule should allow a provider to nonidentify the patient safety work product with respect to a nonauthorizing provider and disclose the patient safety work product with respect to the remaining authorizing providers. However, we rejected that approach as being impracticable. In light of the contextual nonidentification standard proposed in § 3.212, it would seem that there would be very few, if any, situations in which a nonauthorizing provider could be nonidentified without also needing to nonidentify, or nearly so, an authorizing provider in the same patient safety work product. Unless we adopt a less stringent nonidentification standard, disclosing persons can either totally non-identify patient safety work product and disclose under proposed § 3.206(b)(5), or disclose the patient safety work product only if all identified providers in patient safety work product authorize its disclosure.

When all identified providers authorize the disclosure of patient safety work product, the Patient Safety Act permits such disclosure, but remains silent about the identification of patients or reporters in such patient safety work product. As to other persons that make patient safety work product identifiable, i.e., patients and reporters, the Patient Safety Act does not provide a separate right of authorization.

However, as one of the core principles underlying the Patient Safety Act is the protection of the privacy and confidentiality concerns of certain persons in connection with specific patient safety work product (i.e., providers, patients and reporters), we encourage persons disclosing patient safety work product to exercise discretion in the scope of patient safety work product disclosed, even though neither patient nor reporter authorization is required. Disclosers are encouraged to consider whether the disclosure of identifying information regarding patients and reporters is necessary to accomplish the particular purpose of the disclosure. As discussed below, if the disclosing entity is a HIPAA covered entity, the HIPAA Privacy Rule, including the minimum necessary standard when applicable, would apply to the disclosure of protected health information contained within the patient safety work product.

We seek public comment as to whether the proposed approach is sufficient to protect the interests of reporters and patients identified in the patient safety work product permitted to be disclosed pursuant to identifiable provider authorizations. Does this approach sufficiently balance the interests of the patients and reporters and their confidentiality versus the purposes for which the providers are authorizing the disclosures?

The Patient Safety Act does not specify the form of the authorization by a provider to come within this disclosure exception or a timeframe for recordkeeping. We propose that an authorization be in writing, be signed by the authorizing provider, and give adequate notice to the provider of the nature and scope of the disclosures authorized. The content of the authorization should fairly inform the provider as to the nature and scope of the identifiable patient safety work product to be disclosed to ensure the provider is making a knowing authorization. We do not intend that each authorization identify the specific patient safety work product to be disclosed. Such a requirement would be unworkable in complex health care arrangements existing today. Rather, an authorization can be general, (e.g., referring to categories of patient safety work product) and even to patient safety work product to be created in the future, so long as the authorization can be determined to have reasonably informed the authorizing provider of the scope of the authorized disclosure. The authorization requirement also enables providers to place limits on disclosures made pursuant to this proposed exception regarding patient safety work product identifying the provider. Any disclosure must be made in accordance with the terms of the signed authorization, but

we do not require that any specific terms be included, only that such terms regarding the scope of the authorized disclosure of patient safety work product be adhered to. We seek public comment on whether a more stringent standard would be prudent and workable, such as an authorization process that is disclosure specific (i.e., no future application or a one time disclosure only authorization).

We also propose that any authorization be maintained by the disclosing entity or person for a period of six years from the date of the last disclosure made in reliance on the authorization, the limit of time within which the Secretary must initiate an enforcement action. While we recognize that a prudent person disclosing patient safety work product under this disclosure will likely maintain records in order to support a claim that such disclosure was permissible, nonetheless we require a six year retention of authorizations so that, if challenged, the Secretary may examine authorizations to determine whether a disclosure was valid pursuant to this disclosure provision. While we would not be monitoring or penalizing a person for lack of maintenance of an authorization, the failure to present a valid authorization will raise significant concerns regarding the permissibility of a disclosure pursuant to this permission. With respect to compliance with the HIPAA Privacy Rule

for patient safety work product that contains individually identifiable health information, authorization by a provider pursuant to this permitted disclosure does not permit a HIPAA covered entity or such a HIPAA covered entity's business associate to release such protected health information contained in the patient safety work product under the HIPAA Privacy Rule. Therefore, either the individually identifiable health information must be de-identified or the release of the individually identifiable health information must otherwise be permitted under the HIPAA Privacy Rule. Because this disclosure does not limit the purposes for which identifiable patient safety work product may be released with the provider's authorization, a HIPAA covered entity would need to review releases on a case-by-case basis to determine if there is an applicable provision in the HIPAA Privacy Rule that would otherwise permit such disclosure.

(4) Proposed § 3.206(b)(4)—Patient Safety Activities

Section 922(c)(2)(A) of the Public Health Service Act, 42 U.S.C. 299b–22(c)(2)(A), permits the disclosure of identifiable patient safety work product for patient safety activities. Proposed § 3.206(b)(4) permits the disclosure of identifiable patient safety work product for patient safety activities (i) by a provider to a PSO or by a PSO to that disclosing provider; or (ii) by a provider or a PSO to a contractor of the provider or PSO; or (iii) by a PSO to another PSO or to another provider that has reported to the PSO, or by a provider to another provider, provided, in both cases, certain direct identifiers are removed.

Patient safety activities are the core mechanism by which providers may disclose patient safety work product to obtain external expertise from PSOs.

PSOs may aggregate information from multiple providers, and communicate feedback and analyses to providers.

Ultimately, it is through such communications that much of the improvement in patient safety may occur. Thus, the rule needs to facilitate the communication between a provider and one or more PSOs.

To further this essential statutory purpose, we propose to allow providers to disclose identifiable patient safety work product to PSOs; one of the ways that information can become patient safety work product is through reporting of it to a PSO. We also propose to allow PSOs to reciprocally disclose patient safety work product back to such providers for patient safety activities.

This free flow of information will ensure that the statute's goals of collecting, aggregating, and analyzing patient safety event information as well as disseminating recommendations for safety and quality improvements are achieved. Such a dialogue will allow both providers and PSOs to

take a shared role in the advancement of patient safety improvements.

In addition, we recognize that there may be situations where providers and PSOs want to engage contractors who are not agents to carry out patient safety activities. Thus, the proposal would allow disclosures by providers to their contractors who are not workforce members and by PSOs to their contractors who are not workforce members. Contractors may not further disclose patient safety work product, except to the entity from which they first received the information. We note that this limitation does not preclude a provider or PSO from exercising its authority under section 922(g)(4) of the Public Health Service Act, 42 U.S.C. 299b-22(g)(4), to separately delegate its power to the contractor to make other disclosures. Although we do not require a contract between a provider or PSO and its contractor, we expect that most providers and PSOs will engage in prudent practices when disclosing confidential patient safety work product for patient safety activities, (i.e., ensuring such information is narrowly used by the contractor solely for the purpose for which disclosed and adequately protected from wrongful disclosure). While the permission allows the necessary communication as between a single provider and its PSO, such exchanges may not be sufficient. It is possible to conceive of meaningful

patient safety activities occurring between two PSOs or between a PSO and a provider that is different than the original reporting provider, or between two providers. For example, PSOs may be able to more effectively aggregate patient safety work product if such expanded sharing of information is permitted. Aggregation may help PSOs pool sufficient information to achieve contextual nonidentification, in accordance with § 3.212(a)(ii), but keep meaningful data in the information when disclosing to the network of patient safety databases contemplated in section 923 of the Public Health Service Act, 42 U.S.C. 299b-23. Providers may be able to collaborate and learn more efficiently about patient safety solutions if such sharing is permitted. At the same time, we are concerned that, without any limitation on such sharing, providers may be not only reluctant to disclose patient safety work product, but also potentially reticent to participate at all in patient safety activities, given the sensitive nature of the information, and the potential lack of certainty with respect to where the information might ultimately be disclosed. Balancing these concerns, we are proposing that other than the reporting relationship between a provider and a PSO, PSOs be permitted to disclose patient safety work product to other PSOs or to other providers that have reported to the PSO, and providers be permitted to make disclosures to other providers, for patient safety activities, with provider and reporter identifiers in an anonymized (i.e., with certain direct identifiers removed, but not nonidentifiable under the proposed rule) or encrypted but not fully non-identified form. For patient identifiers, the HIPAA Privacy Rule limited data set standard would apply. See 45 CFR 164.514(e). To anonymize the provider or reporter identifiers in the patient safety work product, the disclosing entity must remove the following direct identifiers of any providers and of affiliated organizations, corporate parents, subsidiaries, practice partners, employers, members of the workforce, or household members of such providers: (1) Names; (2) Postal address information, other than town or city, State and zip code; (3) Telephone numbers; (4) Fax numbers; (5) Electronic mail addresses; (6) Social security numbers or taxpayer identification numbers; (7) Provider or practitioner credentialing or DEA numbers; (8) National provider identification number; (9) Certificate/license numbers; (10) Web Universal Resource Locators (URLs); (11) Internet Protocol (IP) address numbers; (12) Biometric identifiers, including finger and voice prints; and (13) Full face photographic images and any comparable images. Removal of such identifiers

may be absolute or may be done through encryption, provided that the disclosing entity does not disclose the key to the encryption or the mechanism for re-identification. We have not proposed an unrestricted disclosure of identifiable patient safety work product to any person for patient safety activities. It is our understanding that disclosures to persons other than those proposed above do not need identifiable patient safety work product and that sufficient information may be communicated with nonidentifiable patient safety work product; we seek comment on this issue. Similarly, we recognize that nonidentifiable patient safety work product may have more limited usefulness due to the removal of key elements of identification; however, we have no basis for opening the patient safety activity disclosure permission further without specific examples of beneficial disclosures prohibited by our proposal.

The exchange of patient safety work product for patient safety activities permits extensive sharing among both providers and PSOs interested in improving patient safety. As patient safety work product is disclosed, however, it continues to be protected by the confidentiality provisions. The permission allows continual exchange of information without breach of confidentiality. At any time and as needed,

information may be non-identified, and the patient safety activities disclosure may be employed for this purpose.

Moreover, providers and PSOs are capable of imposing greater confidentiality requirements for the future use and disclosure of the patient safety work product through private agreements (see section 922(g)(4) of the Public Heath Service Act, 42 U.S.C. 299b-22(g)(4)). However, we note that the government would not be permitted to apply civil money penalties under this Part based on a violation of a private agreement that was not a violation of the confidentiality provisions.

Compliance With the HIPAA Privacy Rule
With respect to compliance with the HIPAA Privacy Rule, the Patient Safety Act establishes that PSOs shall be treated as business associates; and patient safety activities performed by, or on behalf of, a covered provider by a PSO are deemed health care operations as defined by the HIPAA Privacy Rule. A HIPAA covered entity is permitted to use or disclose protected health information as defined at 45 CFR 160.103 without an individual's authorization for its own health care operations and, in certain circumstances (which would include patient safety activities), for the health care operations of another HIPAA covered entity (e.g., HIPAA covered provider) under 45 CFR 164.506. To share protected health information with

another HIPAA covered entity for that entity's health care operations, both HIPAA covered entities must share a patient relationship with the individual who is the subject of the protected health information and the protected health information that is shared must pertain to that relationship.

In addition, in cases where providers and PSOs share anonymized patient safety work product, providers may disclose a limited data set of patient information. Under 45 CFR 164.514(e)(3), a HIPAA covered entity may use or disclose a limited data set for the purpose of health care operations, including patient safety activities. Such disclosures, however, must be accompanied by a data use agreement, ensuring that the limited data set recipient will only use or disclose the protected health information for limited purposes. See 45 CFR 164.514(e)(4).

We seek comment regarding whether the HIPAA Privacy Rule definition for health care operations should contain a specific reference to patient safety activities conducted pursuant to this regulatory scheme. A health care provider that is a HIPAA covered entity may not disclose identifiable patient safety work product that is protected health information to a PSO unless that PSO is performing patient safety activities (as a health care operation) for that provider. Under this exception for patient safety activities, a health care provider that is a HIPAA covered entity may disclose identifiable patient

safety work product that is protected health information to another provider (1) for the sending provider's patient safety activities; (2) for the patient safety activities of an organized health care arrangement (OHCA) (as defined at 45

CFR 160.103) if both the sending and receiving provider participate in the OHCA; or (3) to another provider for the receiving provider's patient safety activities if the protected health information relates to a common patient (including to determine that there is a common patient). We further seek comment regarding whether the provision permitting the disclosure of protected health information for health care operations at 45 CFR 164.506 should be modified to conform to the patient safety work product disclosures for patient safety activities set forth herein. (5) Proposed § 3.206(b)(5)— Disclosure of Nonidentifiable Patient Safety Work Product Proposed § 3.206(b)(5) permits the disclosure of nonidentifiable patient safety work product when the patient safety work product meets the standard for nonidentification in proposed § 3.212. This implements section 922(c)(2)(B) of the Public Health Service Act, 42 U.S.C. 299b–22(c)(2)(B). Under proposed § 3.206(b)(5), nonidentifiable patient safety work product may be disclosed by any entity or person that

holds the nonidentifiable patient safety work product without violating the confidentiality provisions. Moreover, any provider, PSO or responsible person may non-identify patient safety work product. As described in proposed § 3.208(b)(ii), nonidentifiable patient safety work product, once disclosed, loses its privilege and confidentiality protection. Thus, it may be re-disclosed by its recipient without any Patient Safety Act limitations.

Nonidentification Standard

The nonidentification standard is proposed at § 3.212. However, we will discuss that standard at this point in the preamble due to its connection with the disclosure permission for nonidentifiable patient safety work product at proposed § 3.206(b)(5). Proposed § 3.212 would establish the standard by which patient safety work product will be determined nonidentifiable. The determination of what constitutes nonidentifiable patient safety work product is important because the standard for nonidentification effectively creates the boundary between protected and unprotected patient safety work product. Under the Patient Safety Act and this Part, identifiable patient safety work product includes information that identifies any provider or reporter or contains individually identifiable health information under the HIPAA

Privacy Rule (see 45 CFR 160.103). See section 921(2) of the Public Health Service Act, 42 U.S.C. 299b–21(2). By contrast, nonidentifiable patient safety work product does not include information that permits identification of any provider, reporter or subject of individually identifiable health information. See section 921(3) of the Public Health Service Act, 42 U.S.C. 299b–21(3). Because individually identifiable health information as defined in the HIPAA Privacy Rule is one element of identifiable patient safety work product, the de-identification standard provided in the HIPAA Privacy Rule applies with respect to the patient-identifiable information in the patient safety work product. Therefore, where patient safety work product contains individually identifiable health information, that information must be de-identified in accordance with 45 CFR 164.514(a)–(c) to qualify as nonidentifiable patient safety work product with respect to individually identifiable health information under the Patient Safety Act.

We propose that patient safety work product be contextually nonidentifiable in order to be considered nonidentifiable for the purposes of this rule. Contextual nonidentification of both providers and reporters would match the standard of de-identification in the HIPAA Privacy Rule. We are proposing two methods by which noniden-

tification can be accomplished which are similar to the standards for de-identification under the HIPAA Privacy Rule: (1) A statistical method of nonidentification and (2) the removal of 15 specified categories of direct identifiers of providers or reporters and of parties related to the providers and reporters, including corporate parents, subsidiaries, practice partners, employers, workforce members, or household members, and that the discloser have no actual knowledge that the remaining information, alone or in combination with other information reasonably available to the intended recipient, could be used to identify any provider or reporter (i.e., a contextual nonidentification standard). In proposed § 3.212(a)(1), the first method for rendering patient safety work product nonidentifiable with respect to a provider or reporter, we propose that patient safety work product can be non-identified if a person with appropriate knowledge of and experience with generally accepted statistical and scientific principles and methods for rendering information not individually identifiable applying such principles and methods, determines that the risk is very small that the information could be used, alone or in combination with other reasonably available information, by an anticipated recipient to identify an identified provider or reporter.

We believe that this method of nonidentification may sometimes be preferable to the safe harbor method proposed in § 3.212(a)(2) discussed below and may be especially useful when aggregating data for populating the network of patient safety databases referenced in section 923 of the Public Health Service Act, 42 U.S.C. 299b–23.

Under this proposal, if a statistician makes a determination as described above and documents the analysis, patient safety work product could be labeled as nonidentifiable even though it contains detailed clinical information and some potentially identifiable information such as zip codes.

In proposed § 3.212(a)(2), the second method for rendering patient safety work product nonidentifiable with respect to a provider or reporter, we outline a process as a safe harbor requiring that the disclosing entity remove a list of specific typical identifiers and have no actual knowledge that the information to be disclosed could be used, alone or in combination with other information that is reasonably available to the intended recipient, to identify the particular provider or reporter. We have limited the knowledge component to that which is known to be reasonably available to the intended recipient in order to provide data custodians with a workable knowledge standard. With the contextual nonidentification standard in place, providers will have the most confidence that their identities will not be derived from nonidentifiable information and will be more likely to participate in the program. Moreover, requiring that patient safety work product be contextually nonidentifiable is consistent with the de-identification standard for patient identities, as described above.

We recognize that the more stringent the nonidentifiable patient safety work product standard is, the more cost, burden, and risk of error in nonidentification there will be to the disclosing entity. We also acknowledge that our proposal introduces uncertainty and subjectivity into the standard, making it a harder standard to enforce. The proposed standard may require the removal of more clinical and demographic information than would be removed in the absence of the contextual nonidentification requirement, and the resulting information would likely be less useful to a recipient. This outcome would particularly impact the network of patient safety databases of nonidentifiable patient safety work product to be established under section 923 of the Public Health Service Act, 42 U.S.C. 299b–23. In particular, the information that ultimately resides in the network may have reduced utility and a reduced capacity to contribute to the evaluation of patient safety issues.

To mitigate these concerns, this standard would work in conjunction with a separate permission for sharing identifiable patient safety work product through the patient safety activities disclosure. Disclosures as patient safety activities should enable the aggregation of sufficient patient safety work product to allow contextual nonidentification without the removal of all important specific clinical and demographic details. We invite comment on the proposed standards and approaches. For example, we are interested in knowing whether, under a contextual nonidentification standard, it is possible to have any geographical identifiers; and if so, at what level of detail (state, county, zip code). We are also interested in public comments regarding whether there are alternative approaches to standards for entities determining when health information can reasonably be considered nonidentifiable.

Re-identification We permit a provider, PSO, or other disclosing entity or person to assign a code or other means of record identification to allow information made nonidentifiable to be re-identified by the disclosing person, provided certain conditions that further the goal of confidentiality are met regarding such code or other means of record identification. Further, a discloser may not release any key or other information that would enable a recipient to reidentify any provider or reporter or subject of

individual identifiable health information. We propose to permit a reidentification mechanism to facilitate follow-up inquiries regarding, and analysis of, nonidentified patient safety work product that has been disclosed, such as from users of the network of patient safety databases when analyzing national and regional statistics. Such keys would not be for the purpose of permitting re-identification of patient safety work product obtained through the network of databases. Rather, such keys would facilitate the investigation of data anomalies reported to the network, correction of nonidentifiable records, and the potential to avoid duplicate records when richer information may be made available due to aggregation.

Finally, with respect to HIPAA compliance, we note that, because non-identified patient safety work product will, by definition, be de-identified information under the HIPAA Privacy Rule, a disclosure under § 3.206(b)(5) will not violate the HIPAA Privacy Rule. (6) Proposed § 3.206(b)(6)—For Research Proposed § 3.206(b)(6) describes the disclosure of identifiable patient safety work product to entities carrying out research, evaluations, or demonstration projects that are funded, certified, or otherwise sanctioned by rule or other means by the Secretary. This disclosure is not for general research. Any research for which patient safety work product is disclosed under this exception must be sanctioned by the Secretary. See section 922(c)(2)(C) of the Public Health Service Act, 42 U.S.C. 299b–22(c)(2)(C). Research that is not sanctioned by the Secretary is insufficient to be a basis for the disclosure of patient safety work product under this exception. Further, although disclosure can be made for any research, evaluation, or demonstration project sanctioned by the Secretary, we expect that most research that may be subject to this disclosure permission will be related to the methodologies, analytic processes, and interpretation, feedback and quality improvement results from PSOs, rather than general medical, or even health services, research. Patient safety work product disclosed for research under this provision continues to be confidential and privileged.

Section 922(c)(2)(C) of the Public Health Service Act, 42 U.S.C. 299b–22(c)(2)(C), requires that patient safety work product which identifies patients may only be released to the extent that protected health information would be disclosable for research purposes under the HIPAA Privacy Rule. Under 45 CFR 164.512(i), a HIPAA covered entity may use or disclose protected health information for research, without the individual's authorization, provided that there is a waiver (or alteration of waiver) of authorization by either an Institutional Review Board

(IRB) or a Privacy Board. The IRB/Privacy Board evaluates the request against various criteria that measure the privacy risk to the individuals who are the subjects of the protected health information.[17] The HIPAA Privacy Rule only operates with respect to the identifiable health information of patients when held by a HIPAA covered entity or its business associate, and does not address the rights of individuals who may otherwise be the subject of the research.

---

17 The following are the waiver criteria at 45 CFR 164.512(i)(2)(ii):
(A) The use or disclosure of protected health information involves no more than a minimal risk to the privacy of individuals, based on, at least, the presence of the following elements:
a. An adequate plan to protect the identifiers from improper use and disclosure;
b. An adequate plan to destroy the identifiers at the earliest opportunity consistent with conduct of the research, unless there is a health or research justification for retaining the identifiers or such retention is otherwise required by law; and c. Adequate written assurances that the protected health information will not be reused or disclosed to any other person or entity, except as required by law, for authorized oversight of the research study, or for other research for which the use or disclosure of protected health information would be permitted by this subpart;
(B) The research could not practicably be conducted without the waiver or alteration; and
(C) The research could not practicably be conducted without access to and use of the protected health information.

We tentatively conclude that the language in the Patient Safety Act that applies the exception "to the extent that disclosure of protected health information would be allowed for research purposes under the HIPAA [Privacy Rule]" is intended to apply the HIPAA Privacy Rule research provisions at 45 CFR 164.512(i) only to HIPAA covered entities when they release identifiable patient safety work product containing protected health information for research. This interpretation would result in the HIPAA Privacy Rule research standards being preserved in their application to HIPAA covered entities without burdening non-covered entities with HIPAA compliance.

We note that our interpretation of section 922(c)(2)(C) of the Public Health Service Act, 42 U.S.C. 299b–22(c)(2)(C), is not a bar to the disclosure of identifiable patient safety work product by entities or persons that are not HIPAA covered entities. We further note that for providers, reporters and other persons identified in patient safety work product disclosed for research purposes, the Common Rule, which is applicable to research conducted or supported by the Secretary, and the FDA human subjects protection regulations will provide appropriate protections to any natural persons who would be deemed subjects of the research.

With regard to research, the incorporation by reference of

the HIPAA Privacy Rule should provide for the proper alignment of disclosures for research purposes. However, the exception under the Patient Safety Act also refers to evaluations and demonstration projects. Some of these activities may meet the definition of research under the HIPAA Privacy Rule, while other activities may not result in generalizable knowledge, but may nonetheless meet the definition of health care operations under the HIPAA Privacy Rule. Where the disclosure of protected health information for evaluations and demonstration projects are permitted as health care operations under the HIPAA Privacy Rule, HIPAA covered entities disclosing patient safety work product that includes protected health information under this exception could do so without violation of the HIPAA Privacy Rule. (7) Proposed § 3.206(b)(7)— To the Food and Drug Administration Section 922(c)(2)(D) of the Public Health Service Act, 42 U.S.C. 299b-22(c)(2)(D) permits the disclosure by a provider to the FDA with respect to a product or activity regulated by the FDA. Proposed § 3.206(b)(7) permits the disclosing by providers of patient safety work product concerning products or activities regulated by the Food and Drug Administration (FDA) to the FDA or to an entity required to report to the FDA concerning the quality, safety, or effectiveness of an

FDA-regulated product or activity. For example, hospitals and health care professionals may disclose patient safety work product concerning the safety of drugs, medical devices, biological products, and dietary supplements, or vaccine and medical device adverse experiences to the FDA as part of an FDA monitoring or alert system. The proposed provision also permits sharing between the FDA, entities required to report to the FDA concerning the quality, safety, or effectiveness of an FDA-regulated product or activity, and their contractors for the same purposes. Patient safety work product disclosed pursuant to this disclosure permission continues to be confidential and privileged. The FDA has monitoring and alert systems in place to assure the safety of FDA regulated products. These systems rely heavily on voluntary reports from providers, such as hospitals and health care professionals. Most reports that hospitals and health care professionals make directly to the FDA today concerning drugs, medical devices, biological products, and dietary supplements are voluntary, although health care professionals are required to report to FDA certain vaccine adverse experiences, and user facilities such as hospitals must report to FDA some medical device adverse experiences. Manufacturers of drugs, devices, and biological products are required to report to the

FDA concerning adverse experiences, but the manufacturers themselves must rely on information provided voluntarily by product users, including hospitals and health care professionals. There are three provisions of the Patient Safety Act that are implicated for reporting to the FDA: (1) The disclosure for reporting to the FDA (section 922(c)(2)(D) of the Public Health Service Act, 42 U.S.C. 299b-22(c)(2)(D)); (2) the clarification as to what is not patient safety work product which states that information "collected, maintained, or developed separately, or [that] exists separately, from a [patient safety evaluation system]" is not patient safety work product, and which, accordingly, can be reported for public health purposes (section 921(7)(B) of the Public Health Service Act, 42 U.S.C. 299b-21(7)(B)); and (3) the rule of construction which preserves required reporting to the FDA (section 922(g)(6) of the Public Health Service Act, 42 U.S.C. 299b-22(g)(6)). The FDA disclosure provision at proposed § 3.206(b)(7) would be applicable when patient safety work product is at issue. For example, the analysis of events by the provider or PSO that constitutes patient safety work product may generate information that should be reported to the FDA because it relates to the safety or effectiveness of an FDA-regulated product or activity. The exception would allow this patient safety work product to be disclosed to the FDA. Privilege and confidentiality protections would attach to the patient safety work product disclosed when received by FDA and continue to apply to any future disclosures by the FDA.

We tentatively conclude that the statutory language concerning reporting "to the FDA" includes reporting by the provider to the persons or entities regulated by the FDA and that are required to report to the FDA concerning the quality, safety, or effectiveness of an FDA-regulated product or activity. We propose this interpretation to allow providers to report to manufacturers who are required to report to the FDA, such as drug manufacturers, without violating this rule. This interpretation reflects both the rule of construction which preserves required reporting to the FDA and the goals of this statute which are to improve patient safety.

We further propose at § 3.206(b)(7)(ii) that the FDA and entities required to report to the FDA may only further disclose patient safety work product for the purpose of evaluating the quality, safety, or effectiveness of that product or activity; such further disclosures are only permitted between the FDA, entities required to report to the FDA, their contractors, and disclosing providers. This permission is crucial to the effective operation of the FDA's activities and to facilitate the purpose for

which the report was made initially.

Thus, the FDA or a drug manufacturer receiving adverse drug event information that is patient safety work product may engage in further communications with the disclosing provider(s), for the purpose of evaluating the quality, safety, or effectiveness of the particular regulated product or activity, or may work with their contractors. Moreover, an entity regulated by the FDA may further disclose the information to the FDA; without this provision, such reporting would not meet the regulatory intent that disclosures be to the FDA and a narrow interpretation could impede the FDA's ability to effectuate improvements through the use of patient safety work product.

We recognize that there may be situations where the FDA or entities required to report to the FDA want to engage contractors who are not agents for the purpose of evaluating the quality, safety, or effectiveness of that product or activity. Thus, the proposal would allow disclosures to contractors who are not workforce members.

Contractors may not further disclose patient safety work product, except to the entity from which they first received the information. Because Congress did not expressly include disclosure to FDA-regulated entities, we seek public comment on our proposal related to this interpretation of section 922(c)(2)(D) of the Public

Health Service Act, 42 U.S.C. 299b–22(c)(2)(D).

In particular, we question whether this interpretation will cause any unintended consequences to disclosing providers.

The HIPAA Privacy Rule at 45 CFR 164.512(b) permits HIPAA covered entities to disclose protected health information concerning FDA-regulated activities and products to persons responsible for collection of information about the quality, safety, and effectiveness of those FDA-regulated activities and products. Therefore, disclosures under this exception of patient safety work product containing protected health information would be permitted under the HIPAA Privacy Rule.

(8) Proposed § 3.206(b)(8)— Voluntary Disclosure to an Accrediting Body Proposed § 3.206(b)(8) permits the voluntary disclosure of identifiable patient safety work product by a provider to an accrediting body that accredits the disclosing provider.

Voluntary means not compelled, a disclosure that the provider affirmatively chose to make. Patient safety work product disclosed pursuant to this proposed exception continues to be privileged and confidential. Under this proposed disclosure, the identifiable patient safety work product that would be permitted to be disclosed must identify the disclosing provider, given the Patient Safety Act's explicit linkage of the disclosing provider to a body that accredits that specific provider in this permitted disclosure.

We believe that the only information that would be relevant to that provider's accreditation would be information about the disclosing provider (i.e., actions or inactions of the disclosing provider), and not information about the provider's colleagues or any other accredited provider. Thus, a provider may not use this exception to disclose patient safety work product that is unrelated to the actual actions of the disclosing provider, such as information about the provider's colleagues or any other accredited individual or entity.

An issue arises concerning the identities of other providers, reporters, or patients contained within the 0disclosed patient safety work product. We considered whether to require the patient safety work product to be nonidentifiable as to providers other than the disclosing provider, since incidental disclosures of patient safety work product identifying other providers, especially if they were also accredited by the same accrediting institution, would not be a voluntary disclosure by those other providers.

However, we do not believe that such an approach is necessary.

We understand that most providers that are accredited are large institutions, and in general their accreditors seek vast amounts of data during the accreditation process, some of which may include identifiers of practitioners who work in such institutions. We have preliminarily concluded that the disclosure of patient safety work product including practitioners in such circumstances will be harmless because, in many cases, the providers will not be accredited by the institution's accrediting body.

Even in circumstances where a non-disclosing provider identified by a provider voluntarily disclosing to an accrediting body is subject to the accrediting body, we believe the accrediting body will not use the information. First, we believe it is unlikely that a provider may have or seek to disclose patient safety work product containing information about the actions or inactions of a provider also accredited by the same accrediting body. Second, even if such a disclosure occurs, although it may not be voluntary as to the non-disclosing provider, we do not believe the accrediting body will use such information to take accrediting actions against the non-disclosing provider. We would expect that an accrediting body may ignore or give little weight to information about providers not disclosing information directly to the accrediting body. Such second hand information may be incomplete and incorrect. We anticipate that accrediting bodies would seek to obtain information about a provider's actions directly from the subject provider rather than second hand. Furthermore, we propose to limit the accrediting body's permission to further re-disclose such patient safety work product. To ensure that any patient safety work product in the hands of an accrediting body that contains provider identifiers of a provider who did not voluntarily disclose to such body, § 3.206(b)(7)(i) proposes that an accrediting body may not further disclose the patient safety work product that was originally voluntarily disclosed. As an alternative to this approach, we could, as proposed in the patient safety activities disclosure, require that information with respect to non-disclosing providers be anonymized. See preamble discussion at proposed § 3.206(b)(4). We seek comments as to whether the problem of information being disclosed non-voluntarily to an accrediting body by non-disclosing providers requires rendering such information anonymized.

The accrediting body takes the patient safety work product subject to the confidentiality protection, and would therefore be subject to civil money penalties for any re-disclosure. The patient safety work product disclosed under this permission in the hands of the accrediting body remains privileged and confidential, in accordance with the continued confidentiality provisions at proposed § 3.208. Thus, it is incumbent upon the accrediting body to handle and maintain the patient safety work product in a way that preserves its confidential status. Such safeguards may include maintaining this information separately from other accrediting information in a confidential file, if the other information is not similarly held confidential.

Additionally, the Patient Safety Act includes strong provisions limiting the disclosure of patient safety work product to accrediting bodies and limiting the actions an accrediting body may take to seek patient safety work product. Proposed § 3.206(b)(8)(ii) provides that an accrediting body may not take an accreditation action against a provider based on that provider's participation, in good faith, in the collection, reporting or development of patient safety work product. Accrediting bodies are also prohibited from requiring a provider to reveal its communications with any PSO, without regard to whether such provider actually reports information to a PSO.

Thus, a provider may disclose patient safety work product to an accrediting body voluntarily, but cannot be compelled or required as a condition of accreditation to divulge patient safety work product or communications with a PSO. This subsection is based on the statutory requirements at section 922(d)(4)(B) of the Public Health Service Act, 42 U.S.C. 299b–22(d)(4)(B). Under the HIPAA Privacy Rule, a HIPAA covered entity may disclose protected health information to an accrediting body for the HIPAA covered entity's own health care operations, provided there is a business associate agreement with the accrediting body.

Such health care operations include the activity of accreditation for the HIPAA covered entity as well as the accreditation of workforce members.

Thus, providers that are HIPAA covered entities or are workforce members of a HIPAA covered entity that hold the protected health information may voluntarily disclose identifiable patient safety work product containing individually identifiable health information to an accrediting body that accredits that provider, provided there is a business associate agreement between the HIPAA covered entity and the accreditation organization.

(9) Proposed § 3.206(b)(9)— Business Operations Section 922(c)(2)(F) of the Public HealthServiceAct,42U.S.C.299b–22(c)(2)(F), gives the Secretary authority to designate additional disclosures as permissible exceptions to the confidentiality protection if such disclosures are necessary for business operations and are consistent with the goals of the Patient Safety Act. Any patient safety work product disclosed pursuant to a business operations exception so designated by the Secretary continues to be confidential and privileged.

We propose to allow disclosures of patient safety work product by a provider or a PSO to professionals such as attorneys and accountants for the business operations purposes of the provider or PSO. A disclosure to an attorney may be necessary when a provider is seeking outside legal advice in defending against a malpractice claim or other litigation, even though the information would not be admissible as part of a legal proceeding. A provider might also need to disclose patient safety work product to an attorney in the case of due diligence related to a merger, sale or acquisition. Similarly, a provider may need to disclose patient safety work product to an accountant who is auditing the books and records of providers and PSOs. In order to ensure that such routine business operations are possible, we propose to allow disclosures by providers and PSOs for business operations to attorneys, accountants, and other professionals. Professionals such as those identified are usually bound by professional ethics to maintain the confidences of their clients. Such contractors may not further disclose patient safety work product, except to the entity from which it received the information. We note that this limitation does not preclude a provider or PSO from exercising its authority under section 922(g)(4) of the Public Health Service Act, 42 U.S.C. 299b–22(g)(4), to separately delegate its power to the contractor to make other disclosures.

We note that if a provider or PSO were to disclose relevant patient safety work product to such professionals, we would rely upon the professional's legal and ethical constraints not to disclose the information for any unauthorized purpose. Our presumption is that professionals are generally subject to a set of governing rules. Nonetheless, we expect that providers and PSOs who disclose privileged and confidential information to attorneys, accountants or other ethically bound professionals for business purposes will engage in the prudent practice of ensuring such information is narrowly used by the contractor solely for the purpose for which it was disclosed and adequately protected from wrongful disclosure.

Because patient safety work product is specialized and highly confidential information, we have not conceived of any other third parties to whom it would be appropriate to disclose patient safety work product as a business operations disclosure. Because we are not regulating uses, any business operations need within the entity could occur unimpeded. Although we considered whether to adopt an exception for activities in the operation of a patient safety evaluation system, we believe these activities are within the definition of patient safety activities and, thus, within the confidentiality exception proposed at § 3.206(b)(4). We seek public

comment regarding whether there are any other consultants or contractors to whom a business operations disclosure should also be permitted, or whether there are any additional exceptions for the Secretary's consideration under this authority.

Under the HIPAA Privacy Rule, at 45 CFR 164.506, HIPAA covered entities are permitted to disclose protected health information for the HIPAA covered entity's own health care operations. "Health care operations" are certain activities of a HIPAA covered entity that are necessary to run its business and to support the core functions of treatment and payment, including "conducting or arranging for medical review, legal services, and auditing functions * * *." 45 CFR 164.501. Thus, a business operation designation by the Secretary that enables a HIPAA covered entity to disclose patient safety work product containing protected health information to professionals is permissible as health care operations disclosures under the HIPAA Privacy Rule. Generally such professionals would fall within the definition of business associate at 45 CFR 160.103 and would require a business associate agreement.

The Secretary's Business Operations Exception Designation Authority

Section 922(c)(2)(F) of the Public Health Service Act, 42 U.S.C. 299b–

22(c)(2)(F), gives the Secretary broad authority to designate additional exceptions that are necessary for business operations and are consistent with the goals of the Patient Safety Act. At this point, we plan to designate additional exceptions only through regulation. Although the Patient Safety Act establishes that other means are available for adoption by the Secretary, which we interpret as including the publication of letters, notice within the **Federal Register** or publication on the Department Web site, we believe these methods may not provide for sufficient opportunity for public comment or transparency in the development of other business operations exceptions.

Moreover, because an impermissible disclosure that violates a business operations exception can result in a civil money penalty, we believe it is important that any proposed business operations exception be implemented in a way that is unquestionably binding on both the public and the Department. We invite public comments with respect to whether the Secretary should incorporate or preserve other mechanisms for the adoption of business operations exceptions, given that we cannot anticipate all potential business operations needs at this time.

(10) Proposed § 3.206(b)(10)—Disclosure to Law Enforcement Proposed

§ 3.206(b)(10) permits the disclosure of identifiable patient safety work product to law enforcement authorities, so long as the person making the disclosure believes—and that belief is reasonable under the circumstances—that the patient safety work product disclosed relates to a crime and is necessary for criminal law enforcement purposes. Under proposed § 3.208, the disclosed patient safety work product would continue to be privileged and confidential.

We view this exception as permitting, for example, a disclosure by a whistleblower who would initiate the disclosure to law enforcement. The focus of this exception is the state of mind of the subject discloser. In making a disclosure, the discloser must reasonably believe that the event constitutes a crime and that the patient safety work product disclosed is necessary for criminal law enforcement purposes. The discloser need not be correct in these determinations, but his beliefs must be objectively reasonable.

This standard provides some constraint on the discloser, and further protects against a release merely in response to a request by law enforcement.

Patient safety work product received by law enforcement under this exception continues to be confidential and privileged. The law enforcement entity receiving the patient safety work product may use the patient safety work product to pursue any law enforcement purposes; however, because the patient safety work product disclosed to law enforcement entities under the Patient Safety Act and proposed § 3.206(b)(10) remains privileged and confidential, the law enforcement entity can only disclose such patient safety work product—including in a court proceeding—as permitted by this proposed rule.

We further propose that a law enforcement entity be permitted to re-disclose the patient safety work product it receives under this exception to other law enforcement entities as needed for law enforcement activities related to the event that gave rise to the disclosure. We seek comment regarding whether these provisions allow for legitimate law enforcement needs, while ensuring appropriate protections.

We note that disclosure pursuant to this exception does not except patient safety work product from the privilege protection. Thus, patient safety work product cannot be subpoenaed, ordered, or entered into evidence in a criminal or civil proceeding through this exception; nor should a discloser rely solely on a law enforcement agent's statement that such information is necessary for law enforcement purposes. As already discussed, the Patient Safety Act framework permits an exception from privilege protection or law enforcement compulsion only in very narrow circumstances (see above privilege exception discussion). Under section 922(c)(1)(A) of the Public Health Service Act, 42 U.S.C. 299b–22(c)(1)(A), patient safety work product may be disclosed for use in a criminal proceeding, but only after a judge has determined by means of an *in camera* review that the patient safety work product is material to a criminal proceeding and not reasonably available from any other source. Even after its use in such a criminal proceeding, and the lifting of the confidentiality protections with respect to such patient safety work product, the privilege protection continues. In light of the strict privilege protections for this information, we do not interpret this law enforcement disclosure exception as allowing the disclosure of patient safety work product based on a less compelling request by law enforcement for its release. The decision as to whether a discloser reasonably believes that the patient safety work product is necessary for a law enforcement purpose is the discloser's decision alone, provided that the decision is reasonable.

While the HIPAA Privacy Rule permits disclosures by HIPAA covered entities to law enforcement under a variety of circumstances, few align well with the proposed interpretation of this exception as being limited to disclosures to law enforcement initiated by the HIPAA covered entity. Although there is a very narrow set of HIPAA Privacy Rule permissions under which a HIPAA covered entity as a holder of patient safety work product would be allowed to release patient safety work product that contains protected health information to law enforcement, we note that a HIPAA covered entity would be permitted to de-identify the protected health information, in which case only the Patient Safety Act would apply to the disclosure of the patient safety work product. If the protected health information is needed by law enforcement, the HIPAA Privacy Rule has standards that permit the release of protected health information in response to certain law enforcement processes. If such information is not patient safety work product, it would not be subject to the privilege protections of the Patient Safety Act.

(C) Proposed § 3.206(c)—Safe Harbor Proposed § 3.206(c) is based on section 922(c)(2)(H) of the Public Health Service Act, 42 U.S.C. 299b–22(c)(2)(H).
This provision permits the disclosure of identifiable patient safety work product when that information does not include oral or written materials that either contain an assessment of the quality of care of an identifiable provider or describe or pertain to the actions or failure to act of an identifi-able provider.
The use of this exception is limited to persons other than PSOs. This provision

essentially prohibits the disclosure of a subject provider's identity with information, whether oral or written, that: (1) Assesses that provider's quality of care; or (2) identifies specific acts attributable to such provider. Thus, a permissible disclosure may include a provider's identity, so long as no "quality information" about the subject provider is also disclosed and so long as it does not describe or pertain to an action or failure to act by the subject provider.
We propose that the provider identity element under this exception means the identity of any provider that is a subject of the patient safety work product. In other words, if the patient safety work product does not contain quality information about a particular provider or describe or pertain to any actions or failures to act by the provider, such provider could be identifiable within the patient safety work product disclosed pursuant to this exception.
For example, if a nurse reports a patient safety event, but was not otherwise involved in the occurrence of that event, the nurse could be named in the disclosure. Providers that cannot be identified are those about whom the patient safety work product assesses the quality of care or describes or pertains to actions or failures to act of that provider. We propose that the threshold for identification of a provider will be determined in accordance with the nonidentification standard

set forth in proposed § 3.210. Thus, confidential patient safety work product disclosed under this exception may identify providers, reporters or patients so long as the provider(s) that are the subject of the actions described are non-identified. In general, the determination with respect to the content of quality information is straightforward. We also interpret quality information to include the fact that patient safety work product exists, without the specifics of the patient safety event at issue. For example, if a provider employee discloses to a friend that a particular surgeon had an incident reported to the PSO, without actually describing this incident, the fact that the surgeon was associated with patient safety work product would be a prohibited disclosure.
This is the only exception that defines prohibited conduct, rather than permitted conduct. We recognize that institutional providers, even practitioners offices, are communities unto themselves. We preliminarily interpret this exception as creating a narrow safe harbor for disclosures, possibly inadvertent, which may occur by a provider or other responsible person, when the patient safety work product does not reveal a link between a subject provider and the provider's quality of care or an action or failure to act by that subject provider. By proposing this provision as a safe harbor, we seek to

have it available to mitigate harmless errors, rather than as a disclosure permission that may render all other disclosure permissions practically meaningless. Under the HIPAA Privacy Rule, HIPAA covered entities are broadly permitted to disclose protected health information for the HIPAA covered entity's treatment, payment or health care operations. Otherwise, specific standards are described that limit the use and disclosure of protected health information. If such disclosure is made by a HIPAA covered entity, it is possible that the disclosure of protected health information would be permissible as a health care operation, or as incidental to another permitted disclosure. Nevertheless, examination of whether a HIPAA Privacy Rule standard has been violated will need to be made on a case-by-case basis. (D) Proposed § 3.206(d)— Implementation and Enforcement of the Patient Safety Act Proposed § 3.206(d) permits the disclosure of relevant patient safety work product to or by the Secretary as needed for investigating or determining compliance with this Part or for enforcement of the confidentiality provisions of this Subpart or in making or supporting PSO certification or listing decisions under the Patient Safety Act and Subpart B of this regulation. This disclosure parallels the privilege exception under proposed § 3.204(c). Patient safety work product

disclosed under this exception remains confidential. This exception does not limit the ability of the Secretary to disclose patient safety work product in accordance with the exceptions under proposed § 3.206(b) or this Part. Rather, this proposed section provides a specific permission pursuant to which patient safety work product may be disclosed to the Secretary and the Secretary may further use such disclosed patient safety work product for compliance and enforcement purposes. We propose to permit a disclosure of patient safety work product in order to allow the Secretary to obtain such information as is needed to implement and enforce this program, both for the purposes of enforcing the confidentiality of patient safety work product and for the oversight of PSOs. Enforcement of the confidentiality provisions includes the imposition of civil money penalties and adherence to the prohibition against imposing a civil money penalty for a single act that violates both the Patient Safety Act and the HIPAA Privacy Rule. This exception ensures that there will not be a conflict between the confidentiality obligations of a holder of patient safety work product and other provisions that allow the Secretary access to protected information and/ or require disclosure to the Secretary for enforcement purposes. See proposed §§ 3.110, 3.210, and 3.310.

Although the statute does not explicitly address this disclosure, we believe that the authority to disclose to the Secretary for these purposes is inherent in the statute, and that this disclosure is permitted and necessary to meaningfully exercise our authority to enforce against breaches of confidentiality as well as to ensure that PSOs meet their certification attestations if needed. Proposed § 3.312(c) discusses the limitations on what the Secretary may do with any patient safety work product obtained pursuant to an investigation or compliance review regarding an alleged impermissible disclosure. This proposed provision would permit the disclosure of patient safety work product to the Secretary or disclosure by the Secretary so long as such disclosure is limited to the purpose of implementation and enforcement of these proposed regulations. Such disclosure would include the introduction of patient safety work product into proceedings before ALJs or the Board under proposed Subpart D by the Secretary, as well as the disclosure during investigations by the Secretary, or activities in reviewing PSO certifications by AHRQ. Disclosures of patient safety work product made to the Board or other parts of the Department that are received by workforce members, such as contractors operating electronic web portals or mail sorting and paper scanning services, would be permitted as a disclosure to the Secretary under this proposed provision. This provision would also permit the Board to disclose any patient safety work product in order to properly review determinations or to provide records for court review.

We believe strongly in the protection of patient safety work product as provided in the Patient Safety Act and the proposed regulations, and seek to minimize the risk of improper disclosure of patient safety work product by using and disclosing patient safety work product only in limited and necessary circumstances. With respect to disclosures to an ALJ or the Board, we note that the Board has numerous administrative, technical and physical safeguards available to protect sensitive information. For example, the Board has the authority to: Enter protective orders; hold closed hearings; redact records; anonymize names of cases and parties prior to publishing opinions; and put records under seal. It routinely maintains a controlled environment; trains staff about proper handling of confidential information; flags confidential information in records prior to archiving cases and shreds copies of case files, etc. Most importantly, understanding that any patient safety work product that is used in an enforcement proceeding is sensitive, the Board would seek to include only information in an opinion that is necessary to the decision, and omit any

extraneous sensitive information that is not needed for its judgments. This proposed provision also requires that patient safety work product disclosed to or by the Secretary must be necessary for the purpose for which the disclosure is made. We intend that any disclosure made pursuant to this proposed provision be limited in the amount of patient safety work product disclosed to accomplish the purpose of implementation, compliance, and enforcement. We discuss our anticipated uses and protections further in proposed Subpart D.

(E) Proposed § 3.206(e)—No Limitation on Authority To Limit or Delegate Disclosure or Use Proposed § 3.206(e) reflects the Patient Safety Act's rule of construction in section 922(g)(4) of the Public Health Service Act, 42 U.S.C. 299b–22(g)(4), establishing that a person holding patient safety work product may enter into a contract that requires greater confidentiality protections or may delegate its authority to make a disclosure in accordance with this Subpart. For example, a provider may delegate its permission (which it may have as a provider) to disclose to the FDA under proposed § 3.206(b)(7) to a PSO through a contractual arrangement.

In such a case, the PSO would be acting on behalf of the provider in making disclosures to the FDA. Without the delegated permission, it would, in this scenario, be impermissible

for the PSO to disclose identifiable patient safety work product to the FDA, and a PSO that made such a disclosure could be subject to a civil money penalty. However, if a delegation of disclosing authority exists, the delegating person would be responsible for the disclosures of the delegee. Thus, in the example above, if the PSO made an impermissible disclosure, the delegating provider could be liable under the principle of principal liability for the acts of its agent. The PSO making the disclosure could also be liable. See discussion in proposed § 3.402(b).

Neither the statute nor the proposed rule limits the authority of a provider to place limitations on disclosures or uses.

For example, a provider may require that a PSO remove all employee names prior to disclosing any patient safety work product despite such disclosure being permissible under this Subpart with the names included.

3. Proposed § 3.208—Continued Protection of Patient Safety Work Product Proposed § 3.208 provides that the privilege and confidentiality protections continue to apply to patient safety work product when disclosed and describes the narrow circumstances when the protections terminate. Generally, when identifiable patient safety work product is disclosed, whether pursuant to a permitted exception to privilege and/ or confidentiality or disclosed impermissibly, that patient safety work

product continues to be privileged and confidential. Any person receiving such patient safety work product receives that patient safety work product pursuant to the privilege and confidentiality protections. The receiving person holds the patient safety work product subject to these protections and is generally bound by the same limitations on disclosure and the potential civil money penalty liability if he or she discloses the patient safety work product in a manner that warrants imposition of a civil money penalty under proposed Subpart D.

An example would be if identifiable patient safety work product is disclosed to a provider's employee for patient safety activities, the identifiable patient safety work product disclosed to the employee would be confidential and the employee would be subject to civil money penalty liability for any knowing or reckless disclosure of the patient safety work product in identifiable form not permitted by the exceptions. Similarly, if confidential patient safety work product is received impermissibly, such as by an unauthorized computer access (i.e., hacker), the impermissible disclosure, even when unintentional, does not terminate the confidentiality.

Thus, the hacker may be subject to civil money penalty liability for impermissible disclosures of that information. We do not require that notification of the privilege and confidentiality of patient safety work product be made with each disclosure. We also note that the Secretary does not have authority to impose a civil money penalty for an impermissible breach of the privilege protection. Rather, any breach of privilege, permissible or not, would encompass a disclosure and concurrent breach of confidentiality, subject to penalty under the CMP provisions of the Patient Safety Act and this proposed rule, unless a confidentiality exception applied. See the discussion above of confidentiality protections at proposed § 3.206 and the discussion of the enforcement provisions at proposed Subpart D.

Nor do we require notification of either the confidentiality of patient safety work product or the fact that patient safety work product is being disclosed. The Secretary's authority to impose a civil money penalty is not dependent upon whether the disclosing entity or person knows that the information being disclosed is patient safety work product or whether patient safety work product is confidential (see discussion under proposed Subpart D). Thus, we do not require that the disclosure of patient safety work product be accompanied by a notice as to either the fact that the information disclosed is patient safety work product or that it is confidential. Labeling does not make information protected patient safety work product, and the failure to label patient safety work product does not remove the protection. However, we do believe that such a notification would be beneficial to the recipient to alert such recipient to the fact that the information received should be held in a confidential manner and that knowing or reckless disclosure in violation of the confidentiality protection may subject a discloser to civil money penalties.

Labeling patient safety work product may also make it easier for the provider to establish that such information is privileged patient safety work product. Also, a notification may also be prudent management for providers, PSOs, and responsible persons who could be subject to liability under agency principles for actions of disclosing agents. Moreover, such a notification policy may serve as a mitigating factor under the factors outlined under proposed Subpart D. Similarly, labeling of patient safety work product may be a good practice for the internal management of information by an entity that holds protected patient safety work product.

There are two exceptions to the continued protection of patient safety work product which terminate either the confidentiality or both the privilege and confidentiality under section 922(d)(2) of the Public Health Service Act, 42 U.S.C. 299b–22(d)(2). The first exception to continued protection is an exception to continued confidentiality when patient safety work product is disclosed for use in a criminal proceeding, pursuant to proposed §§ 3.204(b)(1) and 3.206(b)(1). Proposed § 3.204(b)(1) is an exception to privilege for the particular proceeding at issue and does not permit the use of such patient safety work product in other proceedings or otherwise remove the privilege protection afforded such information. Thus, in the case of a criminal proceeding disclosure, the privilege continues even though the confidentiality terminates. In other words, when a court makes an *in camera* determination that patient safety work product can be entered into a criminal proceeding, that information remains privileged for any future proceedings, but is no longer confidential and may be further disclosed without restriction.

The second exception to continued protection is when patient safety work product is disclosed in nonidentifiable form, pursuant to proposed §§ 3.204(b)(4) and 3.206(b)(5). Under both of these exceptions, the patient safety work product disclosed is no longer confidential, and may be further disclosed without restriction. The termination of the continued protections is based on section 922(d)(2) of the Public Health Service Act, 42 U.S.C. 299b–22(d)(2).

4. Proposed § 3.210— Required Disclosure of Patient Safety Work Product to the Secretary We are proposing in § 3.210 that providers, PSOs, and other persons that hold patient safety work product be required to disclose such patient safety work product to the Secretary upon a determination by the Secretary that such patient safety work product is needed for the investigation and enforcement activities related to this Part, or is needed in seeking and imposing civil money penalties. Such patient safety work product disclosed to the Secretary will be excepted from privilege and confidentiality protections insofar as the Secretary has a need to use such patient safety work product for the above purposes which include: accepting, conditioning, or revoking acceptance of PSO certification or in supporting such actions. See proposed § 3.206(d).

5. Proposed § 3.212— Nonidentification of Patient Safety Work Product Proposed § 3.210 establishes the standard by which patient safety work product will be determined nonidentifiable. For the ease of the reader, we have discussed this standard within the context of proposed § 3.206(b)(5), the confidentiality disclosure exception for nonidentifiable patient safety work product.

D. Subpart D—Enforcement Program
The authority of the Secretary to enforce the confidentiality provisions of the Patient Safety Act is intended to deter impermissible disclosures of patient safety work product.

Proposed Subpart D would establish a framework to enable the Secretary to monitor and ensure compliance with this Part, procedures for imposing a civil money penalty for breach of confidentiality, and procedures for a hearing contesting a civil money penalty.

The proposed enforcement program has been designed to provide maximum flexibility to the Secretary in addressing violations of the confidentiality provisions to encourage participation in patient safety activities and achieve the goals of the Patient Safety Act while safeguarding the confidentiality and protected nature of patient safety work product under the Patient Safety Act and this part. Failures to maintain confidentiality may be serious, deleterious and broad-ranging, and, if unpunished, may discourage participation by providers in the PSO voluntary reporting system. The Secretary's enforcement authority will be exercised commensurately to respond to the nature of any such failure and the resulting harm from such failures. The proposed regulations seek to provide the Secretary with reasonable discretion, particularly in areas where the exercise of judgment is called for by the statute or proposed rules, and to avoid being overly prescriptive in areas and causing unintended adverse effects where it would be helpful to gain experience with the practical impact of the proposed rules.

The provisions of section 1128A of the Social Security Act, 42 U.S.C. 1320a–7a, apply to the imposition of a civil money penalty under section 922(f) of the Public Health Service Act, 42 U.S.C. 299b–22(f), "in the same manner as" they apply to the imposition of civil money penalties under section 1128A itself. Section 1128A(*l*) of the Social Security Act, 42 U.S.C. 1320a–7a(*l*), provides that a principal is liable for penalties for the actions of its agents acting within the scope of their agency. Therefore, a provider or PSO will be responsible for the actions of a workforce member when such member discloses patient safety work product in violation of the confidentiality provisions while acting within the scope of the member's agency relationship.

Proposed §§ 3.304 through 3.314 are designed to enable the Secretary to assist with, monitor, and investigate alleged failures with respect to compliance with the confidentiality provisions. Proposed §§ 3.304 through 3.314 would establish the processes and procedures for the Secretary to provide technical assistance with compliance, for filing complaints with the Secretary, and for investigations and compliance reviews performed by the Secretary. Proposed §§ 3.402 through 3.426 would provide the legal basis for imposing a civil money penalty, determining the amount of a civil money penalty, implementing the prohibi-

tion on the imposition of a civil money penalty under both HIPAA and the Patient Safety Act, and issuing a notice of proposed determination to impose a civil money penalty and establishing the process that would be relevant subsequent to the issuance of such a notice, whether or not a hearing follows the issuance of the notice of proposed determination. These sections also would contain provisions on the statute of limitations, authority to settle, collection of any penalty imposed for violation of the confidentiality provisions, and public notice of the imposition of such penalties. Finally, proposed § 3.504 addresses the administrative hearing phase of the enforcement process, including provisions for appellate review within HHS of a hearing decision and burden of proof in such proceedings. Generally, proposed Subpart D is based on the HIPAA Enforcement Rule, 45 CFR Part 160, Subparts C, D and E. We have closely followed the HIPAA Enforcement Rule for several reasons. First, because civil money penalties under both the HIPAA Enforcement Rule and Patient Safety Act are based on section 1128A of the Social Security Act, 42 U.S.C. 1320a–7a, we believe there is benefit in maintaining a common approach to enforcement and appeals of such civil money penalty determinations. Second, we believe that these procedures set forth in the HIPAA

Enforcement Rule, which in turn are based on the procedures established by the OIG, work and satisfactorily address issues raised and addressed in prior rulemakings by the Department and the OIG. We do not reiterate those concerns, or their resolutions, here, but they have informed our decision making on these proposed rules. Proposed §§ 3.504(b)–(d), (f)–(g), (i)–(k), (m), (n), (t), (w) and (x) of the proposed rule are unchanged from, or incorporate the provisions of, the HIPAA Enforcement Rule. For a full discussion of the basis for these proposed sections, please refer to the proposed and final HIPAA Enforcement Rule, published on April 18, 2005, at 70 FR 20224 (proposed) and on February 16, 2006, at 71 FR 8390 (final). Although the preamble discussion of the HIPAA Enforcement Rule pertains to the HIPAA Administrative Simplification provisions, HIPAA covered entities, and protected health information under HIPAA, we believe the same interpretations and analyses are applicable to the Patient Safety Act confidentiality provisions, providers, PSOs, and responsible persons, and patient safety work product.

Proposed §§ 3.424 and 3.504(a), (e), (h), (l), (o)–(s), (u) and (v) of the proposed rule also are based on, or incorporate, the HIPAA Enforcement Rule, but include technical changes made in order to adapt these provisions to the Patient

Safety Act confidentiality provisions. We discuss these technical changes below but refer to the proposed and final HIPAA Enforcement Rule for a substantive discussion of these proposed sections.

For the above proposed sections, while we have chosen not to repeat our discussion of the rationale for these regulations, we invite comments regarding whether any further substantive or technical changes are needed to adapt these provisions to the Patient Safety Act confidentiality provisions.

The remaining sections in Subpart D of the proposed rule reprint HIPAA Enforcement Rule provisions in their entirety or constitute substantive changes from the analogous provisions of the HIPAA Enforcement Rule. We discuss these proposed sections in full below.

1. Proposed § 3.304—Principles for Achieving Compliance Proposed § 3.304(a) would establish the principle that the Secretary will seek the cooperation of providers, PSOs, and responsible persons in maintaining and preserving the confidentiality of patient safety work product, relying on the civil money penalty authority when appropriate to remediate violations. Proposed § 3.304(b) provides that the Secretary may provide technical assistance to providers, PSOs, and responsible persons to help them comply with the confidentiality provisions. We will seek to achieve compliance through technical assistance and outreach so that providers, PSOs, and responsible persons that hold patient safety work product may better understand the requirements of the confidentiality provisions and, thus, may voluntarily comply by preventing breaches. However, we believe that the types of events that are likely to trigger complaints are actual breaches of confidentiality which will need remedial action (such events cannot be mitigated through preventive measures alone). Given the existing framework of peer review systems and other similar processes, we believe that most providers and patient safety experts already have well-established mechanisms for using sensitive information while respecting its confidentiality. Moreover, such persons will have incentives to maintain the confidentiality of patient safety work product each such person possesses in the future. Thus, while there may be situations where an issue may be resolved through technical assistance and corrective action, we anticipate that the resolution of complaints of breaches of confidentiality may warrant imposition of a civil money penalty to deter future non-compliance and similar violations. This Subpart preserves the discretion of the Secretary to enforce confidentiality in the manner that best fits the situation.

The Secretary will exercise discretion in developing a technical assistance program that may include the provision of written material when appropriate to assist persons in achieving compliance.

We encourage persons to share "best practices" for the confidential utilization of patient safety work product. However, the absence of technical assistance or guidance may not be raised as a defense to civil money penalty liability.

2. Proposed § 3.306—Complaints to the Secretary We are proposing in § 3.306 that any person may file a complaint with the Secretary if the person believes that a provider, PSO or responsible person has disclosed patient safety work product in violation of the confidentiality provisions. A complaint-driven process would provide helpful information about the handling and disclosure of patient safety work product and could serve to identify particularly troublesome compliance problems on an early basis. The procedures proposed in this section are modeled on those used for the HIPAA Enforcement Rule. We would require: complaints to be in writing; complainants to identify the person(s), and describe the acts, alleged to be out of compliance; and that the complainant file such complaint within 180 days of when the complainant knew or should have known that the act complained of occurred, unless this time limit is waived by the Secretary for good cause shown. We have tried to keep the require-

ments for filing complaints as minimal as possible to facilitate use of this process. The Secretary would also attempt to keep the identity of complainants confidential, if possible. However, we recognize that it could be necessary to disclose the identity of a complainant in order to investigate the substance of the complaint, and the rules proposed below would permit such disclosures.

For the same reason that the HIPAA Enforcement Rule adopted the "known or should have known" standard for filing a complaint, we require that complaints be filed within 180 days of when the complainant knew or should have known that the violation complained of occurred unless this time limit is waived by the Secretary for good cause shown. We believe that an investigation of a complaint is likely to be most effective if persons can be interviewed and documents reviewed as close to the time of the alleged violation as possible. Requiring that complaints generally be filed within a certain period of time increases the likelihood that the Secretary will be able to obtain necessary and reliable information in order to investigate allegations. Moreover, we are taking this approach in order to encourage complainants to file complaints as soon as possible. By receiving complaints in a timely fashion, we can, if such complaints prove valid,

reduce the harm caused by the violation.

In most cases, we expect that the providers, PSOs, responsible persons, and/or their employees will be aware of disclosures of patient safety work product. Nevertheless, other persons may become aware of the wrongful disclosure of patient safety work product as well. For these reasons, we do not limit who may file a complaint.

We will accept complaints alleging violations from any person.

Once a complaint is received, the Secretary will notify the provider, PSO, or responsible person(s) against whom the complaint has been filed (i.e., the respondent), investigate and seek resolution to any violations based on the circumstances of the violation, in accordance with the principles for achieving compliance. In enforcing the confidentiality provisions of the Patient Safety Act, the Secretary will generally inform the respondent of the nature of any complaints received against the respondent. The Secretary will also generally afford the entity an opportunity to share information with the Secretary that may result in an early resolution.

3. Proposed § 3.308—Compliance Reviews We are proposing in § 3.308 that the Secretary could conduct compliance reviews to determine whether a provider, PSO, or responsible person is in compliance. A compliance review could be based on information indicating a possible

violation of the confidentiality provisions even though a formal complaint has not been filed. As is the case with a complaint investigation, a compliance review may examine the policies, practices or procedures of a respondent and may result in voluntary compliance or in a finding of a violation or no violation finding.

We believe the Secretary's ability to conduct compliance reviews should be flexible and unobstructed by limitations or required links to ongoing investigations. We do not establish any affirmative criteria for the conduct of a compliance review. Compliance reviews may be undertaken without regard to ongoing investigations or prior conduct.

We recognize that cooperating with compliance reviews may create some burden and expense. However, the Secretary needs to maintain the flexibility to conduct whatever reviews are necessary to ensure compliance with the rule. We note that, at least in the short term, HHS will be taking a case-based, complaint-driven approach to investigations and enforcement, rather than focusing resources on compliance reviews unrelated to any information or allegations of confidentiality violations.

4. Proposed § 3.310—Responsibilities of Respondents Proposed § 3.310 establishes certain obligations for respondents that would be necessary to enable the Secretary to carry out the statutory role to

determine their compliance with the requirements of the confidentiality provisions. Respondents would be required to maintain records as proposed in this proposed rule, participate as required in investigations and compliance reviews, and provide information to the Secretary upon demand. Respondents would also be required to disclose patient safety work product to the Secretary for investigations and compliance activities. We interpret the enforcement provision at section 922(f) of the Patient Safety Act, 42 U.S.C. 299b-22(f), to allow for such disclosure to the Secretary for the purpose of enforcing the confidentiality provisions.

Proposed § 3.310(b) would require cooperation by respondents with investigations as well as compliance reviews.

Proposed § 3.310(c) would provide that the Secretary must be provided access to a respondent's facilities, books, records, accounts, and other sources of information, including patient safety work product. Ordinarily, the Secretary will provide notice requesting access during normal business hours. However, if exigent circumstances exist, such as where documents might be hidden or destroyed, the Secretary may require access at any time and without notice. The Secretary will consider alternative approaches, such as subpoenas or search warrants, in seeking information from respondents that are not providers,

PSOs, or a member of their workforce.

5. Proposed § 3.312— Secretarial Action Regarding Complaints and Compliance Reviews Proposed § 3.312(a) provides that, if a complaint investigation or compliance review indicates noncompliance, the Secretary may attempt to resolve the matter by informal means. If the Secretary determines that the matter cannot be resolved by informal means, the Secretary will issue findings to the respondent and, if applicable, the complainant. Proposed § 3.312(a)(1) provides that, where noncompliance is indicated, the Secretary could seek to reach a resolution of the matter satisfactory to the Secretary by informal means. Informal means would include demonstrated compliance or a completed corrective action plan or other agreement. Under this provision, entering into a corrective action plan or other agreement would not, in and of itself, resolve the noncompliance; rather, the full performance by the respondent of its obligations under the corrective action plan or other agreement would be necessary to resolve the noncompliance.

Proposed §§ 3.312(a)(2) and (3) address what notifications would be provided by the Secretary where noncompliance is indicated, based on an investigation or compliance review. Notification under these paragraphs would not be required where the only contacts made were with the

complainant to determine whether the complaint warrants investigation. Section 3.312(a)(2) proposes written notice to the respondent and, if the matter arose from a complaint, the complainant, where the matter is resolved by informal means. If the matter is not resolved by informal means, proposed § 3.312(a)(3)(i) would require the Secretary to so inform the respondent and provide the respondent 30 days in which to raise any mitigating factors the Secretary should consider in imposing a civil money penalty. Section 3.312(a)(3)(ii) proposes that, where a matter is not resolved by informal means and the Secretary decides that imposition of a civil money penalty is warranted based upon a response from the respondent or expiration of the 30 day response time limit, the formal finding would be contained in the notice of proposed determination issued under proposed § 3.420.

Proposed § 3.312(b) provides that, if the Secretary finds, after an investigation or compliance review, no further action is warranted, the Secretary will so inform the respondent and, if the matter arose from a complaint, the complainant. This section does not apply where no investigation or compliance review has been initiated, such as where a complaint has been dismissed due to lack of jurisdiction.

Proposed § 3.312(c) addresses how the Secretary

will handle information obtained during the course of an investigation or compliance review. Under proposed § 3.312(c)(1), identifiable patient safety work product obtained by the Secretary in connection with an investigation or compliance review under this Part remains subject to the privilege and confidentiality protections and will not be disclosed except in accordance with proposed § 3.206(d), if necessary for ascertaining or enforcing compliance with this part, or as permitted by this Part or the Patient Safety Act. In other words, the Secretary, as with any other entity or person, would receive patient safety work product subject to the confidentiality and privilege requirements and protections. The proposed rule strikes a balance between these protections and enforcement, providing that the Secretary would not disclose such patient safety work product, except as may be necessary to enable the Secretary to ascertain compliance with this Part, in enforcement proceedings, or as otherwise permitted by this Part. We note that, pursuant to section 922(g)(3) of the Public Health Service Act, 42 U.S.C. 299b-22(g)(3), as added by the Patient Safety Act, the Patient Safety Act does not affect the implementation of the HIPAA confidentiality regulations (known as the HIPAA Privacy Rule). Accordingly, we propose that the Secretary may use patient safety work product obtained in connection with an investigation hereunder to enforce the HIPAA confidentiality regulations. Proposed § 3.312(c)(2) provides that, except for patient safety work product, testimony and other evidence obtained in connection with an investigation or compliance review may be used by HHS in any of its activities and may be used or offered into evidence in any administrative or judicial proceeding.

Such information would include that which is obtained from investigational subpoenas and inquiries under proposed § 3.314. The Department generally seeks to protect the privacy of individuals to the fullest extent possible, while permitting the exchange of records required to fulfill its administrative and programmatic responsibilities. The Freedom of Information Act, 5 U.S.C. 552, and the HHS implementing regulation, 45 CFR Part 5, provide substantial protection for records about individuals where disclosure would constitute an unwarranted invasion of their personal privacy. Moreover, in enforcing the Patient Safety Act and its implementing regulations, OCR plans to continue its current practice of protecting its complaint files from disclosure. These files, thus, would constitute investigatory records compiled for law enforcement purposes, one of the exemptions to disclosure under the Freedom of Information Act. In the case of patient safety work product that is not otherwise subject to a statutory exception permitting disclosure, the Patient Safety Act prohibits the disclosure of such information in response to a Freedom of Information Act request. See section 922(a)(3) of the Public Health Service Act, 42 U.S.C. 299b-22(a)(3).

The Secretary continues to be subject to the existing HIPAA Enforcement Rule with respect to the use and disclosure of protected health information received by the Secretary in connection with a HIPAA Privacy Rule investigation or compliance review (see 45 CFR 160.310(c)(3)); these proposed provisions do not modify those regulations.

6. Proposed § 3.314— Investigational Subpoenas and Inquiries Proposed § 3.314 provides procedures for the issuance of subpoenas to require the attendance and testimony of witnesses and the production of any other evidence, including patient safety work product, during an investigation or compliance review. We propose to issue subpoenas in the same manner as 45 CFR 160.314(a)(1)-(5) of the HIPAA Enforcement Rule, except that the term "this part" shall refer to 42 CFR Part 3.

The language modification is necessary to reference the appropriate authority. We also propose that the Secretary is permitted to conduct investigational inquiries in the same manner as the provisions of 45 CFR 160.314(b)(1)-(9) of the HIPAA Enforcement Rule. The referenced provisions describe the manner in which investigational inquiries will be conducted.

7. Proposed § 3.402—Basis for a Civil Money Penalty Under proposed § 3.402, a person who discloses identifiable patient safety work product in knowing or reckless violation of the confidentiality provisions shall be subject to a civil money penalty of not more than $10,000 for each act constituting a violation. See section 922(f)(1) of the Public Health Service Act, 42 U.S.C. 299b-22(f)(1).

(A) Proposed § 3.402(a)— General Rule Proposed § 3.402(a) would allow the Secretary to impose a civil money penalty on any person which the Secretary determines has knowingly or recklessly violated the confidentiality provisions. This provision is based on the language in section 922(f) of the Public Health Service Act, 42 U.S.C. 299b-22(f), that "a person who discloses identifiable patient safety work product in knowing or reckless violation of subsection (b) shall be subject to a civil money penalty of not more than $10,000 for each act constituting such violation." A civil money penalty may only be imposed if the Secretary first establishes a wrongful disclosure (i.e., (1) the information disclosed was identifiable patient safety work product; (2) the information was disclosed;

and (3) the manner of the disclosure does not fit within any permitted exception). If a wrongful disclosure is established, the Secretary must then determine whether the person making the disclosure acted "knowingly" or "recklessly." The applicable law on the issue of "knowing" provides that "unless the text of the statute dictates a different result, the term 'knowingly' merely requires *proof of knowledge of the facts that constitute the offense* [rather than] a culpable state of mind or [] knowledge of the law." *Bryan* v. *United States,* 524 U.S. 184 (1998) (emphasis added). Applying this meaning in the context of the Patient Safety Act, the Secretary would not need to prove that the person making the disclosure knew the law (i.e., knew that the disclosed information constituted identifiable patient safety work product or that such disclosure did not meet one of the standards for a permissive disclosure in the Patient Safety Act). Rather, the Secretary would only need to show that the person knew a disclosure was being made. Although knowledge that disclosed information is patient safety work product is not required, circumstances in which a person can show no such knowledge and no reason to know such knowledge may warrant discretion by the Secretary. By contrast, as a person's opportunity for knowledge and disregard of that opportunity increases, the Secretary's compulsion to

exercise discretion not to impose a penalty declines. Where a "knowing" violation cannot be established, the Secretary can still impose a civil money penalty by showing that the person was reckless in making the disclosure of identifiable patient safety work product. A person acts recklessly if they are aware, or a reasonable person in their situation should be aware, that their conduct creates a substantial risk of disclosure of information and to disregard such risk constitutes a gross deviation from reasonable conduct. A "substantial risk" represents a significant threshold, more than the mere possibility of disclosure of patient safety work product. Whether a risk is "substantial" is a fact-specific inquiry. Additionally, whether a reasonable person in the situation should know of a risk is based on context. For example, an employee whose job duties regularly involve working with sensitive patient information may be expected to know of disclosure risks of which other types of employees may reasonably be unaware. Finally, the disregarding of the risk must be a gross deviation from reasonable conduct. This gross deviation standard is commonly used to describe reckless conduct. See, e.g., Model Penal Code § 2A1.4(2006), definition of "reckless" for purposes of involuntary manslaughter; Black's Law Dictionary (8th ed., 2004). This does not mean that the conduct itself must be a gross deviation from reasonable conduct. Rather, the standard is whether the disregarding of the risk was a gross deviation (i.e., whether a reasonable person who is aware of the substantial risk of making an impermissible disclosure would find going forward despite the risk to be grossly unreasonable). Thus, disclosures that violate this Part and occur because an individual acted despite knowing of, or having reason to know of, a grossly unreasonable risk of disclosure are punishable by civil money penalty, regardless of whether such conduct may otherwise be widespread in the industry. An example of a reckless disclosure of identifiable patient safety work product would be leaving a laptop unattended in a public area and accessible to unauthorized persons with identifiable patient safety work product displayed on the laptop screen. Such a situation would be reckless because it would create a substantial risk of disclosure of the information displayed on the laptop screen. If a person did not remove the identifiable patient safety work product from the laptop screen or take other measures to prevent the public view of the laptop screen, then leaving the laptop unattended would be a disregard for the substantial risk of disclosure that would be a gross deviation from reasonable conduct. Under these circumstances, the person leaving the laptop unattended could be liable for a civil money penalty.

The use of the term "shall be subject to" in section 922(f) of the Public Health Service Act, 42 U.S.C. 299b–22(f), conveys authority to the Secretary to exercise discretion as to whether to impose a penalty for a knowing or reckless violation of the confidentiality provisions. Based on the nature and circumstances of a violation and whether such violation was done in a knowing or reckless manner, the Secretary may impose a civil money penalty, require a corrective action plan, or seek voluntary compliance with these regulations.

Even in cases that constitute violations of the confidentiality provisions, the Secretary may exercise discretion. For example, in a situation where a provider makes a good faith attempt to assert the patient safety work product privilege, but is nevertheless ordered by a court to make a disclosure, and the provider does so, the Secretary could elect not to impose a civil money penalty. Thus, for example, it is not the Secretary's intention to impose a civil money penalty on a provider ordered by a court to produce patient safety work product where the provider has deliberately and in good faith undertaken reasonable steps to avoid such production and is, nevertheless, faced with compelled production or being held in contempt of court.

Similarly, an individual may innocently come into possession of information, unaware of the fact that the information is patient safety

work product, and may innocently share the information in a manner not permitted by the confidentiality provisions. In such circumstances, the Secretary would look at the facts and circumstances of the case and could elect not to impose a penalty. Relevant facts and circumstances might include the individual's relationship with the source of the information (e.g., whether the information originated with a health care provider or a patient safety organization for which the individual was employed); whether, and the extent to which, the individual had a basis to know the information was patient safety work product or to know that the information was confidential; to whom the information was disclosed; and the intent of the individual in making the disclosure.

(B) Proposed § 3.402(b)— Violations Attributed to a Principal The proposed rule includes a provision, at proposed § 3.402(b), that addresses the liability of a principal for a violation by a principal's agent.

Proposed § 3.402(b) adopts the principle that the federal common law of agency applies when addressing the liability of a principal for the acts of his or her agent. Under this principle, a provider, PSO or responsible person generally can be held liable for a violation based on the actions of any agent, including an employee or other workforce member, acting within the scope of the agency or employment.

This liability is separate from the underlying liability attributable to the agent and could result in a separate and exclusive civil money penalty. In other words, a principal may be liable for a $10,000 civil money penalty and an agent may be liable for a separate $10,000 civil money penalty arising from the same act that is a violation. Section 922(f)(2) of the Public Health Service Act, 42 U.S.C. 299b–22(f)(2), provides that "the provisions of section 1128A * * * shall apply to civil money penalties under this subsection [of the Patient Safety Act] in the same manner as such provisions apply to a penalty or proceeding under section 1128A."

Section 1128A(*l*) of the Social Security Act, 42 U.S.C. 1320a–7a(*l*), establishes that "a principal is liable for penalties * * * under this section for the actions of the principal's agents acting within the scope of the agency." This is similar to the traditional rule of agency in which principals are vicariously liable for the acts of their agents acting within the scope of their authority. See *Meyer* v. *Holley*, 537 U.S. 280 (2003).

Therefore, a provider, PSO or responsible person generally will be responsible for the actions of its workforce members within the scope of agency, such as where an employee discloses confidential patient safety work product in violation of the confidentiality provisions during the course of his or her employment.

The determination of whether or not a principal is responsible for a violation would be based on two fact-dependent determinations. First, the Secretary must find that a principal-agent relationship exists between the person doing the violative act and the principal. If a principal-agent relationship is established, then a second determination, whether the act in violation of the confidentiality provisions was within the scope of the agency, must be made. The determination as to whether an agent's conduct is outside the scope of the agency will be dependent upon the application of the federal common law of agency to the facts.

The purpose of applying the federal common law of agency to determine when a provider, PSO, or responsible person is vicariously liable for the acts of its agents is to achieve nationwide uniformity in the implementation of the confidentiality provisions and nationwide consistency in the enforcement of these rules by OCR. Reliance on State law could introduce inconsistency in the implementation of the patient safety work product confidentiality provisions by persons or entities in different States.

Federal Common Law of Agency A principal's liability for the actions of its agents is generally governed by State law. However, the U.S. Supreme Court has provided that the federal common law of agency may be applied where there is a strong

governmental interest in nationwide uniformity and a predictable standard, and when the federal rule in question is interpreting a federal statute. *Burlington Indus.* v. *Ellerth,* 524 U.S. 742 (1998).

The confidentiality and enforcement provisions of this regulation interpret a federal statute, the Patient Safety Act. Under the Patient Safety Act, there is a strong interest in nationwide uniformity in the confidentiality provisions and how those provisions are enforced. The fundamental goal of the Patient Safety Act is to promote the examination and correction of patient safety events in order to improve patient safety and create a culture of patient safety in the health care system. Therefore, it is essential for the Secretary to apply one consistent body of law regardless of where an agent is employed, an alleged violation occurred, or an action is brought. The same considerations support a strong federal interest in the predictable operation of the confidentiality provisions, to ensure that persons using patient safety work product can do so consistently so as to facilitate the appropriate exchange of information. Thus, the tests for application of the federal common law of agency are met.

Where the federal common law of agency applies, the courts often look to the Restatement (Second) of Agency (1958) (Restatement) as a basis for explaining the common law's application.

While the determination of whether an agent is acting within the scope of its authority must be decided on a case-by-case basis, the Restatement provides guidelines for this determination. Section 229 of the Restatement provides:

(1) To be within the scope of the employment, conduct must be of the same general nature as that authorized, or incidental to the conduct authorized.

(2) In determining whether or not the conduct, although not authorized, is nevertheless so similar to or incidental to the conduct authorized as to be within the scope of employment, the following matters of fact are to be considered;

(a) Whether or not the act is one commonly done by such servants;

(b) The time, place and purpose of the act;

(c) The previous relations between the master and the servant;

(d) The extent to which the business of the master is apportioned between different servants;

(e) Whether or not the act is outside the enterprise of the master or, if within the enterprise, has not been entrusted to any servant;

(f) Whether or not the master has reason to expect that such an act will be done;

(g) The similarity in quality of the act done to the act authorized;

(h) Whether or not the instrumentality by which the harm is done has been furnished by the master to the servant;

(i) The extent of departure from the normal method of accomplishing an authorized result; and

(j) Whether or not the act is seriously criminal.

In some cases, under federal agency law, a principal may be liable for an agent's acts even if the agent acts outside the scope of its authority. Restatement (Second) of Agency section 219 (1958). However, proposed § 3.402(b) would follow section 1128A(l) of the Social Security Act, 42 U.S.C. 1320a–7a(l), which limits liability for the actions of an agent to those actions that are within the scope of the agency. Agents Various categories of persons may be agents of a provider, PSO, or responsible person. These persons include workforce members. We propose a slightly expanded definition of "workforce" from the term defined in the HIPAA Privacy Rule. The proposed definition of "workforce" includes employees, volunteers, trainees, contractors, and other persons whose conduct, in the performance of work for a provider, PSO or responsible person, is under the direct control of such principal, whether or not they are paid by the principal. Because of the "direct control" language of the proposed rule, we believe that all workforce members, including those who are not employees, are agents of a principal. Under the proposed rule, a principal could be liable for a violation based on an act that is a violation by any workforce

member acting within the scope of employment or agency. The determinative issue is whether a person is sufficiently under the control of a person or entity and acting within the scope of the agency.

Proposed § 3.402(b) creates a presumption that a workforce member is an agent of an employer.

8. Proposed § 3.404—Amount of Civil Money Penalty Proposed § 3.404, the amount of the civil money penalty, is determined in accordance with section 922(f) of the Public Health Service Act, 42 U.S.C. 299b–22(f), and the provisions of this Part. Section 922(f)(1) of the Public Health Service Act, 42 U.S.C. 299b– 22(f)(1), establishes a maximum penalty amount for violations of "not more than $10,000" per person for each violation.

The statutory cap is reflected in proposed § 3.404(b). The statute establishes only maximum penalty amounts, so the Secretary has the discretion to impose penalties that are less than the statutory maximum. This proposed regulation would not establish minimum penalties. Under proposed § 3.404(a), the penalty amount would be determined using the factors set forth in proposed § 3.408, subject to the statutory maximum reflected in proposed § 3.404(b).

As stated in the discussion under proposed § 3.402(b), a principal can be held liable for the acts of its agent acting within the scope of the agency. Read together, with proposed § 3.404(b), if a principal and an agent are determined to be liable for a single act that is a violation, the Secretary may impose a penalty of up to $10,000 against each separately. That is, the $10,000 limit applies to each person separately, not the act that was a violation. Thus, in the circumstance where an agent and a principal are determined to have violated the confidentiality provisions, the Secretary may impose a civil money penalty of up to $10,000 against the agent and a civil money penalty of up to $10,000 against the principal, for a total of $20,000 for a single act that is a violation.

9. Proposed § 3.408—Factors Considered in Determining the Amount of a Civil Money Penalty Section 1128A(d) of the Social Security Act, 42 U.S.C. 1320a-7a(d), made applicable to the imposition of civil money penalties by section 922(f)(2) of the Public Health Service Act, 42 U.S.C. 299b-22(f)(2), requires that, in determining the amount of "any penalty," the Secretary shall take into account: (1) The nature of the claims and the circumstances under which they were presented, (2) the degree of culpability, history of prior offenses, and financial condition of the person presenting the claims, and (3) such other matters as justice may require.

This language establishes factors to be considered in determining the amount of a civil money penalty.

This approach is taken in other regulations that cross-reference section 1128A of the Social Security Act, 42 U.S.C. 1320a-7a, which rely on these factors for purposes of determining civil money penalty amounts. See, for example, 45 CFR 160.408. The factors listed in section 1128A(d) of the Social Security Act, 42 U.S.C. 1320a-7a(d), were drafted to apply to violations involving claims for payment under federally funded health programs.

Because Patient Safety Act violations will not be about specific claims, we propose to tailor the section 1128A(d) factors to violations of the confidentiality provisions and further particularize the statutory factors by providing discrete criteria, as done in the HIPAA Enforcement Rule and the OIG regulations that implement section 1128A of the Social Security Act, 42 U.S.C. 1320a-7a. Consistent with these other regulations, and to provide more guidance to providers, PSOs, and responsible persons as to the factors that would be used in calculating civil money penalties, we propose the following detailed factors:

(1) The nature of the violation.

(2) The circumstances and consequences of the violation, including the time period during which the violation occurred; and whether the violation caused physical or financial harm or reputational damage.

(3) The degree of culpability of the respondent, including

whether the violation was intentional, and whether the violation was beyond the direct control of the respondent.

(4) Any history of prior compliance with the confidentiality provisions, including violations, by the respondent, and whether the current violation is the same as or similar to prior violation(s), whether and to what extent the respondent has attempted to correct previous violations, how the respondent has responded to technical assistance from the Secretary provided in the context of a compliance effort, and how the respondent has responded to prior complaints.

(5) The financial condition of the respondent, including whether the respondent had financial difficulties that affected its ability to comply, whether the imposition of a civil money penalty would jeopardize the ability of the respondent to continue to provide health care or patient safety activities, and the size of the respondent.

(6) Such other matters as justice may require.

For further discussion of these factors, please see the preambles to the Interim Final Rule and the Final Rule for the HIPAA Enforcement Rule at 70 FR 20235-36, Apr. 18, 2005, and 71 FR 8407-09, Feb. 16, 2006. Meeting certain conditions, such as financial condition, is a fact-specific determination based upon the individual circumstances of the situation presented.

We seek comments regarding whether the above list of

factors should be expanded to expressly include a factor for persons who self-report disclosures that may potentially violate the confidentiality provisions such that voluntary self-reporting would be a mitigating consideration when assessing a civil money penalty. Voluntary self-reporting may encourage persons to report breaches of confidentiality, particularly breaches that may otherwise go unnoticed, and to demonstrate the security practices that led to the discovery of the breach and how the breach has been remedied.

However, including self-reporting as a factor may be viewed incorrectly as an additional reporting obligation to report every potentially impermissible disclosure, thereby, unnecessarily increasing administrative burdens on the Department and the individuals or entities making the self-reporting, or it may interfere with obligations to identified persons, particularly when a negotiated, contractual relationship between a provider and a PSO exists that addresses how the parties are to deal with breaches.

Respondents are responsible for raising any issues that pertain to any of the factors to the Secretary within 30 days after receiving notice from the Secretary that informal resolution attempts have not resolved the issue in accordance with proposed § 3.312(a)(3)(i). The Secretary is under no obligation to

affirmatively raise any mitigating factor if a respondent fails to identify the issue. See proposed § 3.504(p).

In many regulations that implement section 1128A of the Social Security Act, 42 U.S.C. 1320a–7a, the statutory factors and/or the discrete criteria are designated as either aggravating or mitigating. For example, at 42 CFR 1003.106(b)(3) of the OIG regulations, "history of prior offenses" is listed as an aggravating factor and is applicable as a factor to a narrow range of prohibited conduct. However, because proposed § 3.408 will apply to a variety of persons and circumstances, we propose that factors may be aggravating or mitigating, depending on the context. For example, the factor "time period during which the violation(s) occurred" could be an aggravating factor if the respondent's violation went undetected for a long period of time or undetected actions resulted in multiple violations, but could be a mitigating factor if a violation was detected and corrected quickly.

This approach is consistent with other regulations implementing section 1128A of the Social Security Act, 42 U.S.C. 1320a–7a. See, for example, 45 CFR 160.408. We propose to leave to the Secretary's discretion the decision regarding when aggravating and mitigating factors will be taken into account in determining the amount of a civil money penalty. The facts of each

violation will drive the determination of whether a particular factor is aggravating or mitigating. 10. Proposed § 3.414— Limitations Proposed § 3.414 sets forth the 6-year limitations period on initiating an action for imposition of a civil money penalty provided for by section 1128A(c)(1) of the Social Security Act, 42 U.S.C. 1320a–7a(c)(1). We propose the date of the occurrence of the violation be the date from which the limitation period begins. 11. Proposed § 3.416—Authority to Settle Proposed § 3.416 states the authority of the Secretary to settle any issue or case or to compromise any penalty during the process addressed in this Part, including cases that are in hearing.

The first sentence of section 1128A(f) of the Social Security Act, 42 U.S.C. 1320a–7a(f), made applicable by section 922(f)(2) of the Public Health Service Act, 42 U.S.C. 299b–22(f)(2), states, in part, "civil money penalties * * * imposed under this section may be compromised by the Secretary." This authority to settle is the same as that set forth in 45 CFR 160.416 of the HIPAA Enforcement Rule.

12. Proposed § 3.418— Exclusivity of Penalty Proposed § 3.418 makes clear that, except as noted below, penalties imposed under this Part are not intended to be exclusive where a violation under this Part may also be a violation of, and subject the respondent to, penalties

under another federal or State law. This provision is modeled on 42 CFR 1003.108 of the OIG regulations.

Proposed § 3.418(b) repeats the statutory prohibition against imposing a penalty under both the Patient Safety Act and under HIPAA for a single act or omission that constitutes a violation of both the Patient Safety Act and HIPAA.

Congress recognized that there could be overlap between the confidentiality provisions and the HIPAA Privacy Rule.

Because identifiable patient safety work product includes individually identifiable health information as defined under the HIPAA Privacy Rule, HIPAA covered entities could be liable for violations of the HIPAA Privacy Rule based upon a single disclosure of identifiable patient safety work product.

We tentatively interpret the Patient Safety Act as only prohibiting the imposition of a civil money penalty under the Patient Safety Act when there have been civil, as opposed to criminal, penalties imposed on the respondent under the HIPAA Privacy Rule for the same single act or omission. In other words, a person could have a civil money penalty imposed against him under the Patient Safety Act as well as a criminal penalty under HIPAA for the same act or omission. However, an act that amounts to a civil violation of both the confidentiality provisions and the HIPAA Privacy Rule

would be enforceable under either authority, but not both.

The decision regarding which statute applies to a particular situation will be made based upon the facts of individual situations. HIPAA covered entities that seek to disclose confidential patient safety work product that contains protected health information must know when such disclosure is permissible under both statutes.

13. Proposed § 3.420—Notice of Proposed Determination

Proposed § 3.420 sets forth the requirements for the notice to a respondent sent when the Secretary proposes a penalty under this Part. This notice implements the requirement for notice contained in section 1128A(c)(1) of the Social Security Act, 42 U.S.C. 1320a–7a(c)(1). These requirements are substantially the same as those in the HIPAA Enforcement Rule at 45 CFR 160.420, except for the removal of provisions related to statistical sampling.

The notice provided for in this section must be given whenever a civil money penalty is proposed. The proposed requirements of this section serve to inform any person under investigation of the basis for the Secretary's proposed civil money penalty determination.

These requirements include the statutory basis for a penalty, a description of the findings of fact regarding the violation, the reasons the violation causes liability,

the amount of the proposed penalty, factors considered under proposed § 3.408 in determining the amount of the penalty, and instructions for responding to the notice, including the right to a hearing.

At this point in the process, the Secretary may also send a notice of proposed determination to a principal based upon liability for a violation under proposed § 3.402(b).

14. Proposed § 3.422—Failure To Request a Hearing

Under proposed § 3.422, when a respondent does not timely request a hearing on a proposed civil money penalty, the Secretary may impose the civil money penalty or any less severe civil money penalty permitted by section 1128A(d)(5) of the Social Security Act, 42 U.S.C. 1320a–7a(d)(5).

Once the time has expired for the respondent to file for an appeal, the Secretary will decide whether to impose the civil money penalty and provide notice to the respondent of the civil money penalty. If the Secretary does pursue a civil money penalty, the civil money penalty is final, and the respondent has no right to appeal a civil money penalty imposed under these circumstances. This section is similar to 45 CFR 160.422 of the HIPAA Enforcement Rule.

For purposes of determining when subsequent actions may commence, such as collection of an imposed civil money penalty, we propose that the penalty be final upon receipt of a penalty notice sent by certified mail return receipt requested.

15. Proposed § 3.424—Collection of Penalty
Proposed § 3.424 provides that once a determination to impose a civil money penalty has become final, the civil money penalty must be collected by the Secretary, unless compromised, and prescribes the methods for collection.

We propose that civil money penalties be collected as set forth under the HIPAA Enforcement Rule at 45 CFR 160.424, except that the term "this part" shall refer to 42 CFR Part 3. The modification is made for the provision to refer to the appropriate authority.

16. Proposed § 3.426—Notification of the Public and Other Agencies
Proposed § 3.426 would implement section 1128A(h) of the Social Security Act, 42 U.S.C. 1320a–7a(h). When a civil money penalty proposed by the Secretary becomes final, section 1128A(h) of the Social Security Act, 42 U.S.C. 1320a–7a(h), directs the Secretary to notify appropriate State or local agencies, organizations, and associations and to provide the reasons for the civil money penalty. We propose to add the public generally as a group that may receive notice, in order to make the information available to anyone who must make decisions with respect to persons that have had a civil money penalty imposed for violation of the confidentiality provisions. For instance, knowledge of the imposition of a civil money penalty for violation of the Patient Safety Act could be important to hospitals, other health care organizations, health care consumers, as well as to current and future business partners throughout the industry.

The basis for this public notice portion lies in the Freedom of Information Act, 5 U.S.C. 552. The Freedom of Information Act requires final opinions and orders made in adjudication cases to be made available for public inspection and copying. See 5 U.S.C. 552(a)(2)(A). While it is true that section 1128A(h) of the Social Security Act, 42 U.S.C. 1320a–7a(h), does not require that such notice be given to the public, neither does it prohibit such wider dissemination of that information, and nothing in section 1128A(h) of the Social Security Act, 42 U.S.C. 1320a–7a(h), suggests that it modifies the Secretary's obligations under the Freedom of Information Act. The Freedom of Information Act requires making final orders or opinions available for public inspection and copying by "computer telecommunication * * * or other electronic means," which would encompass a display on the Department's Web site. See 5 U.S.C. 552(a)(2).

A civil money penalty is considered to be final, for purposes of notification, when it is a final agency action (i.e., the time for administrative appeal has run or the adverse administrative finding has otherwise become final). The final opinion or order that is subject to the notification provisions of this section is the notice of proposed determination, if a request for hearing is not timely filed, the decision of the ALJ, if that is not appealed, or the final decision of the Board. Currently final decisions of the ALJs and the Board are made public via the Board's Web site. See *http://www.hhs. gov/dab/search.html*. Such postings, however, would not include penalties that become final because a request for hearing was not filed under proposed § 3.504(a). Under proposed § 3.426, notices of proposed determination under proposed § 3.420 that become final because a hearing has not been timely requested, would also be made available for public inspection and copying as final orders, with appropriate redaction of any patient safety work product or other confidential information, via OCR's Web site. See the OCR patient safety Web site at *http://www.hhs.gov/ocr/PSQIA*. By making the entire final opinion or order available to the public, the facts underlying the penalty determination and the law applied to those facts will be apparent. Given that information, the public may discern the nature and extent of the violation as well as the basis for imposition of the civil money penalty.

The regulatory language would provide for notification in such manner as the Secretary deems appropriate. Posting to a Department Web site and/or the periodic publication of a notice in the **Federal Register** are among the methods which the Secretary is considering using for the efficient dissemination of such information.

These methods would avoid the need for the Secretary to determine which entities, among a potentially large universe, should be notified and would also permit the general public served by providers, PSOs, and responsible persons upon whom civil money penalties have been imposed—as well as their business partners—to be apprised of this fact, where that information is of interest to them. While the Secretary could provide notice to individual agencies where desired, the Secretary could, at his option, use a single public method of notice, such as posting to a Department Web site, to satisfy the obligation to notify the specified agencies and the public.

17. Proposed § 3.504— Procedures for Hearings Proposed § 3.504 is a compilation of procedures related to administrative hearings on civil money penalties imposed by the Secretary. The proposed section sets forth the authority of the ALJ, the rights and burdens of proof of the parties, requirements for the exchange of information and prehearing, hearing, and post-hearing processes. These individual sections are described in greater detail below.

This proposed section crossreferences the HIPAA Enforcement Rule exten-sively due to the similar nature of the enforcement and appeal procedures, the nature of the issues and substance presented, and the parties most affected by these proposed regulations. We intend that the provisions of the HIPAA Enforcement Rule will be applied to the imposition of civil money penalties under this Subpart in the same manner as they are applied to violations of the HIPAA administrative simplification provisions, subject to any modifications set forth in proposed § 3.504. We believe the best and most efficient manner of achieving this result is through explicitly referencing and adopting the relevant provisions of the HIPAA Enforcement Rule. Where modifications are necessary to address the differences between the appeals of determinations under the HIPAA Enforcement Rule and the Patient Safety Act, we have made specific exceptions that we discuss below.

We note that the recently published Notice of Proposed Rulemaking entitled "Revisions to Procedures for the Departmental Appeals Board and Other Departmental Hearings" (see 72 FR 73708 (December 28, 2007)) proposes to modify the HIPAA Enforcement Rule, which we reference extensively in this proposed rule. Our intent for the patient safety regulations would be to maintain the alignment between the patient safety enforcement process and the HIPAA Enforcement Rule, as stated previously.

Should the amendments to the HIPAA Enforcement Rule become final based on that Notice of Proposed Rulemaking, our intent would be to incorporate those changes in any final rulemaking here.

That Notice of Proposed Rulemaking proposes to amend 45 CFR 160.508(c) and 45 CFR 160.548, and to add a new provision, 45 CFR 160.554, providing that the Secretary may review all ALJ decisions that the Board has declined to review and all Board decisions for error in applying statutes, regulations or interpretive policy.

18. Proposed § 3.504(a)— Hearings Before an ALJ Proposed § 3.504(a) provides the time and manner in which a hearing must be requested, or dismissed when not timely requested. This proposed section applies the same regulations as the HIPAA Enforcement Rule cited at 45 CFR 160.504(a)-(d), except that the language in paragraph (c) of 45 CFR 160.504 following and including "except that" does not apply. The excluded provision refers to the ability of respondents to raise an affirmative defense under 45 CFR 160.410(b)(1) for which we have not adopted a comparable provision because the provision implements a statutory defense unique to HIPAA.

19. Proposed § 3.504(b)— Rights of the Parties Proposed § 3.504(b) provides that the rights of the parties not specifically provided elsewhere in this Part shall

be the same as those provided in 45 CFR 160.506 of the HIPAA Enforcement Rule.

20. Proposed § 3.504(c)—Authority of the ALJ Proposed § 3.504(c) provides that the general guidelines and authority of the ALJ shall be the same as provided in the HIPAA Enforcement Rule at 45 CFR 160.508(a)–(c)(4). We exclude the provision at 45 CFR 160.508(c)(5) because there is no requirement under the Patient Safety Act for remedied violations based on reasonable cause to be insulated from liability for a civil money penalty.

21. Proposed § 3.504(d)—Ex parte Contacts Proposed § 3.504(d) is designed to ensure the fairness of the hearing by prohibiting ex-parte contacts with the ALJ on matters at issue. We propose to incorporate the same restrictions as provided for in the HIPAA Enforcement Rule at 45 CFR 160.510.

22. Proposed § 3.504(e)—Prehearing Conferences Proposed § 3.504(e) adopts the same provisions as govern prehearing confer-ences in the HIPAA Enforcement Rule at 45 CFR 160.512, except that the term "identifiable patient safety work product" is substituted for "individually identifiable health information." Under this proposed provision, the ALJ is required to schedule at least one prehearing conference, in order to narrow the issues to be addressed at the hearing and, thus, expedite the formal hearing process, and to

prescribe a timeframe for prehearings.

23. Proposed § 3.504(f)—Authority To Settle Proposed § 3.504(f) adopts 45 CFR 160.514 of the HIPAA Enforcement Rule. This proposal provides that the Secretary has exclusive authority to settle any issue or case at any time and need not obtain the consent of the ALJ.

24. Proposed § 3.504(g)—Discovery We propose in § 3.504(g) to adopt the discovery procedures as provided for in the HIPAA Enforcement Rule at 45 CFR 160.516. These provisions allow limited discovery in the form of the production for inspection and copying of documents that are relevant and material to the issues before the ALJ.

These provisions do not authorize other forms of discovery, such as deposi-tions and interrogatories. Although the adoption of 45 CFR 160.516 would permit parties to raise claims of privilege and permit an ALJ to deny a motion to compel privileged information, a respondent could not claim privilege, and an ALJ could not deny a motion to compel, if the Secretary seeks patient safety work product relevant to the alleged confidentiality violation because the patient safety work product would not be privileged under proposed § 3.204(c).

Under this proposal, a respondent concerned with potential public access to patient safety work product may raise the issue before the

ALJ and seek a protective order. The ALJ may, for good cause shown, order appropriate redactions made to the record after hearing. See proposed § 3.504(s).

25. Proposed § 3.504(h)—Exchange of Witness Lists, Witness Statements, and Exhibits Proposed § 3.504(h) provides for the prehearing exchange of certain documents, including witness lists, copies of prior statements of witnesses, and copies of hearing exhibits. We propose that the requirements set forth in 45 CFR 160.518 of the HIPAA Enforcement Rule shall apply, except that the language in paragraph (a) of 45 CFR 160.518 following and including "except that" shall not apply. We exclude the provisions relating to the provision of a statistical expert's report not less than 30 days before a scheduled hearing because we do not propose language permitting the use of statistical sampling to estimate the number of violations.

26. Proposed § 3.504(i)—Subpoenas for Attendance at Hearing Proposed § 3.504(i) provides procedures for the ALJ to issue subpoenas for witnesses to appear at a hearing and for parties and prospective witnesses to contest such subpoenas. We propose to adopt the same regulations as provided at 45 CFR 160.520 of the HIPAA Enforcement Rule.

27. Proposed § 3.504(j)—Fees Proposed § 3.504(j) provides for the payment of witness

fees by the party requesting a subpoena. We propose that the fees requirements be the same as those provided in 45 CFR 160.522 of the HIPAA Enforcement Rule.

28. Proposed § 3.504(k)—Form, Filing and Service of Papers Proposed § 3.504(k) provides requirements for documents filed with the ALJ. We propose to adopt the requirements of 45 CFR 160.524 of the HIPAA Enforcement Rule.

29. Proposed § 3.504(l)—Computation of Time Proposed § 3.504(l) provides the method for computing time periods under this Part. We propose to adopt the requirements of 45 CFR 160.526 of the HIPAA Enforcement Rule, except the term "this subpart" shall refer to 42 CFR Part 3, Subpart D and the citation "§ 3.504(a) of 42 CFR Part 3" shall be substituted for the citation "§ 160.504."

30. Proposed § 3.504(m)—Motions Proposed § 3.504(m) provides requirements for the content of motions and the time allowed for responses. We propose to adopt the requirements of 45 CFR 160.528 of the HIPAA Enforcement Rule.

31. Proposed § 3.504(n)—Sanctions Proposed § 3.504(n) provides the sanctions an ALJ may impose on parties and their representatives for failing to comply with an order or procedure, failing to defend an action, or other misconduct. We propose to adopt the provisions of 45 CFR 160.530 of the HIPAA Enforcement Rule.

32. Proposed § 3.504(o)—Collateral Estoppel Proposed § 3.504(o) would adopt the doctrine of collateral estoppel with respect to a final decision of an administrative agency. Collateral estoppel means that determinations made with respect to issues litigated and determined in a proceeding between two parties will bind the respective parties in later disputes concerning the same issues and parties. We propose to adopt the provisions of 45 CFR 160.532 of the HIPAA Enforcement Rule, except that the term "a confidentiality provision" shall be substituted for the term "an administrative simplification provision".

33. Proposed § 3.504(p)—The Hearing Proposed § 3.504(p) provides for a public hearing on the record, the burden of proof at the hearing and the admission of rebuttal evidence. We propose to adopt the provisions of 45 CFR 160.534 of the HIPAA Enforcement Rule, except the following text shall be substituted for § 160.534(b)(1): "The respondent has the burden of going forward and the burden of persuasion with respect to any challenge to the amount of a proposed penalty pursuant to §§ 3.404–3.408 of 42 CFR Part 3, including any factors raised as mitigating factors." We propose to adopt this new language for § 160.534(b)(1) because references to affirmative defenses in the excluded text are not

applicable in the context of the Patient Safety Act as such defenses are under the HIPAA Enforcement Rule; nor does the Patient Safety Act include provisions for the waiver or reduction of a civil money penalty in accordance with 45 CFR 160.412.

45 CFR 160.534(c) states that the hearing must be open to the public unless otherwise ordered by the ALJ for good cause shown. In proposed § 3.504(p) of this Subpart, we propose that good cause shown under 45 CFR 160.534(c) may be that identifiable patient safety work product has been introduced into evidence or is expected to be introduced into evidence. Protecting patient safety work product is important and is an issue about which all parties and the ALJ should be concerned.

34. Proposed § 3.504(q)—Witnesses Under proposed § 3.504(q), the ALJ may allow oral testimony to be admitted or provided in the form of a written statement or deposition so long as the opposing party has a sufficient opportunity to subpoena the person whose statement is being offered. We propose to adopt the provisions of 45 CFR 160.538 of the HIPAA Enforcement Rule, except that the citation "§ 3.504(h) of 42 CFR Part 3" shall be substituted for the citation "§ 160.518."

35. Proposed § 3.504(r)—Evidence Proposed § 3.504(r) would provide guidelines for

the acceptance of evidence in hearings. We propose to adopt the provisions of 45 CFR 160.540 of the HIPAA Enforcement Rule, except that the citation "§ 3.420 of 42 CFR Part 3" shall be substituted for the citation "§ 160.420 of this part". In the same manner as the exception to privilege for enforcement activities under § 3.204(c) applies to proposed § 3.504(g), the exception to privilege applies under proposed § 3.504(r) as well. Although the adoption of 45 CFR 160.540(e) would permit parties to raise claims of privilege and permit an ALJ to exclude from evidence privileged information, a respondent could not claim privilege and an ALJ could not exclude identifiable patient safety work product if the Secretary seeks to introduce that patient safety work product because disclosure of the patient safety work product would not be a violation of the privilege and confidentiality provisions under proposed § 3.204(c).

36. Proposed § 3.504(s)—The Record

Proposed § 3.504(s) provides for recording and transcription of the hearing, and for the record to be available for inspection and copying by any person. We propose to adopt the provisions at 45 CFR 160.542 of the HIPAA Enforcement Rule. We also propose to provide that good cause for making appropriate redactions includes the presence of

identifiable patient safety work product in the record.

37. Proposed § 3.504(t)—Post-Hearing Briefs

Proposed § 3.504(t) provides that the ALJ has the discretion to order post-hearing briefs, although the parties may file post-hearing briefs in any event if they desire. We propose to adopt the provisions of 45 CFR 160.544 of the HIPAA Enforcement Rule.

38. Proposed § 3.504(u)—ALJ's Decision

Proposed § 3.504(u) provides that not later than 60 days after the filing of post-hearing briefs, the ALJ shall serve on the parties a decision making specific findings of fact and conclusions of law. The ALJ's decision is the final decision of the Secretary, and will be final and binding on the parties 60 days from the date of service of the ALJ decision, unless it is timely appealed by either party. We propose to adopt the provisions of 45 CFR 160.546 of the HIPAA Enforcement Rule, except the citation "§ 3.504(v) of 42 CFR Part 3" shall be substituted for "§ 160.548."

39. Proposed § 3.504(v)—Appeal of the ALJ's Decision

Proposed § 3.504(v) provides for manner and time for review of an ALJ's decision regarding penalties imposed under this Part and subsequent judicial review. We propose to adopt the same provisions as 45 CFR 160.548 of the HIPAA Enforcement Rule, except the following language in

paragraph (e) of 45 CFR 160.548 shall not apply: "Except for an affirmative defense under § 160.410(b)(1) of this part." We exclude this language because the Patient Safety Act does not provide for affirmative defenses in the same manner as HIPAA.

40. Proposed § 3.504(w)—Stay of the Secretary's Decision Proposed § 3.504(w) provides that a respondent may request a stay of the effective date of a penalty pending judicial review. We propose to adopt the provisions of 45 CFR 160.550 of the HIPAA Enforcement Rule to govern this process.

41. Proposed § 3.504(x)—Harmless Error Proposed § 3.504(x) adopts the "harmless error" standard as expressed in the HIPAA Enforcement Rule at 45 CFR 160.522. This proposed rule provides that the ALJ and the Board at every stage of the proceeding will disregard any error or defect in the proceeding that does not affect the substantial rights of the parties.

IV. Impact Statement and Other Required Analyses
Unfunded Mandates Reform Act
Section 202 of the Unfunded Mandates Reform Act requires that a covered agency prepare a budgetary impact statement before promulgating a rule that includes any Federal mandate that may result in the expenditure by State, local, and Tribal governments, in the aggregate, or by the private sector, of $100 million or more in any one year.

The Department has determined that this proposed rule would not impose a mandate that will result in the expenditure by State, Local, and Tribal governments, in the aggregate, or by the private sector, of more than $100 million in any one year.

Paperwork Reduction Act

This notice of proposed rulemaking adding a new Part 3 to volume 42 of the Code of Federal Regulations contains information collection requirements. This summary includes the estimated costs and assumptions for the paperwork requirements related to this proposed rule. A copy of the information collection request will be available on the PSO Web site (*www.pso.ahrq.gov*) and can be obtained in hardcopy by contacting Susan Grinder at the Center for Quality Improvement and Patient Safety, AHRQ, (301) 427–1111 (o); (301) 427–1341 (fax). These paperwork requirements have been submitted to the Office of Management and Budget for review under number xxxx–xxxx as required by 44 U.S.C. 3507(a)(1)(c) of the Paperwork Reduction Act of 1995, as amended (PRA). Respondents are not required to respond to any collection of information unless it displays a current valid OMB control number. With respect to proposed § 3.102 concerning the submission of certifications for initial and continued listing as a PSO, and of updated information, all such information would be submitted on Form SF–XXXX. To maintain its listing, a PSO must also submit a brief attestation, once every 24-month period after its initial date of listing, submitted on Form SF–XXXX, stating that it has entered contracts with two providers. We estimate that the proposed rule would create an average burden of 30 minutes annually for each entity that seeks to become a PSO to complete the necessary certification forms. Table 1 summarizes burden hours.

TABLE 1.—TOTAL BURDEN HOURS RELATED TO CERTIFICATION FORMS [Summary of all burden hours, by Provision, for PSOs]

Provision Annualized burden hours

3.112 .... 30 minutes.

HHS is working with OMB to obtain approval of the associated burden in accordance with the Paperwork Reduction Act of 1995 (44 U.S.C. 3507(d)) before the effective date of the final rule. Comments on this proposed information collection should be directed to Susan Grinder, by sending an e-mail to *Psosupport@ahrq.hhs.gov* or sending a fax to (301) 427–1341.

Under 5 CFR 1320.3(c), a covered collection of information includes the requirement by an agency of a disclosure of information to third parties by means of identical reporting, recordkeeping, or disclosure requirements, imposed on ten or more persons. The proposed rule reflects the previously established reporting requirements for breach of confidentiality applicable to business associates under HIPAA regulations requiring contracts top contain a provision requiring the business associate (in this case, the PSO) to notify providers of breaches of their identifiable patient data's confidentiality or security. Accordingly, this reporting requirement referenced in the regulation previously met Paperwork Reduction Act review requirements. The proposed rule requires in proposed § 3.108(c) that a PSO notify the Secretary if it intends to relinquish voluntarily its status as a PSO. The entity would be required to notify the Secretary that it has, or will soon, alert providers and other organizations from

TABLE 1. –ESTIMATED HOSPITALS COSTS TO SUBMIT INFORMATION TO PSOs: 2008--2012

Year	2008	2009	2010	2011	2012
Hospital Penetration Rate...	10%..........	40%..........	60%......	75%.......	85%......
Hospital Cost.........................	$7.5M.....	$30.0 M..	$45.0M.	$56.2 M.	$63.7 M.

which it has received patient safety work product or data of its intention and provide for the appropriate disposition of the data in consultation with each source of patient safety work product or data held by the entity. In addition, the entity is asked to provide the Secretary with current contact information for further communication from the Secretary as the entity ceases operations. The reporting aspect of this requirement is essentially an attestation that is equivalent to the requirements for listing, continued listing, and meeting the minimum contracts requirement. This minimal data requirement would come within 5 CFR 1320.3(h)(1) which provides an exception from PRA requirements for affirmations, certifications, or acknowledgments as long as they entail no burden other than that necessary to identify the respondent, the date, the respondent's address, and the nature of the instrument. In this case, the nature of the instrument would be an attestation that the PSO is working with its providers for the orderly cessation of activities. The following other collections of information that would be required by the proposed regulation under proposed § 3.108 are also exempt from PRA requirements pursuant to an exception in 5 CFR 1320.4 for information gathered as part of administrative investigations and actions regarding specific parties: information supplied in response to

preliminary agency determinations of PSO deficiencies or in response to proposed revocation and delisting (e.g., information providing the agency with correct facts, reporting corrective actions taken, or appealing proposed agency revocation decisions).

Federalism

Executive Order 13132 establishes certain requirements that an agency must meet when it promulgates a proposed rule (and subsequent final rule) that imposes substantial direct requirement costs on state and local governments, preempts State law, or otherwise has Federalism implications.

The Patient Safety Act upon which the proposed regulation is based makes patient safety work product confidential and privileged. To the extent this would not be consistent with any state law, including court decisions, the Federal statute would preempt such state law or court order. The proposed rule (and subsequent final rule) will not have any greater preemptive effect on state or local governments than that imposed by the statute. While the Patient Safety Act does establish new Federal confidentiality and privilege protections for certain information, these protections only apply when health care providers work with PSOs and new processes, such as patient safety evaluation systems, that do not currently exist. These Federal data protections provide a

mechanism for protection of sensitive information that could improve the quality, safety, and outcomes of health care by fostering a non-threatening environment in which information about adverse medical events and near misses can be discussed. It is hoped that confidential analysis of patient safety events will reduce the occurrence of adverse medical events and, thereby, reduce the costs arising from such events, including costs incurred by state and local governments attributable to such events. AHRQ, in conjunction with OCR, held three public listening sessions prior to drafting the proposed rule. Representatives of several states participated in these sessions. In particular, states that had begun to collect and analyze patient safety event information spoke about their related experiences and plans. Following publication of the NPRM, AHRQ will consult with appropriate state officials and organizations to review the scope of the proposed rule and to specifically seek input on federalism issues and a proposal in the rule at proposed § 3.102(a)(2) that would limit the ability of public or private sector regulatory entities to seek listing as a PSO.

Regulatory Impact Analysis

Under Executive Order 12866 (58 FR 51735, October 4, 1993), Federal Agencies must determine whether a regulatory action is "significant" and, therefore, subject to OMB review and the requirements of the Executive Order. Executive Order 12866 defines "significant regulatory action" as one that is likely to result in a rule that may:

1. Have an annual effect on the economy of $100 million or more or adversely affect in a material way the economy, a sector of the economy, productivity, competition, jobs, the environment, public health or safety, or state, local, or tribal government or communities.

2. Create a serious inconsistency or otherwise interfere with an action taken or planned by another agency.

3. Materially alter the budgetary impact of entitlements, grants, user fees, or loan programs or the rights and obligations of recipients thereof.

4. Raise novel legal or policy issues arising out of legal mandates, the President's priorities, or the principles set forth in the Executive Order.

AHRQ has accordingly examined the impact of the proposed rule under Executive Order 12866, the Regulatory Flexibility Act (5 U.S.C. 601–612), and the Unfunded Mandates Reform Act of 1995 (Pub. L. 104–4). Executive Order 12866 directs agencies to assess all costs and benefits of available regulatory alternatives and, when regulation is necessary, to select regulatory approaches that maximize net benefits (including potential economic, environmental, public health and safety, and

other advantages; distributive impacts; and equity). A regulatory impact analysis must be prepared for major rules with economically significant effects ($100 million or more in any one year). In the course of developing the proposed rule, AHRQ has considered the rule's costs and benefits, as mandated by Executive Order 12866. Although we cannot determine with precision the aggregate economic impact of the proposed rule, we believe that the impact may approach $100 million or more annually. HHS has determined that the proposed rule is "significant" also because it raises novel legal and policy issues with the establishment of a new regulatory framework, authorized by the Patient Safety Act, and imposes requirements, albeit voluntary, on entities that had not previously been subject to regulation in this area.

Consequently, as required under Executive Order 12866, AHRQ conducted an analysis of the economic impact of the proposed rule.

Background

The Patient Safety Act establishes a framework for health care providers voluntarily to report information on the safety, quality, and outcomes of patient care that to PSOs listed by HHS. The main objectives of the Patient Safety Act are to: (1) Encourage health care providers to collect and examine patient safety events more freely and consistently

than they do now, (2) encourage many provider arrangements or contracts with expert PSOs to receive, aggregate, and analyze data on patient safety events so that PSOs may provide feedback and assistance to the provider to improve patient safety and (3) allow the providers to improve the quality of care delivered and reduce patient risk.

The Patient Safety Act provides privilege from legal discovery for patient safety work product, as well as confidentiality protections in order to foster a culture of patient safety. The Patient Safety Act does not contain mandatory reporting requirements. It does, however, require information submissions by entities that voluntarily seek to be recognized, (i.e., listed) as PSOs by the Secretary.

The cost of an adverse patient safety event can be very high in terms of human life, and it also often carries a significant financial cost. The Institute of Medicine report, *To Err is Human: Building a Safer Health Care System*, estimates that adverse events cost the United States approximately $37.6 billion to $50 billion each year. "Total national costs (lost income, lost household production, disability, and health care costs) of preventable adverse events (medical errors resulting in injury) are estimated to be between $17 billion and $29 billion, of which health care costs represent over one-half."[18]

---

18 Corrigan, J. M., Donaldson, M. S., Kohn, L. T., McKay, T.,

The proposed rule was written to minimize the regulatory and economic burden on an entity that seeks certification as a PSO in order to collect, aggregate, and analyze confidential information reported by health care providers. Collecting, aggregating, and analyzing information on adverse events will allow problems to be identified, addressed, and eventually prevented.

This, in turn, will help improve patient safety and the quality of care, while also reducing medical costs. The following analysis of costs and benefits—both quantitative and qualitative—includes estimates based on the best available health care data and demonstrates that the benefits of the proposed regulation justify the costs involved in its implementation.

The economic impact of an alternative to the proposed rule is not discussed in the following analysis because an alternative to the statutorily authorized voluntary framework is the existence of no new program, which would produce no economic change or have no economic impact, or—alternatively—a mandatory regulatory program for all health care providers, which is not authorized by the Patient Safety Act and which is

necessarily not a realistic alternative and would likely be much more expensive. (A guiding principle of those drafting the regulation was to minimize the economic and regulatory burden on those entities seeking to be PSOs and providers choosing to work with PSOs, within the limits of the Patient Safety Act. Hence this proposed rule represents the Department's best effort at minimal impact while still meeting statutory provisions.)

AHRQ has relied on key findings from the literature to provide baseline measures for estimating the likely costs and benefits of the proposed rule. We believe that the costs of becoming a PSO (i.e., the costs of applying to be listed by the Secretary) will be relatively small, and the costs of operating a PSO will be small, in relation to the possible cost savings that will be derived from reducing the number of preventable adverse medical events each year.

The direct costs to individual providers of working with PSOs will vary considerably. For an institutional or individual provider that chooses to report readily accessible information to a PSO occasionally, costs may be negligible. The proposed rule does not require a provider to enter into a contract with a PSO, establish internal reporting or analytic systems, or meet specific security requirements for patient safety work product. A provider's costs will derive from its own

choice whether to undertake and, if so, whether to conduct or contract for data collection, information development, or analytic functions. Such decisions will be based on the provider's assessment of the cost and benefits it expects to incur and achieve. As we discuss below, hospitals in particular have developed, and can be expected to take advantage of the protections afforded by the Patient Safety Act by expanding data collection, information development, and analytic functions at their institutions. We anticipate that many providers will choose to enter into contracts with PSOs voluntarily. If providers choose to report data routinely to a PSO, a contract will be a good business practice. It provides greater assurance that a provider can demonstrate, if its claims of protections are challenged, that it is operating in full compliance with the statute. It enables the provider to exert greater control over the use and sharing of its data and, in the case of a provider that is a covered entity under the HIPAA Privacy Rule, the provider will need to enter a business associate agreement with a PSO for compliance with that regulation if the reported data includes protected health information.

The following cost estimates represent an effort to develop an "upper bound" on the cost impact of the proposed rule by assuming that providers choosing to work with PSOs will follow

---

Pike, K. C., for the Committee on Quality of Health Care in America. *To Err is Human: Building a Safer Health System*. Washington, DC.: National Academy Press; 2000.

best business practices, take full advantage of the Patient Safety Act's protections, and develop robust internal reporting and analytic systems, rather than meeting the minimal requirements of the proposed rule. The cost estimates below are based on existing hospital-based activities for reporting patient safety events, which are likely to be similar to most events that a PSO will analyze (namely quality and safety activities within hospitals). While the Patient Safety Act is not limited to hospitals, AHRQ has received indications from various stakeholder groups that hospital providers will be the predominant provider type initially interested in working with PSOs.

Affected Entities

To date, AHRQ has no hard information on the exact number of interested parties that may wish to become a PSO. AHRQ estimates, however, that 50 to 100 entities may request to become a listed PSO by the Secretary during the first three years after publication of the final rule. AHRQ anticipates a gradual increase in the number of entities seeking listing as a PSO and estimates that roughly 50 entities will seek PSO certification during Year 1, 25 entities during Year 2, and an additional 25 entities during Year 3, totaling 100 PSOs by the end of Year 3. After Year 3, we anticipate that the number of PSOs will remain about constant, with the

number of new entrants roughly equivalent to the number of PSOs that cease to operate.

Healthcare providers, especially hospitals, currently assume some level of burden to collect, develop, and analyze patient safety event information similar to the information that will be reported to PSOs. We note that most institutional providers (especially larger ones) already do some of this data gathering. AHRQ anticipates that entities that currently operate internal patient safety event reporting systems either may be interested in: (1) Establishing a component organization to seek certification as a PSO; or (2) contracting with a PSO. Using data from the 2004 American Hospital Association, AHRQ conducted an analysis of the burden hours and likely costs associated with reporting patient safety event information to a PSO. See below.

Costs

The proposed rule enables providers to receive Federal protections for information on patient safety events that the providers choose to collect, analyze, and report in conformity with the requirements of the Patient Safety Act and the proposed rule. The proposed rule, consistent with the Patient Safety Act, does not require any entity to seek listing as a PSO and does not require any provider to work with a

PSO. While all holders of patient safety work product must avoid impermissible disclosures of patient safety work product, we do not impose any specific requirements that holders must meet to comply with this obligation. The requirements of the proposed rule apply only to entities that choose to seek listing by the Secretary as a PSO.

Similarly, the proposed rule does not impose requirements on States or private sector entities (including small businesses) that would result in additional spending, that is, the government is not imposing any direct costs on States or the private sector.

The Patient Safety Act, and therefore, the proposed rule, does impose obligations on entities that are listed by the Secretary as PSOs. Every PSO must carry out eight patient safety activities and comply with seven statutory criteria during its period of listing, including requirements related to the provision of security for patient safety work product, the ability to receive and analyze data from providers and assist them in implementing system improvements to mitigate or eliminate potential risk or harm to patients from the delivery of health care services.[19] Because this is a new,

---

19 These 15 requirements from the Patient Safety Act are discussed in proposed § 3.102(b). The eight patient safety activities are defined in proposed § 3.20 and the seven criteria are

untested, and voluntary initiative—coupled with the fact that PSOs currently do not exist—AHRQ does not have data on PSO fees, income, or expenses to estimate the precise monetized and non-monetized costs and benefits of the proposed rule. The following estimates reflect the cost of all incremental activities required (or contemplated) by the proposed rule.

For entities that seek to be listed as a PSO by the Secretary, AHRQ assumes that most of the total costs incurred will be for the establishment of a new organizational structure. AHRQ expects such costs to vary considerably based on the types of entities that request PSO listing (e.g., size; geographic location; setting; academic, professional, or business affiliation; and whether or not the entity is a component of a parent organization). It is antici-pated that the proposed rule's cost to a PSO will likely be highest in the first year due to startup and initial operational costs and establishment of policies and procedures for complying with PSO regulations. PSO operational costs will include the hiring of qualified staff, setting up data collection and reporting systems, establishing policies and procedures for ensuring data security and confidentiality, maintaining a patient safety evaluation system as required by the Patient

specified in proposed § 3.102(b)(2)

Safety Act, and receiving and generating patient safety work product. The fact that PSOs are new entities for which there are no existing financial data means that estimates of the cost or charges for PSO services are a matter of speculation at this time. Additionally, the degree to which PSOs will exercise market power, what services they will offer, and the impact of a competitive environment is not yet known. Based on discussions with stakeholder groups, we believe that there will be a number of business models that emerge for PSOs. We anticipate that many PSOs will be components of existing organizations, which will likely subsidize the operations of their component PSOs for some time. Despite these limitations, AHRQ believes it can construct reasonable estimates of the costs and benefits of the Patient Safety Act. See "Provider—PSO Costs and Charges" for an explanation of why the abovementioned uncertain-ties do not preclude AHRQ from calculating overall costs, benefits, and net benefits of the Patient Safety Act.

As noted above, the proposed rule does not require providers to establish internal reporting or analytic systems.

AHRQ expects, however, that many providers will do so in order to take full advantage of the protections of the Patient Safety Act. As a result, our estimates reflect an upper bound on the potential costs associated

with implementation by assuming that all providers that choose to participate will establish robust internal reporting and analytic systems.

AHRQ recognizes that many state governments, public and private health care purchasers, and private accrediting and certifying organizations already employ voluntary and/or mandatory patient safety event reporting systems.

As health care organizations increasingly focus on the monitoring of adverse events, the use of voluntary reporting systems to detect, evaluate, and track such events has also increased. Preliminary findings from AHRQ's Adverse Event Reporting Survey, conducted by the RAND Corporation (RAND) and the Joint Commission on Accreditation of Healthcare Organizations (JCAHO), show that 98 percent of hospitals are already reporting adverse medical events.[20] This survey was administered to a representa-tive sample of 2,000 hospitals, with an 81 percent response rate. Thus, it is anticipated that the associated costs of the proposed rule for hospitals with existing patient safety event reporting systems will be very minimal, because the majority of these organiza-tions already have the

20 RAND and Joint Commission on Accreditation of Healthcare Organizations. *Survey on Hospital Adverse Event Reporting Systems: Briefing on Baseline Data.* August 16, 2006 Briefing.

institutional infrastructure and operations to carry out the data collection activities of the proposed rule. AHRQ assumes that the estimated 2 percent of hospitals that currently have no reporting system are unlikely to initiate a new reporting system based on the proposed rule, at least in the first year that PSOs are operational.

Hospital Costs We extrapolated findings from the RAND–JCAHO survey in order to calculate the burden hours and monetized costs associated with the proposed rule, using data from the American Hospital Association's 2004 [21] annual survey of hospitals in the United States [22] to estimate the number of hospitals nationwide. This figure served as the denominator in our analysis. We acknowledge that, over time, not all providers working with PSOs will be hospitals; however, it is reasonable to use hospitals as a basis for our initial estimates, given the preliminary indications that hospitals will be the predominant, if not exclusive, providers submitting information to PSOs during the early years in which PSOs are operational.

Based on American Hospital Association data, there are 5,759 registered U.S. hospitals—including community hospitals, Federal hospitals, non-Federal psychiatric hospitals, non-Federal long-term care hospitals, and hospital units of institutions—in which there are 955,768 staffed operational beds. Based on the RAND–JCAHO finding regarding event reporting in hospitals, AHRQ calculates that 98 percent of the 5,759 hospitals (5,644 hospitals with 936,653 staffed beds) already have, and are supporting the costs of, a centralized patient safety event reporting system. AHRQ assumed that an institution will report an average of one patient safety event (including no harm events and close calls) per bed per month.

Based on this assumption, AHRQ estimates that all hospitals nationwide are currently completing a total of 11,239,832 patient safety event reports per year. Based on the assumption that it takes 15 minutes to complete each patient safety event report, we estimate that hospitals are already spending 2,809,958 hours per year on this activity. At a Full-Time Equivalent (FTE) rate of $80 per hour, we estimate that all hospitals nationwide are currently spending approximately $224,796,634 per year on patient safety event reporting activities.

AHRQ estimates that, once collected, it will take an additional five minutes for hospital staff to submit

patient safety event information to a PSO. We, therefore, estimate that the total burden hours for all hospitals nationwide to submit patient safety event information to a PSO totals 936,653 hours annually with an associated cost of $74,932,211 based on the assumption that all hospitals nationwide reported all possible patient safety events (using the heuristic of one event per bed per month). During the first year following publication of the final rule PSOs will be forming themselves into organizations and engaging in startup activities. We assume that there will be a gradual increase in the number of entities seeking listing as PSOs, beginning with a 10 percent participation rate. We assume as many as 25 percent of hospitals may enter into arrangements with PSOs by the end of the first year; however, the overall effective participation rate will only average 10 percent. This assumption translates to 93,665 hours of additional burden for hospitals to report patient safety event information to PSOs with an estimated cost of $7,493,221.

Assuming a 40 percent participation rate of all hospitals nationwide during the second year that PSOs are operational, there would be 374,660 burden hours with an estimated cost of $29,972,884. Assuming there is 60 percent participation rate of all hospitals nationwide during the third year that PSOs are operational, there would be

---

21 American Hospital Association. Fast Facts on U.S. Hospitals from AHA Hospital Statistics. November 14, 2005. Available at: http://www.aha.org/aha/resource_center/fastfacts/fast_facts_US_hospitals.html. Web Page. 22 The 2005 survey results will likely be release in November 2006.

561,990 burden hours nationwide with an estimated cost of $44,959,326. (See Table 1). In summary, the direct costs—which would be voluntarily incurred if all hospitals nationwide that choose to work with PSOs during the first five years also chose to establish systematic reporting systems—are projected to range from approximately $7.5 million to nearly $63.7 million in any single year, based on 10 percent to 85 percent participation rate among hospitals.

These cost estimates may be high if provider institutions, such as hospitals, do not submit all the patient safety data they collect to a PSO. If only a fraction of the data is reported to a PSO, the cost estimates and burden will be proportionately reduced.

PSO Costs

A second category of costs, in addition to incremental costs borne by hospitals, is that of the PSOs themselves.

PSO cost estimates are based on estimates of organizational and consulting capabilities and statutory requirements. We followed the standard accounting format for calculating "independent government cost estimates," although the categories did not seem entirely appropriate for the private sector. In order to estimate PSO costs over a five-year period, we made several assumptions about the size and operations of new PSOs. Specifically, we assumed that PSOs would be staffed modestly, relying on existing hospital activities in reporting adverse events, and that a significant proportion of PSOs are likely to be component PSOs, with support and expertise provided by a parent organization. Our assumptions are that PSOs will hire dedicated staff of from 1.5 to 4 FTEs, assuming an average salary rate of $67/hour. We estimate that a significant overhead figure

of 100%, coupled with 20% for General and Administrative (G&A) expenses, will cover the appreciable costs anticipated for legal, security, travel, and miscellaneous PSO expenses. Although we believe that the above estimates may be conservative, we also believe that PSOs will become more effective over time without increasing staff size. Finally, we estimate that the number of PSOs will increase from 50 to 100 during the first three years in which the Secretary lists PSOs and remain at 100 PSOs in subsequent years.

Table 2 summarizes PSO operational costs for the first five years based on these estimates.

Table 3 presents the total estimated incremental costs related to implementation of the Patient Safety Act, based on new activities on the part of hospitals and the formation of new entities, PSOs, from 2008–2012. Estimates for total Patient Safety Act costs are $80

TABLE 2.—TOTAL PSO OPERATIONAL COSTS: 2008-2012

Year	2008	2009	2010	2011	2012
Number of PSOs.................	50........	75......	100...	100......	100.
PSO Cost	$61.4M..	$92.1M.	$122.8 M	$122.8M	$122.8M.

TABLE 3.—TOTAL PATIENT SAFETY ACT COSTS INCLUDING HOSPITAL COSTS AND PSO COSTS: 2008-2012

Year	2008	2009	2010	2011	2012
Hospital Penetration Rate	10%.........	40%.........	60%......	75%.......	85%......
Hospital Cost	$7.5M.........	$30.0 M..	$45.0M.	$56.2 M.	$63.7 M.
PSO Cost	$641.4M...	$92.1 M..	$122.8 M.	$122.8 M.	$122.8 M.
Total Cost	$68.9M..	$122.1 M	$167.8 M.	$179.0 M.	$186.5 M

million in Year 1, increasing to $186.5 million in Year 5. Provider—PSO Costs and Charges We have not figured into our calculations any estimates for the price of PSO services, amounts paid by hospitals and other health care providers to PSOs, PSO revenues, or PSO break-even analyses. We have not speculated about subsidies or business models. Regardless of what the costs and charges are between providers and PSOs, they will cancel each other out, as expenses to providers will become revenue to PSOs. Benefits The primary benefit of the proposed rule is to provide the foundation for new, voluntary opportunities for health care providers to improve the safety, quality, and outcomes of patient care. The non-monetized benefits to public health from the proposed rule are clear, translating to improvements in patient safety, although such benefits are intangible and difficult to quantify, not only in monetary terms but also with respect to outcome measures such as years added or years with improved quality-of-life. Although AHRQ is unable to quantify the net benefits of this proposed rule precisely, it believes firmly that the proposed rule will be effective in addressing costly medical care problems in the health system that adversely affect patients, their families, their employees, and society in general. Finally, estimating the impact of the proposed rule in terms of measurable

monetized and non-monetized benefits is a challenge due to a lack of baseline data on the incidence and prevalence of patient safety events themselves. In fact, one of the intended benefits of the Patient Safety Act is to provide more objective data in this important area, which will begin to allow tracking of improvement. AHRQ has relied on key findings from the medical professional literature to provide a qualitative description of the scope of the problem. The Institute of Medicine reports that 44,000 to 98,000 people die in hospitals each year as a result of adverse events.[23] The Harvard Medical Practice Study found a rate of 3.7 adverse events per 100 hospital admissions.[24] Similar results were found in a replication of this study in Colorado and Utah; adverse events were reported at a rate of 2.9 per 100 admissions.[25] Adverse events do not occur only in hospitals; they also occur in physician's offices, nursing homes, pharmacies, urgent care centers, ambulatory care settings,

---

23 Institute of Medicine, "To Err Is Human: Building a Safer Health System", 1999
24 Brennan TA, Leape LL, Laird NM, et al. Incidence of Adverse Events and Negligence in Hospitalized Patients. New England Journal of Medicine. 1991. 324: 370–76.
25 Thomas EJ, Studdert DM, Burstin HR, et al. Incidence and Types of Adverse Events and Negligent Care in Utah and Colorado. Medical Care. 2000. 38: 261–71.

and care delivered in the home. The importance of evaluating the incidence and cost of adverse events cannot be underestimated. They are not only related to possible morbidity and mortality, but also impose a significant economic burden on both society and the individual (patient, family, health care workers) in terms of consumption of health care resources and lost productivity, and in many cases avoidable pain and suffering. However, to prevent adverse events, it may take many years for the proposed rule to achieve its full beneficial effects, and it will remain a challenge to track the effect of the proposed rule on the patient population and society, generally. It may be possible to measure improvements in patient safety in general descriptive terms regarding improved health outcomes. However, it is more difficult to translate such improvements to direct monetary savings or outcome measures that can be integrated into a single numerical index (e.g., units of health improvement, years of life gained). By analyzing patient safety event information, PSOs will be able to identify patterns of failures in the health care system and propose measures to eliminate patient safety risks and hazards as a means to improve patient outcomes. As more information is learned about patient safety events through data collection by the PSOs, the care delivery environment

TABLE 4.—TOTAL ESTIMATED COST SAVINGS BY PERCENT REDUCTION IN ADVERSE EVENTS: 2008-2012*

Year	2008	2009	2010	2011	2012
Hospital Penetration Rate	10%.........	40%.........	60%.........	75%..........	85%......
Percent Reduction in Adverse Events	1%	1.5%-----	2%............	2.5%------	3%.......
Savings	$11.5 M...	$69 M...	$138 M...	$215.625M	$293.25 M.

*Source: Baseline figures from IOM Report, To Err is Human, on total national health care costs associated with preventable adverse events (between 8.5 billion and 14.5 billion). Year 1 estimates are based on mid-point figures.

can be redesigned to prevent adverse events in the future. However, PSOs will not have the necessary authority to implement recommended changes to improve patient safety in providers' health care delivery organizations. It will be up to the providers themselves to bring about the changes that will result in a reduction in adverse events and a resultant improvement in the quality of care delivered.

The submission of more comprehensive information by health care providers regarding patient risks and hazards will likely increase the understanding of the factors that contribute to events that adversely affect patients. The expected benefit of this information would be improvements in patient safety event reports and analyses, which would translate to better patient outcomes and possible economic savings attributable to the more efficient use of health care services. Due to the uncertainty of the benefits and costs associated with the proposed rule as delineated above, it is then possible only to make

general estimates of the monetary values of expected improvements in patient outcomes, that is, savings to the healthcare system.

We can estimate monetized benefits by referring to the Institute of Medicine report, To Err Is Human,[26] which estimates total national costs of preventable adverse events to be between $17 billion and $29 billion, of which direct health care costs represent over one-half (totaling between $8.5 billion and $14.5 billion). Based on the assumption that PSOs may be able to reduce the preventable adverse events by between one percent and three percent within their first five years of operation, this reduction would amount to be between $85 million— $145 million in savings at the 1 percent level if the whole nation were affected, and $255 million—$435

26 Corrigan, J. M., Donaldson, M. S., Kohn, L. T., McKay, T., Pike, K. C., for the Committee on Quality of Health Care in America. *To Err Is Human: Building a Safer Health System*. Washington, DC: National Academy Press; 2000.

million at the 3 percent level, if the whole nation were affected. Applying a median figure from the Institute of Medicine range to PSOs, based on an increasing impact from 1%–3% as it grows over the first five years, we see progressively growing savings as shown in Table 4. It should be noted that we are estimating savings by assuming a percentage reduction of adverse events from the overall occurrence rate delineated by the Institute of Medicine report. We are not tying the estimated reduction to those events specifically reported to PSOs.

Events that have already occurred do not represent a potential for savings.

The presumption behind the estimated savings is that the reporting, analysis, and institution of ameliorating policies and procedures will result in fewer adverse events going forward because of such PSO activities.

It is assumed that when the proposed rule is implemented, it will have a beneficial effect on patient outcomes.

TABLE 5.—NET BENEFITS: 2008-2012*

Year	2008	2009	2010	2011	2012
Total Benefits	$11.5 M...	$69 M....	$138 M....	$215.625 M	$293.25 M.
Total Costs	$68.9 M---	$11.1 M..	$167.8 M..	$179.0 M	$186.5 M...
Net Benefits	($57.4) M.	($53.1) M	($29.8) M..	$36.625 M.	$106.75 M.
Discounted net present value at 3%	($55.7) M.	($50.0) M	($27.3) M.	$32.5 M...	$92.1 M....
Discounted net present value at 7%	($53.6) M.	($46.4) M	($24.3) M.	$27.9 M...	$76.1 M....

Eliminating adverse events would help to ensure the greatest value possible from the billions of dollars spent on medical care in the United States.[27] AHRQ concludes that the potential benefits of the Patient Safety Act—which encourages hospitals, doctors, and other health care providers to work voluntarily with PSOs by reporting of health care errors and enabling PSOs to analyze them to improve health care quality and safety—would justify the costs of the proposed rule. During the first five operational years of PSOs, we calculated the net benefits based on total costs and benefits. (See Table 5.) We estimate that costs of implementing the Patient Safety Act will reach break-even after 2010 and provide progressively greater benefits thereafter.

Confidentiality Rule The confidentiality provisions are included in the Patient Safety Act to encourage provider participation. Without such protections, providers will be reluctant to participate in the expanded reporting and analysis of patient safety events, and low participation will severely inhibit the opportunity to reap the benefits from efforts to improve patient safety. The proposed rule requires any holder of patient safety work product to maintain its confidentiality but, with the exception of PSOs, the appropriate security measures are left to the holder's discretion. Proposed § 3.106 establishes a security framework that PSOs must address but, even then, PSOs are given discretion to establish the specific security standards most appropriate to their organization. Violation of the confidentiality provisions under the proposed rule creates a risk of liability for a substantial civil money penalty. If a person makes a knowing or reckless disclosure in violation of the confidentiality provisions, that person will be subject to the enforcement process, and subject to costs including participation in an investigation and payment of a civil money penalty, if imposed.

While participating providers may incur some costs associated with maintaining the confidentiality of patient safety work product (e.g., developing policies/procedures to keep information confidential, safeguarding the information, training staff, etc.), those activities and associated costs are not required by the proposed rule and are likely minimal in light of existing procedures to meet existing requirements on providers to maintain sensitive information as confidential.

We are proposing a scheme that places the least possible amount of regulatory burden on participants while simultaneously ensuring that the confidentiality provisions are effectively implemented and balanced with the objective of encouraging the maximum amount of participation possible. We were mindful of not placing unnecessary regulatory requirements on

27 Corrigan, J. M., Donaldson, M. S., Kohn, L. T., McKay, T., Pike, K. C., for the Committee on Quality of Health Care in America. *To Err Is Human: Building a Safer Health System.* Washington, DC: National Academy Press; 2000.

participating entities because this is a voluntary initiative, and we did not want entities interested in participating to forego participation because of concerns about the associated risk of liability for civil money penalties.

Regulatory Flexibility Act Analysis

The Regulatory Flexibility Act requires agencies to analyze regulatory options that would minimize any significant impact of a rule on small entities. Because the Patient Safety Act enables a broad spectrum of entities—public, private, for-profit, and not-forprofit—to seek certification as a PSO, there may be many different types of organizations interested in becoming certified as a PSO that would be affected by the proposed rule. The proposed rule minimizes possible barriers to entry and creates a review process that is both simple and quick. As a result, AHRQ expects that a broad range of health care provider systems, medical specialty societies, and provider-based membership organizations will seek listing as a PSO by the Secretary. AHRQ preliminarily determines that the proposed rule does not have a significant impact on small businesses because it does not impose a mandatory regulatory burden, and because the Department has made a significant effort to promulgate regulations that are the minimum necessary to interpret and implement the law. As stated previously, working with PSOs is completely voluntary; the proposed rule provides

benefits in the form of legal protections that are expected to outweigh the cost of participation from the perspective of participating providers. AHRQ believes that the proposed rule will not have a significant impact on a substantial number of small entities because the proposed rules do not place small entities at a significant competitive disadvantage to large entities. AHRQ does not anticipate that there will be a disproportional effect on profits, costs, or net revenues for a substantial number of small entities. The proposed rule will not significantly reduce profit for a substantial number of small entities.

Impacts on Small Entities 1. The Need for and the Objectives of the Proposed Rule

The proposed rule establishes the authorities, processes, and requirements necessary to implement the Patient Safety Act, sections 921–926 of the Public Health Service Act, 42 U.S.C. 299b–21 to 299b–26. The proposed rules seek to establish a streamlined process for the Department to accept certification by entities seeking to become PSOs. Under the proposal, PSOs will be available voluntarily to enter into arrangements with health care providers and provide expert advice regarding the causes and prevention of adverse patient safety events.

Information collected or developed by a health care provider or PSO, and reported to or by a PSO, that relate to a patient safety

event would become privileged and confidential. Related deliberations would also be protected.

Persons who breached the confidentiality provisions of the rule could be subject to civil money penalties of up to $10,000.

2. Description and Estimate of the Number of Small Entities Affected For purposes of the Regulatory Flexibility Act, small entities include small businesses, non-profit organizations, and government jurisdictions. Most hospitals and many other health care providers and suppliers are small entities, either because they are nonprofit organizations or because they generate revenues of $6.5 million to $31.5 million in any one year. Individuals and States are not included in the definition of a small entity. The proposed rule would affect most hospitals, and other health care delivery entities, plus all small entities that are interested in becoming certified PSOs. Based on various stakeholder meetings, AHRQ estimates that approximately 50–100 entities may be interested in becoming listed as PSOs during the first three years following publication of the final rule. This figure is likely to stabilize over time, as some new PSOs form and some existing PSOs cease operations.

3. Impact on Small Entities AHRQ believes that the proposed rule will not have a significant impact on a substantial number of small provider or PSO entities

because the proposed rule does not place a substantial number of small entities at a significant competitive disadvantage to large entities. AHRQ does not anticipate that there will be a disproportional effect on profits, costs, or net revenues for a substantial number of small entities.

The proposed rule will not significantly reduce profit for a substantial number of small entities. In fact, when fully implemented, we expect that the benefits and/or provider savings will outweigh the costs.

Compliance requirements for small entities under this proposed rule are the same as those described above for other affected entities. AHRQ has proposed only those regulations that are necessary to comply with provisions and goals of the Patient Safety Act, with the objective of encouraging the maximum participation possible. The proposed rule was written to minimize the regulatory and economic burden on any entity that seeks to be listed as a PSO by the Secretary, regardless of size. It is impossible for AHRQ to develop alternatives to the proposed rule for small entities, as the proposed rule must adhere to statutory requirements. For example, the proposed rule requires confidentiality and privilege protections and places the least amount of regulatory burden on participating players—while simultaneously ensuring that the goals of confidentiality are effectively implemented—with the objective

of encouraging the maximum participation possible. In addition, the proposed rule was written recognizing that many providers will be HIPAA covered entities, and many PSOs will be business associates, which entails certain obligations under the HIPAA Privacy Rule. Thus, this proposed rule is coordinated with existing law, to minimize the burden of compliance.

AHRQ believes that the proposed rule will not have a significant impact on small providers. The proposed rule does not impose any costs directly on providers, large or small, that choose to work with a PSO. To the extent that providers hold patient safety work product, they must prevent impermissible disclosures; however, the proposed rule does not establish requirements for how providers must meet this requirement.

Finally, it is the statutory and supporting regulatory guarantee of the confidentiality of the reporting of adverse events that will enable PSOs to operate and perform their function. Thus, while the compliance costs in the form of start-up operational costs may be substantial, the benefits that will be generated as a result of these costs will exceed the actual costs, as illustrated in Table 5.

The Secretary certifies that the proposed rule will not have a significant economic impact on a substantial number of small entities.

List of Subjects in 42 CFR Part 3

Administrative practice and procedure, Civil money penalty, Confidentiality, Conflict of interests, Courts, Freedom of information, Health, Health care, Health facilities, Health insurance, Health professions, Health records, Hospitals, Investigations, Law enforcement, Medical research, Organization and functions, Patient, Patient safety, Privacy, Privilege, Public health, Reporting and recordkeeping requirements, Safety, State and local governments, Technical assistance.

For the reasons stated in the preamble, the Department of Health and Human Services proposes to amend Title 42 of the Code of Federal Regulations by adding a new part 3 to read as follows:

PART 3—PATIENT SAFETY ORGANIZATIONS AND PATIENT SAFETY WORK PRODUCT Subpart A—General Provisions

Sec. 3.10 Purpose. 3.20 Definitions.

Subpart B—PSO Requirements and Agency Procedures

3.102 Process and requirements for initial and continued listing of PSOs.
3.104 Secretarial actions.
3.106 Security requirements.
3.108 Correction of deficiencies, revocation, and voluntary relinquishment.

Subpart A—General Provisions

§ 3.10 Purpose.

The purpose of this Part is to implement the Patient Safety and Quality Improvement Act of 2005 (Pub. L. 109–41), which amended Title IX of the Public Health Service Act (42 U.S.C. 299 *et seq.*) by adding sections 921 through 926, 42 U.S.C. 299b-21 through 299b-26.

§ 3.20 Definitions.

As used in this Part, the terms listed alphabetically below have the meanings set forth as follows: *AHRQ* stands for the Agency for Healthcare Research and Quality in HHS. *ALJ* stands for an Administrative Law Judge of HHS.

Board means the members of the HHS Departmental Appeals Board, in the Office of the Secretary, who issue decisions in panels of three.

Bona fide contract means:
(1) A written contract between a provider and a PSO that is executed in good faith by officials authorized to execute such contract; or
(2) A written agreement (such as a memorandum of understanding or equivalent recording of mutual commitments) between a Federal, State, Local, or Tribal provider and a Federal, State, Local, or Tribal PSO that is executed in good faith by officials authorized to execute such agreement.

Complainant means a person who files a complaint with the Secretary pursuant to § 3.306.

Component organization means an entity that is either:
(1) A unit or division of a corporate organization or of a multi-organizational enterprise; or
(2) A separate organization, whether incorporated or not, that is owned, managed or controlled by one or more other organization(s), i.e., its parent organization(s).

Component PSO means a PSO listed by the Secretary that is a component organization.

Confidentiality provisions means for purposes of Subparts C and D, any requirement or prohibition concerning confidentiality established by section 921 and 922(b), (d), (g) and (i) of the Public Health Service Act, 42 U.S.C. 299b-21, 299b-22(b)–(d), (g) and (i) and the provisions, at §§ 3.206 and 3.208, that implement the statutory prohibition on disclosure of identifiable patient safety work product.

Disclosure means the release, transfer, provision of access to, or divulging in any other manner of patient safety work product by a person holding the patient safety work product to another.

Entity means any organization or organizational unit, regardless of whether the organization is public, private, for-profit, or not-for-profit.

Group health plan means employee welfare benefit plan (as defined in section 3(1) of the Employee Retirement Income Security Act of 1974 (ERISA)) to the extent that the plan provides medical care (as defined in paragraph (2) of section 2791(a) of the Public Health Service Act, including items and services paid for as medical care) to employees or their dependents (as defined under the terms of the plan) directly or through insurance, reimbursement, or otherwise.

Health insurance issuer means an insurance company, insurance service, or insurance organization (including a health maintenance organization, as defined in 42 U.S.C. 300gg–91(b)(3)) which is licensed to engage in the business of insurance in a State and which is subject to State law which regulates insurance (within the meaning of 29 U.S.C. 1144(b)(2)). The term does not include a group health plan.

Health maintenance organization means:
(1) A Federally qualified health maintenance organization (HMO) (as defined in 42 U.S.C. 300e(a)),
(2) An organization recognized under State law as a health maintenance organization, or
(3) A similar organization regulated under State law for solvency in the same manner and to the same extent as such a health maintenance organization.

HHS stands for the United States Department of Health and Human Services.

HIPAA Privacy Rule means the regulations promulgated under section 264(c) of the Health Insurance Portability and Accountability Act of 1996 (HIPAA), at 45 CFR Part 160 and Subparts A and E of Part 164.

Identifiable patient safety work product means patient safety work product that:
(1) Is presented in a form and manner that allows the identification of any provider that is a subject of the work product, or any providers that participate in, or are responsible for, activities that are a subject of the work product;
(2) Constitutes individually identifiable health information as that term is defined in the HIPAA Privacy Rule at 45 CFR 160.103; or
(3) Is presented in a form and manner that allows the identification of an individual who in good faith reported information directly to a PSO or to a provider with the intention of having the information reported to a PSO ("reporter").

Nonidentifiable patient safety work product means patient safety work product that is not identifiable patient safety work product in accordance with the nonidentification standards set forth at § 3.212.

OCR stands for the Office for Civil Rights in HHS.

Parent organization means an entity that, alone or with others, either owns a provider entity or a component organization, or has the authority to control or manage agenda setting, project management, or day-to-day operations, or the authority to review and override decisions of a component organization.

Patient Safety Act means the Patient Safety and Quality Improvement Act of 2005 (Pub. L. 109–41), which amended Title IX of the Public Health Service Act (42 U.S.C. 299 *et seq.*) by inserting a new Part C, sections 921 through 926, which are codified at 42 U.S.C. 299b–21 through 299b–26.

Patient safety activities means the following activities carried out by or on behalf of a PSO or a provider:
(1) Efforts to improve patient safety and the quality of health care delivery;
(2) The collection and analysis of patient safety work product;
(3) The development and dissemination of information with respect to improving patient safety, such as recommendations, protocols, or information regarding best practices;
(4) The utilization of patient safety work product for the purposes of encouraging a culture of safety and of providing feedback and assistance to effectively minimize patient risk;
(5) The maintenance of procedures to preserve confidentiality with respect to patient safety work product;
(6) The provision of appropriate security measures with respect to patient safety work product;

(7) The utilization of qualified staff; and
(8) Activities related to the operation of a patient safety evaluation system and to the provision of feedback to participants in a patient safety evaluation system.

Patient safety evaluation system means the collection, management, or analysis of information for reporting to or by a PSO.

Patient safety organization (PSO) means a private or public entity or component thereof that currently is listed as a PSO by the Secretary in accordance with Subpart B. A health insurance issuer or a component organization of a health insurance issuer may not be a PSO. See also the exclusion in proposed § 3.102 of this Part.

Patient safety work product (PSWP).
(1) Except as provided in paragraph
(2) of this definition, patient safety work product means any data, reports, records, memoranda, analyses (such as root cause analyses), or written or oral statements (or copies of any of this material)
(i)(A) Which are assembled or developed by a provider for reporting to a PSO and are reported to a PSO; or
(B) Are developed by a PSO for the conduct of patient safety activities; and which could improve patient safety, health care quality, or health care outcomes; or
(ii) Which identify or constitute the deliberations or analysis of, or identify the fact of reporting pursuant

to, a patient safety evaluation system.
(2)(i) Patient safety work product does not include a patient's medical record, billing and discharge information, or any other original patient or provider information; nor does it include information that is collected, maintained, or developed separately, or exists separately, from a patient safety evaluation system. Such separate information or a copy thereof reported to a PSO shall not by reason of its reporting be considered patient safety work product.
(ii) Nothing in this part shall be construed to limit information that is not patient safety work product from being:
(A) Discovered or admitted in a criminal, civil or administrative proceeding;
(B) Reported to a Federal, State, local or tribal governmental agency for public health or health oversight purposes; or
(C) Maintained as part of a provider's recordkeeping obligation under Federal, State, local or tribal law.

Person means a natural person, trust or estate, partnership, corporation, professional association or corporation, or other entity, public or private.

Provider means:
(1) An individual or entity licensed or otherwise authorized under State law to provide health care services, including—
(i) A hospital, nursing facility, comprehensive outpatient rehabilitation facility, home health agency,

hospice program, renal dialysis facility, ambulatory surgical center, pharmacy, physician or health care practitioner's office (includes a group practice), long term care facility, behavior health residential treatment facility, clinical laboratory, or health center; or
(ii) A physician, physician assistant, registered nurse, nurse practitioner, clinical nurse specialist, certified registered nurse anesthetist, certified nurse midwife, psychologist, certified social worker, registered dietitian or nutrition professional, physical or occupational therapist, pharmacist, or other individual health care practitioner;
(2) Agencies, organizations, and individuals within Federal, State, local, or Tribal governments that deliver health care, organizations engaged as contractors by the Federal, State, local, or Tribal governments to deliver health care, and individual health care practitioners employed or engaged as contractors by the Federal State, local, or Tribal governments to deliver health care; or
(3) A parent organization that has a controlling interest in one or more entities described in paragraph (1)(i) of this definition or a Federal, State, local, or Tribal government unit that manages or controls one or more entities described in (1)(i) or (2) of this definition.

Research has the same meaning as the term is defined in the HIPAA Privacy Rule at 45 CFR 164.501.

Respondent means a provider, PSO, or responsible person who is the subject of a complaint or a compliance review.

Responsible person means a person, other than a provider or a PSO, who has possession or custody of identifiable patient safety work product and is subject to the confidentiality provisions.

Workforce means employees, volunteers, trainees, contractors, and other persons whose conduct, in the performance of work for a provider, PSO or responsible person, is under the direct control of such provider, PSO or responsible person, whether or not they are paid by the provider, PSO or responsible person.

Subpart B—PSO Requirements and Agency Procedures
§ 3.102 Process and requirements for initial and continued listing of PSOs.

(a) *Eligibility and process for initial and continued listing.*
(1) *Submission of Certification.* Any entity, except as specified in paragraph (a)(2) of this section, may request from the Secretary an initial or continued listing as a PSO by submitting a completed certification form that meets the requirements of this section, in accordance with the submission requirements at § 3.112. An individual with authority to make commitments on behalf of the entity seeking listing will be required to acknowledge each of the certification requirements, attest that the

entity meets each requirement, provide contact information for the entity, and certify that the PSO will promptly notify the Secretary during its period of listing if it can no longer comply with any of the criteria in this section.
(2) *Restrictions on certain entities.*
Entities that may not seek listing as a
PSO include: health insurance issuers or components of health insurance issuers.
Any other entity, public or private, that conducts regulatory oversight of health care providers, such as accreditation or licensure, may not seek listing, except that a component of such an entity may seek listing as a component PSO. An applicant completing the required certification forms described in paragraph (a)(1) of this section will be required to attest that the entity is not subject to the restrictions of this paragraph.
(b) *Fifteen general PSO certification requirements.* The certifications submitted to the Secretary in accordance with paragraph (a)(1) of this section must conform to the following 15 requirements:
(1) *Required certification regarding eight patient safety activities.* An entity seeking initial listing as a PSO must certify that it has written policies and procedures in place to perform each of the eight patient safety activities, defined in § 3.20. Such policies and procedures will provide for compliance with the confidentiality

provisions of subpart C of this part and the appropriate security measures required by § 3.106 of this subpart. A PSO seeking continued listing must certify that it is performing, and will continue to perform, each of the patient safety activities, and is and will continue to comply with subpart C of this part and the security requirements referenced in the preceding sentence.
(2) *Required certification regarding seven PSO criteria.* In its initial certification submission, an entity must also certify that it will comply with the additional seven requirements in paragraphs (b)(2)(i) through (b)(2)(vii) of this section. A PSO seeking continued listing must certify that it is complying with, and will continue to comply with, the requirements of this paragraph.
(i) The mission and primary activity of a PSO must be to conduct activities that are to improve patient safety and the quality of health care delivery.
(ii) The PSO must have appropriately qualified workforce members, including licensed or certified medical professionals.
(iii) The PSO, within the 24-month period that begins on the date of its initial listing as a PSO, and within each sequential 24-month period thereafter, must have entered into 2 bona fide contracts, each of a reasonable period of time, each with a different provider for the purpose of receiving and reviewing patient safety work product.

(iv) The PSO is not a health insurance issuer, and is not a component of a health insurance issuer.

(v) The PSO must make disclosures to the Secretary as required under § 3.102(d), in accordance with § 3.112 of this subpart.

(vi) To the extent practical and appropriate, the PSO must collect patient safety work product from providers in a standardized manner that permits valid comparisons of similar cases among similar providers.

(vii) The PSO must utilize patient safety work product for the purpose of providing direct feedback and assistance to providers to effectively minimize patient risk.

(c) *Additional certifications required of component organizations.* In addition to meeting the 15 general PSO certification requirements of paragraph (b) of this section, an entity seeking initial listing that is a component of another organization or enterprise must certify that it will comply with the requirements of paragraphs (c)(1) through (c)(3) of this section. A component PSO seeking continued listing must certify that it is complying with, and will continue to comply with, the requirements of this paragraph.

(1) *Separation of patient safety work product.*

(i) A component PSO must: (A) Maintain patient safety work product separately from the rest of the parent organization(s) of which it is a part; and (B) Not have a shared information system

that could permit access to its patient safety work product to an individual(s) in, or unit(s) of, the rest of the parent organization(s) of which it is a part.

(ii) Notwithstanding the requirements of paragraph (c)(1)(i) of this section, a component PSO may provide access to identifiable patient safety work product to an individual(s) in, or a unit(s) of, the rest of the parent organization(s) of which it is a part if the component PSO enters into a written agreement with such individuals or units that requires that: (A) The component PSO will only provide access to identifiable patient safety work product to enable such individuals or units to assist the component PSO in its conduct of patient safety activities, and (B) Such individuals or units that receive access to identifiable patient safety work product pursuant to such written agreement will only use or disclose such information as specified by the component PSO to assist the component PSO in its conduct of patient safety activities, will take appropriate security measures to prevent unauthorized disclosures and will comply with the other certifications the component has made pursuant to paragraphs (c)(2) and (c)(3) of this section regarding unauthorized disclosures and conflicts with the mission of the component PSO.

(2) *Nondisclosure of patient safety work product.* A component PSO must require that members of its

workforce and any other contractor staff, or individuals in, or units of, its parent organization(s) that receive access in accordance with paragraph (c)(1)(ii) of this section to its identifiable patient safety work product, not be engaged in work for the parent organization(s) of which it is a part, if the work could be informed or influenced by such individuals' knowledge of identifiable patient safety work product, except for individuals whose other work for the rest of the parent organization(s) is solely the provision of clinical care.

(3) *No conflict of interest.* The pursuit of the mission of a component PSO must not create a conflict of interest with the rest of the parent organization(s) of which it is a part.

(d) *Required notifications.* PSOs must meet the following notification requirements:

(1) *Notification regarding PSO compliance with the minimum contract requirement.* No later than 45 calendar days prior to the last day of the applicable 24-month assessment period, specified in paragraph (b)(2)(iii) of this section, the Secretary must receive from a PSO a certification that states whether it has met the requirement of that paragraph regarding two bona fide contracts, in accordance with § 3.112 of this subpart.

(2) *Notification regarding a PSO's relationships with its contracting providers.* A PSO must submit to the Secretary a disclosure statement, in

accordance with § 3.112 of this subpart, regarding its relationships with each provider with which the PSO has a contract pursuant to the Patient Safety Act if the circumstances described in either paragraph (d)(2)(i) or (d)(2)(ii) of this section are applicable. The Secretary must receive a disclosure statement within 45 days of the date on which a PSO enters a contract with a provider if the circumstances are met on the date the contract is entered. During the contract period, if a PSO subsequently enters one or more relationships with a contracting provider that create the circumstances described in paragraph (d)(2)(i) of this section or a provider exerts any control over the PSO of the type described in paragraph (d)(2)(ii) of this section, the Secretary must receive a disclosure statement from the PSO within 45 days of the date that the PSO entered each new relationship or of the date on which the provider imposed control of the type described in paragraph (d)(2)(ii).

(i) Taking into account all relationships that the PSO has with the provider, other than the bona fide contract entered into pursuant to the Patient Safety Act, the PSO must fully disclose any other contractual, financial, or reporting relationships described below that it has with that provider.

(A) Contractual relationships which are not limited to relationships based on formal contracts but also encompass relationships based on any oral or written agreement or any arrangement that imposes responsibilities on the PSO.

(B) Financial relationships including any direct or indirect ownership or investment relationship between the PSO and the contracting provider, shared or common financial interests or direct or indirect compensation arrangement, whether in cash or inkind.

(C) Reporting relationships including any relationship that gives the provider access to information or control, directly or indirectly, over the work of the PSO that is not available to other contracting providers.

(ii) Taking into account all relationships that the PSO has with the provider, the PSO must fully disclose if it is not independently managed or controlled, or if it does not operate independently from, the contracting provider. In particular, the PSO must further disclose whether the contracting provider has exercised or imposed any type of management control that could limit the PSO's ability to fairly and accurately perform patient safety activities and fully describe such control(s).

(iii) PSOs may also describe or include in their disclosure statements, as applicable, any agreements, stipulations, or procedural safeguards that have been created to protect the ability of the PSO to operate independently or information that indicates the limited impact or insignificance of its financial, reporting, or contractual relationships with a contracting provider.

§ 3.104 Secretarial actions.
(a) *Actions in response to certification submissions for initial and continued listing as a PSO.* (1) In response to an initial or continued certification submission by an entity, pursuant to the requirements of § 3.102 of thissubpart,theSecretarymay—
(i) Accept the certification submission and list the entity as a PSO, or maintain the listing of a PSO, if the Secretary determines that the entity meets the applicable requirements of the Patient Safety Act and this subpart;
(ii) Deny acceptance of a certification submission and, in the case of a currently listed PSO, remove the entity from the list if the entity does not meet the applicable requirements of the Patient Safety Act and this subpart; or
(iii) Condition the listing of an entity, or continued listing of a PSO, following a determination made pursuant to paragraph (c) of this section.
(2) *Basis of determination.* In making a determination regarding listing, the Secretary will consider the certification submission; any prior actions by the Secretary regarding the entity or PSO including delisting; any history of or current noncompliance by the entity or the PSO with statutory or regulatory requirements or requests from the Secretary; the relationships of the entity or PSO with providers; and any findings made by the Secretary in accordance with paragraph (c) of this section.

(3) *Notification.* The Secretary will notify in writing each entity of action taken on its certification submission for initial or continued listing. The Secretary will provide reasons when an entity's certification is conditionally accepted and the entity is conditionally listed, when an entity's certification is not accepted and the entity is not listed, or when acceptance of its certification is revoked and the entity is delisted.

(b) *Actions regarding PSO compliance with the minimum contract requirement.* When the Secretary receives notification required by § 3.102(d)(1) of this subpart that the PSO has met the minimum contract requirement, the Secretary will acknowledge in writing receipt of the notification and add information to the list established pursuant to paragraph (d) of this section stating that the PSO has certified that it has met the requirement. If the PSO states that it has not yet met the minimum contract requirement, or if notice is not received by the date specified in § 3.102(d)(1) of this subpart, the Secretary will issue to the PSO a notice of a preliminary finding of deficiency as specified in § 3.108(a)(2) and establish a period for correction that extends until midnight of the last day of the PSO's applicable 24-month period of assessment.

Immediately thereafter, if the requirement has not been met, the Secretary will provide the PSO a written notice of proposed revocation and delisting in accordance with § 3.108(a)(3) of this subpart.

(c) *Actions regarding required disclosures by PSOs of relationships with contracting providers.* The Secretary will review and make findings regarding each disclosure statement submitted by a PSO, pursuant to § 3.102(d)(2) of this subpart, regarding its relationships with contracting provider(s), determine whether such findings warrant action regarding the listing of the PSO, and make the findings public.

(1) *Basis of findings regarding PSO disclosure statements.* In reviewing disclosure statements, submitted pursuant to § 3.102(d)(2) of this subpart, the Secretary will consider the nature, significance, and duration of the disclosed relationship(s) between the PSO and the contracting provider and will determine whether the PSO can fairly and accurately perform the required patient safety activities.

(2) *Determination by the Secretary.* Based on the Secretary's review and findings, he may choose to take any of the following actions:
(i) For an entity seeking an initial or continued listing, the Secretary may list or continue the listing of an entity without conditions, list the entity subject to conditions, or deny the entity's certification for initial or continued listing; or
(ii) For a listed PSO, the Secretary may determine that the entity will remain listed without conditions, continue the entity's listing subject to conditions, or remove the entity from listing.

(3) *Release of disclosure statements and Secretarial findings.*
(i) Subject to paragraph (c)(3)(ii) of this section, the Secretary will make disclosure statements available to the public along with related findings that are made available in accordance with paragraph (c) of this section.
(ii) The Secretary may withhold information that is exempt from public disclosure under the Freedom of Information Act.

(d) *Maintaining a list of PSOs.* The Secretary will compile and maintain a publicly available list of entities whose certifications as PSOs have been accepted. The list will include contact information for each entity, a copy of all certification forms and disclosure statements submitted by each entity, the effective date of the PSO's listing, and information on whether a PSO has certified that it has met the two-contract requirement. The list also will include a copy of the Secretary's findings regarding each disclosure statement submitted by an entity, information describing any related conditions that have been placed by the Secretary on the listing of an entity as a PSO, and other information that this Subpart states may be made public. AHRQ will establish a PSO Web site (or a comparable future form of public notice) and may post the list on this Web site.

(e) *Three-year period of listing.*
(1) The period of listing of a PSO will be for a three-year period, unless the listing is revoked or relinquished prior to the expiration of the three-year period, in accordance with § 3.108 of this subpart.
(2) The Secretary will send a written notice of imminent expiration to a PSO at least 45 calendar days prior to the date on which its three-year period of listing expires if the Secretary has not received a certification for continued listing.

(f) *Effective dates of Secretarial actions.* Unless otherwise stated, the effective date of each action by the Secretary pursuant to this subpart will be specified in the written notice of such action that is sent to the entity. When the Secretary sends a notice that addresses acceptance or revocation of an entity's certifications or voluntary relinquishment by an entity of its status as a PSO, the notice will specify the effective date and time of listing or delisting.

§ **3.106 Security requirements.**
(a) *Application.* A PSO must provide security for patient safety work product that conforms to the security requirements of paragraph (b) of this section. These requirements must be met at all times and at any location at which the PSO, its workforce members, or its contractors hold patient safety work product.
(b) *Security framework.* PSOs must consider the following framework for the security of patient safety work product. The framework includes four elements: security management, separation of systems, security monitoring and control, and system assessment. To address the four elements of this framework, a PSO must develop appropriate and scalable security standards, policies, and procedures that are suitable for the size and complexity of its organization.
(1) *Security management.* A PSO must address:
(i) Maintenance and effective implementation of written policies and procedures that conform to the requirements of this section to protect the confidentiality, integrity, and availability of the patient safety work product that is processed, stored, and transmitted; and to monitor and improve the effectiveness of such policies and procedures, and
(ii) Training of the PSO workforce and PSO contractors who access or hold patient safety work product regarding the requirements of the Patient Safety Act, this Part, and the PSO's policies and procedures regarding the confidentiality and security of patient safety work product.
(2) *Separation of Systems.* A PSO must address:
(i) Maintenance of patient safety work product, whether in electronic or other media, physically and functionally separate from any other system of records;

(ii) Protection of the media, whether in electronic, paper, or other format, that contain patient safety work product, limiting access to authorized users, and sanitizing and destroying such media before disposal or release for reuse; and
(iii) Physical and environmental protection, to control and limit physical and virtual access to places and equipment where patient safety work product is stored or used.

(3) *Security control and monitoring.* A PSO must address:
(i) Identification of those authorized to have access to patient safety work product and an audit capacity to detect unlawful, unauthorized, or inappropriate access to patient safety work product, and
(ii) Measures to prevent unauthorized removal, transmission or disclosure of patient safety work product.
(4) *Security assessment.* A PSO must address:
(i) Periodic assessments of security risks and controls, as determined appropriate by the PSO, to establish if its controls are effective, to correct any deficiency identified, and to reduce or eliminate any vulnerabilities.
(ii) System and communications protection, to monitor, control, and protect PSO uses, communications, and transmissions involving patient safety work product to and from providers and any other responsible persons.

§ **3.108 Correction of deficiencies, revocation,**

and voluntary relinquishment.

(a) *Process for correction of a deficiency and revocation*—(1) *Circumstances leading to revocation.*

The Secretary may revoke his acceptance of an entity's certification and delist the entity as a PSO if he determines—
(i) The PSO is not fulfilling the certifications it made to the Secretary that are set forth in § 3.102 of this subpart;
(ii) The PSO has not timely notified the Secretary that it has met the two contract requirement, as required by § 3.102(d)(1) of this subpart;
(iii) The Secretary, based on a PSO's disclosures made pursuant to § 3.102(d)(2) of this subpart, makes a public finding that the entity cannot fairly and accurately perform the patient safety activities of a PSO; or
(iv) The PSO is not in compliance with any other provision of the Patient Safety Act or this Part.
(2) *Notice of preliminary finding of deficiency and establishment of an opportunity for correction of a deficiency.* (i) If the Secretary determines that a PSO is not in compliance with its obligations under the Patient Safety Act or this Subpart, the Secretary must send a PSO written notice of the preliminary finding of deficiency. The notice must state the actions or inactions that encompass the deficiency finding, outline the evidence that the deficiency exists, specify the possible and/or required corrective actions that must be taken, and establish a date by which the deficiency must

be corrected. The Secretary may specify in the notice the level of documentation required to demonstrate that the deficiency has been corrected.
(ii) The notice of a preliminary finding of deficiency is presumed received five days after it is sent, absent evidence of the actual receipt date. If a PSO does not submit evidence to the Secretary within 14 calendar days of actual or constructive receipt of such notice, whichever is longer, which demonstrates that the preliminary finding is factually incorrect, the preliminary finding will be the basis for a finding of deficiency.
(3) *Determination of correction of a deficiency.* (i) Unless the Secretary specifies another date, the Secretary must receive documentation to demonstrate that the PSO has corrected the deficiency no later than five calendar days following the last day of the correction period, that is specified by the Secretary in the notice of preliminary finding of deficiency.
(ii) In making a determination regarding the correction of any deficiency, the Secretary will consider the documentation submitted by the PSO, the findings of any site visit that he determines is necessary or appropriate, recommendations of program staff, and any other information available regarding the PSO that the Secretary deems appropriate and relevant to the PSO's implementation of the terms of its certification.

(iii) After completing his review, the Secretary may make one of the following determinations:
(A) The action(s) taken by the PSO have corrected any deficiency, in which case the Secretary will withdraw the notice of deficiency and so notify the PSO;
(B) The PSO has acted in good faith to correct the deficiency but the Secretary finds an additional period of time is necessary to achieve full compliance and/or the required corrective action specified in the notice of a preliminary finding of deficiency needs to be modified in light of the experience of the PSO in attempting to implement the corrective action, in which case the Secretary will extend the period for correction and/or modify the specific corrective action required; or
(C) The PSO has not completed the corrective action because it has not acted with reasonable diligence or speed to ensure that the corrective action was completed within the allotted time, in which case the Secretary will issue to the PSO a notice of proposed revocation and delisting.
(iv) When the Secretary issues a written notice of proposed revocation and delisting, the notice will specify the deficiencies that have not been timely corrected and will detail the manner in which the PSO may exercise its opportunity to be heard in writing to respond to the deficiencies specified in the notice.
(4) *Opportunity to be heard in writing following a notice of*

proposed revocation and delisting. The Secretary will afford a PSO an opportunity to be heard in writing, as specified in paragraph (a)(4)(i) of this section, to provide a substantive response to the deficiency finding(s) set forth in the notice of proposed revocation and delisting.

(i) The notice of proposed revocation and delisting is presumed received five days after it is sent, absent evidence of actual receipt. The Secretary will provide a PSO with a period of time, beginning with the date of receipt of the notice of proposed revocation and delisting of which there is evidence, or the presumed date of receipt if there is no evidence of earlier receipt, and ending at midnight 30 calendar days thereafter, during which the PSO can submit a substantive response to the deficiency findings in writing.

(ii) The Secretary will provide to the PSO rules of procedure governing the form or transmission of the written response to the notice of proposed revocation and delisting. The Rules may also be posted on the AHRQ PSO Web site or published in the **Federal Register**.

(iii) If a PSO does not submit a written response to the deficiency finding(s) within 30 calendar days of receipt of the notice of proposed revocation and delisting, the notice of proposed revocation becomes final as a matter of law and the basis for Secretarial action under

paragraph (b)(1) of this section.

(5) *The Secretary's decision regarding revocation.* The Secretary will review the entire administrative record pertaining to a notice of proposed revocation and delisting and any written materials submitted by the PSO under paragraph (a)(4) of this section. The Secretary may affirm, reverse, or modify the notice of proposed revocation and delisting and will make a determination with respect to the continued listing of the PSO.

(b) *Revocation of the Secretary's acceptance of a PSO's certifications—(1) Establishing revocation for cause.* When the Secretary concludes, in accordance with a decision made under paragraph (a)(5) of this section, that revocation of the acceptance of a PSO's certification is warranted for its failure to comply with requirements of the Patient Safety Act or of this Subpart, the Secretary will establish the time and date for the prompt revocation and removal of the entity from the list of PSOs, so notify the PSO in writing, and provide the relevant public notice required by § 3.108(d) of this subpart.

(2) *Required notification of providers and status of data.* Within 15 days of being notified of the Secretary's action pursuant to paragraph (b)(1) of this section, an entity subject to paragraph (b)(1) of this section will submit to the Secretary confirmation that it has taken all reasonable

actions to notify each provider, whose patient safety work product it collected or analyzed, of the Secretary's action(s). Confidentiality and privilege protections that applied to patient safety work product while the former PSO was listed continue to apply after the entity is removed from listing.

Data submitted by providers to the former PSO within 30 calendar days of the date on which it is removed from the list of PSOs pursuant to paragraph (b)(1) of this section will have the same status as data submitted while the entity was still listed.

(3) *Disposition of patient safety work product and data.* Following revocation and delisting pursuant to paragraph (b)(1) of this section, the former PSO will take one or more of the following measures:
(i) Transfer such patient safety work product or data, with the approval of the source from which it was received, to a PSO that has agreed to receive such patient safety work product or data;
(ii) Return such work product or data to the source from which it was submitted; or
(iii) If returning such patient safety work product or data to its source is not practicable, destroy such patient safety work product or data.

(c) *Voluntary relinquishment—(1) Circumstances constituting voluntary relinquishment.* A PSO will be considered to have voluntarily relinquished its status as a PSO if the

Secretary accepts a notification from a PSO that it wishes to relinquish voluntarily its listing as a PSO or the Secretary determines that an implied voluntary relinquishment has taken place because the period of listing of a PSO has expired without receipt of a timely submission of certifications for continued listing.

(2) *Notification of voluntary relinquishment.* A PSO's notification of voluntary relinquishment to the Secretary must include the following:

(i) An attestation that all reasonable efforts have been made, or will have been made by a PSO within 15 calendar days of this statement, to notify the sources from which it received patient safety work product or data of the PSO's intention to cease operations, to relinquish voluntarily its status as a PSO, to request that these other entities cease reporting or submitting any further information to the PSO as soon as possible, and inform them that any data submitted after the effective date and time of delisting, that the Secretary sets pursuant to paragraph (c)(3) of this section, will not be protected as patient safety work product under the Patient Safety Act based upon such submissions;

(ii) An attestation that the entity has established a plan, or within 15 calendar days of this statement, will have made all reasonable efforts to establish a plan, in consultation with the

sources from which it received patient safety work product or data, that provides for the disposition of such patient safety work product or data consistent with, to the extent practicable, the statutory options for disposition of patient safety work product or data as set out in paragraphs (b)(3)(i) through (iii) of this section; and (iii) Appropriate contact information for further communications from the Secretary.

(3) *Response to notification of voluntary relinquishment.* (i) After a PSO provides the notification required by paragraph (c)(2) of this section, the Secretary will respond in writing to the entity indicating whether the proposed voluntary relinquishment of its PSO status is accepted. If the voluntary relinquishment is accepted, the Secretary's response will indicate an effective date and time for the entity's removal from the list of PSOs and will provide public notice of the delisting, in accordance with § 3.108(d) of this subpart.

(ii) If the Secretary receives a notification of voluntary relinquishment during or immediately after revocation proceedings for cause under paragraphs (a)(4) and (a)(5) of this section, the Secretary, as a matter of discretion, may accept voluntary relinquishment in accordance with the preceding paragraph or decide not to accept the entity's proposed voluntary relinquishment and proceed with the revocation for cause

and delisting pursuant to paragraph (b)(1) of this section.

(4) *Implied voluntary relinquishment.*

(i) If the period of listing of a PSO lapses without timely receipt and acceptance by the Secretary of a certification seeking continued listing or timely receipt of a notification of voluntary relinquishment of its PSO status in accordance with paragraph (c)(2) of this section, the Secretary will determine that voluntary relinquishment has occurred and will remove the entity from the list of PSOs effective as of midnight on the last day of its three-year period of listing. The Secretary will take reasonable measures to notify the entity of its delisting and will provide public notice of the delisting in accordance with § 3.108(d) of this subpart.

(ii) The Secretary will request in the notice to the entity that it make reasonable efforts to comply with the requirements of paragraph (c)(2) of this section with respect to notification, appropriate disposition of patient safety work product, and the provision of contact information to the Secretary.

(5) *Non-applicability of certain procedures and requirements.* (i) A decision by the Secretary to accept a request by a PSO to relinquish voluntarily its status as a PSO pursuant to paragraph (c)(2) of this section or a decision that voluntary relinquishment has occurred pursuant to paragraph (c)(4) of this section does not constitute a determination

of a deficiency in PSO compliance with the Patient Safety Act or with this Subpart and no opportunity for corrective action by the PSO is required.

(ii) The procedures and requirements of § 3.108(a) of this subpart regarding deficiencies including the opportunity to be heard in writing, and those that are based upon determinations of the Secretary pursuant to § 3.108(b)(1) of this subpart are not applicable to determinations of the Secretary made pursuant to paragraph (c) of this section.

(d) *Public notice of delisting regarding removal from listing.* If the Secretary removes an entity from the list of PSOs following revocation of acceptance of the entity's certification pursuant to § 3.108(b)(1) of this subpart or following a determination of voluntary relinquishment pursuant to § 3.108(c)(3) or (c)(4) of this subpart, the Secretary will promptly publish in the **Federal Register** and on the AHRQ PSO Web site, or in a comparable future form of public notice, established pursuant to § 3.104(d) of this subpart, a notice of the actions taken and the effective dates.

§ 3.110 Assessment of PSO compliance.

The Secretary may request information or conduct announced or unannounced reviews of or site visits to PSOs, to assess or verify PSO compliance with the requirements of this subpart and for these purposes will be allowed to inspect the physical or virtual sites maintained or controlled by the PSO. The Secretary will be allowed to inspect and/or be given or sent copies of any PSO records deemed necessary and requested by the Secretary to implement the provisions of this subpart. Such PSO records may include patient safety work product in accordance with § 3.206(d) of this subpart.

§ 3.112 Submissions and forms.

(a) Forms referred to in this subpart may be obtained on the AHRQ PSO Web site or a comparable future form of public notice or by requesting them in writing by e-mail at *psimplement@ ahrq.hhs.gov,* or by mail from the Agency for Healthcare Research and Quality, CQuIPS, PSO Liaison, 540 Gaither Road, Rockville, MD 20850.

A form (including any required attachments) must be submitted in accordance with the accompanying instructions.

(b) Information submitted to AHRQ in writing, but not required to be on a form, and requests for information from AHRQ, may be submitted by mail or other delivery to the Agency for Healthcare Research and Quality, CQuIPS, PSO Liaison, 540 Gaither Road, Rockville, MD 20850, by facsimile at (301) 427–1341, or by e-mail at *psimplement@ ahrq.hhs.gov.*

(c) If a submission to the Secretary is incomplete or additional information is needed to allow a determina-tion to be made under this subpart, the submitter will be notified if any additional information is required.

Subpart C—Confidentiality and Privilege Protections of Patient Safety Work Product

§ 3.204 Privilege of Patient Safety Work Product

(a) *Privilege.* Notwithstanding any other provision of Federal, State, local, or tribal law and subject to paragraph (b) of this section and § 3.208 of this subpart, patient safety work product shall be privileged and shall not be:

(1) Subject to a Federal, State, local, or tribal civil, criminal, or administrative subpoena or order, including in a Federal, State, local, or tribal civil or administrative disciplinary proceeding against a provider;

(2) Subject to discovery in connection with a Federal, State, local, or tribal civil, criminal, or administrative proceeding, including in a Federal, State, local, or tribal civil or administrative disciplinary proceeding against a provider;

(3) Subject to disclosure pursuant to section 552 of Title 5, United States Code (commonly known as the Freedom of Information Act) or any other similar Federal, State, local, or tribal law;

(4) Admitted as evidence in any Federal, State, local, or tribal governmental civil proceed-ing, criminal proceeding, administrative rulemaking proceeding, or administra-tive adjudicatory proceeding, including any such

proceeding against a provider; or

(5) Admitted in a professional disciplinary proceeding of a professional disciplinary body established or specifically authorized under State law.

(b) *Exceptions to privilege.* Privilege shall not apply to (and shall not be construed to prohibit) one or more of the following disclosures:

(1) Disclosure of relevant patient safety work product for use in a criminal proceeding, subject to the conditions at § 3.206(b)(1) of this subpart.

(2) Disclosure to the extent required to permit equitable relief subject to the conditions at § 3.206(b)(2) of this subpart.

(3) Disclosure pursuant to provider authorizations subject to the conditions at § 3.206(b)(3) of this subpart.

(4) Disclosure of non-identifiable patient safety work product subject to the conditions at § 3.206(b)(5) of this subpart.

(c) *Implementation and Enforcement of the Patient Safety Act.* Privilege shall not apply to (and shall not be construed to prohibit) disclosures of relevant patient safety work product to or by the Secretary if such patient safety work product is needed to investigate or determine compliance with this part or is needed in seeking or imposing civil money penalties, or in making or supporting PSO certification or listing decisions, under the Patient Safety Act.

§ 3.206 Confidentiality of Patient Safety

Work Product.

(a) *Confidentiality.* Subject to paragraphs (b) through (e) of this section, and §§ 3.208 and 3.210 of this subpart, patient safety work product shall be confidential and shall not be disclosed.

(b) *Exceptions to confidentiality.* The confidentiality provisions shall not apply to (and shall not be construed to prohibit) one or more of the following disclosures:

(1) *Criminal proceedings.* Disclosure of relevant patient safety work product for use in a criminal proceeding, but only after a court makes an *in camera* determination that:

(i) Such patient safety work product contains evidence of a criminal act;

(ii) Such patient safety work product is material to the proceeding; and

(iii) Such patient safety work product is not reasonably available from any other source.

(2) *Equitable relief for reporters.* Disclosure of patient safety work product to the extent required to permit equitable relief under section 922 (f)(4)(A) of the Public Health Service Act.

(3) *Authorized by identified providers.*

(i) Disclosure of identifiable patient safety work product consistent with a valid authorization if such authorization is obtained from each provider identified in such work product prior to disclosure. A valid authorization must:

(A) Be in writing and signed by the provider from whom authorization is sought; and

(B) Contain sufficient detail to fairly inform the provider of the nature and scope of the disclosures being authorized;

(ii) A valid authorization must be retained by the disclosing entity for six years from the date of the last disclosure made in reliance on the authorization and made available to the Secretary upon request.

(4) *Patient safety activities—*(i) *Disclosure between a provider and a PSO.* Disclosure of patient safety work product for patient safety activities by a provider to a PSO or by a PSO to that disclosing provider.

(ii) *Disclosure to a contractor of a provider or a PSO.* A provider or a PSO may disclose patient safety work product for patient safety activities to an entity with which it has contracted to undertake patient safety activities on its behalf. A contractor receiving patient safety work product for patient safety activities may not further disclose patient safety work product, except to the entity with which it is contracted.

(iii) *Disclosure by a PSO to another PSO or by a provider to another provider.* Disclosure of patient safety work product for patient safety activities by a PSO to another PSO or to another provider that has reported to the PSO, or by a provider to another provider, provided:

(A) The following direct identifiers of any providers and of affiliated organizations, corporate parents, subsidiaries, practice partners, employers, members of the workforce, or household members of such providers are removed:

(1) Names;

(2) Postal address information, other than town or city, State and zip code;

(3) Telephone numbers;

(4) Fax numbers;

(5) Electronic mail addresses;

(6) Social security numbers or taxpayer identification numbers;

(7) Provider or practitioner credentialing or DEA numbers;

(8) National provider identification number;

(9) Certificate/license numbers;

(10) Web Universal Resource Locators (URLs);

(11) Internet Protocol (IP) address numbers;

(12) Biometric identifiers, including finger and voice prints; and

(13) Full face photographic images and any comparable images; and

(B) With respect to any individually identifiable health information in such patient safety work product, the direct identifiers listed at 45 CFR 164.514(e)(2) have been removed.

(5) *Disclosure of nonidentifiable patient safety work product.* Disclosure of nonidentifiable patient safety work product when patient safety work product meets the standard for nonidentification in accordance with § 3.212 of this subpart.

(6) *For research.* (i) Disclosure of patient safety work product to persons carrying out research, evaluation or demonstration projects authorized, funded, certified, or otherwise sanctioned by

rule or other means by the Secretary, for the purpose of conducting research.

(ii) If the patient safety work product disclosed pursuant to paragraph (b)(6)(i) of this section is by a HIPAA covered entity as defined at 45 CFR 160.103 and contains protected health information as defined by the HIPAA Privacy Rule at 45 CFR 160.103, such patient safety work product may only be disclosed under this exception in the same manner as would be permitted under the HIPAA Privacy Rule at 45 CFR 164.512(i).

(7) *To the Food and Drug Administration (FDA).*

(i) Disclosure by a provider of patient safety work product concerning an FDA regulated product or activity to the FDA or to an entity required to report to the FDA concerning the quality, safety, or effectiveness of an FDA-regulated product or activity.

(ii) The FDA and any entity receiving patient safety work product pursuant to paragraph (b)(7)(i) of this section may only further disclose such patient safety work product for the purpose of evaluating the quality, safety, or effectiveness of that product or activity between each other, their contractors, and the disclosing provider. A contractor receiving patient safety work product pursuant to this paragraph may not further disclose patient safety work product, except to the entity from which it received the patient safety work product.

(8) *Voluntary disclosure to an accrediting body.*

(i) Voluntary disclosure by a provider of patient safety work product that identifies that provider to an accrediting body that accredits that provider. Such accrediting body may not further disclose such patient safety work product.

(ii) An accrediting body may not take an accrediting action against a provider based on a good faith participation of the provider in the collection, development, reporting, or maintenance of patient safety work product in accordance with this Part. An accrediting body may not require a provider to reveal its communications with any PSO.

(9) *Business operations.* (i) Disclosure of patient safety work product by a provider or a PSO for business operations to attorneys, accountants, and other professionals. Such contractors may not further disclose patient safety work product, except to the entity from which they received the information.

(ii) Disclosure of patient safety work product for such other business operations that the Secretary may prescribe by regulation as consistent with the goals of this part.

(10) *Disclosure to law enforcement.*

(i) Disclosure of patient safety work product to an appropriate law enforcement authority relating to an event that either constitutes the commission of a crime, or for which the disclosing person reasonably believes constitutes the commission of a crime, provided that the disclosing person believes, reasonably under the circumstances, that the patient safety work product that is disclosed is necessary for criminal law enforcement purposes.

(ii) Law enforcement personnel receiving patient safety work product pursuant to paragraph (b)(10)(i) of this section may disclose that patient safety work product to other law enforcement authorities as needed for law enforcement activities related to the event that gave rise to the disclosure under paragraph (b)(10)(i) of this section.

(c) *Safe harbor.* A provider or responsible person, but not a PSO, is not considered to have violated the requirements of this subpart if a member of its workforce discloses patient safety work product, provided that the disclosure does not include materials, including oral statements, that:

(1) Assess the quality of care of an identifiable provider; or

(2) Describe or pertain to one or more actions or failures to act by an identifiable provider.

(d) *Implementation and Enforcement of the Patient Safety Act.* The confidentiality provisions shall not apply to (and shall not be construed to prohibit) disclosures of relevant patient safety work product to or by the Secretary if such patient safety work product is needed to investigate or determine compliance with this part or is needed in

seeking and imposing civil money penalties, or in making or supporting PSO certification or listing decisions, under the Patient Safety Act.

(e) *No limitation on authority to limit or delegate disclosure or use.* Nothing in subpart C of this part shall be construed to limit the authority of any person to enter into a contract requiring greater confidentiality or delegating authority to make a disclosure or use in accordance with this subpart.

§ 3.208 Continued protection of Patient Safety Work Product.

(a) Except as provided in paragraph

(b) of this section, patient safety work product disclosed in accordance with this subpart, or disclosed impermissibly, shall continue to be privileged and confidential.

(b)(1) Patient safety work product disclosed for use in a criminal proceeding pursuant to section 922(c)(1)(A) of the Public Health Service Act and/or pursuant to § 3.206(b)(1) of this subpart continues to be privileged, but is no longer confidential.

(2) Non-identifiable patient safety work product that is disclosed is no longer privileged or confidential and not subject to the regulations under this part.

(3) Paragraph (b) of this section applies only to the specific patient safety work product disclosed.

§ 3.210 Required disclosure of Patient

Safety Work Product to the Secretary.

Providers, PSOs, and responsible persons must disclose patient safety work product upon request by the Secretary when the Secretary determines such patient safety work product is needed to investigate or determine compliance with this part or is needed in seeking and imposing civil money penalties or making determinations on certifying and listing PSOs.

§ 3.212 Nonidentification of Patient Safety Work Product.

(a) Patient safety work product is nonidentifiable with respect to a particular identified provider or a particular identified reporter if:

(1) A person with appropriate knowledge of and experience with generally accepted statistical and scientific principles and methods for rendering information not individually identifiable:

(i) Applying such principles and methods, determines that the risk is very small that the information could be used, alone or in combination with other reasonably available information, by an anticipated recipient to identify an identified provider or reporter; and (ii) Documents the methods and results of the analysis that justify such determination; or

(2)(i) The following identifiers of such provider or reporter and of affiliated organizations, corporate parents, subsidiaries, practice partners, employers, members of the workforce, or household members of such providers or reporters are removed:

(A) Names;

(B) Geographic subdivisions smaller than a State, including street address, city, county, precinct, zip code and equivalent geocodes, except for the initial three digits of a zip code if, according to the current publicly available data from the Bureau of the Census, the geographic unit formed by combining all zip codes with the same three initial digits contains more than 20,000 people;

(C) All elements of dates (except year) for dates directly related to a patient safety incident or event;

(D) Telephone numbers;

(E) Fax numbers;

(F) Electronic mail addresses;

(G) Social security numbers or taxpayer identification numbers;

(H) Provider or practitioner credentialing or DEA numbers;

(I) National provider identification number;

(J) Certificate/license numbers;

(K) Web Universal Resource Locators (URLs);

(L) Internet Protocol (IP) address numbers;

(M) Biometric identifiers, including finger and voice prints;

(N) Full face photographic images and any comparable images; and, (O) Any other unique identifying number, characteristic, or code except

as permitted for re-identification; and

(ii) The provider, PSO or responsible person making the disclosure does not have actual knowledge that the information could be used, alone or in combination with other information that is reasonably available to the intended recipient, to identify the particular provider or reporter.

(3) *Re-identification.* A provider, PSO, or responsible person may assign a code or other means of record identification to allow information made nonidentifiable under this section to be re-identified by such provider, PSO, or responsible person, provided that:

(i) The code or other means of record identification is not derived from or related to information about the provider or reporter and is not otherwise capable of being translated so as to identify the provider or reporter; and

(ii) The provider, PSO, or responsible person does not use or disclose the code or other means of record identification for any other purpose, and does not disclose the mechanism for reidentification.

(b) Patient safety work product is nonidentifiable with respect a particular patient only if the individually identifiable health information regarding that patient is de-identified in accordance with the HIPAA Privacy Rule standard and implementation specifications for the de-identifica-

tion at 45 CFR 164.514 (a) through (c).

Subpart D—Enforcement Program

§ 3.304 Principles for achieving compliance.

(a) *Cooperation.* The Secretary will, to the extent practicable, seek the cooperation of providers, PSOs, and responsible persons in obtaining compliance with the applicable confidentiality provisions.

(b) *Assistance.* The Secretary may provide technical assistance to providers, PSOs, and responsible persons to help them comply voluntarily with the applicable confidentiality provisions.

§ 3.306 Complaints to the Secretary.

(a) *Right to file a complaint.* A person who believes that patient safety work product has been disclosed in violation of the confidentiality provisions may file a complaint with the Secretary.

(b) *Requirements for filing complaints.* Complaints under this section must meet the following requirements:

(1) A complaint must be filed in writing, either on paper or electronically.

(2) A complaint must name the person that is the subject of the complaint and describe the act(s) believed to be in violation of the applicable confidentiality provision(s).

(3) A complaint must be filed within 180 days of when the complainant knew or should have known that the act complained of occurred, unless this time limit is

waived by the Secretary for good cause shown.

(4) The Secretary may prescribe additional procedures for the filing of complaints, as well as the place and manner of filing, by notice in the **Federal Register**.

(c) *Investigation.* The Secretary may investigate complaints filed under this section. Such investigation may include a review of the pertinent policies, procedures, or practices of the respondent and of the circumstances regarding any alleged violation. At the time of initial written communication with the respondent about the complaint, the Secretary will describe the act(s) that are the basis of the complaint.

§ **3.308 Compliance reviews.**

The Secretary may conduct compliance reviews to determine whether a respondent is complying with the applicable confidentiality provisions.

§ **3.310 Responsibilities of respondents.**

(a) *Provide records and compliance reports.* A respondent must keep such records and submit such compliance reports, in such time and manner and containing such information, as the Secretary may determine to be necessary to enable the Secretary to ascertain whether the respondent has complied or is complying with the applicable confidentiality provisions.

(b) *Cooperate with complaint investigations and compliance*

reviews. A respondent must cooperate with the Secretary, if the Secretary undertakes an investigation or compliance review of the policies, procedures, or practices of the respondent to determine whether it is complying with the applicable confidentiality provisions.

(c) *Permit access to information.* (1) A respondent must permit access by the Secretary during normal business hours to its facilities, books, records, accounts, and other sources of information, including patient safety work product, that are pertinent to ascertaining compliance with the applicable confidentiality provisions. If the Secretary determines that exigent circumstances exist, such as when documents may be hidden or destroyed, a respondent must permit access by the Secretary at any time and without notice.

(2) If any information required of a respondent under this section is in the exclusive possession of any other agency, institution, or person, and the other agency, institution, or person fails or refuses to furnish the information, the respondent must so certify and set forth what efforts it has made to obtain the information.

§ **3.312 Secretarial action regarding complaints and compliance reviews.**

(a) *Resolution when noncompliance is indicated.* (1) If an investigation of a complaint pursuant to § 3.306 of this subpart or a compliance review pursuant to § 3.308 of this subpart indicates

noncompliance, the Secretary may attempt to reach a resolution of the matter satisfactory to the Secretary by informal means. Informal means may include demonstrated compliance or a completed corrective action plan or other agreement.

(2) If the matter is resolved by informal means, the Secretary will so inform the respondent and, if the matter arose from a complaint, the complainant, in writing.

(3) If the matter is not resolved by informal means, the Secretary will—

(i) So inform the respondent and provide the respondent an opportunity to submit written evidence of any mitigating factors. The respondent must submit any evidence to the Secretary within 30 days (computed in the same manner as prescribed under § 3.504(l) of this subpart) of receipt of such notification; and

(ii) If, following action pursuant to paragraph (a)(3)(i) of this section, the Secretary decides that a civil money penalty should be imposed, inform the respondent of such finding in a notice of proposed determination in accordance with § 3.420 of this subpart.

(b) *Resolution when no violation is found.* If, after an investigation pursuant to § 3.306 of this subpart or a compliance review pursuant to § 3.308 of this subpart, the Secretary determines that further action is not warranted, the Secretary will so inform the respondent and, if the matter arose from a complaint, the complainant, in writing.

(c) *Uses and disclosures of information obtained.* (1) Identifiable patient safety work product obtained by the Secretary in connection with an investigation or compliance review under this subpart will not be disclosed by the Secretary, except in accordance with § 3.206(d) of this subpart, or if otherwise permitted by this part or the Patient Safety Act.

(2) Except as provided for in paragraph (c)(1) of this section, information, including testimony and other evidence, obtained by the Secretary in connection with an investigation or compliance review under this subpart may be used by HHS in any of its activities and may be used or offered into evidence in any administrative or judicial proceeding.

§ 3.314 Investigational subpoenas and inquiries.

(a) The Secretary may issue subpoenas in accordance with 42 U.S.C. 405(d) and (e), and 1320a–7a(j), to require the attendance and testimony of witnesses and the production of any other evidence including patient safety work product during an investigation or compliance review pursuant to this part.

The Secretary will issue and serve subpoenas pursuant to this subpart in accordance with 45 CFR 160.314(a)(1) through (5), except the term "this part" shall refer to 42 CFR part 3.

(b) Investigational inquiries are nonpublic investigational proceedings conducted by the Secretary. The Secretary will conduct investigational proceedings in accordance with 45 CFR 160.314(b)(1) through (9).

§ 3.402 Basis for a civil money penalty.

(a) *General rule.* A person who discloses identifiable patient safety work product in knowing or reckless violation of the confidentiality provisions shall be subject to a civil money penalty for each act constituting such violation.

(b) *Violation attributed to a principal.* A principal is independently liable, in accordance with the federal common law of agency, for a civil money penalty based on the act of the principal's agent, including a workforce member, acting within the scope of the agency if such act could give rise to a civil money penalty in accordance with § 3.402(a) of this subpart.

§ 3.404 Amount of a civil money penalty.

(a) The amount of a civil money penalty will be determined in accordance with paragraph (b) of this section and § 3.408 of this subpart.

(b) The Secretary may impose a civil money penalty in the amount of not more than $10,000.

§ 3.408 Factors considered in determining the amount of a civil money penalty.

In determining the amount of any civil money penalty, the Secretary may consider as aggravating or mitigating factors, as appropriate, any of the following:

(a) The nature of the violation.

(b) The circumstances, including the consequences, of the violation, including:

(1) The time period during which the violation(s) occurred; and

(2) Whether the violation caused physical or financial harm or reputational damage;

(c) The degree of culpability of the respondent, including:

(1) Whether the violation was intentional; and

(2) Whether the violation was beyond the direct control of the respondent.

(d) Any history of prior compliance with the Patient Safety Act, including violations, by the respondent, including:

(1) Whether the current violation is the same or similar to prior violation(s);

(2) Whether and to what extent the respondent has attempted to correct previous violations;

(3) How the respondent has responded to technical assistance from the Secretary provided in the context of a compliance effort; and

(4) How the respondent has responded to prior complaints.

(e) The financial condition of the respondent, including:

(1) Whether the respondent had financial difficulties that affected its ability to comply;

(2) Whether the imposition of a civil money penalty would jeopardize the ability of the respondent to continue to provide health care or patient safety activities; and

(3) The size of the respondent.

(f) Such other matters as justice may require.

§ 3.414 Limitations.

No action under this subpart may be entertained unless commenced by the Secretary, in accordance with § 3.420 of this subpart, within 6 years from the date of the occurrence of the violation.

§ 3.416 Authority to settle.

Nothing in this subpart limits the authority of the Secretary to settle any issue or case or to compromise any penalty.

§ 3.418 Exclusivity of penalty.

(a) Except as otherwise provided by paragraph (b) of this section, a penalty imposed under this part is in addition to any other penalty prescribed by law.

(b) Civil money penalties shall not be imposed both under this part and under the HIPAA Privacy Rule (45 CFR parts 160 and 164).

§ 3.420 Notice of proposed determination.

(a) If a penalty is proposed in accordance with this part, the Secretary must deliver, or send by certified mail with return receipt requested, to the respondent, written notice of the Secretary's intent to impose a penalty.

This notice of proposed determination must include:

(1) Reference to the statutory basis for the penalty;

(2) A description of the findings of fact regarding the violations with respect to which the penalty is proposed;

(3) The reason(s) why the violation(s) subject(s) the respondent to a penalty;

(4) The amount of the proposed penalty;

(5) Any factors described in § 3.408 of this subpart that were considered in determining the amount of the proposed penalty; and

(6) Instructions for responding to the notice, including a statement of the respondent's right to a hearing, a statement that failure to request a hearing within 60 days permits the imposition of the proposed penalty without the right to a hearing under § 3.504 of this subpart or a right of appeal under § 3.504(v) of this subpart, and the address to which the hearing request must be sent.

(b) The respondent may request a hearing before an ALJ on the proposed penalty by filing a request in accordance with § 3.504 of this subpart.

§ 3.422 Failure to request a hearing.

If the respondent does not request a hearing within the time prescribed by § 3.504 of this subpart and the matter is not settled pursuant to § 3.416 of this subpart, the Secretary may impose the proposed penalty or any lesser penalty permitted by 42 U.S.C. 299b–21 through 299b–26. The Secretary will notify the respondent by certified mail, return receipt requested, of any penalty that has been imposed and of the means by which the respondent may satisfy the penalty, and the penalty is final on receipt of the notice. The respondent has no right to appeal a penalty under § 3.504(v) of this subpart with respect to which the respondent has not timely requested a hearing.

§ 3.424 Collection of penalty.

Once a determination of the Secretary to impose a penalty has become final, the penalty will be collected by the Secretary in accordance with 45 CFR 160.424, except the term "this part" shall refer to 42 CFR Part 3.

§ 3.426 Notification of the public and other agencies.

Whenever a proposed penalty becomes final, the Secretary will notify, in such manner as the Secretary deems appropriate, the public and the following organizations and entities thereof and the reason it was imposed:

The appropriate State or local medical or professional organization, the appropriate State agency or agencies administering or supervising the administration of State health care programs (as defined in 42 U.S.C. 1320a–7(h)), the appropriate utilization and quality control peer review organization, and the appropriate State or local licensing agency or organization (including the agency specified in 42 U.S.C. 1395aa(a), 1396a(a)(33)).

§ 3.504 Procedures for hearings.

(a) *Hearings before an ALJ.* A respondent may request a hearing before an ALJ. Hearings must be requested in accordance with 45 CFR 160.504(a) through (c), except the language in paragraph (c) following and including "except that" shall not apply. The ALJ must dismiss a hearing request in accordance with 45 CFR 160.504(d).

(b) *Rights of the parties.* The hearing rights of the parties will be determined in accordance with 45 CFR 160.506.

(c) *Authority of the ALJ.* The ALJ will conduct a fair and impartial hearing in accordance with 45 CFR 160.508(a) through (c)(4).

(d) *Ex parte contacts.* Ex parte contacts are prohibited in accordance with 45 CFR 160.510.

(e) *Prehearing conferences.* Prehearing conferences will be conducted in accordance with 45 CFR 160.512, except the term "identifiable patient safety work product" shall apply in place of the term "individually identifiable health information."

(f) *Authority to settle.* The Secretary has authority to settle issues in accordance with 45 CFR 160.514.

(g) *Discovery.* Discovery will proceed in accordance with 45 CFR 160.516.

(h) *Exchange of witness lists, witness statements, and exhibits.* The parties will exchange hearing material in accordance with 45 CFR 160.518, except the language in paragraph (a) following and including "except that" shall not apply.

(i) *Subpoenas for attendance at hearing.* The ALJ will issue a subpoena for the appearance and testimony of any person at the hearing in accordance with 45 CFR 160.520.

(j) *Fees.* Fees and mileage for subpoenaed witnesses will be paid in accordance with 45 CFR 160.522.

(k) *Form, filing, and service of papers.* Hearing documents will be filed and serviced in accordance with 45 CFR 160.524.

(l) *Computation of time.* Computation of time shall be in accordance with 45 CFR 160.526, except the term "this subpart" shall refer to 42 CFR part 3, Subpart D, and the citation "§ 3.504(a) of 42 CFR part 3" shall apply in place of the citation "§ 160.504."

(m) *Motions.* Procedures for the filing and disposition of motions will be in accordance with 45 CFR 160.528.

(n) *Sanctions.* The ALJ may sanction a person in accordance with authorities at 45 CFR 160.530.

(o) *Collateral estoppel.* Collateral estoppel will apply to hearings conducted pursuant to this subpart in accordance with 45 CFR 160.532, except the term "a confidentiality provision" shall apply in place of the term "an administrative simplification provision."

(p) *The hearing.* Hearings will be conducted in accordance with 45 CFR 160.534, except the following text shall apply in place of § 160.534(b)(1): "The respondent has the burden of going forward and the burden of persuasion with respect to any challenge to the amount of a proposed penalty pursuant to §§ 3.404–3.408 of 42 CFR part 3, including any factors raised as mitigating factors." Good cause shown under 45 CFR 160.534(c) may be that identifiable patient safety work product has been introduced into evidence or is expected to be introduced into evidence.

(q) *Witnesses.* The testimony of witnesses will be handled in accordance with 45 CFR 160.538, except that the citation "§ 3.504(h) of 42 CFR part 3" shall apply in place of the citation "§ 160.518."

(r) *Evidence.* The ALJ will determine the admissibility of evidence in accordance with 45 CFR 160.540, except that the citation "§ 3.420 of 42 CFR part 3" shall apply in place of the citation "§ 160.420 of this part."

(s) *The record.* The record of the hearing will be created and made available in accordance with 45 CFR 160.542. Good cause under 45 CFR 160.542(c) through (d) may include the presence in the record of identifiable patient safety work product.

(t) *Post hearing briefs.* Post-hearing briefs, if required by the ALJ, will be filed in accordance with 45 CFR 160.544.

(u) *ALJ's decision.* The ALJ will issue a decision in accordance with 45 CFR 160.546, except the citation "§ 3.504(v) of 42 CFR part 3" shall apply in place of "§ 160.548."

(v) *Appeal of the ALJ's decision.* Any party may appeal the decision of the ALJ in accordance with 45 CFR 160.548, except the following language in paragraph (e) shall not apply: "Except for an affirmative defense under § 160.410(b)(1) of this part."

(w) *Stay of the Secretary's decision.*
Pending judicial review, a stay of the Secretary's decision may be requested in accordance with 45 CFR 160.550.

(x) *Harmless error.* Harmless errors will be handled in accordance with 45 CFR 160.552.

Dated: October 5, 2007.

Michael O. Levitt, *Secretary.*

[FR Doc. E8–2375 Filed 2–11–08; 8:45 am]

BILLING CODE 4153–01–P

APPENDIX C

VHA National Patient Safety Improvement Handbook

Department of Veterans Affairs	VHA HANDBOOK 1050.1
Veterans Health Administration	Transmittal Sheet
Washington, DC 20420	January 30, 2002

VHA NATIONAL PATIENT SAFETY IMPROVEMENT HANDBOOK

1. **REASON FOR ISSUE:** This Veterans Health Administration (VHA) Handbook provides guidance for minimizing the chance of the occurrence of untoward outcomes consequent to medical care.

2. **SUMMARY OF MAJOR CHANGES:** This is a new handbook that incorporates Root Cause Analysis, a widely understood methodology for dealing with patient safety-related issues allowing for clear and more rapid communication of information up and down the organization, thus speeding the process of safety improvement.

3. **RELATED DIRECTIVE:** VHA Directive 1051/1.

4. **RESPONSIBLE OFFICE:** The National Center for Patient Safety (10X) is responsible for the contents of this VHA Handbook. Questions may be referred to 734-930-5890.

5. **RESCISSION:** VHA Handbook 1051/1 dated January 13, 1998, is rescinded.

6. **RECERTIFICATION:** This document is scheduled for recertification on or before the last working date of January 2007.

S/Thomas L. Garthwaite, M.D.
Under Secretary for Health

DISTRIBUTION   CO: E-mailed 1/31/2002
FLD: VISN, MA, DO, OC, OCRO, and
200 – E-mailed 1/31/2002

283

CONTENTS

VHA NATIONAL PATIENT SAFETY IMPROVEMENT HANDBOOK

VHA NATIONAL PATIENT SAFETY IMPROVEMENT HANDBOOK

1. PURPOSE

This Veterans Health Administration (VHA) Patient Safety Improvement Handbook provides a roadmap that can be used to guide the VHA in the accomplishment of its goal of minimizing the chance of the occurrence of untoward outcomes consequent to medical care.

2. BACKGROUND

a. It has been reported in the medical literature that as many as 180,000 deaths occur in the United States each year due to errors in medical care, many of which are preventable. In order to take actions that will improve this situation, it is necessary to have a clear picture as to what is actually happening so that appropriate steps can be taken to prevent such occurrences. For this prevention effort to be effective, it is necessary to establish methods of gathering and analyzing data from the field that allows the formation of the most accurate picture possible. It is believed that only by viewing the health care continuum as a 'system' can truly meaningful improvements be made. A systems approach that emphasizes prevention, not punishment, as the preferred method to accomplish this goal will be used. Armed with this type of information, the most appropriate conclusions can be drawn from which prudent solutions can be formulated, tested, and implemented. *NOTE: Ultimately, this effort can be successful only if emphasis on safety and responsibility for improving it resides at all levels of the organization. This activity requires a true team effort.*

b. Through the use of procedures, methods, clarifying examples, and appropriate feedback loops at all levels of the organization (with accompanying rationale), it is hoped that this overall goal can be achieved. Incorporation of a widely understood methodology for dealing with these safety-related issues allows for a clear and a more rapid communication of information up and down the organization, thus speeding the process of safety improvement. *NOTE: For this to occur training must take place to complement the contents of this handbook; reading it alone is not sufficient.*

3. SCOPE

This handbook:

a. Delineates what types of events are to be considered within the Patient Safety Program and how they should be dealt with, as well as defining the disposition of other Adverse Events resulting from a criminal act; a purposefully unsafe act; an act related to alcohol or substance abuse by an impaired provider and/or staff; or events involving alleged or suspected patient abuse of any kind.

b. Specifies the method by which the need for conducting a Root Cause Analysis (RCA) will be determined and the procedure for communicating related findings throughout the organization. These procedures address the management component as well as the frontline needs. *NOTE: Directions in this handbook for reporting Adverse Events and Close Calls do not eliminate the need for the provider to document or report events related to a patient as applicable by other requirements.*

4. DEFINITIONS

a. **Adverse Events.** Adverse Events that may be candidates for an RCA are untoward incidents, therapeutic misadventures, iatrogenic injuries, or other adverse occurrences directly associated with care or services provided within the jurisdiction of a medical center, outpatient clinic, or other VHA facility.

(1) Adverse Events may result from acts of commission or omission (e.g., administration of the wrong medication, failure to make a timely diagnosis or institute the appropriate therapeutic intervention, adverse reactions or negative outcomes of treatment).

(2) Some examples of more common Adverse Events include: patient falls, adverse drug events, procedural errors and/or complications, completed suicides, parasuicidal behaviors (attempts, gestures, and/or threats), and missing patient events. *NOTE: All Adverse Events require reporting and documentation in the Patient Safety Information System. However, the type of review required is determined through the Safety Assessment Code (SAC) Matrix scoring process, as outlined in Appendix D.*

b. **Sentinel Events.** Sentinel Events are a type of Adverse Event. Sentinel Events, as defined by the Joint Commission on Accreditation of Healthcare Organizations (JCAHO), are unexpected occurrences involving death, serious physical or psychological injury, or risk thereof. Serious injury specifically includes loss of limb or function. The phrase "risk thereof" includes any process variation for which a recurrence would carry a significant chance of serious adverse outcomes.

(1) Sentinel Events signal the need for immediate investigation and response. Immediate investigations may be an RCA, or, in the case of an intentionally unsafe act, administrative action.

(2) Some examples of reviewable Sentinel Events include:

(a) Death resulting from a medication error or other treatment related error;

(b) Suicide of a patient in a setting where they receive around-the-clock care;

(c) Surgery on the wrong patient or body part regardless of the magnitude of the operation; and

(d) Hemolytic transfusion reaction involving the administration of blood or blood products having major blood group incompatibilities.

NOTE: Events considered to be JCAHO reviewable "Sentinel Events" are included in the catastrophic severity category of the SAC Matrix; also see Appendix D.

c. **Close Calls.** A Close Call is an event or situation that could have resulted in an Adverse Event but did not, either by chance or through timely intervention (see App. A). Such events have also been referred to as "near miss" incidents.

(1) An example of a Close Call would be a surgical or other procedure almost performed on the wrong patient due to lapses in verification of patient identification, but caught at the last minute by chance.

(2) Close Calls are opportunities for learning and afford the chance to develop preventive strategies and actions: they receive the same level of scrutiny as Adverse Events that result in actual injury; and they require reporting and documentation in the Patient Safety Information System. *NOTE: However, the same as for Adverse Events, the SAC Matrix scoring process and score determines the type of review.*

d. Intentionally Unsafe Acts

(1) Intentionally unsafe acts, as they pertain to patients, are any events that result from: a criminal act; a purposefully unsafe act; an act related to alcohol or substance abuse by an impaired provider and/or staff; or events involving alleged or suspected patient abuse of any kind.

(2) Intentionally unsafe acts are to be dealt with through avenues other than those defined in this handbook (i.e., Administrative Investigation (AI) or other administrative methods as determined by the facility Director and by applicable directives and regulations). The goal of these investigations, as it is with RCAs, needs to focus on answering the questions of what happened, why did it happen, and what do we do to prevent it from happening again. *NOTE: Guidance on what to do when criminal or intentionally unsafe acts are suspected is described in paragraph 6.*

(3) Facilities must maintain a log of all such events, including the disposition of all these cases.

e. RCA.

RCA is a process for identifying the basic or contributing causal factors that underlie variations in performance associated with Adverse Events or Close Calls. An RCA is a specific type of focused review that is used for all Adverse Events or Close Calls requiring analysis. Consistent use of RCAs further refines the implementation and increases the quality and consistency of focused reviews. To avoid confusion, the term RCA is used to denote this type of focused review and will adhere to the guidelines provided in this Handbook. Root Cause Analyses need to be initiated with a specific charter memo, and the term "Root Cause Analysis" needs to be used in documents so that they will be protected and confidential under Title 38 United States Code (U.S.C.) 5705 and its implementing regulations.

(1) RCAs have the following characteristics:

(a) The review is interdisciplinary in nature with involvement of those knowledgeable about the processes involved in the event.

(b) The analysis focuses primarily on systems and processes rather than individual performance.

(c) The analysis digs deeper by asking "what" and "why" until all aspects of the process are reviewed and contributing factors are considered.

(d) The analysis identifies changes that could be made in systems and processes through either redesign or development of new processes, or systems that would improve performance and reduce the risk of the Adverse Event or Close Call recurrence.

(2) To help adhere to these characteristics, the following five guidelines need to be considered when developing root cause statements:

(a) Root cause statements need to include the cause and effect.

(b) Negative descriptions are not to be used in root cause statements.

(c) Each human error has a preceding cause.

(d) Violations of procedure are not root causes, but must have a preceding cause.

(e) Failure to act is only a root cause when there is a pre-existing duty to act.

(3) To be thorough, an RCA must include:

(a) A determination of the human and other factors most directly associated with the event or Close Call and the processes and systems related to its occurrence (there is rarely only one underlying cause).

(b) Analysis of the underlying systems through a series of "why" questions to determine where redesigns might reduce risk.

(c) Identification of risks and their potential contributions to the Adverse Event or Close Call.

(d) Determination of potential improvement in processes or systems that would tend to decrease the likelihood of such events in the future, or a determination, after analysis, that no such improvement opportunities exist.

(4) To be credible, an RCA must:

(a) Include participation by the leadership of the organization (this can range from chartering the RCA team, to direct participation on the RCA team, to participation in the determination of the corrective action plan) and by individuals most closely involved in the processes and systems under review. In cases where the facility Director serves on the RCA team, final concurrence is to come from the Veterans Integrated Service Network (VISN) Director, or designee.

(b) Be internally consistent (i.e., not contradict itself or leave obvious questions unanswered).

(c) Include consideration of relevant literature.

(d) Include corrective actions, outcome measures, and top management approval.

(e) Meet the National Center for Patient Safety (NCPS) and JCAHO requirements. NCPS provides a computer-assisted tool that must be used to guide RCA teams, document the RCA, and communicate to NCPS and VISNs. It is referred to in this Handbook as the Patient Safety Information System.

(f) **Employee Rights.** RCAs do not involve sworn testimony. They can generate written confidential quality assurance documents if this is appropriately indicated in writing at the outset of the review (as in the RCA charter memo). Facility staff represented by an exclusive representative must be afforded all rights in accordance with their collective bargaining agreement.

5. GOALS

The goal of the Patient Safety Program is to prevent injuries to patients, visitors, and personnel. This is accomplished by taking small steps in the way things are done so that the level of faith and trust in the VHA patient safety system is established and these behaviors become a part of all employee behavior. This is a never-ending process. In this way a "culture of safety" can be formed. The key building blocks for accomplishing these goals are:

a. Comprehensive identification and reporting of Adverse Events, Sentinel Events, and Close Calls (see par. 6).

b. Reviewing Adverse Events, Sentinel Events, and Close Calls to identify underlying causes and system changes needed to reduce the likelihood of recurrence (see paragraph 7). The determination of cause is aimed at the system issues and is not to be used as a punitive tool. The requirements for initiating a review is determined by the prioritization method defined by the Safety Assessment Code (see App. D).

c. Disseminating patient safety alerts and lessons learned regarding effective system modifications throughout VHA (see par. 7) in an effective manner.

d. Prospective analysis of service delivery systems before an Adverse Event occurs to identify system redesigns that will reduce the likelihood of harm. These would include potential system weaknesses that were identified through prospective hypothetical analyses ("what if" types of questions) using techniques such as Healthcare Failure Mode and Effects Analysis (HFMEA™).

6. IDENTIFICATION AND REPORTING OF ADVERSE EVENTS, SENTINEL EVENTS, AND CLOSE CALLS; HOW TO ADDRESS INTENTIONALLY UNSAFE ACTS

a. Each VISN must ensure that its designated facilities report at least the following events to NCPS (and to the local VISN, if this is the VISN policy):

(1) Adverse Events (see subpar. 4a).

(2) Sentinel Events (see, subpar. 4b).

(3) Close Calls (see, subpar. 4c).

b. Facility staff must report, as per local policy, any unsafe conditions of which they are aware, even though the conditions have not yet resulted in an Adverse Event or Close Call.

c. Adverse Events and Sentinel Events shall be reported within the facility to the Patient Safety Manager (PSM), or designee. Facility staff are strongly encouraged to report Close Calls to the PSM, or designee. The PSM, or designee, then uses the Safety Assessment Code Matrix (SAC) to determine what action is required.

(1) This action could range from reporting to the VISN, NCPS, and JCAHO with the associated RCA performed and corrective action plan, to a decision to do nothing at the present time due to the low priority accorded the event from its SAC score.

(2) Appendix D details how the SAC score is used and paragraph 7 and Figures 1 and 2 show the procedure that must be followed for handling events that are reported along with the associated time constraints and products required, as well as what actions will or may be taken. If a safety alert to other

facilities seems needed, this needs to be indicated. Events affecting personnel or visitors that could reveal vulnerabilities that could cause Adverse Events to patients need to be reported within the facility to the PSM, or designee.

d. Any report of an Adverse Event, Sentinel Event, or Close Call, as defined in subparagraphs 4a, 4b, and 4c, received by the PSM, or designee, is protected from disclosure under 38 U.S.C. 5705, as part of a medical quality assurance program. The only exception to this protection would be in the case of an intentionally unsafe act as defined as a criminal act; a purposefully unsafe act; an act related to alcohol or substance abuse by an impaired provider and/or staff; or events involving alleged or suspected patient abuse of any kind (see subpar. 4d).

e. If in the course of conducting an RCA it appears that the event under consideration is the result of an Intentionally Unsafe Act, the RCA team must refer the event to the facility Director for appropriate further consideration as described in subparagraph 4d. In such a situation the RCA team discontinues their efforts, since the facility Director has assumed the responsibility for any further fact finding or investigation.

(1) The RCA team still maintains the information they have already collected confidentially as per 38 U.S.C. 5705. This means that members of the RCA team in question could not serve on an Administrative Investigation (AI) team that might be convened by the Facility Director to consider this particular issue.

(2) All facilities must maintain a record of all events that have been referred to top management for consideration and the final disposition of the case.

f. If a crime is suspected to have been committed, appropriate officials (e.g., facility Director, Department of Veterans Affairs (VA) Police and Security) are to be notified as soon as possible by management (Title 38 Code of Federal Regulations (CFR) Sections 14.560 and 14.563, MP-1, Pt. I, Ch. 16, and MP-1, Pt. I, Ch. 2, subpar. 208.02). To the best extent possible, the surrounding area is not disturbed so that evidence is available for review by the police and other authorities. However, care needed by the patient is always to be provided as quickly as possible, regardless of its effect on the facility.

(1) As required by 38 CFR Sections 14.560 and 14.563, allegations of crimes against the person or property, or other non-fraudulent criminal matters must be referred to the Regional Counsel, who then refers the matter to the appropriate law enforcement agency.

(2) Serious crimes (felonies or misdemeanors) committed on hospital or domiciliary grounds must be reported directly to the United States Attorney, or a local agent of the Federal Bureau of Investigation.

(3) Allegations of fraud, corruption, or other criminal conduct involving VA programs and operations must be referred to the Office of the Inspector General. *NOTE: Notification is also to be given to the Deputy Assistant Secretary for Security and Law Enforcement and to the VISN office. The VISN office must inform the Assistant Deputy Under Secretary for Health (10N).*

g. If a crime is suspected to have been committed, facility security and medical staff may need to assist law enforcement agencies with preserving evidence (e.g., blood alcohol levels, weapons, controlled substances, etc.). Local policies and procedures for maintaining the chain of custody of evidence apply in these instances.

h. Staff who submit Close Call and Adverse Event reports that result in an RCA will receive feedback on the actions being taken as a result of their report. The feedback is to be of a timely nature and come from the PSM, or other appropriately designated party. Prompt feedback to reporters has been credited, in other reporting systems, with being one of the cornerstones that establishes trust in the system. It demonstrates the seriousness and commitment on the part of the organization to the importance of the reporting effort. Reporters are to be made acutely aware that their effort of reporting was not just a paperwork drill. The nature of this feedback can range from a simple acknowledgement that the event is under consideration, to providing information as to the corrective action that is planned or has been accomplished. *NOTE: Feedback should only be given to individuals that remain on staff at the time when the information from the RCA is available.*

i. Each VISN and facility is to adopt strategies to encourage and advocate staff identification and reporting of Adverse Events and Close Calls. Emphasis is to be placed on the value of Close Calls in identifying needed system redesigns. Identification and reporting of Adverse Events and Close Calls, including those that appear to result from practitioner error, need to be a routine part of everyday practice. Employees need to understand that events that are often referred to as human errors are commonly due to systems-type problems. They especially need to understand that even the most conscientious, knowledgeable, and competent professionals can make errors and that the goal is to understand these in order to prevent them from causing harm to patients.

j. VA medical centers with a Nuclear Regulatory Commission license or other authorization to use radioactive materials must ensure compliance with the license and pertinent regulations. The VHA National Health Physics Program (NHPP) is to be contacted for assistance, if needed, to clarify license or regulatory requirements. *NOTE: The NHPP can be contacted by telephone at (501) 257-1571, by e-mail at vhconhpp@med.va.gov.*

k. The Patient Safety Information System must be used to track and monitor reported events. Designated staff at VA medical centers will enter data into the Patient Safety Information System, thereby ensuring the accuracy of the data recorded. *NOTE: This may also avoid translation and transcription errors that could occur if others performed this function.*

7. REVIEW AND ANALYSIS OF REPORTED EVENTS

a. A procedure has been worked out so that the review and analysis system for handling reports proceeds in an understandable manner and takes into account the various requirements of VHA and accrediting organizations. The RCA process is detailed schematically in Figure 1, which provides a detailed view of the RCA process. The following description will 'walk you through' Figure 1:

(1) When an Adverse Event or Close Call occurs, VA personnel may use any available or locally accepted method to notify the PSM and begin the facility's consideration of the event. The first step taken by the PSM after any required immediate action is to assign actual and potential SAC scores (see App. D) that then define what further actions are necessary.

(2) Events receiving a score of one or two will be acted on as thought appropriate by the facility. One needs to eliminate, control, or accept the risks associated with these events. These actions can range from performing an RCA to "no further action required."

(3) All events receiving a SAC score of three will receive either a traditional RCA or an Aggregated Review as described in subparagraph 7a(4) and the initial report of the event must be entered into the Patient Safety Information System. Events that have received a SAC score of three based on what has actually occurred, must have an RCA performed; the aggregated approach may not be used.

(4) A quarterly Aggregated Review may be used for the events as described in Appendix C, Aggregated Reviews. The use of aggregated analysis serves two important purposes.

(a) First, this will provide a greater utility of the analysis as trends or patterns not noticeable in individual case analysis are more likely to show up as the number of cases increases.

(b) Second, it makes wise use of the RCA team's time and expertise. NCPS uses this information to compare with other data and to determine if any immediate action as far as the issuance of alerts or other action is indicated. **NOTE:** *Any event may be subjected to a traditional RCA if this course of action is thought to be appropriate, even though it is in a category that permits an aggregated review.*

(5) If the event in question is an actual Adverse Event meeting the JCAHO definition of Reviewable Sentinel Event, the facility makes the determination to report it to JCAHO. This may entail consultation with other entities such as the VISN as is defined by local policy. In either case, the event receives an RCA and results are reported to the Patient Safety Information System and if previously reported to JCAHO, to them as well. The report of the outcome of the RCA must be completed within 45 calendar days and forwarded as described.

(6) To summarize, facilities have the option to report to JCAHO as explained in JCAHO policy (see App. B and the JCAHO web page: http://www. jcaho.org/ptsafety_frm.html). The RCA report will be retained by the facility even after the results have been entered into the Patient Safety Information System so that the report can be made available for future review and learning as appropriate.

(7) All events must be entered into the Patient Safety Information System. In this way all events reported are captured in the Patient Safety Information System even if they have SAC scores less than three. Those that receive a score of three (actual or potential) must receive RCA or aggregate review. Accordingly, the

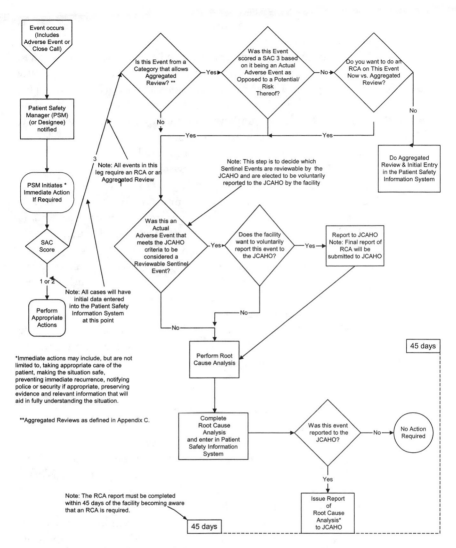

Figure 1. A Detailed View of the Root-Cause Analysis Process

opportunity will then exist to better understand the system and appropriately focus attention in the future.

b. The real benefit of this review process is realized after the RCA is completed and the corrective actions are defined and implemented that prevent the future occurrence of similar events. These corrective actions are classified as eliminate, control, or accept based upon their projected impact on the identified system vulnerabilities. Once implemented, a plan for evaluating the effectiveness of the implemented change must be enacted to ensure that this change has the desired effect. The subsequent results must also be communicated to the VISN and NCPS through entry in the Patient Safety Information System or through other appropriate means. *NOTE: Figure 2, provides a simplified view of the RCA process.*

c. NCPS is responsible for disseminating important information learned from RCAs and the Patient Safety Information System. National Alerts and Advisories to VHA facilities are issued by the Office of the Assistant Deputy Under Secretary for Health in concert with NCPS.

d. The Office of Medical Inspector (OMI) monitors RCAs and AIs to assess their adequacy and to identify problems with processes of care that warrant attention. The OMI may conduct reviews and site visits at the request of the Secretary of Veterans Affairs, the Under Secretary for Health, the Deputy Under Secretary for Health, the Inspector General, veterans and their families, the VISNs and medical facilities, and to other stakeholders, such as Congress and Veterans Service Organizations. The OMI may also conduct reviews and site visits based on its own judgment.

8. INFORMING PATIENTS ABOUT ADVERSE EVENTS
a. **Background Information**
(1) Clinicians and organizational leaders must work together to ensure that disclosure is a routine part of the response to Adverse Events. Telling patients that their health has been harmed rather than helped by the care provided is never easy, and disclosure must be undertaken with skill and tact. Nonetheless, VHA requires disclosure to patients who have been injured by Adverse Events.

(2) Disclosing Adverse Events to patients and their families is consistent with VHA core values of trust, respect, excellence, commitment, and compassion. Clinicians are ethically obligated to be honest with their patients. Honestly discussing the difficult truth that an Adverse Event has occurred demonstrates respect for the patient and a commitment to improving care. Disclosure of Adverse Events can be combined with reaffirming VHA's commitment to continuing to provide health care.

(3) VHA policy requiring disclosure is consistent with JCAHO requirements that hospitalized patients and their families be told of "unanticipated outcomes" of care (Standard RI 1.2.2, July 2001). JCAHO's requirement demonstrates a policy commitment that clinicians and health care organizations are disclose Adverse Events to patients and families.

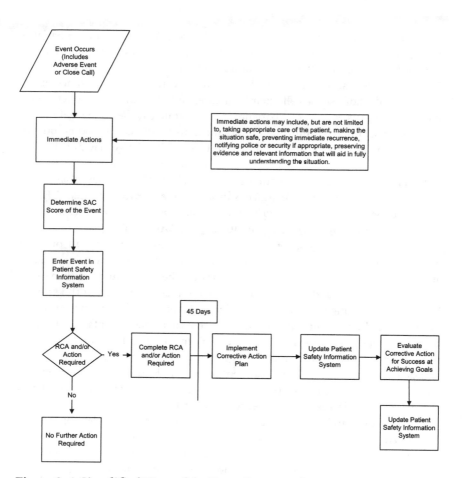

Figure 2. A Simplified View of the Root-Cause Analysis Process

(4) Despite the general obligation to disclose Adverse Events to patients and families, there are legal restrictions that limit disclosures that violate patient privacy. Specifically, the Privacy Act limits disclosures to families, and 38 U.S.C. 7332 limits disclosures related to the patient's treatment for substance abuse (including alcohol), sickle cell anemia disease, and Human Immunodeficiency Virus (HIV) status even after a patient's death. Similarly, there are legal limitations on disclosure of information obtained from RCAs and other quality improvement activities protected under 38 U.S.C. 5705. VHA may not disclose information obtained from RCAs and other quality improvement activities protected under 38 U.S.C. 5705 to patients and families. *NOTE: Questions about release of information to the patient and the patient's family are to be referred to the facility's Health Information Service; consultation with local or regional counsel may also be necessary.*

    b. <u>**Communication with Patients Regarding Adverse Events**</u>

(1) VISNs must ensure that their facilities have a process in place to promptly inform patients and their families about pertinent clinical facts associated with injuries resulting from Adverse Events. The patient and family need to be assured that measures have been taken to minimize the impact of the Adverse Event. The attending physician, or a designated member of the treatment team, needs to initially communicate the Adverse Event to the patient or family. Further disclosures and discussions of the Adverse Event need to be undertaken with input from regional counsel, risk management staff, patient safety officers, facility leaders, and members of the treatment team. Disclosure of Adverse Events to patients and/or family members need to be undertaken using methods similar to those used by clinicians to give other types of "bad news."

(2) VISNs and facilities must ensure that their staff provides appropriate and timely communication with patients and their families regarding Adverse Events that involve potential organizational liability. Potential organizational liability is to be assessed based on discussions with practitioners and the Regional Counsel. The patients and their families must be advised of appropriate remedial options. These options can include locally available interventions (e.g., arranging for second opinions, expediting clinical consultations, inpatient admission) and referral of patients to the 38 U.S.C. 1151 claims process and the tort claims process.

(3) A collaborative relationship between Regional Counsel and VA medical center staff is necessary to ensure appropriate and timely communication with patients. Each VISN needs to ensure that their staffs develop an understanding with its Regional Counsel regarding the procedures for obtaining Regional Counsel input prior to discussing an Adverse Event with a patient.

9. COMPENSATION FOR INJURED PATIENTS

    a. The two primary options available to injured patients, or their survivors, are claims for compensation under 38 U.S.C., Chapter 11, Section 1151, and tort claims under the Federal Tort Claims Act, 28 U.S.C., Sections 1346 (b), 2671–2680.

(1) Claims under 38 U.S.C. 1151 can result in payment of monthly benefits for additional disability or death incurred as the result of VHA facility care, medical or surgical treatment or examination, if the disability or death was proximately caused by negligence or an unforeseen event. Claims under 38 U.S.C. 1151 provide for the payment of a monthly benefit based on the percentage of disability and eligibility for VA medical care. *NOTE: Claims for 38 U.S.C.1151 benefits are processed by Veterans Benefits Administration (VBA) Regional Offices.*

(2) Tort claims may result in a settlement by Regional Counsels, General Counsel, United States Attorney, or in a judgment by a Federal court which has determined that negligence by medical practitioners caused injury or death (and jurisdictional requirements are met). *NOTE: Tort claims are processed by the Regional Counsels. In some cases subsequent review by the VHA Forensic Medicine Strategic Healthcare Group's (11F) Office of Medical-Legal Affairs may result in a recommendation that a practitioner be reported to the National Practitioner Data Bank based on a finding of substandard care, professional incompetence, or professional misconduct. Information contained in RCAs and other quality improvement materials is protected from disclosure in response to tort claims under 38 U.S.C. 5705 and may not be used by the VHA Office of Medical-Legal Affairs.*

(3) Veterans and survivors may pursue both 38 U.S.C 1151 and tort claims. However, if both claims are successful, 38 U.S.C. 1151 benefits will be offset until the amount that would have been paid equals the amount of the tort claim settlement or judgment.

CLOSE CALL SYSTEM DEFINITIONS

What is a Close Call?

1. <u>A Close Call is an event or situation that could have resulted in an adverse event but did not, either by chance or through timely intervention.</u>

2. All have experienced Close Calls on the job, whether they have recognized them or not. Two examples are listed as follows:

a. A nurse almost gives an overdose of insulin, but recognizes it and prevents the overdose when double-checking the order. *NOTE: During the double-check, they realize that they had confused the "U" for units, with a "0."*

b. An environmental management employee notices a jug of industrial strength cleaner mistakenly left in the shower stall on a locked psychiatric unit. They return it to proper storage before any patient can use it inappropriately.

THE JOINT COMMISSION ON ACCREDITATION OF HEALTHCARE ORGANIZATIONS' (JCAHO) DEFINITION OF REVIEWABLE SENTINEL EVENTS THAT MAY BE REPORTED TO JCAHO

The following criteria define the subset of Sentinel Events that are voluntarily reportable, at the facility's discretion to the Joint Commission on Accreditation of Healthcare Organizations (JCAHO). *NOTE: As JCAHO policies are dynamic, it is important to be sure that the most recent JCAHO Sentinel Event Policies and definitions are used in making any determination. The text below was taken from the JCAHO web page: http://www.jcaho.org/ptsafety_frm.html, and this site should be checked periodically for updates or changes in policies.*

1. Only those Sentinel Events that affect recipients of care (i.e., patients, clients, and Veterans Health Administration (VHA) nursing home and domiciliary residents) and that meet the following criteria fall into the subset of Sentinel Events that are voluntarily reportable to JCAHO:

2. The event has resulted in an unanticipated death or major permanent loss of function, not related to the natural course of the patient's illness or underlying condition. *NOTE: A distinction is made between an adverse outcome that is related to the natural course of the patient's illness or underlying condition (not reviewable under the Sentinel Event Policy) and a death or major permanent loss of function that is associated with the treatment, or lack of treatment, of that condition (reviewable). "Major permanent loss of function" means sensory, motor, physiologic, or intellectual impairment not present on admission requiring continued treatment or life-style change. When "major permanent loss of function" cannot be immediately determined, applicability of this policy is not established until either the patient is discharged with continued major loss of function, or two weeks have elapsed with persistent major loss of function, whichever occurs first.*

Or

3. The event is one of the following (even if the outcome was not death or major permanent loss of function):

a. Suicide of a patient in a setting where the patient receives around-the-clock care (e.g., hospital, residential treatment center, crisis stabilization center).

b. Infant abduction or discharge to the wrong family.

c. Rape. *NOTE: The determination of "rape" is to be based on the healthcare organization's definition, consistent with applicable law and regulation. An allegation of rape is not reviewable under the policy. Applicability of the policy is established when a determination is made that a rape has occurred.*

d. Hemolytic transfusion reaction involving administration of blood or blood products ving major blood group incompatibilities.

e. Surgery on the wrong patient or wrong body part. *NOTE: All events of surgery on the wrong patient or wrong body part are reviewable under the policy, regardless of the magnitude of the procedure.*

QUARTERLY AGGREGATED REVIEWS FALLS, ADVERSE DRUG EVENTS, MISSING PATIENTS, AND PARASUICIDAL BEHAVIOR

1. **Quarterly Aggregated Reviews**. Quarterly Aggregated Reviews completed within 45 days of the end of the quarter and conducted by a chartered Root Cause Analysis (RCA) Team, may be used for four types of reported Adverse Events or Close Calls (potential Safety Assessment Code (SAC) score of three). The four types of events that may be handled by Aggregated Reviews are falls, adverse drug events, missing patients, and parasuicidal behaviors. All Adverse Events with an actual SAC score of three require individual RCAs.

a. The use of Aggregated Reviews serves two important purposes. First, it provides greater utility of the analysis as trends or patterns not noticeable in individual case analysis are more likely to show up as the number of cases increases. Second, it makes wise use of the RCA team's time and expertise.

b. Of course, a facility may elect to perform an individual RCA rather than an Aggregated Review on any of these four types of Adverse Events or Close Calls that they think merits that attention, regardless of the actual SAC score.

c. A tailored, real-time minimum data set (Aggregated Review Log) must be compiled for falls, missing patients, adverse drug events, and parasuicidal behaviors by designated staff in follow-up to reported events or Close Calls, during each quarter. Capturing this data may require medical record review, medication administration record review, and a brief discussion with staff members most knowledgeable about the events or Close Calls. The Aggregated Review Logs are to be provided to the designated RCA Teams as soon as they are convened, and serve as their initial data source. *NOTE: By using these logs the RCA teams may not routinely need to retrospectively consult individual patient profiles or individual medical records.*

d. It is anticipated that by utilizing this aggregated approach and building the reviews over succeeding quarters, common themes may be more readily identified enabling evaluation of the effectiveness of actions taken to prevent these events or Close Calls. *NOTE: Descriptions of each Aggregated Review Log are provided on the following pages. See the National Center for Patient Safety (NCPS) website for the most current form of the aggregate logs at http://vaww.ncps.med.va.gov/training/ AggRevLog.doc.*

2. **Falls.** Falls are defined according to local or facility definition.

a. An individual RCA must be performed for any reported inpatient or outpatient fall occurring on facility property that results in an actual SAC 3, for all enrolled patients.

b. Reported falls and Close Calls (potential SAC score of 3) involving enrolled patients will be included in an Aggregated Review on a quarterly basis (completed by the RCA Team within 45 days after the end of the quarter). These

Aggregated Reviews will be entered in the Patient Safety Information System. Of course, a facility may elect to perform an individual RCA rather than an Aggregated Review on any Adverse Event or Close Call that merits that attention, regardless of the actual SAC score.

    c. The following elements are included in the <u>Falls Aggregated Review Log</u>:

    (1) Case number.

    (2) Age.

    (3) Sex.

    (4) Event (day, date, time).

    (5) OPT or INPT/Unit (designation of outpatient or inpatient status at time of event, and if inpatient, unit where the patient was assigned at the time of the event).

    (6) Functional and cognitive factors (a listing of factors related to falls, requires a "yes" or "no" response for all applicable items: prior fall; designation as "high risk" for falls; needs assistance with activities of daily living (ADLs) mobility, transfer, toileting, dressing, eating; gait or balance limitations; incontinence; confused or memory limitations; related medical conditions; medication effect, etc.).

    (7) Assistive Devices (a listing of devices related to falls, requires a "yes" or "no" response for all applicable items: cane; crutches; transfer device; walker; wheelchair; bathing device; mechanical lift; eye glasses; hearing aid, etc.).

    (8) Communication Issues (a short list of areas where communication or information exchange can break down, requires a "yes" or "no" response for all applicable items: staff to staff, staff to patient, and staff to family and/or other).

    (9) Environmental Factors (a listing of physical plant issues related to falls, requires a "yes" or "no" response for all applicable items: use of restraints, use of protective devices, inadequate footwear, bed side rails, floor condition, obstacles, fall while the patient was reaching for a needed item, inadequate patient or family or other education, unfamiliarity with the environment, inadequate lighting, and other).

    (10) A free narrative entitled "What Happened and Treatment Plan Changes."

    (11) Comments (free narrative).

NOTE: The current forms of the aggregated review logs can be seen at http://vaww.ncps. med.va.gov/training/AggRevLog.doc

    3. <u>**Adverse Drug Events.**</u>　The VHA report: "Consensus Report for Nomenclature and Taxonomy of Adverse Drug Events (ADEs)," issued December 27, 2000 defines an ADE as "an injury associated with the use or nonuse of a drug."

    a. An individual RCA mustbe performed for any reported inpatient or outpatient ADE that results in an actual SAC 3, for all patients receiving pharmaceutical care from a Department of Veterans Affairs (VA) health care system provider.

b. Reported ADEs or Close Calls (potential SAC 3 score) involving patients receiving pharmaceutical care from a VA health care system provider will be included in an Aggregated Review on a quarterly basis (completed by the RCA Team within 45 days after the end of the quarter). These Aggregated Reviews will be entered in the Patient Safety Information System. Of course, a facility may elect to perform an individual RCA rather than an Aggregated Review on any Adverse Event or Close Call that merits that attention, regardless of the actual SAC score.

c. The following elements are included in the <u>Medication Aggregated Review Log</u>:

(1) Case number.

(2) Age.

(3) Sex.

(4) Event (day, date, time).

(5) OPT or INPT/Unit (designation of outpatient or inpatient status at time of event, and if inpatient, unit where the patient was assigned at the time of the event)

(6) Processes related to the event (i.e., a listing of key steps in the medication process, requires a "yes" or "no" response for all applicable items: ordering, transcribing, dispensing, administering, and documenting).

(7) What happened? (A listing of ADEs, requires a "yes" or "no" response for all applicable items: medication given despite known allergy, omission, overdose, incorrect patient identification, incorrect medication identification, incorrect dose, incorrect route, incorrect schedule, and equipment failure.)

(8) Medication (name, dose, route, schedule for the correct medication, and the actual and/or Close Call medication).

(9) Treatment plan changes (free narrative).

(10) Comments (free narrative).

NOTE: The current forms of the aggregated review logs can be seen at http://vaww.ncps. med.va.gov/training/AggRevLog.doc

4. Parasuicidal Behaviors. There are two primary categories of suicidal events: completed suicides, and parasuicidal events (any suicidal behavior with or without physical injury [i.e., short of death], including the full-range of known or reported attempts, gestures, and threats).

a. An individual RCA will be performed for any completed inpatient suicide (at the time it occurs) and for any completed outpatient suicide (at the time of facility notification) for all enrolled patients who have received clinic care services from VA. In other words, all actual known suicides of enrolled patients who have received clinic care services from VA must receive an RCA and must be reported in the Patient Safety Information System.

b. All reported parasuicidal events or Close Calls (potential score of three) involving enrolled patients who have received clinic care services from VA will be included in an Aggregated Review on a quarterly basis. The RCA Team will complete this within 45 days after the end of the quarter. These Aggregated Reviews must be entered in the Patient Safety Information System. Of course, a facility may elect to perform an individual RCA rather than an Aggregated Review on any Adverse Event or Close Call that merits that attention, regardless of the actual SAC score.

c. The following elements are included in the <u>Parasuicidal Aggregated Review Log</u>:

(1) Case number.

(2) Age.

(3) Sex.

(4) Event (day, date, time).

(5) OPT or INPT/Unit (designation of outpatient or inpatient status at the time of event, and if inpatient, unit where the patient was assigned at the time of the event).

(6) Date of last OPT TX (date of most recent prior outpatient treatment; this does not include an appointment that was scheduled, but was a "no show").

(7) Diagnoses (a listing of current and active diagnoses).

(8) Tx Team (a short list of treatment team options for providers that were assigned to the patient at the time of the event; requires a "yes"/"no" response for all applicable items: mental health and/or psychiatry, specialty and/or sub-specialty, and primary care).

(9) What happened? (free narrative).

(10) Family and other supports (free narrative).

(11) Treatment plan changes (free narrative).

(12) Comments (free narrative).

NOTE: *The current forms of the aggregated review logs can be seen at http://vaww.ncps. med.va.gov/training/AggRevLog.doc*

5. Missing Patients. A missing patient is "a high-risk patient who disappears from an inpatient or outpatient treatment area or while under control of VA, such as during transport." A high-risk patient is one who is "incapacitated because of frailty, or physical or mental impairment."

a. An individual RCA must be completed for any missing patient who is classified as an actual 3 using the SAC matrix. All missing patients that receive a SAC potential score of three must be included in the Aggregated Review on a quarterly basis. The RCA Team must complete the Aggregate Review RCA within 45 days after the end of the quarter. The Aggregated Reviews must be entered in the Patient Safety Information System. Of course, a facility may elect to perform an individual RCA rather than an Aggregated Review on any Adverse Event or Close Call that merits that attention, regardless of the actual SAC score.

  b. The following elements are included in the **Missing Patient Aggregated Review Log:**

   (1) Case number.

   (2) Age.

   (3) Date reported missing (day, date).

   (4) Time reported missing.

   (5) Location reported missing from.

   (6) Length of time missing (days, hours).

   (7) Level of privileges (full, partial, none).

   (8) Previous episodes.

   (9) Order of treatment plan required supervision (Yes or No).

   (10) Primary diagnosis.

   (11) Person notified (name, date, and time).

   (12) Type of search conducted (general, grid).

   (13) Date found.

   (14) Location found.

   (15) Condition (injuries).

   (16) Barriers to prevent escape or elopement.

   (17) Activity at time of elopement or escape.

NOTE: The current forms of the aggregated review logs can be seen at http://vaww.ncps. med.va.gov/training/AggRevLog.doc.

THE SAFETY ASSESSMENT CODE (SAC)

The Severity Categories and the Probability Categories that are used to develop the Safety Assessment Codes (SACs) for Adverse Events and Close Calls are presented below, and are followed by information on the SAC Matrix.

SEVERITY CATEGORIES

1. Key factors for the severity categories are extent of injury, length of stay, level of care required for remedy, and actual or estimated physical plant costs. These four categories apply to actual Adverse Events and potential events (Close Calls). For **actual Adverse Events**, assign severity based on the patient's actual condition.

2. If the event is a **Close Call**, assign severity based on a reasonable "worst case" systems level scenario. *NOTE: For example, if you entered a patient's room before they were able to complete a lethal suicide attempt, the event is catastrophic, because the reasonable "worst case" is suicide.*

Catastrophic	Major
Patients with Actual or Potential:	**Patients with Actual or Potential:**
Death or major permanent loss of function (sensory, motor, physiologic, or intellectual) **not related to the natural course of the patient's illness or underlying condition** (i.e., acts of commission or omission). This includes outcomes that are a direct result of injuries sustained in a fall; or associated with an unauthorized departure from an around-the-clock treatment setting; or the result of an assault or other crime. Or any of the following:	Permanent **lessening** of bodily functioning (sensory, motor, physiologic, or intellectual) **not related to the natural course of the patient's illness or underlying conditions** (i.e., acts of commission or omission) **or** any of the following:
• Suicide (inpatient or outpatient) • Rape • Hemolytic transfusion reaction • Surgery or procedure on the wrong patient or wrong body part • Infant abduction or infant discharge to the wrong family	• Disfigurement • Surgical intervention required • Increased length of stay for 3 or more patients • Increased level of care for 3 or more patients
	Visitors: Hospitalization of 1 or 2 visitors
Visitors: A death; **or** hospitalization of 3 or more visitors	**Staff:** Hospitalization of 1 or 2 staff **or** 3 or more staff experiencing lost time or restricted duty injuries or illnesses_
Staff: A death or hospitalization of 3 or more staff*	**Equipment or facility:** Damage equal to or more than $100,000**, *
Fire: Any fire that grows larger than an incipient stage‡	

Moderate	Minor
Patients with Actual or Potential: Increased length of stay **or** increased level of care for 1 or 2 patients	**Patients with Actual or Potential:** No injury, nor increased length of stay nor increased level of care
Visitors: Evaluation **and** treatment for 1 or 2 visitors (less than hospitalization)	**Visitors:** Evaluated and no treatment required **or** refused treatment
Staff: Medical expenses, lost time or restricted duty injuries or illness for 1 or 2 staff	**Staff:** First aid treatment only with no lost time, nor restricted duty injuries nor illnesses
Equipment or facility: Damage more than $10,000 but less than $100,000**,	**Equipment or facility:** Damage less than $10,000 or loss of any utility without adverse patient outcome (e.g., power, natural gas, electricity, water, communications, transport, heat and/or air conditioning)**,
Fire – Incipient stage or smaller‡	

*Title 29 Code of Federal Regulations (CFR) 1960.70 and 1904.8 requires each Federal agency to notify the Occupational Safety and Health Administration (OSHA) within 8 hours of a work related incident that results in the death of an employee or the in-patient hospitalization of three or more employees. Volunteers are considered to be non-compensated employees.

**The Safe Medical Devices Act of 1990 requires reporting of all incidents in which a medical device may have caused or contributed to the death, serious injury, or serious illness of a patient or another individual.

‡ An incipient fire is a fire that is smaller than a burning waste paper basket. It is easily extinguished by using a single portable fire extinguisher (or equivalent) and it is not necessary to take evasive action (stooping, etc.) when approached to avoid heat or smoke.

The effectiveness of the facilities disaster plan must be critiqued following each implementation to meet the Joint Commission on Accreditation of Healthcare Organizations (JCAHO) Environment of Care Standards.

PROBABILITY CATEGORIES

1. Like the severity categories, the probability categories apply to actual Adverse Events and Close Calls.

2. In order to assign a probability rating for an Adverse Event or Close Call, it is ideal to know how often it occurs <u>at your facility</u>. Sometimes the data will be easily available because it is routinely tracked (e.g., falls with injury, ADEs, etc.). Sometimes, getting a feel for the probability of events that are not routinely tracked will mean asking for a quick or informal opinion from staff most familiar with those events. Sometimes it will have to be your best educated guess.

> a. **Frequent** – Likely to occur immediately or within a short period (may happen several times in 1 year).
> b. **Occasional** – Probably will occur (may happen several times in 1 to 2 years).
> c. **Uncommon** – Possible to occur (may happen sometime in 2 to 5 years).
> d. **Remote** – Unlikely to occur (may happen sometime in 5 to 30 years).

3. <u>How the Safety Assessment Codes (SAC) Matrix Looks</u>

Severity & Probability	Catastrophic	Major	Moderate	Minor
Frequent	3	3	2	1
Occasional	3	2	1	1
Uncommon	3	2	1	1
Remote	3	2	1	1

4. <u>How the SAC Matrix Works.</u> When you pair a severity category with a probability category for either an actual event or Close Call, you will get a ranked matrix score (3 = highest risk, 2 = intermediate risk, 1 = lowest risk). These ranks, or SACs can then be used for doing comparative analysis and for deciding who needs to be notified about the event.

5. <u>Notes</u>
> a. All known reporters of events, regardless of SAC score (one, two, or three), will receive appropriate and timely feedback.
> b. The Patient Safety Manager, or designee, will refer Adverse Events or Close Calls related solely to staff, visitors, or equipment and/or facility damage to rele-

vant facility experts or services on a timely basis, for assessment and resolution of those situations.

c. A quarterly Aggregated Root Cause Analysis (RCA) may be used for four types of events (this includes all events or Close Calls <u>other than actual SAC score of three</u>, since all actual SAC score of three require an individual RCA). These four types are falls, adverse drug events, missing patients, and parasuicidal behavior. The use of aggregated analysis serves two important purposes. First, it provides greater utility of the analysis as trends or patterns not noticeable in individual case analysis are more likely to show up as the number of cases increases. Second, it makes wise use of the RCA team's time and expertise. *NOTE: Of course, the facility may elect to perform an individual RCA rather than Aggregated Review on any Adverse Event or Close Call that merits that attention, regardless of the SAC score.*

APPENDIX D

Patient Safety Plan

Generic Safety Plan

COMPREHENSIVE MEDICAL SAFETY PROGRAM

INTRODUCTION

PURPOSE

The Medical Safety Program is designed to support and promote the mission and vision of the _____ as it pertains to patient/visitor/employee safety. This plan will be implemented through the integration and coordination of the medical safety activities of multiple departments and patient care/ patient support services at the _____ having responsibility for various aspects of patient and employee safety, including, but not limited to:

- Quality Improvement
- Epidemiology
- Pharmacy
- Environment of Care
- Risk Management
- Occupational Health Services
- Corporate Compliance
- Purchasing/Procurement
- Laboratory
- Patient Care Services
- Physicians
- Ad Hoc Members

GUIDING STATEMENTS

The _____ is committed, as a component of newly designed and redesigned activities, to promoting the safety of all patients, visitors, volunteers, health-care workers, and trainees. The organization-wide medical safety program is designed to reduce medical/health system errors and hazardous conditions by utilizing continuous improvement to support an organizational safety climate as part of an ongoing, proactive effort in response to actual occurrences.

DEFINITIONS

NEAR MISS: Any process variation that did not affect the outcome but for which a recurrence carries a significant chance of a serious adverse event.

HAZARDOUS CONDITION: Any set of circumstances (exclusive of the disease or condition for which the patient is being treated) that significantly increases the likelihood of a serious adverse outcome.

OVERVIEW

The _____ leadership, through the designation of a Medical Safety Subcommittee, promotes an organization safety climate that:

- Encourages recognition, reporting, and acknowledgement of risks to patient/visitor and employee safety and medical/healthcare errors
- Initiates/monitors actions to reduce these risks/errors
- Internally reports findings and actions taken
- Promotes nonpunitive environment for reporting and follow-up of medical errors
- Supports staff who have been involved in a medical/healthcare error
- Educates staff to assure that all members of the healthcare team participate in the program
- Assures that patients/families are informed about the results of care, including unexpected outcomes and medical/healthcare errors

A. SCOPE OF PROGRAM

1. Data from internal monitoring of patient/employee safety
   - Processes that affect a large percentage of patients/employees
   - Processes that place patients/employees at risk:
     a. If not performed well
     b. If performed when not indicated
     c. If not performed when indicated
   - Processes that have been or are likely to be problem-prone
   - The types of occurrences to be addressed include, but are not limited to, near misses and actual events related to:
     a) Patient safety
     b) Adverse drug events (medication errors and adverse drug reactions)
     c) Nosocomial infections
     d) Patient falls
     e) Pressure ulcers
     f) Transfusion reactions/blood/blood product administration
     g) Communicable disease exposures
     h) Surgical mishaps
     i) Antimicrobial resistance patterns
     j) Immunization programs

    k) Use of restraints
    l) Other patient incidents/unexpected clinical events
   m) Hazardous conditions
    n) Visitor safety
- Visitor incidents

    o) Employee safety
- Blood/body fluid exposures
- Occupational diseases
- Communicable disease exposures
- Musculoskeletal injuries
- Immunization programs
- Other employee incidents

    p) Environmental safety
- Product recalls
- Drug recalls
- Product/equipment malfunction
- Construction – Infection Control Risk Assessment
- Water quality
- Air quality
- Disaster planning
- Security incidents
- Workplace violence

2. Data from external sources, including but not limited to:
   a. Agency for Healthcare Research and Quality (AHRQ)
   b. Centers for Disease Control and Prevention (CDC)
   c. Institute for Healthcare Improvement (IHI)
   d. Institute for Safe Medication Practices (ISMP)
   e. JCAHO Standards and Sentinel Event Alerts
   f. National Forum for Healthcare Quality Measurement and Reporting (NQF)
   g. Occupational Safety and Health Administration (OSHA)
   h. Published literature

B. STRUCTURE

MEDICAL SAFETY INFRASTRUCTURE

The _____ supports a continuous improvement philosophy for medical safety, which promotes ongoing improvement of all processes relating to patient, visitor, volunteer, healthcare worker, and trainee safety. Leadership throughout the organization supports all medical safety efforts. Improvement in medical safety at the _____ is system-, hospital, and department-based. Information flow occurs as outlined in the Organizational Performance Improvement Policy. The _____ provides adequate resources for an ongoing comprehensive medical safety program.

ROLES AND RESPONSIBILITIES:

Governing Body Leadership: Final authority and responsibility for the medical safety of patients and healthcare workers at the _____ rests with its Board of Trustees. This authority is delegated to the Joint Conference Committee (JCC) for review of medical safety program activities. The JCC has empowered the hospital leadership and management teams with the responsibility for implementing performance improvement strategies in conjunction with the medical staff.

The Executive Management Team (EMT) and System Quality-Medical Safety Council (SQ-MSC): The EMT will ensure integration and assessment of medical safety needs through data collection and measurement. The EMT delegates specific responsibility for medical safety improvement efforts to the site leadership and medical staff and makes final recommendations regarding medical safety to the Board of Trustees.

The SQ-MSC established by the EMT is responsible for:
- Overseeing the efforts of the Medical Safety Subcommittee
- Structuring the flow of information to ensure appropriate reporting and communication of key issues
- Prioritizing medical safety improvement activities
- Reviewing data and information
- Allocating resources, including resources for education and training

Medical Safety Subcommittee (MSS) of the SQ-MSC: The SQ-MSC delegates medical safety improvement efforts to the MSS. The MSS is an organization-wide multidisciplinary committee with representation from all departments with responsibility for aspects of patient and employee medical safety as outlined above. The MSS responsibilities include the following:
- Initiates and develops a consistent organization-wide medical safety program and identifies the involvement of other departments
- Oversees comprehensive medical safety program to reduce adverse health events and makes recommendations for reductions in such events
- Coordinates and oversees data collection, analysis, reporting (internal and external), improvement, and follow-up activities related to medical safety
- Reviews and evaluates services of the _____ that are affected by safety/regulatory issues, identifies problems, makes recommendations for improvements, and monitors services to ensure that safety/regulatory recommendations are instituted and the desired results are obtained
- Provides interpretation and can implement policies/practices related to medical safety, in accordance with external regulatory requirements
- Proactively educates site-responsible individuals regarding medical safety issues, regulatory requirements, and new statutes/guidelines

- Serves as a resource for medical safety/regulatory issues and for the regulatory component of accrediting agencies
- Institutes monitoring programs to ensure compliance with external regulatory requirements
- Reports activities on an ongoing basis to the SQ-MSC
- Deputy Chief Quality Officer chairs the MSS

Medical Executive Committee and Medical Staff Operations Committees: The _____ Medical Executive Committee receives reports from hospital Medical Staff Operations Committees related to medical safety. Hospital medical staff is engaged in activities to measure, assess, and improve medical safety on a departmental, divisional, and system-wide basis.

(Consider applicability for systems with multiple sites)

Site Management and Site Leadership: Leaders will ensure ongoing evaluation of medical safety and support processes. In addition, leaders retain accountability for implementation and maintenance of medical safety improvement initiatives. Summaries of these activities will be reported to the local site Leadership Performance Improvement Coordinating Committee (LPICC) or committees with oversight for PI functions.

Leadership and Performance Improvement Coordinating Committees: LPICCs are site-specific, multidisciplinary, and representative of site departments and functions. Site medical safety activities will be reported to the LPICC as outlined in the Organizational Performance Improvement Policy.

Hospital Boards: Hospital Boards, when existent, are responsible for the quality improvement activities at the site. Information will flow to the Boards as outlined in the Organizational Performance Improvement Policy.

APPROACH AND METHODOLOGY

(Option: consider referring to the organization's Plan for Performance Improvement)

THE ORGANIZATION-WIDE APPROACH

The _____ maintains a system-wide approach to all medical safety improvement activities. Medical safety is the responsibility of every healthcare provider at the_____. Improvement teams are multidisciplinary whenever possible. The methodology for this approach is based on a process improvement cycle.

METHODOLOGY

1. Create a positive environment.
2. Define objectives.
3. Identify measurement characteristics.

4. Manage process variation.
5. Improve the process.

MEASUREMENT PLAN

A medical safety measurement plan is utilized to define the measure. The measurement plan defines the dimensions of performance that are important to a process or outcome, numerator, denominator, data source, benchmarks, and responsible persons.

MEDICAL SAFETY EDUCATION AND TRAINING

To support medical safety efforts and to ensure that all members of the healthcare team are involved in improving medical safety, all employees of the _____ will receive yearly education as part of performance improvement education and training. Education includes, but is not limited to, the _____'s nonpunitive approach to medical errors, responsibility to report errors and near misses when they occur, and process for reporting medical safety concerns/ medical errors. All new hires to the _____ will receive the same education and training as part of the orientation process. Ongoing education and just-in-time training will be provided to committees, groups, and individuals as necessary.

DOCUMENTATION AND COMMUNICATION

DOCUMENTATION

Documentation of measures reflects performance over time and identifies performance targets and variances. Analytical tools are used to interpret and display data. System-wide medical safety measures are compared within the organization and with external benchmarks, where available. Interpretation of data includes identification of areas for improvement as well as barriers to improvement.

REPORTING/COMMUNICATION

Reporting will occur as outlined in the Organizational Performance Improvement Policy. Data will be collected as appropriate. Trending and analysis shall occur at least quarterly, with recommendations for improvement opportunities as appropriate. The leaders of teams and committees are responsible for ensuring that medical safety activities are reported as scheduled.

CONFIDENTIALITY

To continue to fulfill the _____ commitment to medical safety, the committees must be allowed to review and evaluate medical safety information in a confidential manner. To effectively evaluate medical safety practices, confidentiality must be maintained to enable the committees to provide constructive recommendations without the fear of public disclosure.

Records, data, and knowledge collected by or for the committees for their review purposes, including committee minutes, reports, and information provided for or by legal council, shall be confidential and maintained in a confidential manner. They are protected from disclosure pursuant to one or more of the provisions of (state statutes for confidentiality provisions) and other state and federal laws. Unauthorized disclosure or duplication is absolutely prohibited.

Confidential committee and legal information will be stored in a locked file cabinet in a room that is to remain locked outside of regular business hours.

AUTHORIZATION FOR RELEASE OF CONFIDENTIAL INFORMATION

(Consider and reference state-specific guidance for confidentially)

The senior vice-president for quality, Legal Affairs, or Corporate Compliance (or designee) should be consulted prior to the release of confidential information.

1. RELEASE OF INFORMATION: (including access to and duplication of documents) may be authorized in the following manner:

   - By the chairperson of each committee to its membership and staff; or
   - By the chairperson of the committee in consultation with Corporate Compliance for the purpose of obligatory reporting in accordance with written policy or by law to another individual or entity assigned a similar review function; or
   - By the president and chief executive officer; or
   - By an executive officer of the Medical Center Board; or
   - Medical staff that the president designates in writing, to act on his/her behalf to an individual committee or other entity assigned a care-review function by the Medical Center and/or having a legitimate need to know (eg, legal counsel for the Medical Center). Records shall be maintained and disclosure made pursuant to this provision.

2. LEGAL PROCEEDINGS:

In the event of legal proceedings that seek production of committee or legal information, the president and chief executive officer or his/her designee shall be empowered and shall authorize Legal Affairs/ Corporate Compliance to review the matter and determine whether it is appropriate to release such information. If it is not appropriate to do so, then Legal Affairs/ Corporate Compliance shall authorize legal counsel to take such steps as are reasonably necessary and advisable to lawfully resist document production, including the making of motions or taking of appeals.

3. SANCTIONS FOR UNAUTHORIZED DISCLOSURE

Unauthorized disclosure of committee or legal information designated as confidential may result in:

- Progressive discipline, up to and including termination, or loss of committee membership for any hospital employees; and
- Corrective action, including loss of committee membership, reprimand, or non-reappointment for any medical staff members

In determining the sanction appropriate, the degree of inadvertence or willfulness of the disclosure, the manner of disclosure, the likelihood of recurrence, and the magnitude of harm done by the disclosure to the Medical Center activities, patients, and/or staff members will be considered.

METHOD FOR EVALUATION

The Medical Safety Program Plan, including the written plan and criteria employed in the review process, shall be reviewed and evaluated at least annually. Revisions to the Medical Safety Program Plan shall occur as appropriate in line with the findings of committee activities and new regulations/statutes and guidelines from external agencies. Documentation associated with the annual review and evaluation shall be maintained, and appropriate findings shall be reported as outlined in the Organizational Performance Improvement Policy.

Premier Safety Institute. www.premierinc.com/safety. http://www.premierinc. com/quality-safety/tools-services/safety/topics/patient_safety/downloads/16_generic_safety_plan_07-09-02.DOC . Reprinted with permission.

APPENDIX E

HOSPITAL BOARD QUALITY COMMITTEE

Overall Roles and Responsibilities

The Quality Committee is responsible for assisting the board to carry out its responsibilities for overseeing and ensuring the quality of clinical care, patient safety, and customer service provided throughout the organization.

Specific Responsibilities for clinical quality, performance improvement, patient safety, customer service, and organizational culture

1. Review and recommend to the board a multi-year Strategic Quality Plan with long-term and annual improvement targets.
2. Review and recommend to the board quality/safety-related policies and standards.
3. Approve and monitor a "dashboard" of key performance indicators compared to organizational goals and industry benchmarks. Report in a summary fashion to the full board.
4. Review sentinel events and root cause analyses; if appropriate, recommend corrective action.
5. Monitor summary reports of hospital and medical staff quality and patient safety activities. Take appropriate action with regard to negative variances and serious errors.
6. Oversee compliance with quality- and safety-related accreditation standards.
7. Engage in education on current national priorities in quality and patient safety.
8. Review and make recommendations to the board on any other matter pertaining to the quality of care, patient safety, customer service or organizational culture.

Meetings

The committee meets at least six times a year, or when necessary at the call of the committee chairperson. The meeting schedule for the committee for the following year is as follows: (meeting dates and times should be specified one year in advance.)

Annual Committee Goals

- The Quality Committee should establish goals each year specifying several areas of focus. Examples include:
- Overseeing program to reduce medication errors
- Oversight of and support for IHI Campaign to Save 5 Million Lives
- Becoming educated about how improvements in information technology could improve the quality of care and patient safety.
- Providing strong support and oversight to an initiative to improve customer service in the emergency department.

Reports

The committee will report to the board at least quarterly, including an in-depth annual quality review. Regular reports will include:
- Progress reports on committee goals
- Quality indicator report in dashboard format (including measures of clinical quality, patient safety, and customer service) (quarterly)
- Progress on major performance improvements and patient safety goals (twice a year)
- Sentinel event summary (at least quarterly)
- Customer perceptions (annual in-depth report)
- Organizational culture (annual in depth report)
- Accreditation (when received)

Bader & Associates. www.GreatBoards.org; http://www.greatboards.org/pubs/ Charter_Hospital_Board_Quality_Committee.pdf Reprinted with permission.

APPENDIX F

AHRQ Hospital Survey on Patient Culture

HOSPITAL SURVEY ON PATIENT SAFETY CULTURE

INSTRUCTIONS

This survey asks for your opinions about patient safety issues, medical error, and event reporting in your hospital and will take about 10 to 15 minutes to complete.

- An "_event_" is defined as any type of error, mistake, incident, accident, or deviation, regardless of whether or not it results in patient harm.
- "_Patient safety_" is defined as the avoidance and prevention of patient injuries or adverse events resulting from the processes of health care delivery.

SECTION A: Your Work Area/Unit

In this survey, think of your "unit" as the work area, department, or clinical area of the hospital where you spend _most of your work time or provide_ _most of your clinical services_.

What is your primary work area or unit in this hospital? Mark ONE answer by filling in the circle.

○ a. Many different hospital units/No specific unit

○ b. Medicine (non-surgical)

○ c. Surgery

○ d. Obstetrics

○ e. Pediatrics

○ f. Emergency department

○ g. Intensive care unit (any type)

○ h. Psychiatry/mental health

○ i. Rehabilitation

○ j. Pharmacy

○ k. Laboratory

○ l. Radiology

○ m. Anesthesiology

○ n. Other, please specify:

Please indicate your agreement or disagreement with the following statements about your work area/unit. Mark your answer by filling in the circle.

Think about your hospital work area/unit...	Strongly Disagree ▼	Disagree ▼	Neither ▼	Agree ▼	Strongly Agree ▼
1. People support one another in this unit	①	②	③	④	⑤
2. We have enough staff to handle the workload	①	②	③	④	⑤
3. When a lot of work needs to be done quickly, we work together as a team to get the work done	①	②	③	④	⑤
4. In this unit, people treat each other with respect	①	②	③	④	⑤
5. Staff in this unit work longer hours than is best for patient care	①	②	③	④	⑤
6. We are actively doing things to improve patient safety	①	②	③	④	⑤
7. We use more agency/temporary staff than is best for patient care	①	②	③	④	⑤
8. Staff feel like their mistakes are held against them	①	②	③	④	⑤

319

	Strongly Disagree	Disagree	Neither	Agree	Strongly Agree
9. Mistakes have led to positive changes here	①	②	③	④	⑤
10. It is just by chance that more serious mistakes don't happen around here	①	②	③	④	⑤
11. When one area in this unit gets really busy, others help out	①	②	③	④	⑤
12. When an event is reported, it feels like the person is being written up, not the problem	①	②	③	④	⑤

SECTION A: Your Work Area/Unit (continued)

Think about your hospital work area/unit...

	Strongly Disagree	Disagree	Neither	Agree	Strongly Agree
13. After we make changes to improve patient safety, we evaluate their effectiveness	①	②	③	④	⑤
14. We work in "crisis mode" trying to do too much, too quickly	①	②	③	④	⑤
15. Patient safety is never sacrificed to get more work done	①	②	③	④	⑤
16. Staff worry that mistakes they make are kept in their personnel file	①	②	③	④	⑤
17. We have patient safety problems in this unit	①	②	③	④	⑤
18. Our procedures and systems are good at preventing errors from happening	①	②	③	④	⑤

SECTION B: Your Supervisor/Manager

Please indicate your agreement or disagreement with the following statements about your immediate supervisor/manager or person to whom you directly report. Mark your answer by filling in the circle.

	Strongly Disagree	Disagree	Neither	Agree	Strongly Agree
1. My supervisor/manager says a good word when he/she sees a job done according to established patient safety procedures	①	②	③	④	⑤
2. My supervisor/manager seriously considers staff suggestions for improving patient safety	①	②	③	④	⑤
3. Whenever pressure builds up, my supervisor/manager wants us to work faster, even if it means taking shortcuts	①	②	③	④	⑤
4. My supervisor/manager overlooks patient safety problems that happen over and over	①	②	③	④	⑤

SECTION C: Communications

How often do the following things happen in your work area/unit? Mark your answer by filling in the circle.

Think about your hospital work area/unit...

	Never	Rarely	Sometimes	Most of the time	Always
1. We are given feedback about changes put into place based on event reports	①	②	③	④	⑤
2. Staff will freely speak up if they see something that may negatively affect patient care	①	②	③	④	⑤

3.	We are informed about errors that happen in this unit	①	②	③	④	⑤
4.	Staff feel free to question the decisions or actions of those with more authority	①	②	③	④	⑤
5.	In this unit, we discuss ways to prevent errors from happening again	①	②	③	④	⑤
6.	Staff are afraid to ask questions when something does not seem right	①	②	③	④	⑤

SECTION D: Frequency of Events Reported
In your hospital work area/unit, when the following mistakes happen, *how often are they reported?*
Mark your answer by filling in the circle.

	Never ▼	Rarely ▼	Some-times ▼	Most of the time ▼	Always ▼
1. When a mistake is made, but is *caught and corrected before affecting the patient*, how often is this reported?	①	②	③	④	⑤
2. When a mistake is made, but has *no potential to harm the patient*, how often is this reported?	①	②	③	④	⑤
3. When a mistake is made that *could harm the patient*, but does not, how often is this reported?	①	②	③	④	⑤

SECTION E: Patient Safety Grade
Please give your work area/unit in this hospital an overall grade on patient safety. Mark ONE answer.

O	O	O	O	O
A	**B**	**C**	**D**	**E**
Excellent	Very Good	Acceptable	Poor	Failing

SECTION F: Your Hospital
Please indicate your agreement or disagreement with the following statements about your hospital. Mark your answer by filling in the circle.

Think about your hospital…	Strongly Disagree ▼	Disagree ▼	Neither ▼	Agree ▼	Strongly Agree ▼
1. Hospital management provides a work climate that promotes patient safety	①	②	③	④	⑤
2. Hospital units do not coordinate well with each other	①	②	③	④	⑤
3. Things "fall between the cracks" when transferring patients from one unit to another	①	②	③	④	⑤
4. There is good cooperation among hospital units that need to work together	①	②	③	④	⑤
5. Important patient care information is often lost during shift changes	①	②	③	④	⑤
6. It is often unpleasant to work with staff from other hospital units	①	②	③	④	⑤

7. Problems often occur in the exchange of information across hospital units	①	②	③	④	⑤
8. The actions of hospital management show that patient safety is a top priority	①	②	③	④	⑤
9. Hospital management seems interested in patient safety only after an adverse event happens	①	②	③	④	⑤
10. Hospital units work well together to provide the best care for patients	①	②	③	④	⑤
11. Shift changes are problematic for patients in this hospital	①	②	③	④	⑤

SECTION G: Number of Events Reported

In the past 12 months, how many event reports have you filled out and submitted? Mark ONE answer.

O a. No event reports   O d. 6 to 10 event reports
O b. 1 to 2 event reports   O e. 11 to 20 event reports
O c. 3 to 5 event reports   O f. 21 event reports or more

SECTION H: Background Information

This information will help in the analysis of the survey results. Mark ONE answer by filling in the circle.

1. How long have you worked in this <u>hospital</u>?

O a. Less than 1 year   O d. 11 to 15 years
O b. 1 to 5 years   O e. 16 to 20 years
O c. 6 to 10 years   O f. 21 years or more

2. How long have you worked in your current hospital <u>work area/unit</u>?

O a. Less than 1 year   O d. 11 to 15 years
O b. 1 to 5 years   O e. 16 to 20 years
O c. 6 to 10 years   O f. 21 years or more

3. Typically, how many <u>hours per week</u> do you work in this hospital?

O a. Less than 20 hours per week   O d. 60 to 79 hours per week
O b. 20 to 39 hours per week   O e. 80 to 99 hours per week
O c. 40 to 59 hours per week   O f. 100 hours per week or more

4. What is your staff position in this hospital? Mark ONE answer that best describes your staff position.

O a. Registered Nurse
O b. Physician Assistant/Nurse Practitioner
O c. LVN/LPN
O d. Patient Care Assistant/Hospital Aide/Care Partner
O e. Attending/Staff Physician
O f. Resident Physician/Physician in Training
O g. Pharmacist

O h. Dietician
O i. Unit Assistant/Clerk/Secretary
O j. Respiratory Therapist
O k. Physical, Occupational, or Speech Therapist
O l. Technician (e.g., EKG, Lab, Radiology)
O m. Administration/Management
O n. Other, please specify:

5. In your staff position, do you typically have direct interaction or contact with patients?

O a. YES, I typically have direct interaction or contact with patients.
O b. NO, I typically do NOT have direct interaction or contact with patients.

6. How long have you worked in your current specialty or profession?

O a. Less than 1 year   O d. 11 to 15 years
O b. 1 to 5 years   O e. 16 to 20 years
O c. 6 to 10 years   O f. 21 years or more

SECTION I: Your Comments

Please feel free to write any comments about patient safety, error, or event reporting in your hospital.

7. Problems often occur in the exchange of information across hospital units	①	②	③	④	⑤
8. The actions of hospital management show that patient safety is a top priority	①	②	③	④	⑤
9. Hospital management seems interested in patient safety only after an adverse event happens	①	②	③	④	⑤
10. Hospital units work well together to provide the best care for patients	①	②	③	④	⑤
11. Shift changes are problematic for patients in this hospital	①	②	③	④	⑤

SECTION G: Number of Events Reported
In the past 12 months, how many event reports have you filled out and submitted? Mark ONE answer.

- ○ a. No event reports
- ○ b. 1 to 2 event reports
- ○ c. 3 to 5 event reports
- ○ d. 6 to 10 event reports
- ○ e. 11 to 20 event reports
- ○ f. 21 event reports or more

SECTION H: Background Information
This information will help in the analysis of the survey results. **Mark ONE answer by filling in the circle.**

1. How long have you worked in this hospital?
   - ○ a. Less than 1 year
   - ○ b. 1 to 5 years
   - ○ c. 6 to 10 years
   - ○ d. 11 to 15 years
   - ○ e. 16 to 20 years
   - ○ f. 21 years or more

2. How long have you worked in your current hospital work area/unit?
   - ○ a. Less than 1 year
   - ○ b. 1 to 5 years
   - ○ c. 6 to 10 years
   - ○ d. 11 to 15 years
   - ○ e. 16 to 20 years
   - ○ f. 21 years or more

3. Typically, how many hours per week do you work in this hospital?
   - ○ a. Less than 20 hours per week
   - ○ b. 20 to 39 hours per week
   - ○ c. 40 to 59 hours per week
   - ○ d. 60 to 79 hours per week
   - ○ e. 80 to 99 hours per week
   - ○ f. 100 hours per week or more

4. What is your staff position in this hospital? Mark ONE answer that best describes your staff position.
   - ○ a. Registered Nurse
   - ○ b. Physician Assistant/Nurse Practitioner
   - ○ c. LVN/LPN
   - ○ d. Patient Care Assistant/Hospital Aide/Care Partner
   - ○ e. Attending/Staff Physician
   - ○ f. Resident Physician/Physician in Training
   - ○ g. Pharmacist
   - ○ h. Dietician
   - ○ i. Unit Assistant/Clerk/Secretary
   - ○ j. Respiratory Therapist
   - ○ k. Physical, Occupational, or Speech Therapist
   - ○ l. Technician (e.g., EKG, Lab, Radiology)
   - ○ m. Administration/Management
   - ○ n. Other, please specify:

5. In your staff position, do you typically have direct interaction or contact with patients?
   - ○ a. YES, I typically have direct interaction or contact with patients.
   - ○ b. NO, I typically do NOT have direct interaction or contact with patients.

6. How long have you worked in your current specialty or profession?
   - ○ a. Less than 1 year
   - ○ b. 1 to 5 years
   - ○ c. 6 to 10 years
   - ○ d. 11 to 15 years
   - ○ e. 16 to 20 years
   - ○ f. 21 years or more

SECTION I: Your Comments

Please feel free to write any comments about patient safety, error, or event reporting in your hospital.

APPENDIX G

Checklist for Patient Safety and JCAHO Standards

Patient Safety Program/Plan	Done	Pending
Designated individual or individuals (team) To coordinate and oversee the patient safety program		
Scope of program Definition of the scope of the program activities		
Safety culture Statements that focus of program is to improve patient safety processes, not take punitive measures against staff who commit errors		
Program components Description of how organization has integrated safety-related elements into organization-wide effort, including participation from appropriate departments and services		
Adverse Events (medical errors) Plan provides for:		
Procedures for immediate response to medical/health care errors Response procedures are in place for:		
Care of the affected patient(s)		
Containment of risk to others		
Preservation of factual information for subsequent analysis		
Definition of the systems in place for internal and external reporting of information relating to medical/healthcare errors		
Definition of mechanisms in place for responding to unexpected clinical events including sentinel events (SE) (eg, root cause analysis [(RCA]) or other mechanisms for conducting proactive risk-reduction activities		
Description of procedures for support of staff who have been involved in an SE		

(continued)

Patient Safety Program/Plan	Done	Pending
Annual report to governing body: Summary of healthcare error occurrences and actions taken to improve patient safety Report includes:		
Response to actual occurrences and outcomes		
Proactive patient safety improvement activities and outcomes		
SE policy and procedures :		
Definition of a sentinel event and a "near miss"		
Definition includes events listed by JCAHO as sentinel events		
Definition is approved by organizational leaders, medical staff		
Definition is communicated throughout the organization		
Reporting of SEs within the organization and to external agencies		
Process for conducting RCA that focuses on process and system factors		
Policy addresses required documentation for a risk-reduction strategy and action plan, including measuring effectiveness of action plan; system improvements to reduce risk		
Performance improvement		
Proactive risk assessment of *one high-risk* process on annual basis Proactive risk assessment process must show:		
Selection process for proactive risk assessment and include information from JCAHO *SE Alerts* (see www. JCAHO.org listing most frequently occurring types of sentinel events and patient safety risk factors)		
Assessment of the intended and actual implementation of the process to identify the steps in the process where there is, or may be, undesirable variation		
Identification of the possible effects on patients and the seriousness of the possible effects for each identified variation		
RCA conducted for most critical variations that could or do occur with selected process		

Patient Safety Program/Plan	Done	Pending
Redesign of the process and/or underlying system(s) to minimize the risk of the variation (failure mode) or to protect patients from the effects of the variation		
Testing and implementation of the redesigned process		
Identification and implementation of measures of the effectiveness of the redesigned process		
Implementation of strategy for maintaining effectiveness of redesigned process over time		
New processes, functions, or services designed or redesigned Must consider potential risks to patient safety		
Inclusion of information related to patient safety and unanticipated adverse events (AE) affecting patients in process planning for performance improvement priorities. The data include:		
Processes that affect a large percentage of patients		
Processes that place patients at risk if not performed well, if performed when not indicated, or if not performed when indicated		
Processes that have been or are likely to be problem-prone		
Evidence of participation of the organization's leaders/directors in the program to measure, assess, and improve performance and patient safety effectively and on a continuous basis		
Evidence of coordination/ integration of patient care and patient safety as an interdisciplinary approach		
Measurement and analysis		
Actual processes identified as error-prone or high-risk regarding patient safety Critical steps in at least one *actual* high-risk process are measured and analyzed on an ongoing basis		
Corrective actions for significant variation identified in error-prone or high-risk processes		
Resource allocation		
Allocation of adequate resources for measuring, assessing, and improving patient safety		
Assignment of adequate personnel (number and competence) to participate in activities to improve patient safety		

(*continued*)

Patient Safety Program/Plan	Done	Pending
Allocation of adequate time for personnel to participate in activities to improve patient safety		
Provision of information systems and data management process for improvement of patient safety		
Leadership assessment of the adequacy of allocation of resources Human, information, physical, and financial resources to support safety improvement		
Leadership measurement and assessment Measure effectiveness of individuals' contributions to improving patient safety by:		
Objectives: Setting measurable objectives for improving patient safety Data collection: Gathering information to assess effectiveness in improving patient safety Criteria: Using pre-established objective process criteria to assess their effectiveness Conclusions: Drawing conclusions from data; implementing improvement in activities Evaluation: Evaluating performance in supporting *sustained* improvement		
Opinions, needs, and perceptions of risks to patients Suggestions for improving patient safety from patients, families, staff are assessed		
Information about staff willingness to report medical/healthcare errors Information is collected and assessed		
Information about barriers to effective communication Efforts are made to reduce barriers and improve communication among caregivers		
Information analysis of major adverse events or medical errors Evidence that intensive analysis is carried out if the following occur:		
Confirmed transfusion reactions Significant adverse drug reactions Significant medication errors and hazardous conditions Major discrepancies or patterns of discrepancies between preoperative and postoperative diagnosis Significant adverse events associated with anesthesia use		

Patient Safety Program/Plan	Done	Pending
Knowledge-based systems		
Processes for ensuring accurate, timely, and complete verbal and written communication among caregivers and others involved with the utilization of data		
Knowledge-based information systems, resources, and services support information related to reducing risk to patients		
Knowledge-based information consists of current authoritative print and nonprint information resources that include successful practices		
Patient and family		
Disclosure mechanism to inform patients and, when appropriate, their families about significant unanticipated outcomes Mechanism (policy or plan component) should include:		
Definition of significant unanticipated outcomes Responsibility of licensed independent practitioner (LIP) to inform patient/family or designee Determination of level of licensure approved by facility and medical staff as LIPs designee		
Patient education includes education regarding:		
The patient's role in helping to facilitate the safe delivery of care The patient's/family's responsibility for reporting perceived risk to their care		
Communication and transfer of information Evidence that throughout *all* phases of care (entry, assessment, diagnosis, care planning, treatment, and transfer/discharge), communication and transfer of information among healthcare professionals provides for a seamless, safe, and effective process		
Orientation process For staff and volunteers includes specific job-related aspects of patient safety		
Ongoing education and training: Improve staff competence Support an interdisciplinary approach to patient care Provide reinforcement of the need and ways to report medical/healthcare errors		

(continued)

Patient Safety Program/Plan	Done	Pending
Approval of safety program by medical staff, administration, and governing body Whether facility develops and functions according to a specific Patient Safety Program Plan, utilizes various policies and procedures to outline program components, or incorporates patient safety components into an existing plan, the patient safety process that outlines your Patient Safety Program must be approved by the medical staff, the organization's administration, and the governing body.		

Premier Safety Institute, Inc. www.permireinc.com/safety. http://www.premierinc. com/quality-safety/tools-services/safety/topics/patient_safety/downloads.jsp www. Reprinted with permission.

THANK YOU FOR COMPLETING THIS SURVEY.

APPENDIX H

Organizational Diagrams

Figure 1.

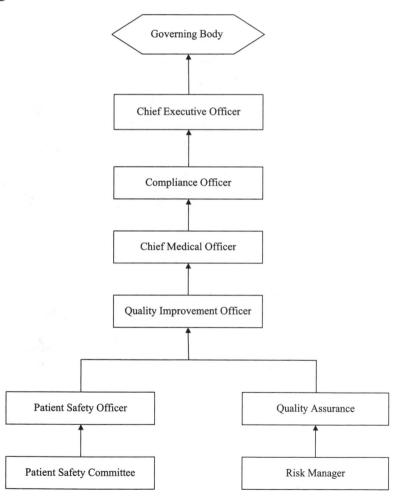

Figure 2.

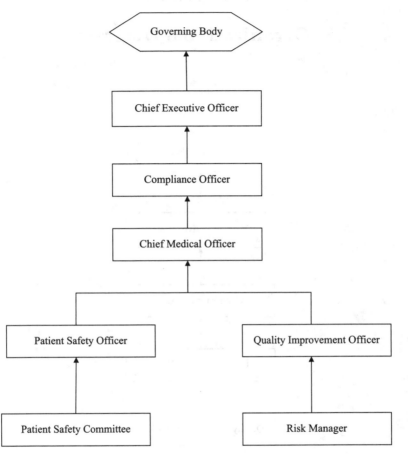

Figure 3.

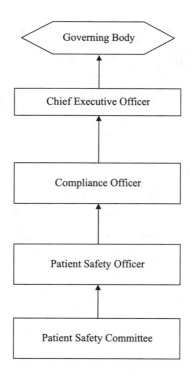

Figure 4.

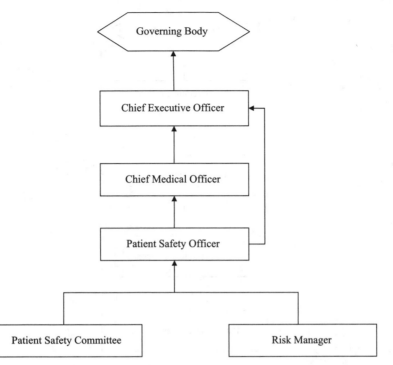

Figure 5.

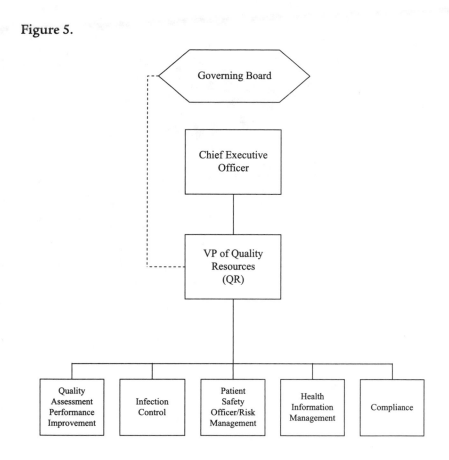

APPENDIX I

Chief Patient Safety and Quality Officer

Position Description

Description

The Chief Patient Safety and Quality Officer (CPSQO) working in partnership with [_____] administrative and medical staff leadership provides leadership in the development of a culture of safety and the measurement of the quality of care identifying opportunities and strategies for performance improvement (PI).

Directs and coordinates accreditation, policy and regulatory affairs initiatives for [_____], serves as the liaison with JCAHO, state and other pertinent regulatory agencies.

Duties and Responsibilities

Initiates and oversees the development of a comprehensive safety/quality/performance improvement program inclusive of the analysis and trending of data related to initiatives.

Provides strategic oversight for patient safety and quality committees with accountability for distribution of organizational communication vertically and horizontally within [_____], as appropriate.

Provides overall direction necessary to ensure that clinical services are provided in accordance with standards established through state and federal regulations and JCAHO accreditation standards, including the National Patient Safety Goals, and that clinical services are evidence-based.

Provides strategic oversight of proactive and reactive patient safety activities including root cause analyses, failure mode effects analyses and Sentinel Event Alerts in regards to the facilitation of process, planning, implementation and evaluation of effectiveness of process changes.

Prepares annual reports to and seeks consultation from the [_____] Board of Trustees regarding patient safety and performance improvement program, and other reports as requested.

Assesses entity compliance with accreditation standards and regulations related to clinical care in collaboration with entity leadership and staff, identifies areas of vulnerability and directs the development of strategies to enhance compliance.

In conjunction with the medical staff and system leadership, directs and coordinates safety/quality/performance improvement initiatives.

In collaboration with clinical staff and service chiefs, participates in the monitoring, reporting, and improvement activities related to clinical guidelines, health care quality/safety/initiatives, accreditation and regulatory requirements.

Fosters and maintains collaborative relationships within [_____] and with external agencies, purchasers, and stakeholders related to quality/performance initiatives.

Proactively educates leadership and staff regarding regulatory issues, new statutes/guidelines, and safety/quality/PI activities.

Regularly communicates PI and quality/safety activities to leadership and staff.

Manages the departmental budget effectively and determines fiscal requirements and prepares budgetary recommendations.

Performs staff performance evaluations establishing a development plan for each employee.

Performs other related duties incidental to the work described herein.

Required Qualifications at this Level

Experience: A minimum of 5 years of direct patient care experience as a healthcare professional. Three years in accreditation/regulatory affairs/performance improvement/patient safety in healthcare. Five years managerial experience.

Education: Advanced degree in a health related field.

Knowledge, Skills: Knowledge of accreditation standards, health care regulations, performance improvement, patient safety and policy formulation.

And Abilities: Effective organizational, oral and written communication skills, problem solving, program development, computer skills, strong leadership, and team building skills.

Ability to work with a variety of disciplines and levels of staff across departments and the health system is required.

Reporting

The Chief Patient Safety and Quality Officer maintains a direct reporting relationship with the Chief Executive Officer (CEO). The CEO carries final authority in all matters. The CPSQO maintains collaborative working relationships throughout the hospital and medical staff.

APPENDIX J

A Framework for a Root-Cause Analysis and Action Plan in Response to a Sentinel Event

Level of Analysis		Questions	Findings	Root Cause?	Ask "Why?"	Take Action
What happened?	Sentinel Event	What are the details of the event? (Brief description)				
		When did the event occur? (Date, day of week, time)				
		What area/service was impacted?				
Why did it happen?	The process or activity in which the event occurred.	What are the steps in the process, as designed? (A flow diagram may be helpful here)				
What were the most proxi-mate factors? (Typically "special cause" variation)		What steps were involved in (contributed to) the event?				
	Human factors	What human factors were relevant to the outcome?				
	Equipment factors	How did the equipment performance affect the outcome?				

339

Controllable environmental factors	What factors directly affected the outcome?			
Uncontrollable external factors	Are they truly beyond the organization's control?			
Other	Are there any other factors that have directly influenced this outcome?			
	What other areas or services are impacted			

This template is provided as an aid in organizing the steps in a root cause analysis. Not all possibilities and questions will apply in every case, and there may be others that will emerge in the course of the analysis. However, all possibilities and questions should be fully considered in your quest for "root cause" and risk reduction.

As an aid to avoiding "loose ends," the three columns on the right are provided to be checked off for later reference:

- "Root cause?" should be answered "yes" or "No" for each finding. A root cause is typically a finding related to a process or system that has a potential for redesign to reduce risk. If a particular finding that is relevant to the event is not a root cause, be sure that it is addressed later in the analysis with a "Why?" question. Each finding that is identified as a root cause should be considered for an action and addressed in the action plan.

- "Ask 'Why?'" should be checked off whenever it is reasonable to ask why the particular finding occurred (or didn't occur when it should have) – in other words, to drill down further. Each item checked in this column should be addressed later in the analysis with a "Why?" question. It is expected that any significant findings that are not identified as root causes themselves have "roots".

- "Take action?" should be checked for any finding that can reasonably be considered for a risk reduction strategy. Each item checked in this column should be addressed later in the action plan. It will be helpful to write the number of the associated Action Item on page 3 in the "Take Action?" column for each of the findings that requires an action.

Level of Analysis	Questions	Findings	Root Cause?	Ask "Why?"	Take Action
Why did that happen? What systems and processes underlie those proximate factors? (Common cause variation here may lead to special cause variation in dependent processes)	Human Resources issues				
	To what degree are staff properly qualified and currently competent for their responsibilities?				
	How did actual staffing compare with ideal levels?				
	What are the plans for dealing with contingencies that would tend to reduce effective staffing levels?				
	To what degree is staff performance in the operant process(es) addressed?				
	How can orientation and in-service training be improved?				

Level of Analysis	Questions	Findings	Root Cause?	Ask "Why?"	Take Action
Information management issues	To what degree is all necessary information available when needed? Accurate? Complete? Unambiguous?				
	To what degree is communication among participants adequate?				
Environmental management issues	To what degree was the physical environment appropriate for the processes being carried out?				
	What systems are in place to identify environmental risks?				
	What emergency and failure-mode responses have been planned and tested?				

Leadership issues: - Corporate culture	To what degree is the culture conducive to risk identification and reduction?			
- Encouragement of communication	What are the barriers to communication of potential risk factors?			
- Clear communication of priorities	To what degree is the prevention of adverse outcomes communicated as a high priority? How?			
Uncontrollable factors	What can be done to protect against the effects of these uncontrollable factors?			

(Continued)

Action Plan	Risk Reduction Strategies	Measures of Effectiveness
For each of the findings identified in the analysis as needing an action, indicate the planned action expected, implementation date and associated measure of effectiveness. OR. …	Action Item #1:	
If after consideration of such a finding, a decision is made not to implement an associated risk reduction strategy, indicate the rationale for not taking action at this time.	Action Item #2:	
Check to be sure that the selected measure will provide data that will permit assessment of the effectiveness of the action.	Action Item #3:	
Consider whether pilot testing of a planned improvement should be conducted.	Action Item #4:	
Improvements to reduce risk should ultimately be implemented in all areas where applicable, not just where the event occurred. Identify where the improvements will be implemented.	Action Item #5:	
	Action Item #6:	
	Action Item #7:	
	Action Item #8:	

Cite any books or journal articles that were considered in developing this analysis and action plan:

© The Joint Commission, 2008. Reprinted with permission.

APPENDIX K

VHA Directive—Disclosure of Adverse Events to Patients

Department of Veterans Affairs
Veterans Health Administration
Washington, DC 20420

VHA DIRECTIVE 2005-049

October 27, 2005

DISCLOSURE OF ADVERSE EVENTS TO PATIENTS

1. PURPOSE: This Veterans Health Administration (VHA) Directive provides policy pertaining exclusively to the disclosure of adverse events related to clinical care to patients or their representatives. *NOTE: Information pertaining to adverse events in research can be found in* <u>VHA Handbook 1200.5</u> *and* <u>VHA Handbook 1058.1</u>.

2. BACKGROUND

a. VHA facilities and individual VHA providers have an obligation to disclose adverse events to patients who have been harmed in the course of their care, including cases where the harm may not be obvious or severe, or where the harm may only be evident in the future. The patient is free to involve family members in the disclosure process. *NOTE: If the patient is deceased, incapacitated, or otherwise unable to take part in a process of adverse event disclosure, the process needs to involve the patient's representative and anyone who is designated by the representative.*

b. Disclosure of adverse events to patients or their representatives is consistent with VHA core values of trust, respect, excellence, commitment, and compassion. Providers have an ethical obligation to be honest with their patients. Honestly discussing the difficult truth that an adverse event has occurred demonstrates respect for the patient, professionalism, and a commitment to improving care.

c. Clinicians and organizational leaders must work together to ensure that appropriate disclosure to patients or their representatives is a routine part of the response to a harmful or potentially harmful adverse event. Telling patients or their representatives about harmful or potentially harmful adverse events is never easy, and it must be done with skill and tact.

d. Disclosure of adverse events and the reporting of adverse events are separate requirements. Actions taken to disclose adverse events to patients according to this Directive in no way obviate the need to report adverse events (and close calls) as required under VHA Handbook 1050.1. Internal reporting through the adverse event and close call reports are protected from disclosure under Title 38 United States Code (U.S.C.) Section 5705. Records protected under 38 U.S.C. Section 5705, that is, quality management and safety activities records, may not be subsequently used as the source of information communicated in the disclosure of an adverse event. The information communicated must come from those involved in the adverse event and from factual information in the patient's medical record.

NOTE: This Directive is consistent with the Joint Commission on Accreditation of Healthcare Organizations (JCAHO) requirement that hospitalized patients and their families be told of "unanticipated outcomes" of care (Standard - Ethics, Rights, and Responsibilities (RI) 2.90,

THIS VHA DIRECTIVE EXPIRES OCTOBER 31, 2010

2005). JCAHO requires that clinicians and health care organizations inform patients and families of adverse events.

e. Despite the general obligation to disclose adverse events to patients, there are some legal restrictions on the information that can be shared:

(1) Confidentiality statutes and regulations, such as the Privacy Act and the Health Insurance Portability and Accountability Act (HIPAA) Privacy Rule, limit disclosure of any record containing a patient's personal information to others without the patient's authorization or other legal authority. *NOTE: The patient's personal representative is authorized to have access to the patient's protected health information except as noted in this subparagraph and subparagraph 2e(2).*

(2) Under 38 U.S.C. Section 7332, VHA may not disclose information related to the patient's treatment for substance abuse (including alcohol), sickle cell anemia disease, or infection with the Human Immunodeficiency Virus (HIV) to others even after a patient's death without a "special authorization" or other exception. Questions about release of such information in the case of an adverse event are to be referred to the facility's Privacy Officer. *NOTE: Consultation with VHA's Privacy Officer may also be necessary.*

(3) Under 38 U.S.C. Section 5705, VHA may not communicate to patients, or their representatives, information that is obtained from documentation of certain quality management activities, such as root cause analyses or patient safety registry records. Rather, the information communicated must come from those involved in the adverse event and from factual information in the patient's medical record. *NOTE: Specific questions regarding sources of information that may not be disclosed or released to the patient or representative may be found in VHA Handbook 1605.1. Other guidance is available from VHA's Privacy Officer.*

f. Definitions

(1) **Adverse Event.** An adverse event is any untoward incident, therapeutic misadventure, iatrogenic injury, or other undesirable occurrence directly associated with care or services provided within the jurisdiction of a medical center, outpatient clinic, or other VHA facility.

(2) **Disclosure of Adverse Events.** For the purpose of this Directive, the phrase "disclosure of adverse events" refers to the forthright and empathetic discussion of clinically significant facts between providers and/or other VHA personnel and patients or their representatives about the occurrence of an adverse event that resulted in patient harm, or could result in harm in the foreseeable future. VA recognizes two types of disclosure of adverse events:

(a) <u>Clinical Disclosure of Adverse Events.</u> An informal process for informing patients or their representatives of harmful adverse events related to the patient's care. In a clinical disclosure, one or more members of the clinical team provides factual information to the extent it is known, expresses concern for the patient's welfare, and reassures the patient or representative that steps are being taken to investigate the situation, remedy any injury, and prevent further harm. The clinical disclosure of adverse events needs to be considered a routine part of clinical care, and needs to be made by the attending or senior practitioner, or designee.

(b) <u>Institutional Disclosure of Adverse Events.</u> In cases resulting in serious injury or death, or those involving potential legal liability, a more formal process is needed. This process is called institutional disclosure of adverse events. In an institutional disclosure the patient or representative and any family members designated by the patient or representative are invited to meet with institutional leaders and others, as appropriate. An apology is made, and information about compensation and procedures available to request compensation is provided, when appropriate. Additional guidance on what must be disclosed, when and how is provided in Attachment A. Documentation of institutional disclosure using the Computerized Patient Record System (CPRS) template is mandatory (see Att. B).

(3) **Patient's Personal Representative.** Representatives of the individual are any person(s) who, under applicable law, has authority to act on behalf of the individual when making decisions related to health care or to act on behalf of a deceased individual. The personal representative of an individual has the ability to exercise the individual's rights. A personal representative for the purposes of this handbook does not necessarily equate to a surrogate for the informed consent process (see Title 38 Code of Federal Regulations (CFR) §17.32(e) for authorized surrogates for informed consent; see VHA Handbook 1605.1 for details on personal representatives).

3. POLICY: It is VHA Policy that each medical center develop and establish a policy, by April 1, 2006, to ensure health care providers communicate adverse events openly and promptly with their patients, and/or the patients' representatives.

4. ACTION

a. **The Veterans Integrated Service Network (VISN) Director.** The VISN Director, or designee, is responsible for:

(1) Promoting an ethical health care environment in which appropriate disclosure of adverse events becomes routine practice.

(2) Ensuring that a collaborative relationship between Regional Counsel and VA medical center staff is established to ensure appropriate and timely disclosure of adverse events to patients.

b. **Facility Director.** The facility Director is responsible for:

(1) Promoting an ethical health care environment in which appropriate disclosure of adverse events becomes routine practice.

(2) Ensuring that a local facility policy, based on this national policy, is developed by April 1, 2006.

(3) Ensuring that clinical staff are aware of this Directive and are implementing it. *NOTE: Practitioners are encouraged to confer with the local ethics consultation service, their Service Chief, Regional Counsel, or Risk Manager to clarify any concerns about how best to communicate this information and what adverse events are applicable to the disclosure of adverse event process.*

(4) Ensuring that staff members involved in adverse events and subsequent disclosure processes are provided with adequate support systems and for ensuring that staff members are aware of them.

(5) Ensuring that harmful adverse events are appropriately disclosed in collaboration with the Chief of Staff, Risk Manager, and the treatment team. Appropriate disclosure includes:

(a) Ensuring that as part of the disclosure process, patients or their representatives are offered appropriate options, such as arrangements for a second opinion, additional monitoring, expediting clinical consultations, bereavement support, or whatever might be appropriate depending on the adverse event.

(b) Ensuring that patients or their representatives are made aware of their rights under 38 U.S.C. Section 1151, made aware of the Tort Claim process, and provided information concerning where to obtain assistance in filling out the necessary forms.

(6) Ensuring that harmful adverse events are documented in CPRS.

(a) Institutional disclosure of adverse events must be documented in CPRS utilizing the "Disclosure of Adverse Event Note" template (see Att. B). Specific documentation in CPRS is not required for all clinical disclosures, as clinical disclosure is considered a part of routine care; however, for significant adverse events, it is appropriate to document the clinical disclosure of the adverse event in the template or a progress note.

(b) In cases requiring reporting, documentation such as the report of contact or incident report may be kept in some other file at the facility's discretion and entitled "Adverse Event and Close Call Report." This information must not be retrieved by patient identifier and must be identified by a case number.

NOTE: The Adverse Event and Close Call Report is protected under 38 U.S.C. Section 5705.

(c) Documenting information in records protected under 38 U.S.C. Section 5705 should never be done to shield information to which a patient is entitled. Likewise, the fact that information may be documented in records protected under 38 U.S.C. Section 5705 does not mean that the identical information, documented in CPRS, cannot be retrieved by patients.

c. **Risk Manager.** The Risk Manager is responsible for:

(1) Immediately notifying the Chief of Staff about the discovery of a significant adverse event.

(2) Establishing a regular dialogue with Regional Counsel and requesting that Regional Counsel educate providers about the legal dimensions of institutional disclosure of adverse events, its documentation, and its relationship to the Federal Tort Claims Act.

5. REFERENCES

a. American Society for Healthcare Risk Management of the American Hospital Association. "Perspective on Disclosure of Unanticipated Outcome Information," April 2001.

b. American Society for Healthcare Risk Management of the American Hospital Association. "Disclosure of Unanticipated Events: The Next Step In Better Communication With Patients," May 2003.

c. American Society for Healthcare Risk Management of the American Hospital Association. "Disclosure of Unanticipated Events: Creating An Effective Patient Communication Policy," November 2003.

d. American Society for Healthcare Risk Management of the American Hospital Association. "Communication: What Works Now and What Can Work Even Better," February 2004.

e. JCAHO Accreditation Manual for Hospitals, Ethics, Rights and Responsibilities, RI 2.90, 2005.

f. JCAHO Accreditation Manual for Hospitals, Leadership Standards, LD 4.40, 2005.

g. VA Handbook 6300.4, Procedures for Processing Requests for Records Subject to the Privacy Act.

h. VHA Handbook 1050.1, VHA National Patient Safety Improvement Handbook.

i. VHA Handbook 1004.1, VHA Informed Consent for Clinical Treatments and Procedures.

j. VHA Handbook 1605.1 Privacy and Release of Information.

k. VHA National Ethics Committee, Disclosing Adverse Events to Patients, March 2003.

l. Andrews, Lori B., Carol Stocking, Thomas Krizek, et al, "An alternative strategy for studying adverse events in medical care." The Lancet. Volume 349:313–7, February 1, 1997.

m. Kraman, Steve S. and Ginny Hamm, "Risk Management: Extreme Honesty May Be the Best Policy," Annals of Internal Medicine. Volume 131:963–7, December 1. 1999.

n. Levinson, Wendy, Debra L. Roter, John P. Mullooly, et al., "Physician-Patient Communication: The Relationship With Malpractice Claims Among Primary Care Physicians and Surgeons," Journal of American Medical Association. Volume 277:553–9, February 19, 1997.

o. Wu, Albert W., "Handling Hospital Errors: Is Disclosure the Best Defense?" Annals of Internal Medicine. Volume 131:970–2, December 21, 1999.

p. Wu, Albert W., et al., "To Tell the Truth: Ethical and Practical Issues in Disclosing Medical Mistakes to Patients," The Journal of General Internal Medicine. Volume 12:770–5, December 1997.

6. FOLLOW-UP RESPONSIBILITY: The Deputy Under Secretary for Health for Operations and Management (10N) and the National Center for Ethics in Health Care (10E) are jointly responsible for this Directive. Questions about operational issues may be addressed to (202) 273-5852. Questions about the ethical content may be addressed to (202) 501-0364.

7. RESCISSION: None. This VHA Directive expires October 31, 2010.

Jonathan B. Perlin, MD, PhD, MSHA, FACP
Under Secretary for Health

DISTRIBUTION:　　CO:　　E-mailed 11/02/05
　　　　　　　　　　FLD:　　VISN, MA, DO, OC, OCRO, and 200　E-mailed
　　　　　　　　　　　　　　11/02/05

VHA DIRECTIVE 2005–049
October 27, 2005

ATTACHMENT A

WHAT ADVERSE EVENTS WARRANT DISCLOSURE?
WHEN SHOULD DISCLOSURE OF AN ADVERSE EVENT OCCUR?
HOW SHOULD ADVERSE EVENTS BE COMMUNICATED?

1. WHAT ADVERSE EVENTS WARRANT DISCLOSURE?

a. Patients and/or their representatives must be informed of the <u>probable</u> or <u>definite</u> occurrence of any adverse event that has resulted in, or is expected to result in, harm to the patient, including the following:

(1) Adverse events that have had or are expected to have a clinical effect on the patient that is perceptible to either the patient or the health care team. For example, if a patient is mistakenly given a dose of furosemide (a diuretic that dramatically increases urine output), disclosure is required because a perceptible effect is expected to occur.

(2) Adverse events that necessitate a change in the patient's care. For example, a medication error that necessitates close observation, extra blood tests, extra hospital days, or follow-up visits that would otherwise not be required, or a surgical procedure that necessitates further (corrective) surgery.

(3) Adverse events with a known risk of serious future health consequences, even if the likelihood of that risk is extremely small. For example, accidental exposure of a patient to a toxin associated with a rare, but recognized serious long-term effect (e.g., HIV infection or increased incidence of cancer).

(4) Adverse events that require providing a treatment or procedure without the patient's consent. For example, if an adverse event occurs while a patient is under anesthesia, necessitating a deviation from the procedure the patient expected, the adverse event needs to be disclosed. Patients have a fundamental right to be informed about what is done to them and why.

b. Disclosure of other adverse events is optional and at the discretion of the providers involved. Cases need to be considered individually and in relation to the specific circumstances.

c. Disclosure of "close calls" to patients is also discretionary, but is advisable at times, such as when the patient or family becomes aware that something out of the ordinary has occurred. For example, a nurse sets a patient up for a blood transfusion and, discovering that the patient is about to receive the wrong unit of blood, abruptly stops the transfusion just before the blood enters the patient's vein. The patient deserves an explanation, even if this would not be considered a clinical disclosure of adverse events. ***NOTE:*** *Although the disclosure of a close call to the patient is optional, its reporting under <u>VHA Handbook 1050.1</u> is required.)*

2. WHEN SHOULD DISCLOSURE OF AN ADVERSE EVENT OCCUR?

Optimal timing of disclosure of adverse events varies with the specific circumstances of the case. If a patient needs urgent treatment to minimize injuries resulting from an adverse event, clinical disclosure must occur quickly. If immediate corrective action is not required, disclosure may be delayed, but only long enough to give staff members time to collect preliminary information and plan the best way to disclose. Clinical disclosure of adverse events needs to occur within 24 hours of a practitioner's discovery of the adverse event. Institutional disclosure of adverse events, when necessary, needs to take place as soon as possible (generally within 24 hours, but no more than 72 hours) after a practitioner's discovery of the event. For patients who are aware of, or suspect, an adverse event, more time prior to disclosure increases the chance that patients will think information is being deliberately withheld.

3. HOW SHOULD ADVERSE EVENTS BE COMMUNICATED?

a. Disclosure of an adverse event needs to occur in an appropriate setting and be done face-to-face. The location needs to be a quiet, private place and adequate time needs to be set aside, with no interruptions.

b. In general, communication about the adverse event needs to be done through a clinical disclosure of adverse events, when one or more members of the clinical team provides preliminary factual information to the extent it is known, expresses concern for the patient's welfare, and reassures the patient or representative that steps are being taken to investigate the situation, remedy any injury, and prevent further harm. Social workers, chaplains, patient advocate, or other staff may be present to help the patient or representative cope with the news and to offer support, if needed. The patient's treating practitioner is responsible for determining who shall communicate this information.

c. Sometimes, given the nature, likelihood, and severity of injury, and the degree of risk for legal liability, there will be a need for institutional disclosure of adverse events either instead of, or in addition to, clinical disclosure. Institutional disclosure includes the following elements:

(1) Institutional Leaders (e.g., the Chief of Staff or facility Director) invite the patient or personal representative to meet for an Institutional Disclosure of Adverse Event Conference. Institutional leaders may only invite the representative if he or she is involved in the patient's care (and the patient does not object), or the representative is the personal representative as outlined in VHA Handbook 1605.1. *NOTE: The facility Risk Manager, treating physician, or other VHA personnel deemed appropriate, may be included in this conference at the discretion of facility leadership.*

(2) Institutional disclosure of adverse events should not take place until organizational leaders, including, as appropriate, the facility Director, Chief of Staff, and members of the treatment team, have conferred with Regional Counsel and addressed what is to be communicated, by whom and how.

(3) Any request by a patient or personal representative to bring an attorney must be honored, but may influence whether providers will participate.

(4) The Risk Manager or organizational leaders need to engage in ongoing communication with the patient or personal representative to keep them apprised, as appropriate, of information that emerges from the investigation of the facts.

NOTE: If the patient is not capable of understanding the disclosure of adverse event, and the patient does not have a personal representative as defined in VHA Handbook 1605.1, the facility may make the institutional disclosure to a family member involved in the patient's care. Consult the facility's or VHA's Privacy Office for additional guidance.

(5) Institutional disclosure of adverse events must include:

(a) An apology including a complete explanation of the facts.

(b) An outline of treatment options.

(c) Arrangements for a second opinion, additional monitoring, expediting clinical consultations, bereavement support, or whatever might be appropriate depending on the adverse event.

(d) Notification that the patient or representative has the option of obtaining outside legal advice for further guidance.

(e) After complete investigation of the facts, the patient or representative is to be given information about compensation under Title 38 United States Code (U.S.C.) Section 1151 and the Federal Tort Claims Act claims processes, including information about procedures available to request compensation and where and how to obtain assistance in filing forms. In the event that the investigation is not complete, information about compensation may be given based on the current understanding of the facts or information may be deferred until the investigation is competed. There should be no assurance that compensation will be granted, as the adverse event may not give rise to and meet legal criteria for compensation under 38 U.S.C. Section 1151 and the Federal Tort Claims Act.

(f) If a patient or personal representative asks whether an investigation will be conducted and whether the patient or representative will be told of the results of an investigation, the patient or representative is to be informed that only the results of an administrative board of investigation (AIB) may be released.

ATTACHMENT B

VHA DIRECTIVE 2005–049
October 27, 2005

DISCLOSURE OF ADVERSE EVENT TEMPLATE

APPENDIX L

Recommended Elements of a Disclosure Policy

The Disclosure Process

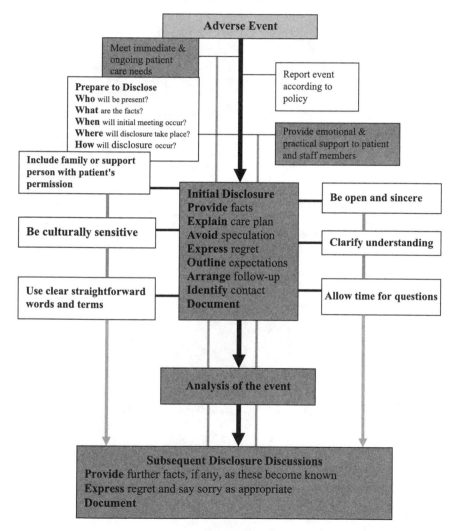

Adverse Event

Meet immediate & ongoing patient care needs

Prepare to Disclose
Who will be present?
What are the facts?
When will initial meeting occur?
Where will disclosure take place?
How will disclosure occur?

Report event according to policy

Provide emotional & practical support to patient and staff members

Include family or support person with patient's permission

Be culturally sensitive

Use clear straightforward words and terms

Initial Disclosure
Provide facts
Explain care plan
Avoid speculation
Express regret
Outline expectations
Arrange follow-up
Identify contact
Document

Be open and sincere

Clarify understanding

Allow time for questions

Analysis of the event

Subsequent Disclosure Discussions
Provide further facts, if any, as these become known
Express regret and say sorry as appropriate
Document

APPENDIX M

Recommended Elements of a Disclosure Policy

1. **Policy Statement/Objectives**—a positively worded statement that sets out what the policy is, when it applies, and what it is intended to do.
2. **Definitions of Key Terms** in the policy, particular to your state or organization
3. **Provision for Patient Support**—list supports and resources
4. **Provision for Healthcare Provider Support and Education**—list supports and resources
5. **The Disclosure Process, outlined with the necessary steps**
   a. Threshold for Disclosure—a brief statement of what warrants disclosure and a definition of the levels of severity/harm as applicable to an organization
   b. Preparing to disclose
   c. Who should disclose and the participants involved
   d. When should disclosure take place
   e. Where should disclosure take place: setting and location—give examples of private, comfortable, and interruption-free areas
   f. What should be disclosed—the facts and applicable legal requirements and limitations
   g. How should disclosure be communicated—initial and subsequent disclosure that includes expressing regret and/or saying sorry as appropriate
   h. What should be documented
6. **Provision for Particular Circumstances**—general and applicable to your organization

APPENDIX N

Checklist for Disclosure Process

☐ The immediate patient care needs are met
☐ Ensure patient, staff and other patients are protected from immediate harm

DISCLOSURE PROCESS PLAN

☐ Gather existing facts
☐ Establish who will be present and who will lead the discussion
☐ Set when the initial discussion will occur
☐ Formulate what will be said and how the disclosure will be communicated
☐ Locate a private area to hold disclosure meeting, free of interruptions
☐ Be aware of your emotions and seek support if necessary
☐ Anticipate patient's emotions and ensure support is available including who the patient chooses to be part of the discussion such as family, friends or religious representatives
☐ Contact your organization's support services for disclosure if uncertain on how to proceed

DISCLOSURE DISCUSSION

☐ Introduce the participants to the patient, functions and reasons for attending the meeting
☐ Use language and terminology that is appropriate for the patient
☐ Describe the facts of the adverse event and its outcome known at the time
☐ Describe any actions that are taken as a result of internal investigations such as system improvements
☐ Describe the steps that were and will be taken in the care of the patient (changes to care plan as applicable)
☐ Avoid speculation or blame
☐ Express sympathy or regret, a statement that one is sorry, as appropriate
☐ Inform the patient of the process for investigating and what the patient can expect to learn from the investigation, with appropriate timelines

- ☐ Allow time for questions and clarify whether the information is understood
- ☐ Be sensitive to cultural and language needs
- ☐ Offer to arrange subsequent meetings along with sharing key contact information
- ☐ Offer practical and emotional support such as spiritual care services, counseling and social work, as needed
- ☐ Facilitate further investigation and treatment if required

- ☐ *DOCUMENT* the disclosure discussion as per organizational policies and practices and include:
- ☐ The time, place and date of disclosure discussion
- ☐ The names and relationships of all attendees
- ☐ The facts presented in the discussion
- ☐ Offers of assistance and the response
- ☐ Questions raised and the answers given
- ☐ Plans for follow-up with key contact information for the organization

Canadian Patient Safety Institute, Saskatchewan Health, ISMP Canada, Hoffman, Carolyn, Beard, Paula, Greenall, Julie, U, David, and White, Jennifer. *Canadian Root Cause Analysis Framework: a tool for identifying and addressing the root causes of critical incidents in healthcare.* Canadian Patient Safety Institute, Edmonton, AB; 2006. Retrieved September 12, 2007 from: http://www.patientsafetyinstitute.ca/uploadedFiles/Resources/RCA_March06.pdf Reprinted with permission.

APPENDIX O

Disclosure of Unanticipated Events and Outcomes Sample Disclosure Policy

Disclosure of Unanticipated Events and Outcomes

PURPOSES:

1. To clarify the role of various disciplines in disclosing information about unanticipated events and outcomes to patients and families in a manner that is supportive, helpful, and informative.
2. To provide a framework for interdisciplinary collaboration and communication for disclosure of unanticipated outcomes or events that cross disciplines to provide optimal care for the patient and family in the aftermath.
3. To comply with regulatory agencies (JCAHO), professional associations (American Medical Association's Code of Ethics, the American College of Physicians) and Medical Board Rules & Regulations.

SUPPORTIVE DATA:

1. Hospital A believes that open and truthful communication is an integral part of patient and family centered care delivery.
2. Disclosure of adverse events is associated with decreased patient/family anxiety, ability to provide informed consent for follow up tests or treatments associated with the adverse event, and promotes ongoing cooperation from the patient and family (ASHRM, 2001; Wu, 1997).
3. The risk of litigation doubles, there is a loss of patient/family trust and the statute of limitations could be extended with non-disclosure of adverse incidents that result in patient harm. (ASHRM, 2001)
4. The AMA and the ACP supports physician disclosure to patients about procedural or judgement errors. The ACP further states that errors do not necessarily constitute improper, negligent or unethical behavior, but failure to disclose them may.

5. Healthcare providers involved with non-disclosure of adverse events associated with errors are reported to have anxiety after the event, loss of confidence, depression and unresolved guilt. Those who participate in disclosure of adverse events associated with errors also are reported to make better adjustments after an error, are in an improved position for litigation and are more apt to make constructive changes to practice that will reduce the risk of future errors (Meurier, 1997; Wu, 1991).

6. Patients and families expect healthcare providers to accept responsibility for their errors, provide simple, honest explanations and apologize for the fact that there was an unanticipated event or outcome.

7. An unanticipated outcome is defined as a result that significantly differs from what was anticipated as a result of treatment or procedures. Unanticipated outcomes may or may not be associated with errors.

8. An unanticipated event is defined as any event that is intercepted prior to completion or actual harm, which is not part of the plan. These events are frequently near miss events. Examples include but are not limited to the following events:

   a. The wrong patient that is taken to a diagnostic department but the error is discovered before any tests are done.

   b. A patient sustains an ecchymosis of the neck and face after an unsuccessful attempt at a neck line insertion.

   c. A mother is presented with the wrong infant and the error is discovered prior to the infant being fed.

   d. The infant security system is non-functional and manual systems need to be implemented.

Unanticipated events involve events where the patient is directly affected. Errors intercepted prior to any patient involvement are not disclosed. Examples include but are not limited to the following:

   a. The wrong medication is found in the patient's medication cassette and is returned to the pharmacy without being administered.

   b. A prescriber enters an order in the wrong patient's HIS record and this is discovered prior to the order being carried out.

9. An unanticipated outcome is defined as a result that significantly differs from what wasanticipated as a result of treatment or procedures. Unanticipated outcomes may or may not be associated with errors.

10. Unanticipated outcomes or events are divided into two severity levels:

   a. **Severity Level 1** is an unanticipated outcome associated with no obvious injury and no need for follow up diagnostic test, monitoring or interventions.

   Examples are as follows:

   A patient falls and sustains no apparent injury; it is determined that there is no need for x-ray.

A patient has a chest x-ray performed that was intended for another patient.

b. **Severity Level 2** is an unanticipated outcome that is associated with the need for diagnostic testing, a higher level of care and/or treatment or intervention to mitigate the adverse events associated with it.

Examples are as follows:

A patient who receives an overdose of insulin with decrease in glucose level that requires a bolus of dextrose with continuous IV glucose infusion and frequent glucose monitoring.

A patient who requires a carotid doppler after the carotid artery is punctured during an attempted intra-jugular line placement.

11. See also **Interdisciplinary Structure Standard**

VII, E. Documentation by Health Care Providers Interdisciplinary Process Standards

Protocol:

Disclosure of Unanticipated Outcomes/Events

Guidelines

Occurrence Report (ARCA)

Documentation for physician

Rules and Regulations of the Medical Board for Documentation Recommendations of Adverse Patient Events.

I. COLLABORATIVE ACCOUNTABILITIES:

All disciplines are responsible for the following activities:

1. Taking prompt action to mitigate the negative effects of the outcome upon discovery.
2. Providing disclosure in a manner that provides support and information to patients and families to ensure ongoing understanding of care delivery.
3. Apologizing for the outcome without acknowledging fault or criticizing other care providers, expressing compassion, and offering comfort to the patient and/or family with disclosure of the incident.
4. Using non-medical terminology that is easily understood by the patient and/or family.
5. Employing a translator and/or interpreter as necessary to maximize understanding.
6. Documenting information provided and patient/family response to disclosure of the unanticipated outcome and events in the medical record.
7. Notifying Risk Management of all Level 2 unanticipated outcomes.

II. PHYSICIAN ACCOUNTABILITIES:

The physician or Licensed Independent Provider (Nurse Practitioners) is responsible for the following activity:

1. The Primary or Covering Attending is ultimately responsible for disclosing Level I incidents and events. The Primary Attending may delegate responsibility for disclosure of Severity level 2 outcomes to the Nurse Practitioner or the Resident.

2. Procedural specialists (e.g., GI Endoscopists, Interventional Cardiologists and Radiologists etc,) and Consultative Physicians (e.g., Anesthesiologists, etc.) are responsible for disclosing Severity Level 2 unanticipated outcomes that may occur during the course of the procedural/interventional phase of care to the patient/family and the primary or covering attending. The Procedural/Consultative Physician is responsible for documenting the disclosure and the name of the attending notified.

3. Discussing the unanticipated outcome inclusive of the follow-up plan and treatment as indicated with the patient taking into consideration the patient's medical status and ability to understand the information.

4. Involving the patient as appropriate about what information is to be given to the family.

5. If it is determined that the family is to be notified the designated professional is responsible for contacting the family via phone in as timely a manner as possible or meeting with the family in person if the family is on the premises.

6. The Primary Attending is responsible for documenting the disclosure of Severity Level 2 outcomes or reviewing notes documenting unanticipated outcomes by other attendings and cosigning notes when disclosure of Severity Level 2 outcomes is delegated to residents or nurse practitioners. Documentation includes the individuals present, the information provided to the patient, family member(s) notified by phone, and response to the disclosure.

7. Covering attendings and procedural specialists are responsible for communicating to the primary attending the disclosure of an unanticipated outcome and the interventions or treatment provided.

8. The primary attending or designee is available to the patient and the family for follow up if questions later arise or to reinforce information that may not be understood during the initial disclosure (e.g., for patients post procedure who are still under the influence of sedatives or anesthesia).

9. If the attending physician expresses concerns or is unable to disclose the event, or if the investigation determines that the physician involvement could exacerbate the problem, the Chief of Service and Risk Management will work with administration to identify the appropriate person to handle the responsibility of disclosure.

III. NURSING ACCOUNTABILITIES:

The Registered Nurse is responsible for:

1. Notifying the covering resident, nurse practitioner or attending, and nursing leadership about an unanticipated event or an outcome of Severity Level 1 and 2.

2. Collaborating with the medical team and nursing leadership to develop a plan for notifying the patient and family of an unanticipated event and Severity Level 1 unanticipated outcome and seeking assistance from the covering resident, nurse practitioner or attending if the family exhibits signs of distress that may require further explanation or support.

3. Providing teaching and explanations about rationales for procedures or diagnostic tests that are being performed as a result of an unanticipated outcome.

4. Contacting the patient representative and/or the social worker to provide ongoing support as necessary.

5. For those unanticipated outcomes of Severity Level 2 associated with a nursing error, the nurse is responsible for collaborating with leadership and the physician or nurse practitioner to be present during disclosure of the incident. If the nurse involved expresses concern or is unable to disclose the event, or investigation determines that the nurse's involvement could exacerbate the problem, nursing leadership and the medical team determine the appropriate person to handle the responsibility of disclosure. Risk management and Nursing Administration may be consulted for assistance if the medical team and nursing leadership deem this appropriate.

6. Documenting the individuals present for the disclosure, the information provided to the patient, the family member(s) notified and response to the disclosure for unanticipated events and Severity Level 1 unanticipated outcomes. For Severity Level 2 outcomes, for documenting the name of the medical team that is notified and provides disclosure to the family and patient.

SELECTED REFERENCES:

American Society for Healthcare Risk Management. (2001). *ASHRM Perspective on Disclosure of Unanticipated Outcome Information.*

Greely, H. (1999). Do physicians have a duty to disclose? *Western Journal of Medicine* 171, 81–83.

Joint Commission on Accreditation of Healthcare Organizations. (2003). *Hospital Accreditation Standards.* Oakbrook, IL: JCAHO.

Hospital A Center. (2003). Rules & Regulations of the Medical Board.

Meurier, C., Vincent, C. et al. (1997). Learning from errors in nursing practice. *Journal of Advanced Nursing,* 26(1): 111–9.

Vincent, J. (1998). Information in the ICU: are we being honest with our patients? The results of a European questionnaire. *Intensive Care Medicine*, 24, 1251–1256.

Witman, A., Park, D., & Hardin, S. (1996). How do patients want physicians to handle mistakes? A survey of internal medicine patients in an academic setting. *Archives of Internal Medicine*, 156 (2), 2565–2569.

Wu, A., Folkman, S., McPhee, S., & Lo, B. (1991). Do house officers learn from their mistakes? *JAMA*, 265 (16), 2089–2094.

Wu, A. (1999). Handling hospital errors, is disclosure the best defense? *Annals of Internal Medicine*, 131(12), 970–972.

Wu, W., Cavanaugh, T., McPhee, S., Lo, B. & Micco, G. To tell the truth: Ethical and practical issues in disclosing medical mistakes to patients. *Journal of General Internal Medicine*, 131(12), 970–972.

DEVELOPED BY:

    APPROVED BY: Patient Safety & Satisfaction Committee
                                Executive Nursing Council
                                Patient Care Standards Council

_____

Senior Vice President & Chief Nursing Officer

_____

Senior Vice President & Chief Medical Officer

_____

Senior Vice President & Chief Operating Officer

DATE ISSUED: **REVIEW DATE:**

DISTRIBUTION: Patient Care & Nursing Standards Manuals

APPENDIX P

Culpability Matrix Flowchart

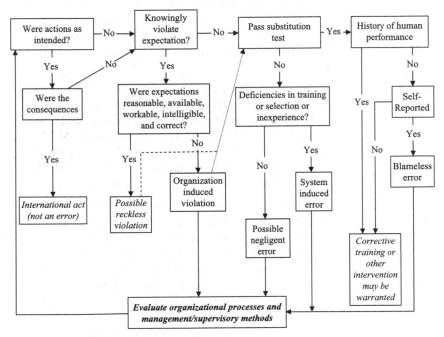

NOTE: Would other employees have made the same error?

Source: Project Hanford Management System. Human Performance Culpability Matrix. HNF-GD-29950 (January 15, 2007).

Culpability Matrix Flowchart Block Information

Block	Instructions
Were Actions As Intended	If both the actions and consequences were intended, we are out of the error realm and into the arena of intentional acts. These acts are possibly sabotage, malevolent damage, willful violation, etc. If the actions were not as intended (I meant to push Button "A", but somehow pushed Button "B"), then we are probably dealing with a mental slip or lapse. These generally are skill-based errors.
Were the Consequences Intended?	If the actions were as intended, but the consequences were not, then the error was most likely a mistake or violation (not willful). These are rule and knowledge-based errors. If the answer to this question is "NO", then proceed to the next section. If "YES", you are probably not dealing with an error at all (intentional act) and should consult your management.
Knowingly Violating Expectation	Reasonable expectations consist of guidance communicated through procedures, policies, work practices, verbally, or just plain common sense. Once again, it is necessary to establish the "intent" of the individual being evaluated. If it is established that the individual was aware of the expectations, but consciously elected not to conform to those expectations, then the answer would be "YES." If the answer is "YES", proceed to the next section. If "NO", proceed to the substitution test. "Intent" will come into play later.
Were Expectations Reasonable, Available, Workable, Intelligible and Correct	The availability, workability, and accuracy of reasonable expectations are an important concept. Once again, this must be evaluated from the perspective of the immediate user. Gaining an understanding of the worker's perception on this matter is important. If it is established that the reasonable expectations were readily available, workable, intelligible and correct, then the answer would be "YES." If it is established or suspected that non-compliance has become more or less automatic (as happens in the case of routine short-cuts) you should question the accuracy of the expectations.

Block	Instructions
	Violations generally involve a conscious decision on the part of the individual to bend or break the rules. However, while the actions are deliberate, the potential bad consequences are not, in contrast to sabotage, etc. If in establishing the intent (or motive) of the violation it can be argued that "the individual was attempting to achieve the proper desire outcome but the situation at hand rendered the expectations unsuitable", then the answer will most likely be "NO" to this question.
	If the answer to this question is "YES", then there was a possible reckless violation. If the answer was "NO" or cannot be established, then the error or violation may have been system induced.
	If it is determined that the violation may have been system induced, proceed to the substitution test. You must also consider another error or violation at this point. The expectation to stop and seek additional guidance in situations like these (unworkable procedures) is generally understood by workers. Failure to adhere to this and other expectations of this nature should be evaluated as separate acts.
Pass Substitution Test	This is probably the most critical, and difficult evaluation to conduct. To evaluate this question we need to perform the following mental test. Substitute the individual concerned with someone else coming from the same domain of activity, possessing comparable qualifications and experience. Then ask the following question, "In the light of how events unfolded and were perceived by those involved *in real time*, is it likely that this new individual would have behaved any differently?" If the answer is "probably not", then apportioning blame has no material role to play other than possibly to obscure potential systemic deficiencies and blame one of the victims.

Block	Instructions
	One method of conducting the substitution test is to ask approximately ten of the individual's peers, "Given the circumstances that prevail at the time, could you be sure that you would not have committed the same or similar unsafe act (error)."
	If the answer again is "probably not", then blame is inappropriate. The answer to the substitution test is "YES." If the answer to the substitution test is "YES", then the error is most likely blameless and you should proceed to the section addressing whether or not the individual has a history of unsafe acts.
	If the substitution test is not passed, proceed along the "NO" path and evaluate the next section.
Deficiencies in Training and Selection or Inexperience	If it is established that there were no deficiencies in the individual's training, selection or experience, then a possible negligent error must be considered. In other words, should this task have been assigned to this person in the first place? If there are questions about the person's training, qualification or selection for the task, then there is a good likelihood that the unsafe act was a largely system induced error.
History of Human Performance Problems	People vary widely and consistently in their liability to everyday slips and lapses. Some individuals are considerably more absentminded than others. For the purpose of determining a "history", one would only consider the documented events involving this individual in the previous six months. If the person in question has a history of unsafe acts or errors, it does not necessarily bear upon the culpability of the error committed on this particular occasion. However, it probably indicates the necessity for corrective training or other intervention to reinforce desire performance and take full advantage of lessons learned. Absentmindedness has nothing to do with ability or intelligence. Someone who continually commits errors along these lines would obviously require some individual assistance in overcoming these tendencies. The emphasis here is on improving this individual's performance in their current position or considering other career options that they may be more suited to. Discipline should not be an automatic response. It should only be implemented after carefully considering all options, and in response to a specific problem.

Block	Instructions
Self-Reporting	Self-reporting can be when the individual notifies management of the error OR when the individual acknowledges that an error was made. Self-reporting indicates that the individual is willing to change behaviors and to assist in development of corrective actions. In a just culture, individuals should feel encouraged to self-report without undue concern for negative consequences.

NOTE: *The dotted lines from Possible Reckless Violation and Organization Induced Violation blocks to Pass Substitution Test block indicate the need to perform the Pass Substitution Test to determine the degree the organization has influenced the behavior.*

Source: Project Hanford Management System, Human Performance Culpability Matrix. HNF-GD-29950 (January 15, 2007).

Index